BRITISH INDIA

IN ITS RELATION TO THE

DECLINE OF HINDOOISM,

AND THE

PROGRESS OF CHRISTIANITY

BRITISH INDIA

IN ITS RELATION TO THE

DECLINE OF HINDOOISM,

AND THE

PROGRESS OF CHRISTIANITY:

CONTAINING REMARKS ON THE

Manners, Customs, and Literature of the People

WILLIAM CAMPBELL

GYAN

Published by

GYAN

Gyan Publishing House
5, Ansari Road
Daryaganj, New Delhi-110002
Phone: 011-47034999, 9811692060
E-mail: books@gyanbooks.com

Distribution Network
gyanbooks.com
India, USA, Canada, UK, Australia, France

ISBN: 978-81-212-9360-0 (PB)
First Published, 1839

2nd Impression 2023

Printed at: Gyan Press, Delhi.

BRITISH INDIA IN ITS RELATION TO THE DECLINE OF HINDOOISM, AND THE PROGRESS OF CHRISTIANITY

AUTHOR: WILLIAM CAMPBELL

View from the Mission House Bangalore

BRITISH INDIA

IN ITS RELATION TO THE

DECLINE OF HINDOOISM,

AND THE

PROGRESS OF CHRISTIANITY:

CONTAINING REMARKS ON THE

Manners, Customs, and Literature of the People;

ON THE

EFFECTS WHICH IDOLATRY HAS PRODUCED;

ON THE SUPPORT WHICH THE BRITISH GOVERNMENT HAS AFFORDED TO THEIR SUPERSTITIONS;

ON EDUCATION, AND THE MEDIUM THROUGH WHICH IT SHOULD BE GIVEN.

BY THE

REV. WILLIAM CAMPBELL,

Missionary to India.

Representation of a Suttee

Illustrated with Engravings on Wood,

BY G. BAXTER.

LONDON: JOHN SNOW, 35, PATERNOSTER ROW.

1839.

TO THE

Directors of the London Missionary Society;

TO

MISSIONARY BRETHREN IN FOREIGN LANDS;

TO THE

MINISTERS AND CHURCHES AT HOME;

AND TO THE

FRIENDS OF EDUCATION;

THIS WORK IS RESPECTFULLY DEDICATED,

BY THEIR FRIEND AND SERVANT,

THE AUTHOR.

PREFACE.

After a residence of nearly twelve years in India, exclusively devoted to the work of a Missionary, the Author was under the necessity of returning to his native land, and of leaving that sphere of labour in which he greatly delighted. In visiting the churches of England, Scotland, Ireland and Wales, the vast importance, and the urgent necessities of our Eastern Empire, have constituted the great theme of his sermons and addresses; the deliverance of Hindoos from priestcraft and superstition, is still the burden of his thoughts, his prayers, and his toils; and whether, in the good providence of God, he is directed to return to his field of labour, or is obliged to occupy a different sphere at home, the claims, the welfare and the conversion of India are bound up with his mortal existence, and must ever have a warm place in his heart.

As there was no book on India which associated the progress of missions with the history, the literature, the customs, and the mythology of its people, and which combined a general view of this interesting field, with the advancement of the truth, many friends expressed a hope that some work would appear upon India, similar to those which have been published, by our brethren, upon other parts of the missionary vineyard.

In addition to this, it is, to the Author, a matter of deep and daily regret that, after fifty years of occupation by British power, India should be so unknown to the public at home, and that her transcendent interests should receive so little attention from the political, commercial and Christian world. Her immense distance from the seat of government, may, in some measure, account for this neglect; but as steam-communication has, for some years, been established, and the mails pass, with considerable regularity, between England and Bombay, there is now some hope, that our Eastern Empire will soon receive that public attention which her great interests demand.

Should the present volume be useful in awakening more general interest in the affairs of India, in exciting greater compassion for the ignorance, degradation, and misery which prevail among its people, and in provoking the wise and the good of every denomination to increased exertion, and to fervent prayer for the conversion of its nations, the Author will not have written, nor published in vain.

To the Directors of the London Missionary Society, and to the friends of missions in general, no apology need be offered for the imperfections of the work; their agents have little time to polish their composition and embellish their thoughts; and those who contend for the truth, ought to be prepared to meet the shafts of the enemy, rather than renounce the imperative duty of pleading the cause of the oppressed, and advancing the interests of humanity.

The Author has to acknowledge his obligations to the Rev Dr. Bennett, for many kind suggestions.

To the gracious care and blessing of that Master whom he desires to serve, the writer commends this attempt to advance the interests of his kingdom; and hopes that a Christian public will receive it, in the spirit of the gospel, as the effort of one who reckons it his highest honour to be a missionary to the heathen, a friend of humanity, and an advocate of the rights, the liberties, and spiritual interests of India.

5, Barnsbury Street, Islington,
November 12, 1839.

CONTENTS.

CHAPTER I.

EXTENT AND CONDITION OF INDIA.

CHAPTER II.

THE POLITICAL DEGENERACY OF INDIA.

CHAPTER III.

THE BRITISH POWER IN INDIA.

CHAPTER IV.

THE MYTHOLOGY OF INDIA.

CHAPTER V.

THE SANGUINARY SUPERSTITION OF INDIA.

CHAPTER VI.

EFFECTS OF IDOLATRY.

CHAPTER VII.

ON CASTE.

CHAPTER VIII.

THE LITERATURE OF INDIA.

CHAPTER IX.

THE SYRIAN CHRISTIANS.

CHAPTER X.

THE DANISH MISSIONS.

CHAPTER XI.

SUCCESS AMONG EUROPEANS.

CHAPTER XII.

ON TRANSLATIONS AND ORIGINAL WORKS IN THE VERNACULAR TONGUES.

CHAPTER XIII.

DIFFERENT DENOMINATIONS.

CHAPTER XIV.

ON THE TAMUL MISSIONS.

CHAPTER XV.

TRAVANCORE.

CHAPTER XVI.

ON THE TAMUL MISSIONS.

CHAPTER XVII.

THE TELLOOGOO MISSIONS.

CHAPTER XVIII.

CUDDAPAH.

CHAPTER XIX.

THE CANARESE MISSIONS.

CHAPTER XX.

BELGAUM.

CHAPTER XXI.

THE MYSORE.

CHAPTER XXII.

BANGALORE.

CHAPTER XXIII.

BANGALORE.

CHAPTER XXIV.

GOVERNMENT SUPPORT OF IDOLATRY.

CHAPTER XXV.

GOVERNMENT SUPPORT OF IDOLATRY.

LIST OF ENGRAVINGS.

BRITISH INDIA, &c.

CHAPTER I.

EXTENT AND CONDITION OF INDIA.

LANDING AT MADRAS—DESCRIPTION OF A PALANKEEN—THE AUTHOR'S FIRST IMPRESSIONS—WHAT INDIA WAS TO THE ANCIENTS AND WHAT TO THE MODERNS—HOW THE NAME "WEST INDIES" WAS GIVEN TO SOUTH AMERICA—THE EXTENT OF THE EMPIRE—THE EXTERNAL APPEARANCE OF THE COUNTRY AND ITS INHABITANTS—SOME MARKS OF IMPROVEMENT IN THE INTERIOR—THE EFFECTS OF WAR MORE VISIBLE—MEASURES OF AMELIORATION NECESSARY TO THE PROSPERITY OF THE COUNTRY.

A VOYAGE to India has hitherto been regarded as a very arduous undertaking. After being confined for five months in a ship, crossing the equator twice, rounding the Cape of Good Hope, and being exposed to many of the trials and dangers of the ocean, one is quite prepared to welcome the sight of the port whither he is bound. No sooner is the anchor cast in the Madras Roads, than we seem in a new world; natives crowd the vessel, show you a number and variety of testimonials which they have received from gentlemen both in and out of India, and describe to you, in strange English, the inconveniences to which you must be exposed, should you venture to land without their guidance and protection.* Both sides of the ship now appear in a state of siege. Catamarans and Masula boats wait to be engaged, and their owners are anxious to gain your approbation. You can scarcely keep your gravity while you look at the grotesque appearance of the natives on the Catamarans, sitting on a small and contemptible raft in the midst of the sea, and steering the frail bark in triumph through the waves. It is a more serious concern when you descend into the Masula boat, which is to bear you through a surf that often dashes, with tremendous violence, upon the shore. Sitting under an awning which shelters you from the sun, and embarked in a boat which, though strong and serviceable, is entirely under the management of a Hindoo pilot and Hindoo sailors, you advance in safety, through the breakers, in which a jolly-boat or a wherry, though

* Young Mr. Munro, afterwards Sir Thomas Munro, on his arrival at Madras, engaged one of these men, and congratulated himself on meeting with such a clever fellow. His servant, after looking into his sea-chest, said, "Oh, sir! this will never do; nobody in this country wears buff waistcoats, and breeches, and thread stockings, nor sleeps upon mattresses: sheets and blankets are useless in this warm climate. You must get a table and chairs, and a new bed." He carried off all the clothes, which he valued at six guineas, to dispose of them, and never returned.

manned with British tars, would be dashed to pieces in a moment; where many a brave man has been lost, and where many more would have perished, but for the expertness and enterprise of the natives on the Catamarans, who dive into the deep, lay hold of the sufferers, and bear them in safety to the beach. Sure as you are that they will deceive you, if possible, and that for money alone such deeds are performed, yet the first services which the natives render to you, inspire you with confidence: you feel yourselves secure under their superintendence, in the midst of danger; and some of the best feelings of your nature are called into exercise, while the missionary remembers that he is the ambassador of mercy to them.

As soon as you have landed, palankeens are in readiness to carry you to the house of your friends. What can be more indulgent, more agreeable, and perhaps more suited to the climate, than this mode of conveyance! It is found a good seat, or a comfortable bed. In shape it is oblong: on both sides there are two sliding doors, which you may shut or open at pleasure. A wooden canopy above shelters you from the sun; a long pole fixed in either end, and fastened with iron rods to the body of the palankeen, becomes the support, with which three bearers before and three behind carry you to your home, while they forget not to answer to one another, first in a low murmur, and then in a regular shout—not from any oppression which they feel, but to encourage one another in their labour, and to keep time and tune together as they advance.*

But whatever may be the delight which this new scene is calculated to inspire, very solemn were the feelings with which the writer and his companion, landed in India. A famine prevailed over the country, and was consigning hundreds of natives to the grave; the cholera was raging with frightful violence at Madras, and had cut down some of the highest and most influential members of European society. Every acquaintance and stranger you met with seemed to ask, with an anxious and enquiring look, "Have you the cholera?" and a deep im-

* A missionary, on landing at Madras, engaged a palankeen, and ordered the bearers to take him to a gentleman's house at Vepery. When they came within sight of the house, they grounded the palankeen, and the head-bearer coming up to him, said, "Master, please to walk into the garden, that is the house; but we are not allowed to carry the palankeen into gentlemen's compounds. If master will just walk this little distance, it will be very good." "Oh, yes," replied the missionary, in ignorance of the customs, "what is your charge?" "Master give five rupees, that will do very well." The five rupees were given, and the missionary walked up to the house. His friend saw him advancing, and ran out to give him a hearty welcome. "But how," he enquired, "have you come?" "Oh, replied the stranger, "I came in a palankeen, but the bearers told me it was against the law to carry me into your compound." "Oh, what cheats!" exclaimed the gentleman; "such a thing was never heard of: what have they charged you?" "Five rupees," said the missionary. "Nearly ten times more than you ought to have given them," said his friend. As the Teloogoo bearers are remarkable for their honesty, these bearers, I should think, were of a different caste and origin.

pression of the nearness and the solemnity of death and judgment, appeared to rest on the community. But to behold the whole city given up to idolatry; what a sight! Every object brings their gross and degrading superstition to your view; the mark of the beast is engraven on their foreheads. Their pagodas, their muntapas,* their altars, and their idols of stone, meet your eye, on every side. If they adorn their houses, it must be with figures of their deities. Their dress, their very ornaments, their trades and occupations, their shops and merchandize, their schools of learning, their public edifices, their manners and customs, and intercourse, —all remind you of their debasing mythology. Your heart sickens within you, while you pass through the streets of Black Town, and behold crowds of immortal beings busy upon the trifles of an hour, almost ready to devour one another to obtain the riches and vanities of earth, panting after worldly fame and renown, and many of them inflicting the most excruciating tortures upon themselves, to become the idols of the multitude, or to propitiate an offended deity; but all without God and without hope, famishing for want of the bread that endureth to life everlasting, and perishing in their sins.

In every age, India has been the region of re-

* A muntapa is a small house built upon the road-side, and containing an idol, at whose shrine, travellers may pay their devotions.

nown, and the admiration of mankind. To the ancients it was a fairy land; the garden of Asia; a country where gold and silver, gems and pearls and precious stones abounded; and a paradise where all that was pleasant to the eye, and sweet to the smell, and agreeable to the taste, were to be enjoyed. To the moderns, it has been the theatre of arms and conquest; the field where fortune and fame waited upon their votaries; the region where commercial enterprise and speculation were sure to be crowned with success; the empire where crowns were to be bought, and kingdoms to be won. While the passage round the Cape was yet unknown, the extent of the eastern continent was a comparative mystery. The great Columbus fancied that, in the new world which he was destined to discover, he would find the Indies stretching out their interminable borders, and that he would bring home to Europe, from the West, the same gold and rubies which had so long been the characteristic of the East. Acting upon this geographical delusion, he returned to Spain, to lay at the feet of Ferdinand and Isabella, the productions of the Indies; and they in return crowned the zeal and industry and perseverance of the navigator, with a charter to hold the *West Indies* as their rightful dominions; and thus did ignorance and fancy give to the South American colonies, that name by which they are still recognized among European nations.

But as soon as Vasco de Gama rounded the Cape

of Good Hope, and ploughed the Eastern seas, the illusion was dispelled. America was found to be a continent, and India was henceforth reduced to her proper dimensions: she stood in no need of such a notion to make her great and powerful. Stretching from Cape Comorin on the south, to the Himalaya on the north, and from the Indus on the west, to the Brahmapootra on the east, she is a most rich and splendid empire, a hive of nations, a multitude of kindreds and people and tongues. This immense extent of territory is now under the sway and the authority of Great Britain. It is composed of as many kingdoms, and perhaps as large, as are to be found in Europe. The Punjaub, the Deccan, Bengal, the Carnatic, the Mysore, the Baramhal, the Ceded districts, the Northern Circars, the Concan, the Nizam's territory, the Maharratta states Travancore, and Tanjore, are so many countries over which native princes were accustomed to reign, and which, whether under Hindoo or Mahomedan rulers, seem to have rendered tribute to an Emperor, as an acknowledgment of their subjection to his authority.

On taking a rapid survey of the exterior of the empire, every thing appears on a magnificent scale.*

* The banyan, or Indian fig-tree, has a stem branching to a great height and vast extent, with heart-shaped entire leaves, ending in acute points. This tree is beautifully described by Milton:—

Whether it be the tigers, the bears, or the elephants that range through its jungles, or the ghauts and mountains and glens which diversify its scenery, or the rivers and cataracts which pour their torrents

> "Branching so broad and long that in the ground
> The bending twigs take root, and daughters grow
> About the mother-tree, a pillar'd shade
> High overarched, and echoing walks between."

Of all trees it is the most charming of nature's productions, and contrary to many other things in animal and vegetable life, it seems to be exempt from decay. It is continually increasing. The Hindoos look upon the banyan-tree as an emblem of the Deity, from its long duration, outspreading arms, and overshadowing beneficence. I have reposed under the Cubbeer Burr, which is the name of a banyan-tree in Guzerat of prodigious size. More than five regiments might be accommodated under the delightful shade of its canopy, impervious to the hottest beams of the sun. It is about 2000 feet in circumference, measured round the principal stems; the overhanging branches not yet struck down, cover a much larger space. The chief trunks of this single tree (which in size greatly exceed our English elms and oaks) amount to 350; the smaller stems, formed into strong supporters, are more than 3,000. It is filled with green wood-pigeons, doves, peacocks, and feathered songsters; crowded with squirrels and families of monkies, and shaded by bats of large size, many of them measuring upwards of six feet from the extremity of one wing to the other. These hang in its upper branches in a torpid state during the day. The tree affords shelter and sustenance to all its inhabitants; being covered amidst its bright foliage with small figs of rich scarlet, which are exceedingly pleasant to the taste. Many animals in it live upon each other, and continual warfare and stratagem are kept up between birds, snakes, monkies, &c.—*See Wallace's Memoirs of India.*

through its plains, there is always something noble and majestic. The sun shines in effulgent splendour; the heavens exhibit a clearness and a brilliancy unknown in a western clime; the moon pours a tide of lustre over the shadows of night; the showers descend, in floods, to water and refresh the ground; the fields produce their abundance almost spontaneously; and all nature seems to shout for joy. The inhabitants alone seem to be out of harmony with this scene. In the lower countries, the Hindoos are small in power, slight in form, indolent in habit, and timid in exertion. In the high lands, they are more powerful and courageous; and, under the influence of a salubrious climate, they excel in energy, become athletic in body, and superior in mind. But the whole race is destitute of that spirit and firmness, and that courageous daring which distinguish their European conquerers. To behold a battalion of Seapoys passing through their evolutions, and to remark the light and timid and feeble step with which they march, and compare it with the steady and powerful tread with which a British regiment make the ground under them to tremble, is sufficient at once to show, that whether it be the influence of climate, or the effect of their depravity, or the fruit of their superstition, or the effeminacy which a long career of despotism is sure to produce, the present Hindoos are the children of a degenerate age, and are the veriest dwarfs, when compared with the heroes and the giants of which their history can boast, and who seemed to be more in keeping with the grandeur and magnificence of their country.

Advancing into the interior, you look out for the improvements which commerce, half a century of British rule, progressive liberty, and measures of amelioration have made among this interesting people, and upon the face of the empire at large. Many large pools are built to accommodate travellers, to supply water to the villages, and to be used as bathing-places for the weary, and for those who wish to refresh themselves. Numerous Choultries* are seen, in the line of road, to afford lodging and repose for pilgrims, and for the poor and destitute on their journeys; and are usually filled at night with persons from all parts and of all descriptions. Tanks or reservoirs of spacious dimensions burst, now and then, upon the view of the traveller, and add greatly to the beauty and to the diversity of the scenery; they are formed in suitable localities, to facilitate the labours of the husbandman and the gardener: mounds are raised to stem the overflowing of their streams in the rainy season; and, at a suitable period, their flood-gates are opened, and allow their waters to pour down in rills upon the paddy-fields and other grounds. Topes, or plantations of large trees are met with in every direction, and form an agreeable shade to merchants engaged

* A convenient resting-place, built of stone, and the erection of which is considered by the natives, as a work of merit.

in traffic, to the Brinjaries * in their expeditions, and to the weary passenger, who prefers, in the heat of the day, a cool and a pleasant retreat, to the close and heated atmosphere of a building. The roads, in many parts, are lined on both sides with large trees, and are splendid avenues, stretching sometimes from one town to another; thus enabling the people to prosecute their journeys in the meridian of day. Now and then, you come to a poor-house, or a charitable establishment, where Bramins are fed, where the poor are refreshed and have their wants supplied, and where great villany is practised by those who are entrusted with its management. But all these are either the fruits of superstition, and the deeds of those who hoped, in this way, to obtain fame in the present world and happiness in the next; or the benefits which former rulers conferred upon their subjects, and with which they were content that their administration should be judged of by future generations.

Still, the effects of war, rapine, and anarchy are far more manifest than the benefits of peace. You pass through large tracts of country which, with little trouble, would yield thirty or fifty fold to the farmer, lying barren and waste; because they have

* Brinjaries are the gipsies of India; carry on merchandize between one country and another; convey their goods upon asses; bring supplies to armies in time of war, and enjoy the privilege, in such seasons, of having their rights and property, and their persons respected by all parties.

not been furnished with the necessary premium upon industry, or because their inhabitants have been reduced to a remnant, and have not been able to contend with the exactions of despotism and misrule. You visit towns and villages which are still surrounded with walls of defence, or with dense and impassable hedges, which were originally planted to defend their inhabitants from the Pindarries,* and which are still deemed necessary as a defence against robbers and banditti, in the absence of a police establishment, whose vigilance and protection ought to be extended to the peasant and to the farmer, as well as to the citizen. You travel through jungles and through deserts almost in the neighbourhood of large towns, and which the tiger, the elephant, the wolf, and the jackal occupy as their dwelling, since the progress of civilization has been so small and so slow, that the people have not been able to reclaim them, and drive their ferocious tenants into more distant abodes. You sojourn in provinces rich in ores and in metals, abounding with natural resources, qualified to bestow treasures of wealth upon the laborious and enterprising adven-

* A tribe of freebooters who arose in India during the eighteenth century. Generally well mounted, a band of them would attack a town during the night, pillage its inhabitants, and commit the greatest excesses, and in the morning be sixty or seventy miles distant from the scene of their depredations. The Mahratta powers took them under their protection, and as they would not surrender these Ishmaelites, it brought on the Mahratta war.

turer; but yielding nothing: nay, sometimes overrun with famine and with pestilence, because their former and present rulers have dug no mines, have cut no canals, have formed no railroads, have erected no granaries, and have adopted no measures to draw forth their exhaustless stores. You live among a most interesting people, whose villages are so many little republics, and who really possess, among themselves, many of the elements of comfort and of happiness; but their children grow up, like their fathers, ignorant, superstitious, sanguinary, and idolatrous, because colleges have not been established to enlighten them, a general system of education has not been granted to emancipate them from error, and pains have not been taken to spread among them that information which would contribute to their present and eternal welfare.

I see Bungalows,* erected for the accommodation of European travellers, provided often with a table, and couch and chairs, and furnished with servants, who are civil and anxious to obtain supplies for your comfort. But where are the alms-houses for the indigent natives? Where are the infirmaries

* These are buildings erected by the government, every ten or fifteen miles in the line of road, affording a good shelter during the day; but as they are not furnished, like our Inns at home, you are obliged to bring your crockery, and some furniture and supplies which your table may require; while the attendants who have charge of the bungalow, can usually find milk, eggs, fowls, a sheep, vegetables, &c. on moderate terms.

for the sick and afflicted? Where are the asylums for the insane, the orphan, and the widow?

The native army has been greatly improved; it has submitted to European discipline, and, under the command of British officers, it is reckoned a match for any oriental troops, however valiant and courageous. But why does the ryot* still cultivate his ground with the same rude implements?—why does the artizan still work at his trade with the same rough and antiquated tools that were used by his forefathers?—why does the merchant carry on his commerce at the same slow and tedious rate as before? Why?—because they have had no models of improvement to emulate, no machinery to show them the superiority of European science, and no measures to accelerate merchandize and save time and trouble and expense.

The Government is liberal; great is the freedom granted to the press; the authorities, generally speaking, are intelligent and meritorious officers; many of the judges and magistrates are superior men, wish well to the community, and would be an honour to any country; and a new criminal code has been adopted for the empire. But the land-tax is, in many parts, high and oppressive; law and justice are, in some instances, slow, expensive, and administered with indifference; exaction, rapacity, and bribery, often attend the collection of the revenues, by the native officers: and wherever Europeans are

* Ryot is the name generally applied to the agriculturists.

not numerous, and not very watchful, the native authorities would feel no hesitation in using the rack, the stone, the thumb-screw, and other modes of torture, to extort money for themselves, as well as for the treasury.

In reply, it may be said, that the British government has not yet had time to consolidate their power; that improvement is slow in its growth; and that, in a country so immense, the development of its energies must be waited for with patience. This is granted; but we long to see the *beginning* of better days—the promise and the pledge of improvement. If three or four millions of money are to be withdrawn annually from India, and imported to England to pay the dividends, and to meet the expenses of the Indian government at home, why should not a similar amount be expended upon the country, to improve its moral, its commercial, and its agricultural interests? Will not the better cultivation of the soil, and the discovery of its riches secure their own reward of prosperity, peace, and gratitude? Will not the Hindoos deem themselves happy under such a rule, co-operate with the agents of the government, and be excited to rivalry and to emulation in the career of improvement? Will not a capital, expended upon works of public utility, yield a good return, lessen the burdens of the people, give additional stimulus to commerce, and ameliorate the condition of those who are, in reality, the strength and riches of the nation?

I cannot join with those who represent the present government of India as the worst that the empire ever saw; as oppressive to its subjects in the highest degree; and as the author of every calamity that happens to the country!—No: many causes are at work besides.* Some parts of the territory may be more exposed to oppressions than others; but I must say, in reference to those parts in which I have travelled, that evil reports, when applied to them, could not be sustained. But a system of amelioration ought to advance,—not with a slow and feeble step, but with rapid and gigantic strides,—not as the public mind at home or in India would urge it on, and render it imperative, but with an honest purpose, a hearty good will, and unflinching exertion;—not as the stewards of an estate would have it proceed, who have their own interests to attend to, more than those of the landlord and the tenant, but as patriots and benevolent philanthropists would like to behold it, who wish, above every thing, the prosperity of their country, and the welfare of their race.

* When the British commission was established in the Mysore, the Bramins, the Mahommedans, and those who had been in power under the Rajah, did their utmost to oppose the Government, to neutralize its efforts, and to render it unpopular with the people.

CHAPTER II.

THE POLITICAL DEGENERACY OF INDIA.

THE HISTORY OF THE HINDOOS INVOLVED IN MYSTERY—THE FABULOUS NATURE OF THEIR WRITINGS—SUPERSTITION, THE CAUSE OF THEIR POLITICAL DEGENERACY—THE SYSTEM MORE DEGRADING THAN THAT OF NATIONS IN FORMER TIMES—THAN THAT OF EUROPEAN KINGDOMS—THE EFFECTS OF IDOLATRY UPON THEIR MORALS,—ILLUSTRATED BY A SCENE IN THE HOUSE OF A GOOROO—BEAR A RESEMBLANCE TO VIEWS OF IDOLATRY GIVEN IN THE BIBLE.

THE early history of India, like that of all other countries, is involved in the deepest obscurity. Fable has given millions of years to its inhabitants, to develope their energies, and to allow space for the wonderful performances of their gods. Little can be said of them prior to the days of Alexander. Under the reign of the Princes of the Sun, or under the dominion of the Princes of the Moon, the people seem to have made advances in the arts and sciences, in civilization, and in the measures which are necessary to secure peace and order, and good government, unknown, at that time, among the nations of the west. But alas! this day of prosperity seems to have been short, and was succeeded by a long night of terror, misrule, and degradation. Their own shasters and pooranas may serve to exhibit their career in as correct a light as it can perhaps be described. Ever and anon, the earth is brought into subjection to demons and to giants; peace and liberty and happiness are driven from the abodes of man; war, murder, rapacity, deeds of violence, and oppressions of every kind, make up the history of the age; monsters wrench the sceptre of rule from the hands of the inferior gods, and carry ruin, and devastation, through the universe; till the earth groans under this burden of impiety, sends forth a howl of lamentation to Vishnoo, entreats him to interpose for her deliverance, and obtains emancipation by his appearance in the form of Rama, of Chrishnu, or some other hero.

An imaginative people, residing in Asia, and recording the exploits of their sages and their gods in poetry, were even more likely, than the poets of Greece, to convert their oppressors into giants, their heroes into deities, their national quarrels into wars between the powers of good and of evil, and their times of peace and tranquillity into the days of paradise. "Who," said a missionary one day to a Hindoo, "is to be the tenth incarnation of Vishnoo?" "Why," said the man, "do you not know that our European rulers are that incarnation?" This is a trivial circumstance, but it is a key, I conceive, to their whole system of mythology. While the Hindoo dynasties were supreme, there was sure to be among the protegées at every court, a poet whose business it was to celebrate the virtues of the prince, and as flattery is not more a national characteristic of Hindoos, than it is extravagant in its diction, and outrageous in its panegyric, there was no restraint upon the poet's fancy. The nature of the sovereign was divine; whatever might be his origin, some fortunate accident was sure to connect him and his ancestors with the gods; however inferior might be his talents and acquirements, he became, in the lines of the poet, another Vicramaditya;* and perchance an epic poem consecrated his memory as an incarnation of Vishnoo. If in such countries as England and Ireland and Scotland, so enlightened and free, so blest with liberal institutions, and so highly favoured with the light of Christianity, it is impossible to trace with any confidence our origin and history, though we go back no further than two thousand years; why should we be surprised that nations whose origin, and customs, and language and annals are so mixed up with idolatry and crime, should be involved in oblivion, or enveloped in the absurdities of fable and romance?

It is impossible to look at the political degeneracy of India, without grief and sorrow, and not to regard idolatry as the cause of its degra-

* An illustrious prince who is thought to have reigned in India about the first century of the Christian era.

dation. As a nation, the Hindoos would have been more than men to have retained, under such a system of superstition, the spirit of freedom, the supremacy of their country, and their political rights and institutions. The very principles upon which the Bramins established their power, and the laws and usages with which they have endeavoured to support it, were sure to sap the foundations of any empire. To say that the habits and customs of the people are the same, that the laws and institutions are the same, that the divisions into castes is the same, that the system of idolatry is the same, which they were in the days of Alexander, is just to say that Hindoo society has been stationary, that right and liberty are long lost and forgotten, that the natives have been so long exposed to the fury and wrath of the invader, and that the sun of India's prosperity went down while it was yet day. As soon, therefore, as this system obtained an ascendency, there was no longer the hardy valour, and chivalrous exploits which characterise barbarians. The spirit and liberty which distinguish the ancient Germans and modern Caffers, were extinguished. Already enslaved by their superstition, they fell an easy prey to the violence and rapacity of the conqueror. Terrified at the signs of heaven, at the changes in the seasons, and at the fury of the elements which they had converted into deities, no wonder that they trembled at the sound of the warrior, and fancied that, in the forms of men like themselves, they beheld giants and furies. They confided more in the number of their chariots, their horsemen and their elephants than, in the valour and discipline of their troops, and entered the field, only to be overthrown.

It has been so with every idolatrous nation, and in every age. Nineveh! where art thou? Once triumphant in battle, determined in council, and overwhelming in power, thou wast a scourge to the nations, thou didst seize the captive and didst divide the spoil; but idolatry was thy bane, and thou didst fall from the summit of dominion. Babylon! where art thou?—where now are thy gorgeous palaces, thy brazen gates, thy majestic walls, thy victorious kings and courageous armies? Thou gavest not God the glory; thou didst exalt the gods of silver and of gold, of wood and of stone, and therefore thou hast fallen never to rise. Mighty Rome! where art thou?—what has become of thy imperial senate, thy lofty Capitol, thy triumphal arches, the Cæsars that fought thy battles, and the legions that won thy victories, and thy heroes who wished to render thee immortal? Ah! they have fallen, and with thy superstition are buried in the grave; thy liberties were not consecrated by Christianity; idolatry was thy curse and thy ruin. But in all these countries, liberty flourished for a season; their institutions were such, that they allowed the state time to respire; and their overthrow was more of a judicial kind, than inherent in the political establishments. But can as much be said of India? Alas!—no. As soon as the Braminical system, began to work, it secured the degradation of the people, and prepared them for a long career of shame and oppression.

From the days of the great Alexander to the present period, their superstition has been the same; but so it appears has been the history of their empire. During the same eventful era, the western nations, under the Grecian and Roman idolatries, sank into ruin and decay, but rose again under the happy genius of Christianity, and attained a state of peace and prosperity worthy of that age. No sooner did a baneful superstition exert its influence, than the dark ages commenced, and the kingdoms were again immersed in ignorance and barbarity; but they burst their shackles at the glorious Reformation, and have long been upon the high-road to freedom and civilization and happiness; and in proportion as true religion has exercised its supremacy over them, in the same proportion have their rights and privileges, and peace and prosperity been consolidated and advanced. But the nations of the East have a very different record to unfold. Throughout these ages, they have remained the slaves of despotism as well as the dupes of superstition. Under the rule of their own princes, what disunion! what wars! what massacres! what revolutions! They became an easy prey to every invader; and while the institutions of Brumha maintained their full force, it was to extinguish the sparks of liberty, and to keep the people in bondage, to a succession of tyrants and calamities. No doubt, there arose occasionally there, as there must in such circumstances, a hero who animated with the love of freedom himself, inspired his countrymen to set the power of their masters at defiance, and roused them to deeds of renown; but such instances were rare, and only occurred to render their degradation more deep, and their chains more galling. In a word, their institutions are incompatible with true liberty, and as sure as slavery in the West has brutalized the minds of its votaries, as well as its subjects, has rendered them callous and indifferent to the interests of others, and has smothered the aspirations of independence and self-respect; so idolatry in the East has prostrated the finest feelings of our nature, —has thrown the chains of slavery and degradation around her votaries,—has extinguished the sparks of patriotism,—and has rendered her beautiful dominions an arena for the despot and the fiend. Nay, she may remain under the sway of Great Britain to the latest generation; but never till her idolatry is destroyed;—never till the Braminical system is broken and annihilated;—never till the religion of the Bible has imparted to her intelligence, and power, and deliverance from moral bondage, will she imbibe the spirit of independence, and be restored to the enjoyment of the rights and privileges to which God and nature have given her a claim.

But however ruinous may be the effects which their idolatry produces upon their constitutions as individuals, upon their civil relations, and upon their public institutions, far more dreadful are its effects upon their morals. From gods who are represented as selfish, cruel, malicious and tyrannical;—who are held up, in the very shasters, as monsters of vice, of debauchery, murder, rapine, and all kinds of abomination;—who are perpetually engaged in broils and quarrels, invading each other's rights, and thwarting each other's purposes, delighting in mischief and demanding a worship which is polluted and degrading; what can we expect to find in the lives, the principles and the dispositions of their votaries? Nothing surely but their own image reflected;—nothing but an imitation of all their villanies and their crimes. As soon might we think of finding the mild and meek and gentle nature of the lamb, among the wild beasts of the forest, as to find truth and honour, virtue and honesty, justice and temperance, meekness and humility, purity, compassion and benevolence, among such a people.

Well may it be said in reference to this land, that the Lord our God looked down to see whether there were any among the race who did understand, or who sought after God; but no. "They are all gone aside; they are all together become filthy; there is none that doeth good; no, not one. Their throats are an open sepulchre; with their tongues they use deceit; the poison of asps is under their lips; their mouths are full of cursing and bitterness; their feet are swift to shed blood; destruction and misery are in their ways; the way of peace they have not known; there is no fear of God before their eyes." Not only have they changed the truth of God into a lie, but they worship and serve the creature more than the Creator who is blessed for ever. They have changed the glory of the incorruptible God, into an image made like to corruptible man, and to birds, and four-footed beasts, and to creeping things; and what has been the consequence? Not liking to retain God in their knowledge, he has given them up to a reprobate mind, and to do those things which are not convenient. They are filled with all unrighteousness, fornication, wickedness, covetousness, maliciousness; they are full of envy, murder, debate, deceit, malignity; they are whisperers, backbiters, haters of God, despiteful, proud, boasters, inventors of evil things, disobedient to parents; they are without understanding, covenant-breakers; they are without natural affection, implacable, and unmerciful.

It is impossible to write as we ought of Hindooism. As its festivals are a rendezvous where the furies assemble, and where riot and vice and debauchery throw aside their restraint; as their temples are covered with figures which are a disgrace even to our fallen nature, and which represent every diabolical crime that the annals of depravity can record; as their worship consists either in a frantic madness, or in a disgusting lasciviousness, or in a murderous cruelty, or in a bachanalian riot, what must be the moral and spiritual state of the people? It is a shame to speak of those things that are done of them in public, as well as in secret. During a short residence at Bellary, I accompanied a friend to one of their ceremonies, that I might see with my own eyes, and estimate for myself, the nature of their worship. The place of assembly was the residence of a Jungum priest, and the occasion was that of a man and his wife, who, in consequence of having obtained a son through the favour of their gooroo, determined to present to his feet an oblation of flowers. It was shocking to see a poor, dying, and contemptible worm occupy a chair as an object of worship, and to behold so many immortal beings profess to be his disciples and his adorers. It was disgusting to witness the airs, and the attitudes with which the dancing-women paid their devotions to their deity, and to hear the songs and din of instruments with which the musicians celebrated his praise. It was fearful to see a man and a woman bring their basin of flowers, and lave them upon the feet of a creature, as an offering of thanksgiving, and prostrate themselves in the dust before him as their divinity. But how shall I describe the scene that followed? Well might the old priest send limes to me and to my friend, and express his hope that we would squeeze some of the juice into our eyes, that we might witness no more of their performances. A dancing woman who seemed to have been reserved for this closing scene, began now her operations. What a sink of infamy! So indecent, so licentious, so degrading were the gestures and the dance of this female, that no harlot in Sodom could ever equal them. But the old gooroo appeared intoxicated with delight; the people seemed in a perfect frenzy; and as she advanced in her dance, and became more disgusting in her attitudes, they responded to her with their shouts of approbation. I was ashamed of my nature; but woe to the land that is cursed with such priests, and that has chosen such bestiality for its religion!

Alas! India, notwithstanding her connection with Britain, and the privileges which she enjoys, is still the dark valley of the shadow of death; she is still, like mystical Babylon, the habitation of devils, the hold of every foul spirit, and the cage of every unclean and hateful bird; she is still the Tophet of Ben-Hinnom, where the children pass through the fire unto Moloch, and the diabolical shouts are to be heard and the fumes of abominable sacrifices infect the air; she is still the chamber of imagery, where the form of creeping things and abominable beasts, and every sort of idol are pourtrayed upon the walls, where the ancients and the young unite to hold their censors, and send up clouds of incense to Baal, where all the women sit weeping for Tammuz, and where not seventy, not a million, but where all the men have their backs turned to the temple of the Lord, and are worshipping the sun, and the host of heaven; and she is still the mighty continent of the East, swarming with a hundred millions of enslaved freemen, heaving with the evils, and the calamities which Satan and his agents have inflicted for many an age, and prepared, like the cities of the plain, to be visited with snares, fire and brimstone as the portion of her cup. Who would not weep and mourn over the guilt, the superstitions, and the idolatry of India?

CHAPTER III.

THE BRITISH POWER IN INDIA.

THE TRANSFER OF INDIA TO GREAT BRITAIN—THE MEANS ADOPTED TO GAIN IT, MUCH TO BE CONDEMNED—THE STATE OF INDIA UNDER FORMER CONQUERORS—THE DESIGN OF GOD IN PUTTING HER INTO OUR POWER—THE OBSTACLES TO THE ENTRANCE OF THE TRUTH—THE GRACIOUS INTERPOSITION OF PROVIDENCE—CHRISTIANITY NOT LIKELY TO OVERTHROW OUR RULE—THE PROSPERITY OF OUR POWER—THE OPINION OF SIR THOMAS MUNRO.

IN traversing the plains of India, and in contemplating the number and character of its inhabitants, how often have I reflected, with astonishment, on the strange and political phenomenon presented to my view. It is very easy to see how a country placed, in the centre of kingdoms, may become so powerful as to obtain their supremacy, and to render them all tributary to its aggrandizement. It is not difficult to comprehend how a conquering nation, whether it occupy an island, or the extremity of a continent, may extend its dominion over the territories of its neighbours, and make them tremble under its frown, or rejoice in its protection. But that an island of the western sea,—that a country which scarcely contained twenty millions of inhabitants,—that a nation which has been called to struggle with accumulated difficulties in its own government, should,—at a time when America asserted her independence, and withdrew her support from the mother-land,—at a time when, with all the kingdoms of Europe leagued against her, she was obliged to struggle for her own existence,—obtain the supremacy over the eastern continent, and bring the powerful kingdoms of which it is composed into subjection, and, at a distance of fifteen thousand miles, hold them in her paternal sway, is not to be accounted for on the ordinary principles of worldly calculation and of political economy. No; the man who would so account for it, would strangely overlook the divine administration of affairs. The fear of the Lord has unquestionably been upon the people; the distrust and disunion which have prevailed among them, have been our strength and security; and while their confidence in our truth, and honour and honesty, is a very strong ground of attachment to us, yet the Lord fought the battle and gave us the victory. He introduced divisions into their councils and rendered them weak in enterprise; he caused the sword and the hand of every man to be turned against his neighbour; and he made the events of his providence contribute to the growth and establishment of our power, that he might exalt us, and make us the agents of his love.

Titus, the son of Vespasian, besieged and destroyed Jerusalem. After he entered the city, he viewed her walls, he inspected her bulwarks, he stood astonished at the strength of her fortifications, he acknowledged the omnipotent arm of the God of Israel, and in rapture he exclaimed, "It is manifest that the Almighty has fought for us, and has driven the Jews from these towers, since neither human force nor all the engines of the world could have effected it." But what are the walls and fortifications of Jerusalem, when compared with the fortresses which required to be stormed, and the battles which were to be fought, and the formidable obstacles which had to be surmounted in taking possession of our Indian empire? Nothing but the power of the Almighty could have made us the rulers of such a continent. To Him, then, be the glory, the honour, the power and the victory.

In making such remarks, I do not wish to justify the measures which have often been pursued, in the acquisition of our Indian territories. Not at all. Our methods have been too much in accordance with the system which heathen and Mahommedan conquerors have adopted. If truth and honour and justice have sometimes prevailed; gold, injustice, and oppression have more frequently triumphed; and while the governor of the universe has the most benign and gracious designs in view, the agents who have accomplished his purposes have not thought so, nor have they reasoned so.

From time immemorial, India has been an oppressed, an afflicted, and a misgoverned country. As the Goths, the Vandals and the northern barbarians made eruptions into the Roman empire, spread ruin and devastation in their march, laid waste the beautiful fields of Italy, and took possession of the provinces, so the Persians, the Afghans, and the Tartars from the north poured in their hordes, with the violence of a hurricane, upon the continent of India—spreading terror, and destruction in their course. It matters not whether it was the armies of the great Alexander and the victorious generals who followed out his schemes of ambition; or whether it was the fleet and terrific cavalry of Mahmood and his successors of the Ghasnian dynasty; it matters not whether it was the fierce and barbarous Pindarees under a Mahratta confederacy, or the brave and conquering bands of British soldiers, under a Clive and a Cornwallis; the effects were nearly the same. Fire and sword spread their ravages on every side. Nothing was heard of but the burning of cities, the massacre of the young and the old, whole provinces given up to the spoiler, large and powerful armies cut to pieces. War brought the famine in its train, and the famine brought the pestilence, and the pestilence spread the ravages of death, till the population of the fairest provinces was often reduced to a mere remnant, till countries, once like the garden of the Lord, became an aceldama—a field of blood, and till a people, once happy and free, became abject and enslaved.

What were the causes of these terrible calamities? The gold and silver, the rubies and the diamonds with which India abounded and for which she was renowned, were no doubt a splendid lure to the robber and the spoiler. Her rich and prosperous plains, were a powerful temptation to the bands who left behind them, nothing but the barren mountain and the arid desert. But these were secondary causes. Her idolatry was the first, and most important reason. These armies were only the instruments of executing upon her, the wrath and vengeance of the Almighty. These wild and destructive invasions, were only the means of visiting upon her idols, upon her temples, and upon her people, the punishment due to their iniquities and their crimes. The Lord put her into the furnace of his wrath—not for seventy—but for seven hundred years; he sent upon her one storm of vengeance after another to humble her for her idolatry, and rebellions.

And why now is he giving to her a revival in her bondage?—why now, in opposition to the professed principles of our Indian government, and in defiance of express orders from the Court of Directors not to increase our territory and extend our frontier, has he put her into the hands of Great Britain—a humane and a Christian land?—why now is he granting to her peace and order and good government; causing her trade and commerce to revive; restoring to her the arts and the sciences; and giving her a protection and prosperity which she has not enjoyed for many an age? Is it merely to gratify the pride and vanity of her conquerors? to increase our wealth and our aggrandizements, and to afford a theatre for our arms in war, and our legislation in peace?—No! It is because the time—the set time—to favour India is come, and her nations are born who are to praise the Lord. It is because she is soon to forget her idolatry for ever, and the vile divinities are to perish out of her abodes. It is because the Lord has determined to add her, as another gem, to the mediatorial crown of his Son; and to confer upon her the best boon which heaven can bestow upon a country—the gospel and religion of Jesus Christ.

Never, in its introduction to a country, has the missionary enterprise met with greater difficulties, than in India. Nothing but a gracious Providence could have overcome them, and given to his people, the victory. As though it were not enough that we had 15,000 miles of the ocean to traverse, and stand exposed to the storms and dangers of the deep, and that we had to contend with an insalubrious climate, and master the difficulties of a strange language; as though it were not enough that the heathen, in their attachment to caste, and to their superstition, were against us; that our own countrymen, in their prejudices, their infidelity, and in their predilections for customs hostile to the gospel, were against us; and that the powers of darkness and spiritual wickedness in high places were against us; the government, in its policy and in its laws, were in direct hostility to our entrance into the field. It was impossible to go in a ship from Britain, bound to any of our Indian presidencies. Dr. Bogue, Mr. Ewing, and other noble-minded and benevolent men were interdicted from leaving our native country at all. Those who were not put under the bann, and whose zeal and intrepidity led them to brave every obstacle, had to find their way to Holland, or to America, or to the Cape of Good Hope, that from thence they might embark, and peradventure be smuggled like contraband goods, upon the shores of Hindosthan. The Baptist missionaries, on their arrival at Calcutta, were not suffered to remain on British ground, and were obliged to take refuge in Serampore, a Danish settlement—where they were permitted to carry on their labours in peace. The American brethren whose names are embalmed in the memory of the churches, were driven from Christian protection, and were exposed to a long night of trial, privation and suffering.

When our dear brother Hands reached Madras in 1809, he was more than once summoned before the authorities to know with what design he had come to India; and had it not been for the interposition of a most excellent chaplain who pleaded for his stay, he would unquestionably have been ordered home. After he had gone into the interior, and had settled at Bellary, he wrote to the Missionary Society, entreating them to send him assistance. Mr. Thompson was appointed as his coadjutor; but unable to procure a passage to Madras, he was obliged to take one for Calcutta, and embarking in a different vessel there, came back to the port of his destination. The Governor-general of that day heard of the event, and sent an express to the Governor of Fort St. George, giving peremptory instructions to put Mr. Thompson, on his arrival, under the bann of the government, and to send him from the country by the first ship bound for England. So far could the power and tyranny of man extend, but no further. They laid Mr. Thompson under arrest, but Providence rescued him from their grasp, and set him at liberty. This servant of the Lord was seized with a violent fever, and before the messengers of despotism could accomplish their purpose, he died in peace; and his brethren consigned him to the tomb, in sure and certain hope of a glorious resurrection to immortality. Thus as Abraham and Isaac and Jacob took possession of the land of Canaan in their sepulchre, so did Mr. Thompson and so have many of his brethren, in their burial-place, taken possession of India, as the land which is, in due time, to be given to the spiritual Israel.

But what were the effects which were produced by this policy? It turned out rather for the furtherance of the gospel. The Lord made the wrath of man to praise Him, and the remainder thereof He restrained. These facts roused the British and religious public, and, on the renewal of the charter in 1813, the conflict was transferred from India, to the British parliament, and metropolis. Major Twining and his band thundered forth their anathemas against the missionaries and their cause. The Vellore mutiny was attributed to their influence and exertions; they were denounced as traitors, firebrands, and conspirators. Nothing but rebellions among the natives, it was predicted, must arise from their efforts; and our Indian empire must be lost, if such enthusiasts were allowed to reside in the land. But what availed this noisy and fiery opposition, when the purposes of Jehovah were to be accomplished? No. The angel of the covenant stood up for the conversion of India, and showed that He was mightier than all they who could be against it; and as a triumph to the contest, Mr. Wilberforce, who was then the friend of the slaves and enemy of slavery, appeared as the advocate of liberty and truth, and introduced into the charter, a clause in virtue of which missionaries were permitted to go out among the heathen, and range through the length and breadth of the empire, to propagate the gospel. What then, though the heathen rage and the people imagine a vain thing? what though the kings of the earth, and the princes thereof take counsel against the Lord and against his anointed, saying, "Let us break their bands asunder, and cast away their cords from us!" He that sitteth in heaven shall laugh at them; the Lord shall have them in derision; He will speak to them in his wrath and vex them in his sore displeasure; and notwithstanding all their hostility, and their combined efforts to thwart his counsels, "He will set his king upon his holy hill of Zion; and he will give his Son, the heathen for his inheritance, and the uttermost parts of the earth for his possession."

What, more than this struggle, could resemble the conflict which the few fishermen of Galilee had to maintain with the Jewish state and the Roman Empire in the first propagation of the truth? In defiance of pains and penalties which were to be visited upon every offender; in the face of a system of espionage carried on by the Indian government at home, and a system of exclusion which was scarcely ever departed from abroad, a few of the men who threatened to turn the world upside down, find their way to India. The power of the empire is arrayed against them. While some are allowed, on neutral ground, to carry on their labours unknown and disregarded, others are driven out of the country. India is to be hermetically sealed against the gospel. A system of calumny and persecution, threatens to annihilate every hope of storming the strong-holds of Satan. The laws of the Sanhedrim and the decisions of councils, forbid the servants of God to speak in the name of Jesus. Everywhere, they are denounced as pestilent fellows, as movers of sedition and as ringleaders of the sect of the Nazarene, and who will venture to advocate their cause? No; it is not by might, nor by power, but by the spirit of the Lord. At his word, the hills and mountains of difficulty are made to bow; and a highway is prepared for the chariot of salvation. The very persecutions of Herod and the Jews, are the means of opening a wider and more effectual door among the Gentiles. The hand of the Lord is with the missionaries, as it was with the evangelists and the believers. It is the counsel of heaven and who shall disannul it? His purpose shall stand and He will do all his pleasure; and His church and his servants are therefore permitted to take possession of India, as a kingdom which is, in due time, to become his own.

It has long been laid down in India, as an incontrovertible axiom, that the progress of our religion among the natives, is incompatible with the maintenance of our rule. On this ground, what laws to disqualify Christian natives for the service of the state! what zeal in support of idolatry and superstition! what oppressive enactments against the natives who have professed Christianity! what contempt and opprobrium and even persecution to frown real religion among our own countrymen into obscurity! Could any thing be more intolerant, more opposed to every wise and beneficent principle of government, or more deserving of the disapprobation of the Almighty? Human nature is blind to reason and to wisdom, otherwise the Indian government must have seen, before this time, the influence of Christianity upon their rule, and the intimate connexion which must subsist between its advancement, and the prosperity of the empire. Since the year 1813, when missionaries were permitted to land in India, and proclaim mercy to the heathen, what, I ask, has been the state of our political, our commercial and our military interests? what! but one of unparalleled prosperity? Victory has crowned our arms in the field. The Pindarries have been hunted into oblivion, and their Maharatta confederacy broken and brought to an end. The haughty Burmese who threatened to overwhelm us with confusion, have been humbled and obliged to yield a tributary acknowledgment to our power. The strong-hold of Bhurtpore which, on former occasions, was deemed impregnable to our assaults, and terrible to our troops, has fallen before British valour, and has been levelled with the ground. Instead of mutinies and plots ending as that of Vellore,* in deeds of horror, they have

* In 1806, a dreadful massacre took place at Vellore. The Seapoys were then in the habit of taking home their muskets; and in the dead of night while the British officers were reposing in security at home, and the soldiers in their barracks, the cowardly assassins poured in their fire through the windows upon the slumbering victims. Sixteen officers, and about a hundred soldiers were murdered; and for a time, the insurgents had

been exploded by Providence, and their authors brought to light and to punishment. The Rajahs of Coorg and Goomsoor and their adherents who boasted so loudly of their power, and talked so contemptuously of the Christians and of the Galilean, were speedily driven from their bulwarks, and reduced to subjection. And though in such an immense empire as India, there will be many events to agitate, the Lord has prospered us for his own name sake, and to uphold his glory in the sight of the heathen.

It is at present with our Eastern possessions, as it was, with Judea, under some of her kings. Their reign was a blessing; judges were appointed to administer the laws in truth and righteousness; the Levites were allowed to go through the land to instruct the people; and the worship of the God of Israel was maintained and acknowledged at Jerusalem. Nevertheless, the high-places were not

possession of the fort. But, at the head of the 19th dragoons, and a regiment of native cavalry, Colonel Gillespie soon compelled them to surrender. Some enemies of the truth, wished to attribute this plot to missionary exertions. But besides that there was no English missionary then in the Peninsula, and not a Danish one almost within a hundred miles, the event was easily accounted for. Tipoo's sons were prisoners; many of their adherents in the army, wished for an occasion to rise in their favour; a government order had proposed some change in the uniform, the turban and the marks of caste; and taking advantage of this regulation, the Musselmen proclaimed that the government wished to make the native army Christians by force, and the night after this order was issued, the horrid conspiracy was carried into execution.

taken away; the altars erected to Baal were not thrown to the ground; and what was the consequence? The Lord subdued their enemies before them, but his favour was not fully enjoyed; peace and prosperity were the privileges of their times, but the curses which the prophets had pronounced, were not repealed; judgments were suspended for a time, but were laid up in store for posterity. So our Eastern rule has been blest; measures of amelioration have been adopted for the benefit of the people; judges and magistrates administer the laws in equity and righteousness; Christianity is acknowledged and, to a certain extent, the worship of Jehovah is maintained; missionaries are permitted to go through the land, declaring the truth; what then hinders that the divine blessing, in all its extent, should be granted? Alas! the high-places of Jugernaut and Gya and Allahabad have not been taken away; the pilgrim-tax has not been abolished; the government is still in league with idolatry; and a revenue is collected from the festivals which are celebrated to Moloch. But let these evils be done away; let the lands and endowment of idolatry be given back to the management of their natural trustees; and let Christian authorities wipe away this reproach from the British name and nation; and what, then, may we expect? That the blessing of the Lord will be more fully enjoyed; that peace and prosperity will be our crown of joy; that the empire will be consolidated and its interests advanced; that a long and glorious career will attend our rule over that people; that the curse which is sure to rest upon the abettors of idolatry, will be removed from our own land; and that our prosperity at home and abroad will be great and lasting.

Nothing it appears to me can be more absurd, than to suppose that the progress of our religion will become the bane of our Indian rule. Where could such an opinion originate? The natives who are already converted, and profess attachment to the truth, are they become enemies of Britain and its government? No, they feel identified with its welfare; it is the ground of their security; and though they are the only class who have to complain of its intolerance, there are none, among its subjects, so devoted to its rule, and so likely to take its side in the day of trial. What then would be the feelings and the sentiments of the millions, were they, instead of the hundreds, to abandon their idols and submit to the power of the gospel? Exactly the same. Whatever insurrections might arise in the empire; they would invariably be found on the side of a Christian, and a Protestant government; since the establishment of a heathen or a Mahomedan rule must be to them oppression, persecution, and death.

Most gladly do I avail myself of the support which these sentiments receive, from similar opinions recorded by the wise and intelligent Sir Thomas Munro. In an address to the government of Fort

St. George, he thus writes: "The facts which I have described seem to authorise the conclusion—a conclusion which, I am convinced, will be further confirmed the more the subject is examined and studied—that whatever impediments may be opposed to the progress of Christianity, will proceed from political not religious jealousy. They who cherish sentiments of hostility against the British power, and hopes of instability will, of course, decry any measures calculated to unite the interest of a body of the people with its permanency. That power is exposed to greater danger from secret conspiracy, than from open resistance; and this danger must increase with the extension of the British possessions, which augments the disproportion in numbers, already so immense between the rulers, and the subjects. But in establishing a body of native subjects connected with the mass of the people by a community of language, occupations and pursuits, and united to the British government by the stronger ties of religion, and mutual safety; ample means would be acquired of procuring information of the proceedings of the people, and of all machinations against the British power. In the course of time still greater advantages would arise; the support of a respectable body of Christian subjects would contribute to strengthen the British power in those junctures of commotion and difficulty which must be expected to occur in a country like India that has been in a state of revolution for ages. The introduction of Christianity in some of the provinces, may be attended with delays; but in Travancore and Cochin, there is already a numerous body of Christian inhabitants, who with moderate assistance and encouragement from the British government, will firmly attach themselves to its interests, and may prove of material service in supporting its power."

CHAPTER IV.

THE MYTHOLOGY OF INDIA.

THE FEARFUL SYSTEM TO BE OVERTHROWN—THE GREAT BRUM—THE IMMENSE NUMBER OF THEIR GODS—THE EXPECTATIONS OF THE PEOPLE—THE PRIESTHOOD—THE POWER OF THE BRAMINS ON THE DECLINE—THE JOGEES—THEIR ESTIMATION IN FORMER TIMES, COMPARED WITH THEIR PRESENT CHARACTER AND INFLUENCE.

In what terms shall I describe the Hindoo Mythology? There never was, in any age, nor in any country, a superstition so cruel, so atrocious and so diabolical as that which has reigned over this people. It is a personification of evil. Satan seems to have used all his ingenuity, his malice and his gigantic power to create a system which would represent all his own attributes upon the earth, render its votaries as much like his angels as possible, and make Hindosthan an image of the infernal regions. No one can imagine the mountains of difficulty which, in India, oppose the progress of the truth. It is not here, as it is in England, where though iniquity abounds in the hearts and in the lives of men, there is a conscience to arraign, and to support the claims of truth, and where the individual has to overturn the barriers of reason, of religion, of example and of privilege in his mad career. It is not here as in the South Sea Islands where, notwithstanding the natural ferocity and barbarism of the people, their superstition was so gross that it was easily exposed; their priesthood was more dependent upon its own cunning and deceit for its stability, than upon its hereditary succession and its despotic control; their mythology was contained in the traditions which memory could retain, more than in writings which could boast of antiquity; and their whole system held its sway only over a scattered population which it was fast exterminating from the soil. It is not here as it is in Africa and the West Indies where the sons of Ham have been broken into wandering tribes, where a few imaginary beings have presided over their destiny, and where, under the oppression of barbarism on the one side, or under the yoke of slavery on the other, that gospel which proclaims liberty to the captive and the opening of the prison to them that are bound, and brings glad tidings to the meek and binds up the broken-hearted, appeared a welcome balm to heal their woes.—No! In India there is a system venerable for its antiquity; imposing in its ritual and its ceremonies; boasting of its sages, philosophers, its heroes and its martyrs; enshrined in vedas, shasters and pooranus; renowned for the splendour of its temples, the grandeur of its festivals, and the exploits of its deities; binding its hundreds of millions together, by the chains of caste, as with fetters of iron; and sending forth, upon the whole world, from its bulwarks and its strongholds, a scowl of defiance. It will be necessary to take a short review of this system in various particulars, and contrast its former power with its present condition.

In the Mythology of the Hindoos, Brum is the great, the self-existent, the independent and eternal one. Residing in perpetual silence he takes no interest whatever in the affairs of the universe; his happiness consists in eternal and undisturbed repose; he is the soul of the world; his essence pervades all space; he is the life-giving energy in angels, in men, in devils, in the animate and inanimate creation; he fills all with his nature, and since the human soul is a part of his essence, and more of the latter is to be found in Bramins and ascetics than in any others, he receives divine honour and worship, in proportion as it is rendered to them. Absorption, therefore, into the Deity is considered supreme happiness, and so long as the spirit is associated with matter, and struggles through its various births, and is disunited from the great spirit, so long it is considered a miserable wanderer from good and from felicity.

Brum gave existence to Brumha the creator, to Vishnoo the preserver, and to Sceva the destroyer, who, with their wives, have become incarnate in

SEEVA. BRAMHA, VEESHNOO.

forms, at times, and for objects almost without number. After them, there are arranged, in the Hindoo Pantheon, the deities who preside over the eight points of the heavens, over the elements, over mountains and seas, and lakes and rivers. Then follow the heavenly bodies, the planets, their heroes, devils, men, beasts, birds, serpents, stocks and stones; and amidst their three hundred and thirty millions of divinities, there is no want of those who are suited to the number, to the passions and the fears, to the prejudices and the wishes of their votaries. What, to a sober and reflecting mind, would be the value of these gods many and lords many? That they are all of yesterday; that they are vanity and a lie; that they are "nothing in the world;" that they are only the creatures of a base and puerile imagination. But they are not so in the estimation of Hindoos. Whatever may be the contempt in which they are held, and the derisions which their votaries may sometimes heap upon them, their gods were the creators of the world; at the churning of the sea, they performed their respective parts in the framing of the universe; millions of years are recounted in their existence, as so many days; the history of time, is the developement of their religion; Yoog is added to Manuwantra, and Manuwantra to Culpa, to bestow on their superstition an indefinite antiquity.

But the system is not now what it once was. External calamities have, long since, shorn it of its glory; and internal feuds and divisions have weakened its power, and dried up its resources. It cannot boast any longer of the fervour of youth, nor the vigour of manhood. It is hoary with years; decrepitude has seized upon its limbs; decay and consumption have settled upon its vitals; and its age, instead of rendering it venerable, has prepared it for dissolution, and for the oblivion of the tomb. Dissatisfied with its promises and groaning under its exactions, its votaries are ready to throw off its yoke. It can afford no peace to their troubled consciences and their restless spirits. They now pant for a better system, and thirst for a greater salvation. With universal desire and expection, they turn to the tenth incarnation as the day-star of their hopes. At the time of his birth, an illustrious goddess is to be born, and is to become his consort in trouble and in prosperity. In consequence of the sin, and impiety which prevail throughout the world, the first days of their rule, are to be those of sorrow; war, strifes, and commotions are, for a season, to gain the ascendency; but after the storm, peace and happiness are to crown the earth; the golden age is to return; the days of paradise are to be restored; and love and union, good will and religion are to bind mankind in a universal brotherhood. What strange expectations these at such a time! may we not hope that they are to resemble those which pervaded the Gentile world, as well as the ancient church, previous to the advent of our Lord; and since the Redeemer and his church are, in the millennial age, to reign in universal empire over mankind, and render the earth an image of the heavenly Canaan, may we not hope that these are the cries, the groans, and the pangs of the whole creation which waits for deliverance and is ready to be set free.

Their priesthood next demands our attention. The Bramins of India are divided into two general classes, called the Loukeekaroo, and the Weideekaroo—that is the secular and the regular Bramins. The former class are given up to business, and are employed as schoolmasters, instructors of their language, clerks in offices, servants of the government, and sometimes as farmers and merchants. The latter or Weideekaroo, are, on the other hand, entirely devoted to the study of the vedas, to the worship of the gods, to the services of the temples, and to various duties of the priesthood. Their occupations thus differ, but their natures are one; their state and character are the same; and in former times, their power was supreme. Supposed to have sprung from the head of Brumha, while the Chetriyas only sprang from his shoulders; the Veisheas from his thighs, and the Shoodras from his feet, the Bramins have been regarded as the demi-gods of the earth; and they have received the honour and the worship which are due to the Almighty alone. No matter what might be their character and their principles, what the number of falsehoods they had told, and adulteries in which they had indulged, and murders which they had committed, they were regarded as the best, the wisest and the most benevolent of men. Their smile, in the eyes of the people, was better than the approbation of heaven, their anathema more dreadful than the prospect of hell. As they passed through the streets of the city, the inferior castes might be seen rushing from their houses, falling prostrate at their feet, invoking their blessing and deprecating their curse. It was when their power was paramount in India, that a Bramin, as I have heard, committed upon the western coast, a most horrid murder. Instead of allowing the culprit to walk at large, and set all law at defiance as such characters had been accustomed to do, the judge of the district, who was a determined man, ordered the criminal to be apprehended, committed him to prison, brought him to the bar of justice, entered into a full investigation of his case, and when he found him guilty, pronounced upon him the sentence of death. As this intelligence circulated through the community, the whole province seemed in a state of insurrection. "What! will the British government," said the populace, "venture to execute a Bramin? It is evident that the wrath and the vengeance of the gods are about to descend on them. After such an act of criminality, it is impossible they can maintain their authority in this land. Their power must pass away as their predecessors' has done. Woe be to the parties who would do violence to a Bramin!" One memorial followed another to the judge, entreating him to set the culprit free, and to restore him to his liberty and his family again, and warning him of the consequences, should he persevere in his course. But no. The judge was a resolute man; law and justice in his view, were supreme; and on the morning of the execution, he went himself to the gallows and saw the sentence carried into effect. That moment the spell was broken, and the enchantment was dissolved. The eyes of the people were opened; they began to see that if a Bramin committed a murder, or was guilty of a crime deserving of death, he ought to suffer the penalty of the law, as well as the poorest Pariah in the land.

Similar cases have occurred in other parts of India, and have been attended with similar effects. The delusion has been dispelled from the minds of the people that the Bramins are immaculate, that they are above all ordinary laws and subject to no other, and that they may riot, with impunity, in their iniquities and their crimes. No circumstances, perhaps, more than these, have contributed to humble the power of the Bramins and to emancipate the people from their grasp. In the more retired districts of the empire where the influence of knowledge and of the British power are comparatively unknown and unfelt, the Bramins may still hold their despotic sway over the other classes, but in the provinces under the British dominion, their influence and their superiority are fast wasting away. Nay more. Only let the measures which have been sanctioned by the government at home, be carried into effect by the executive abroad; let the pilgrim-tax be abolished; let the connexion which has hitherto subsisted between the state and idolatry be dissolved; leave Hindooism to its own endowments, its resources and the support of its admirers; and what shall we speedily hear? That the idols have perished out of the land; that they have no food to eat, no water to drink, and no raiment to wear; that they have no light to illuminate their darkness; that they have no votaries to present to them offerings and sacrifices; that they have no devotees to throw themselves under the wheels of their murderous cars. No; as sure as the gods of Greece and of Rome have perished out of the earth; as sure as the gods of Arphad and Hamath and Sepharvaim have come to an end, so sure it is that the day will come when the gods of India will be recognized only in story and in song. The hand of the Lord is upon the idols to exterminate them from the earth; every Dagon must fall before the ark of the covenant;

and Jesus Christ must have the glory the honour and the praise.

The ascetics or Jogees form a considerable class of devotees in India. A few of them perhaps, under a sense of sin, thirsting after immortality, and seeking absorption into the Deity as their supreme good, are led to forsake their homes, and practise the austerities which a cruel superstition requires. But the great majority are animated by no such motives. Ambition, vanity, love of admiration, and thirst for fame and for honour and renown, the hope of being worshipped now, and of being elevated into a divinity after death, are unquestionably the ruling passions of those who embark in this arduous enterprise. One man lies on a bed of spikes or travels to Benares upon shoes whose irons lacerate his flesh, and thus he inflicts tortures upon his body for the good of his soul; another undertakes a long and wearisome pilgrimage from the extreme north to Rameeshwarum in the south, or from the extreme south to Benares in the north, measuring, with his body, the extent of his journey, oppressed often with hunger and starvation, and falling an easy prey to every calamity. This man sits in the midst of four fires, while the sun is sending down his heat, like a furnace, upon his head, during the day, stands up to his neck in a river, or in a tank, during the night, that thus the juices of his body may be dried up and he may obtain emancipation from his passions and his sins; that one forsakes a comfortable and happy home, resides, like a miserable hermit, among the beasts of the forest, lives upon the roots of the desert, and perseveres in his tortures, till his arm is paralyzed and stiffened, or till his nails have grown out from the back of his hand, or till his limbs are unable to bear him from his cell. Chrisna goes to the Himalaya, that standing in the midst of their frost and their snow, the cold may seize upon his vitals, and he may throw himself down from some terrible precipice, and may sink into the arms of death in pursuit of a phantom, and a lie. Ramasamee attends the swinging festival, as a suneyasee; he receives the plaudits of the multitude; he imposes upon himself a vow of perpetual silence; the hook is thrust through the tendons of his back; he is suspended in the air, and is swung round as a votary to propitiate the favour of some exasperated deity.

In former times, the greatest reverence was paid to ascetics; the people worshipped them as divinities; their blessings and their instructions were deemed of the highest value; and their tortures and austerities were not only regarded as meritorious, but were celebrated in poetry and prose. What now is the general estimate that is formed of them? The few may still be disposed to pay them reverence, but the many regard them either as fools to part with their comforts, or as knaves who wish to practise upon their brethren. It is the general belief that there are no real Jogees now, and that those who make pretensions to it, are hypocrites and deceivers. I once had an exemplification of this credulity while attending a swinging festival in the neighbourhood of Bangalore. Thousands were assembled to witness the spectacle. Much time was spent in breaking cocoa-nuts before the idol; a sheep was then offered in sacrifice, and its blood was sprinkled around as an expiation. On a very strong and substantial pedestal, there was raised, upon a swivel, a very large tree which could thus be lowered or elevated as required, and a rope, to which a large hook was attached, was suspended from the end of it. We waited long, but no votaries appeared. At length some merry and mischievous fellows who longed for a game of play, turned the whole ceremony into ridicule. Professing to be Jogees, they put the iron hook through their cotton girdle, they mounted the step, were hoisted into the air, and holding fast by the rope, they were swung round, to the great amusement of the spectators. The whole assembly were convulsed with laughter. It was a real farce, and the caricature was complete. Nothing was heard but shouts of approbation. "Capital ascetics these!" said one; "They take good care of their flesh," said another; "That is the best way of swinging," said a third. I have never seen any thing that placed the ceremony of those Jogees in a more ridiculous light, and when a people once begin to caricature and contemn their religion, and hold up its solemn institutions to laughter; it has no longer any hold on their affections; they will soon cease to reverence it; and another more suited to their wants and to their reasòn must be chosen in its place.

CHAPTER V.

THE SANGUINARY SUPERSTITION OF INDIA.

THE SUPERSTITIOUS INFLUENCE OF HINDOOISM ON ITS VOTARIES—THE JUGGLERS—THE FEARS WHICH A GIANTESS INSPIRED—CHRISTIANS EMANCIPATED FROM SUCH EVILS—HUMAN SACRIFICES OF GOOMSUR—DEEDS OF BLOOD MINGLED WITH THE HABITS OF THE PEOPLE—THE SYSTEM OF THE THUGS—A DESCRIPTION OF THEIR DEITY—ATROCITIES REGARDED AS ACTS OF RELIGION—HORRID MURDERS—THE SYSTEM LICENSED BY FORMER AUTHORITIES—THE EFFORTS OF THE BRITISH GOVERNMENT TO PUT IT DOWN—HINDOOISM AS IT NOW APPEARS COMPARED WITH FORMER REPRESENTATIONS.

THE superstitions of the Hindoos, exercise an extraordinary influence over their minds, fill them with fear and terror, and give a surprising advantage to impostors, to astrologers, to magicians, and to others who are in league with the wicked one. It is impossible to enter fully into this subject, or to make a Christian people understand and appreciate aright, all the privileges which our holy religion has conferred upon the community at large. What has become of the ghosts, the witches, the fairies and all the strange and mysterious beings of other days? The light of the gospel has chased them away, and their visits and their influence are now comparatively unknown. But in India, there is a darkness that may be felt; Satan reigns supreme over the minds, and among the habitations of its people. Individuals said to be possessed of the devil, obtain incredible power, and will run for miles, with a stone upon their heads, which would require many men to lift; and the land is full of jugglers, necromancers, and alchymists who, in your presence, will perform most incredible feats. I was one of those who are disposed to laugh at such deeds, and regard them as childish manœuvres. But a juggler called one day at my house, and I asked him to show me some of his exploits. After making ribbons, and performing some very curious deeds, he asked me if I had a rupee. Yes, I replied, I have one, and taking a rupee out of my pocket, I showed it, to him, in my hand. He was sitting on the carpet, and I was standing not less than five or six feet from him. "Well! sir," said he, "you are sure you have it?" "O yes," I replied, and held it with a firmer grasp. "Now," he said, "open your hand." I did so, very cautiously, lest any trick should be played; but all my caution was vain; my hand drew back with an involuntary shudder; there leaped out of it, a small snake, and sprang about on the floor. The juggler laid hold of the reptile and consigned it to his bag, and afterwards took my rupee out of his bag and gave it to me. How this was done, was always a mystery to me.

But amazing is the influence which their superstitions give to impostors and to knaves of every description, who work upon their fears and their apprehensions, and turn them to their own advantage. In the year 1831, and when the cholera was raging with terrific fury throughout the province, there came to Bangalore an immense giantess. Frightful in her appearance, she pretended to be the divinity who presided over the cholera; she passed through the streets and lanes of the town, and inspiring the people with terror, she cried aloud in the Canarese language, "Give me your plantains and cocoa-nuts, bring me out your fowls, hand me your money; depend upon it if you do not gratify all my wishes, I will enter into your houses, to-night, and destroy you all with the cholera." Then the people might be seen rushing out of their houses, falling prostrate at the feet of this infamous woman, and be heard crying aloud in reply, "Oh thou illustrious goddess! Have mercy upon us! have mercy upon us! pardon our iniquities; send not the cholera into our houses to destroy us and our children; preserve us, preserve us, O thou illustrious goddess!" After she had fleeced the people well, she commanded them to go to a certain part of the town and erect there a pandal or shed, to make an image to resemble her, and to bring their offerings and sacrifices to present them before her. Such was the terror with which she had inspired them, that they had only to obey her orders. She came and sat down as the presiding divinity; and they brought their sheep, their fowls, their goats and their buffaloes, and slew them, in order to propitiate her favour. After she had imposed upon the credulous people in Bangalore, she went off to the capital to act a similar part with its inhabitants.

In this manner, does idolatry and its superstitions exercise a debasing and pernicious influence over its votaries. They are afraid at the signs of heaven, at the changes of the seasons, at the fury of the elements, at the events of providence, at beings seen and unseen. An evil eye troubles them; the flight of a crow, or a similar unfavourable omen, will prevent them from undertaking a journey; their cattle and their children often die, as they suppose, from witchcraft; necromancers inspire them with terror; and Satan leads them, like his slaves, captive at his will. But strange is the effect which Christianity produces upon them in this respect. No sooner are heathens turned from darkness to light, and from the power of Satan unto God, than they set the powers of evil at defiance; they are emancipated from this thraldom; they seem to come under a new dispensation, and they rejoice in Christ as their great Deliverer. I have known the native teachers to stand in the porch of their temples, call upon the priests and devotees to do their worst, and show how little they regarded their power and their enchantments. Like the children of Israel while they were in Egypt, Pharaoh and his taskmasters ground them to the dust, made their lives bitter in hard bondage, and caused them to cry aloud for deliverance, but now that, like Israel, God has led them forth with a mighty hand and an outstretched arm, and has set them free from the power of their enemies, they stand upon the shores of the Red Sea, sing, in triumph, the new song of Moses and the Lamb, and render praise and glory to the God of their salvation.

The human sacrifices which Hindooism demands are frightful and appalling. Whatever may be the character of the people; and however quiet, and passive and submissive they appear, their superstition is the most cruel and barbarous that has ever been established. In Goomsoor, a province which has lately fallen into the hands of the British, the horrid scenes which have been discovered, are almost beyond credibility. Whenever a disease raged in the family of the monarch, a human sacrifice was demanded to appease the offended deity, and nothing less precious than the life of an only son would gratify the demon. Immured in houses and in dungeons, there were found hundreds of poor children who had been stolen from the adjoining territories; and for what purpose were they concealed and preserved? that they might be fattened like so many sheep and oxen for the slaughter, and might, at a suitable season, be offered up to the Moloch of the country.

At the seed-time, the farmers of a district would assemble together; a human victim was selected, was bound as a sacrifice, to the altar, and was devoted to the most barbarous death. While the priest proclaimed the omens to be propitious, one farmer would come, and with a large knife, would take a slice from the victim, would carry it away to his field, and would press the blood out of it while it was yet warm, and then bury it in the earth. A second, and a third, and a fourth, would come and act a similar part, till the wretched man was sliced in pieces while he was yet alive, and was consigned to various parts of the ground. But why this barbarity? That the favour of Maree might be obtained, and that no curse, nor blight might rest upon their land; and that a richer harvest might arise from fields watered by the blood of sacrifice. Oh! these dark places of the earth are still full of the habitations of cruelty.

Deeds of blood and atrocity are mixed up with the habits and customs of the people, and fail to produce any great sensation. In England, if a mother strangles her infant; if a father murders his son; if a brother puts a sister to death, a thrill of horror passes through the community; the public voice is lifted up, in loud and terrible denunciations, against such a diabolical act; and the wonder is expressed how such a monster is permitted to live. But in India, such deeds are so common that they have failed to make any impression upon the community, and are often regarded by their authors as actions of merit, rather than of infamy.

In the province of Benares, two Bramins named Beechuk and Adher, lived on very bad terms with a man of the name of Goury and his confederates. The quarrel arose out of the general superintendence of the village, having been conferred on Goury. Unable to tolerate such an arrangement, the mother of the Bramins continued, by threats, to intimidate the government-officer, compelled him to revoke the appointment, and to transfer it to her sons.

While the Bramins were absent from home one day, the companions of Goury are said to have entered their house, and carried away forty rupees which belonged to them. As soon as Beechuk returned, his mother, his wife and his sister-in-law, related to him what had occurred. He delayed not his revenge; but how did he take it? Did he enter an action against the parties in the court of justice? Did he send for police-officers to apprehend the guilty?—No! He conducted his mother—his aged and grey-headed mother—to an adjacent rivulet, and joined there at the dawn of the morning by his brother, they shouted to the people of the village: "Now we can overlook the assault, as that cannot be remedied; but we cannot forgive the seizure of these forty rupees; restore them to us, or the blood of this woman be upon your heads." The shout was neither heard, nor replied to, and how did Beechuk take his revenge? He drew his scimitar, and at one stroke, severed his mother's head from her body, and consigned both to the ground, that her spirit, excited by the beating of a large drum, might continue to haunt and torment Goury and his associates, till they committed the crime of suicide, or till some fearful calamity befell them.*

Much as we should wish for the sake of humanity, that this was a solitary and a very uncommon case, yet experience and the records of history show that it is not. The horrid system which the Thugs have pursued, has been but recently discovered, but it is no new feature of Hindoo idolatry. Speak of the evils attendant upon slavery in the West! what are these? Speak of the ferocity and barbarism which characterize some of the tribes in Africa, who resemble more the lions and the tigers of the wilderness, than the race of man! what are these? Speak of the murders, the atrocities and the savage cannibalism for which the New Zealanders and such pagans are distinguished! what are these? No; such ferocity springs from the horrid depravity of man, and is to be accounted for by the sanguinary habits which they have learned from the beasts of the forest. But here is a system of wholesale murder and robbery, under the sanction

* Asiatic Researches.

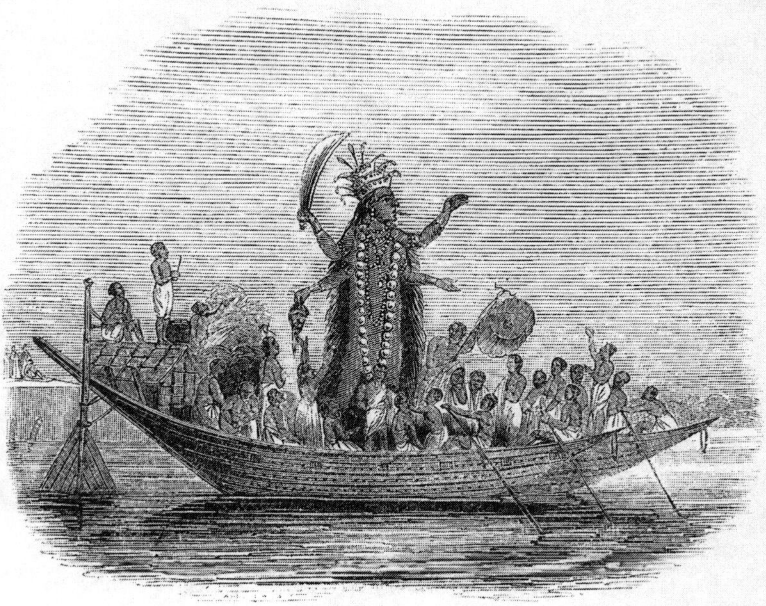

KALEE POOJAH.

WORSHIP OF THE SERPENT IN INDIA

of religion, springing out of the laws and ordinances of the people, pursued by a sect who assert it to be of divine origin, and who think that, in strangling their fellow-citizens, they are discharging a duty to their divinity, and have committed no crime of which conscience can accuse them. Ye admirers of Paganism and of the Hindoo mythology! listen to these men.

"Mahan-Kallee—the wife of Sceva—the goddess who stands upon the body of her husband, who holds a scimitar in her right hand, and a head just severed from its body in her left, whose hair is dishevelled, whose eyes are like balls of fire, who wears, as a garland, a necklace of skulls, and whose tongue thirsts for the blood of her victims, is the divinity whom we adore, and who is our protector in the discharge of our duties. In former times, a demon destroyed mankind as fast as they were created. The Devi took her scimitar, and in wrath beheaded the monster; but from every drop of blood that fell to the ground, there grew up a demon as wicked and as destructive as Rukut Beej Dhana himself. Still, their increase only gave power to her arm and edge to her weapons; but her efforts were vain; the demons multiplied in proportion to the number whom she slew. Her skill was more effectual than her power. She created two men, to whose hands she entrusted the sacred noose. 'Now,' said she, 'strangle these demons for me, and allow not a drop of their blood to be shed.' As soon as they executed her orders, she gave them the *romala** as a reward for their toil, with the permission to take the half of the race, and dispose of it for their own advantage, since through their efforts men were allowed to exist. Nay more, so long as they attended to her will and were guided by her counsels, all whom they would sacrifice were to be regarded as victims, to propitiate her favour, while all the booty which might be realized, would become their inheritance."

Such is the origin of Thuggee—a system more cruel, more shocking and more barbarous, because carried on under the mask of religion and often under sanction of law. The Gooroo inducted the stranglers into their office; rites and ceremonies were performed to obtain direction in the sacred duties; it was only when the omens were favourable, the parties were permitted to act; many of the leaders and renowned men, are talked of as the most pious, faithful and devoted; the pickaxe was not only endowed with supernatural powers, but was consecrated to the service, and its votaries swore under the most fearful sanctions, to use it with fidelity; the victims were all certain of happiness eternal, in consequence of their being offered up, in sacrifice, to the goddess; many of the bands, living in villages, have been regarded as the most peaceful, quiet, industrious, and benevolent citizens;

* A native turban.

and so long as the Thugs were faithful to their Kallee; so long as they attended to all the rites, the ceremonies and offerings by which they rendered to her worship and honour; so long as the order remained pure, and was not contaminated by the low and disreputable castes who never fail to infect those with whom they are associated; so long they prospered in their profession, and so long did they enjoy the favour and the protection of their deity. But now in consequence of these corruptions, they have fallen under her displeasure, and their system is likely to be exploded.

What a description do these assassins give of their murders! The traveller was arrested on his journey; the ascetic was strangled on his road to Juggernaut; the young sometimes have had their brains dashed out against a stone, and the old have had no mercy shown to them on account of their infirmities; the beautiful female and the pregnant mother have been treated with the same ferocity as the bold and the daring: the wealthy merchant has lost his life as well as his gains and his riches; and the Rajah, equipped for his journey, attended by his friends, his servants and his train of followers, accompanied by his elephants, his horses, his camels, his oxen, and all the paraphernalia of Eastern grandeur, has, with all his attendants, been murdered in a moment, and sixty persons have been consigned to one common grave. What to them was the kindness of friendship; the claims of hospitality; the interchange of social intercourse; the solemn promise; vows of protection to the young, the infirm and the lovely; and the sympathies excited by the woes and the calamities of others! all these were disregarded; and when a kind host has been entertaining them at his table and reposing his confidence in their brotherly regard, many of his guests have been engaged, outside the tent, in preparing his tomb, and have given him and his relatives a sepulchre, as a reward for his entertainment.

How, it may well be asked, could such a fraternity grow up in Hindoosthan, and be permitted to carry on their depredations for so many ages? But the same religion that allowed the mother to strangle her infant, that suffered the Bramins to offer up their human sacrifices, that commanded the helpless female to mount the funeral pile, that encouraged the devotee to throw himself under the wheels of Juggernaut, patronized the Thugs in their assassinations and gave them the license of plunder at their will. What class in the community then could dispute their right; or question their authority? So long too as these murders did not disturb their respective neighbourhoods, and their own friends and relatives were not seized as victims, what did Hindoos care about their country, their race, and the universal prosperity? Such is their apathy and indifference about the public good, that so long as the calamity does not affect themselves, they care very little about the amount of trials and sorrows and sufferings which others may be called to endure. This as I have observed elsewhere, is one of the great evils which arise from caste—it dissolves all those ties which ought to unite men together for the common welfare; and no human laws nor regulations will lead the natives of India to take the trouble, to manifest the interest, to make the sacrifice, and to supply the expenses which are necessary, in order to accomplish some great good which has more a reference to others, than to themselves, and to avert some evil which threatens the prosperity of all. Selfishness is their nature, and their superstition sanctions it to the fullest extent.

It is a frightful view that is given us of society; but it is not more frightful than true, that many of the native Rajahs had licensed the infamous system; a certain tax was levied upon every house which was known to be inhabited by a Thug; and under the sanction of the law and the government, the assassin was permited to carry on his atrocious deeds throughout the country. Nay, such was the encouragement which these murderers received, and so useful were they reckoned to the public treasury, that, when the British government resolved to put them down, and applied to the independent princes to co-operate with it in accomplishing this object, the Rajah of Joudpoor contended that he had a right to grant Thugs protection, and refused to give up the number who had taken refuge in his territory; and had it not been for the firmness of Lord William Bentinck who ordered an army to assemble on the frontier of his dominions, and showed him that it was impossible the Joudpoor province should become the rendezvous of a banditti who would commit their depredations with impunity, upon the other states of the empire, the system would have flourished under such protection to this day.

"The following is a brief summary of what has been effected for the suppression of Thuggee. In nine years more than two thousand Thugs have been arrested, one thousand four hundred and seventy have been tried and convicted in one hundred and sixty-seven trials, for the murder of nine hundred and forty-seven persons. Of these, three hundred and eighty-two have been hanged, nine hundred and nine transported, seventy-seven imprisoned for life, ninety-two imprisoned for certain periods, and twenty-one acquitted. Besides these, eleven have escaped, thirty-one died before sentence, and nearly two hundred and fifty have at different times been admitted king's evidences, and exempted from death or transportation—first, to secure the conviction of those already in custody; and secondly to aid in arresting their associates at large. In Malwa, Guzerat, Rajpootana and Delhi, Thuggee has in a great measure been suppressed. Great progress has also been made in the Lower Doab, in Oude, Hydrabad, and the Decan. In the Concan and Malabar, it appears never to have existed. But much yet remains to be done throughout the whole of Southern India, in the Carnatic, Mysore, and the Circars, also in Gwalior and Bundlecund, in Orissa, Behar, and Bengal. Captain Sleeman anticipates the greatest difficulty in dealing with the river Thugs of Bengal, who are supposed to be three hundred strong, and who he thinks will probably defy the efforts of our government, unless some special measure be sanctioned for their suppression. In the convictions of all the above trials, the Bhurtote, or strangler has been invariably executed, as the Bhurtote is the most experienced of the party, and must have given proofs of his judgment and skill, before he is permitted to undertake the office; he is always an exceeding villain. The Shumseas, or those employed to hold the hands of the victim, are considered to be a lower order of villains, and with these the sentence has often been commuted to transportation."*

What a system of horror does Hindooism appear to us now, when compared with the representations of other days! Very few years have elapsed since Satan and his emissaries attempted to deceive the church and the world, with the delusion that the Hindoos were a quiet, a mild, a harmless and a happy people; that their system of mythology was admirably suited to advance their welfare and pros-

* Asiatic Journal, 1836.

perity; and that, by the introduction of Christianity among them, we should only disturb their repose. The hideous deformities of the system were concealed from our view, and Satan thus hoped to maintain his place in peace. But God, in his providence, has strangely disappointed the wicked designs, and time after time, has exposed the crimes and the diabolical deeds, of this monster of depravity. As the atrocious Pharaoh, as the cruel oppressor, and as the bloodthirsty despot of the East, this fiend has been seen causing the children to pass through the fire unto Moloch, he has made the lives of his slaves bitter with hard bondage, and has tried to overwhelm them in ruin. But what is the blood of infants to satiate his cruelty! No; he has been seen dragging the helpless, the aged and the infirm to the banks of the Ganges to be offered up as victims to his voracious and his murderous appetite. But what is the blood of the aged and the feeble and the dying to quench his insatiable thirst for human sacrifices! He has been seen mounted on the murderous car of Juggernaut, lashing his votaries to their task, driving, in fury his ponderous wheels over the bodies of his victims, and whitening the fields of Aceldama with their bones; he has been seen raising the funeral-pile, and compelling thousands of poor and wretched females to throw themselves into the flames; he has been seen standing at the shrine of Mahin Kallee, demanding his human sacrifices, and practising on the hecatombs the most barbarous cruelty. But as though these victims were not numerous enough, as though his sanguinary chapter were not half unfolded, and as though he wished to consummate his triumph and consolidate his reign by multiplying the emissaries of his vengeance, he has scattered the Thugs through the empire, has commanded them to kill, plunder and destroy, and has given them a licence to execute in secret those horrible deeds which the voice of humanity, and public opinion, and good government, and the friends of society, were likely to exterminate, had they been rendered more public. But the villanies which he has thus attempted to perpetrate in secret, have now been published on the house-tops; providence has brought the system of infamy to light; the votaries of superstition themselves are alarmed at the accursed nature of his despotism; and the eyes of the Christian world are opened, and their sympathies are aroused, by the tremendous evils to which so many of their race and of their fellow-subjects are exposed; the strong arm of law and justice have followed his agents into their hiding-places; the system has been arrested in its progress and almost annihilated; and stronger and more determined bands of Christian heroes are advancing to attack an enemy whose villanies are so diabolical, and an empire whose inhabitants suffer such wrongs from the powers of darkness.

CHAPTER VI.

EFFECTS OF IDOLATRY.

THE GENERAL EFFECTS OF IDOLATRY DEPLORABLE—FEMALE DEGRADATION—THE PREVALENCE OF INFANTICIDE—THE SUTTEE—DESCRIPTION OF ONE—ABOLISHED BY LAW—GREATER EFFORTS REQUIRED TO ANNIHILATE SUCH ENORMITIES—FEMALE EXERTIONS GREATLY REQUIRED—THE SOCIETY FOR SENDING OUT FEMALES TO SUPERINTEND SCHOOLS.

SAD is the character of heathenism, and very deplorable are the prospects of its votaries. Their distance from God; their degradation; their prostration to dumb idols of wood and of stone, their services rendered to diverse lusts and pleasures; their strong delusions to believe a lie; their superstitions and abominable idolatries; and their exposure to the wrath and the condemnation of the Almighty; all are calculated to fill us with pity and compassion for their state, and to lead us to stretch forth the arm of deliverance for their rescue. But if there be one part of this system more cruel and diabolical than another, and which bears more the impress of him who has been a liar and a murderer from the beginning, it is the bearing which it has upon the female part of the community. Nothing can be more evident, than that the demons who established this system intended to support the strong in their mirth, their revelries, and their debaucheries, while they determined to trample the weak and the timid and the helpless in the dust.

As soon, therefore, as a Hindoo female has entered into existence, it is to be frowned upon by her parents merely on account of her sex. Her whole life is a series of insults and of disgrace. In the days of her childhood, she is made the drudge of the family, and every one thinks he has a right to despise her. If she is betrothed to an individual who is to become her future husband, she is sold like a slave to a man who loves her not and who cares for her not. Should her intended happen to die before the marriage be consummated, then she is doomed to perpetual widowhood—that is to perpetual infamy. In case he should survive, and she should enter the state of wedlock, it is to repair to the house of her mother-in-law where she is scolded, and buffeted, and treated almost like a beast of burden. Let her be hungry, she is obliged to wait till her master is satisfied. Should she fall into an error, there is no correction but an appeal to the lash. When they undertake a journey, she is not suffered to walk by the side of her husband; she must come up behind him, bearing the burden, as well as the heat of the day. Every step is to her a step of degradation. Her very sex has disqualified her for giving her testimony in a court of justice, and since no widow is there permitted to marry again, it is no extraordinary thing to see children of ten or twelve years of age, married to individuals of fifty or of sixty.

But these are mere trifles, and we might pass them by in silence, were it not that effects more diabolical remain behind. Speak you of the curse which in England rests upon the woman, it is a double—it is a ten-fold curse that rests upon her in Hindoosthan. For many a day, our ears were pained and our hearts were sickened with the tales of woe which reported to us the baseness of slavery, in heaping so many atrocities upon the female slaves in the West Indies; but what are these when compared with the calamities and the degradation which, according to law, and according to their mythology, fall to the lot of the daughters of India?

Infanticide, it is well known, still prevails to a very horrible extent throughout Hindoosthan. Among the Nairs upon the western coast; in Malwa and Rajapootan; in Oude and the northern provinces, it is impossible to calculate the amount of murder which is perpetrated upon female offspring. A few years ago, a gentleman belonging to the Bengal service was deputed by the government to make a tour through the northern and independent kingdoms, and to calculate the amount of evil which might arise from this source; and the report which he presented upon the subject, was sufficient to harrow up the feelings of the most hardened man, and to rend the heart of the most profligate female. In all the provinces through which he passed, the principal chiefs, not only acknowledged that this horrid rite existed among them, but that it was rooted in the affections of the people; that, with their own hands, they had murdered many of their own children, and that they knew their neighbours had destroyed many of theirs.

The following is a list of the proportions which were found in many of the villages between male and female children under twelve years of age: —There were found in Barilahori in eighty-five families, fifty-one boys, only fourteen girls; Cho-tilahori in fifty-eight families, sixty-six boys, and only fourteen girls; Garoli in seventy-nine familes seventy-nine boys and only twelve girls; Gurrum-garh in twelve families ten boys and only two girls; Manshargarh in seventy-one families fifty-eight boys and only four girls; Paprula in fifteen families twenty-two boys and no girls whatever.

Now, if the calculation be correct which shows that female births in our world, are equal, if they are not superior in number to those of the male; what an amount of murder is here committed upon female children! Oh! the vile and cruel parents, with what vengeance will the God of mercy find "in the skirts of their garments, the blood of the souls of these poor innocents?"

In riding through one of these villages, accompanied by his friend, this gentleman was clamourously attacked by a female who demanded of him to desist from making any further attempts to put down this horrible custom. As he turned to reason with her upon the subject, and show her the impropriety of her conduct, "No," said she, "it has existed from time immemorial; it has the support and sanction of the shasters; there are predictions upon record which show that female births must be calamitous to our tribe; and I demand of you, therefore, to desist from making any further attempts to put it down." Oh! what an infamous system must that be which turns mothers into monsters, which deprives them of all those feelings and affections which the brute creation never fail to exercise, and which robs so many hundreds and thousands of infants of life and of happiness? Such deeds of atrocity and blood are attributed, I am aware, to their high regard to *caste*, and to the superior rank which they imagine they sustain and which will not suffer them to give their daughters in marriage to those whom they regard as inferior in rank to themselves. But no; it is the system—it is this accursed system which has established this caste—it is this caste which generates this pride—it is this pride which begets this cruelty—it is this cruelty which steels the heart against compassion and which leads these parents to imbrue their hands in the blood of their female offspring.

No wonder that a system which is thus established in murder, and which is watered with the blood of infants, should pursue its victim throughout her life, and then attempt to bury her in flame. It is so, according to precepts of Hindoo mythology. No sooner is a Hindoo female of any rank deprived by death of her husband, than she is immediately surrounded by her priests and Bramins; for what purpose? Is it to pour into her widowed heart, the balm of sympathy, on this occasion of sorrow and anguish? Ah no! Is it to invite her to their homes that they may there give her the comforts and the consolations which their own absurd system might afford? By no means. It is to give her the dreadful alternative, to have her head shaved and to retire into a state of perpetual infamy, or to go to the funeral-pile of her husband, and there offer herself in sacrifice. When we think of the shame and the degradation which are the sure attendants upon the one, we need not be surprised that so many thousands have embraced the other.

Never shall I forget the evening when, at Bangalore, I was called to be the witness of such a horrid murder. As though it were not a deed of infamy and shame, but one of morality and religion; as though there were not space and opportunity enough in their own burning-ground to perpetrate this deed of darkness; as though they would outrage the feelings of humanity and benevolence and celebrate the orgies of their system in the face of day; as though they would insult the whole European community and show to British females to what a thorough degradation, they had reduced their sex, they brought forth their victims to the borders of the lake which is overlooked by the European cantonment; and there, in the face of day,—at a time when ladies and gentlemen were taking their drives for air and exercise—beneath the waving plumes and the scarlet dress and the golden epaulets which distinguish the general staff of the army, to give it the stamp and the sanction of British authority—and under the satrap of native power—and amidst thousands of spectators, they raised the funeral-pile. No words and no arguments which could be used by the writer, would prevail on the infatuated woman to relinquish her purpose. No. I saw her pacing her appointed circuits around that pile; I saw her ascend the bed of death and tied to the dead body of her husband; I saw her take her jewels from her ears, and her neck, and the various members of her body and distribute them as parting memorials to her friends; I saw her son—the child of her bowels—the boy whom she had nurtured and whom she had nursed, take the torch into his hand, and, in several places, kindle the flame that was to consume his mother; I saw the servants of iniquity cut the ropes to let the canopy of faggots fall upon her to crush her and to prevent her escape; and as these flames ascended, and as that pile became one mass of fire, I heard the horrid yell and the shout of exultation from the surrounding multitude, to drown the shrieks of their victim in the plaudits of their joy. Oh! I thought I was standing on the borders of the infernal lake; I wondered that the earth did not open her mouth to devour the perpetrators of this horrid murder!! ye mothers in Israel! ye whom the gospel of Jesus has elevated to your proper rank in society! pity your sex who are thus degraded in India, stand boldly forth for their relief, attempt to pluck them as brands from the everlasting burning.

It may be said, that this custom has been abolished by law, and that the power and authority of government have been exerted to prevent the recurrence of such deeds in our own provinces. Thanks to a gracious providence for this boon. During the administration of Lord William Bentinck, this abominable suttee was frowned into its hiding-place. But this is not enough. Since that period, many instances of this horrid custom, have occurred in the independent provinces, and some females, instigated by the Bramins, have not long ago, left the British territories, and in order to evade the law, have gone into the adjoining districts to immolate themselves upon the funeral-pile. The British government has, I rejoice to learn, not only protested against such acts of perfidy, but have declared to the ruling powers in these districts, that such deeds will not hereafter be suffered to pass with impunity. But this renders it quite plain that, whatever may be the law, this atrocious custom is not destroyed in the affections of the people. No. The hour, I trust, will never come when the British power will be withdrawn, or overthrown in India, till we have given to her people our religion and Christianity, as well as a specimen of our rule. But what if the hand-writing upon the wall should be against us?—what if we should be weighed in the balances and be found wanting?—what if in consequence of running counter to the gracious designs of providence, that empire should be wrested from our hands?—what, then, would avail these rules and regulations?—what would signify these acts of parliament to put down this abominable rite? They would only resemble an embankment which had been raised to stem the torrent for a time; but behind which, the waters had accumulated in greater force and violence and abundance, and which, when overturned, would allow not a stream, not a current, but a cataract of blood to descend to deluge the land. There would be no public opinion to stop it; there would be no power of the gospel to retard it; and in proportion as strangers and foreigners had exerted their authority and influence to put it down, in the same proportion would the Bramins and the priests and superstition riot in their freedom from restraint, and exult in their deeds of atrocity and blood.

What then, is necessary to be done? It is not enough that we abolish this horrid rite by acts of law and of parliament; we must destroy the system to which it belongs. It is not enough that we extinguish these flames; we must cause the waters of life and salvation to flow in such abundance through the country, that under any circumstances, they will never be rekindled. It is not enough that Hindoos are subject to the laws and ordinances, and statutes of men; we must disseminate among them the laws and gospel and injunctions of Jesus Christ, that when human power fails to uphold its acts, the power of the Bible may be there to enforce them. The enemy is not dead; it is only asleep. It waits for our missionaries, for the gospel, and for the distribution of our tracts and our scriptures; it waits for the establishment of schools, for the education of a native ministry and for the whole machinery of missions to be brought into operation; it waits for our fervent and importunate prayers and for the outpouring of the Holy Spirit from above to break its power and bring it into complete subjection. Let us not be afraid of the contest. The conscience of the world is now upon our side. Pity and compassion and all the best affections of our nature are in league with us. Humanity and benevolence tender us their support; the past triumphs of the gospel assure us of victory; all the wise and holy and good upon the earth animate us onward in this struggle; angels bending from their thrones rejoice over every sinner and every heathen that repenteth; and God the Father the Son and the Holy Ghost have pledged us their assistance in the hour of need, and their blessing to every effort that is made in their name.

In a special manner will it devolve upon our mothers and our sisters, upon our wives and our daughters, and upon our female friends to labour in this sacred cause, with a zeal, a diligence and perseverance commensurate with the great undertaking. No laurels, may indeed, in this struggle, decorate their brow; the honours and awards of fame may not wait upon their achievements; their names and their labours may very speedily be forgotten; and neglect and disappointment and similar evils may even be their present reward. But if it be true that the righteous shall shine as the brightness of the firmament, and they who turn many to righteousness as the stars for ever and ever; if it be true that the faithful servant to whose care five or ten talents have been entrusted and who has put them out to usury, will in the end be made ruler over as many cities; if it be true that the names of Clarkson and Wilberforce—men who stood forth, in the midst of scorn and contumely, as the advocates of the slaves, and toiled and fought for the destruction of slavery, will go down to posterity covered with honour and renown; will be held in everlasting remembrance, while the memory of the wicked shall rot; then, what will be the joys, what the awards of grace, what the exalted honours which await those pious and excellent females who will rise up like a host to extricate the daughters of India from their misery and their degradation?

I rejoice to find that a society has existed for some years, to send out ladies to superintend female schools in India, China, and the East. From the facts which are stated in this chapter, and from the utter neglect that is shown to female education in these heathen lands, no object can be of greater importance, and every one who desires the welfare of his race, must wish that great success may crown the undertaking. Difficulties will, no doubt, arise in the prosecution of the scheme, and such a society will, in its infancy, have to struggle with adversities similar to those which every benevolent institution has been obliged to submit to. Great wisdom, prudence, and devotedness will be required on the part of its directors and its friends to overcome prejudices, to surmount the scorn and contempt of the world, and to remove the fears and apprehensions which many of the best friends of Zion entertain respecting it. But should it outlive, as I trust it will do, all the anxieties of its friends, and all the scandals of its foes, what a heavenly spectacle will it present to our view of pious and devoted females—not only overcoming the weakness and timidity natural to their sex—not only leaving their homes, their friends and their country to which their warm affections render them so attached, and casting themselves almost without protection, and without guardians, upon the care of their Heavenly Father to pursue a career of mercy—but exposing themselves to the storm and the tempest for the sake of their Lord, braving the dangers of the ocean, and the toils and difficulties of a foreign clime to bring back the wanderers to the fold, and venturing to contend, on a dangerous strand, with the powers of evil, to rescue their sex from infamy and shame. My heart warms to this sister band. May they never want the protection, the friendship, the care, and the superintendence of their Almighty friend; and since theirs is a cause beset with greater trials, privations and sorrows, than ours, may grace and strength and power continually rest upon them from above. I hail them, with delight, on their career of benevolence. What though there should be no earthly reward! the Lord will be their inheritance. What though no honour nor favour, nor applause of men should animate their minds in the day of exertion and trial! the light of heaven, the approbation of their Master and a harvest of precious souls will be a higher recompense. What though peculiar temptations, and disasters and sufferings should threaten sometimes to overwhelm their spirits!

yet goodness and mercy will follow them all the days of their life; their dwelling-place will be in the house of our God for ever; and an entrance will be administered to them abundantly into the everlasting kingdom of our Lord and Saviour.

CHAPTER VII.

ON CASTE.

CASTE—ITS DIVISIONS—CONNECTS EVERY INDIVIDUAL WITH THE PAST AND THE FUTURE—A BRAMIN AT BELLARY—THE BANEFUL INFLUENCE OF CASTE ON TRADE AND COMMERCE HAS KEPT SOCIETY STATIONARY—THE GOOD EFFECTS OF IMPROVEMENT—THE GOVERNMENT MIGHT DO MUCH TO ABOLISH CASTE—PERNICIOUS EFFECTS UPON THE PRINCIPLES OF THE PEOPLE—A GREAT OBSTACLE TO THE PROGRESS OF THE GOSPEL—EXPOSES THE CONVERTS TO GREAT WORLDLY LOSS—HOW SUCH CONVERTS SHOULD BE REGARDED BY MISSIONARIES.

WHAT is caste? is a question which is often put to a missionary, in his visits to the churches, at home; and it is one which is really difficult to answer, since its ramifications, in the Hindoo system, are so deep, and its evils so numerous and appalling. Some have considered it a civil rite, while others have maintained that it is a religious one. But the truth is, it is so incorporated with the whole superstition, that it is both civil and religious, as far as Hindoo society can be said to partake of the one and the other. It is the adamantine chain which binds the distinct masses of the community together, and links them to their gross superstition; it is the foundation on which the fabric of their idolatry rests, and without which it must fall; it is that fatal, that retributive, that irresistible destiny which connects them with the life that was, the life that is, and the life that is to come. In the division which Bramha has made of mankind, the Bramins are the priesthood—the first order among men—the most sacred and divine of the race—and the most fortunate in securing every right and privilege to themselves; the Cheitras are the nobility to whose care are entrusted the kingly office, the affairs of government, the military and civil departments of the state; the Veishas are the merchants, the farmers, and those who, in England, would be denominated the respectable classes of society; the Shoodras are the great body of the people, and constitute the artificers, the tradesmen, the inferior agriculturists, and the working classes of all kinds. But these four tribes are divided and subdivided into many other castes who eat and drink together, intermarry among themselves, and have little intercourse with their kinsmen of the same general order. In addition to these, there are the Pariars who are esteemed the outcasts of society, the refuse of mankind, the serfs of the soil—the men of infamy and degradation—the beings who are unworthy of the divine protection, and of a name or a dwelling among the offspring of Bramha, and who are consigned to ignominy and subjection for ever.

This, they say, is not the appointment of man, but the decree of the Creator; and woe be to the individual who would be dissatisfied with the arrangement and would venture to disturb it. The present state of existence is not regarded as one of probation—it is one of rewards and punishments. The Bramin is happy in his present lot, but it is the fruit of some meritorious actions which he performed in a former birth; while the perpetration of some dreadful crime has consigned the Shoodra to his labour, and the Pariar to his degradation and vassalage. For a Shoodra to aspire to the rank of a Veisha, or for a Veisha to envy the caste of a Cheitra, or for a Cheitra to wish to become a Bramin would be an unpardonable crime. Fate has fixed the position of every one in the universe. So pure, so rich, so honourable and excellent is the blood which flows in the veins of the Bramin, that it is a dignity conferred upon the monarch sitting upon his throne, and surrounded by his nobles and his senators, to have the feet of the most abject and worthless of the tribe upon his head; and happy indeed is the day in which a Shoodra is permitted to drink of the water where a Bramin has bathed his feet. Let the descent of the individual be high or low, noble or contemptible, his destiny has fixed it; his future history is written upon his forehead; the decrees of Bramha are inevitable; and to the control of fate he must submit. At Bellary, I once visited a Bramin who was under sentence of death.

For a trifle of money which he knew his friend possessed, and while he entertained him as his guest, he had risen in the night and murdered him. I endeavoured to bring home the crime to his conscience; but it was of no use. "Bramha," he said, "has written it all in my forehead; it was my fate to murder my friend, and to be hanged for it; it is no concern of mine. I must suffer, it is true; but the Creator must account for it all." His destiny had given him his birthright; had allotted him his career, had exempted him from his responsibility, had made him what he was, and would make him what he would be.

On the same principle, the caste of the individual determines his trade, or his profession. Whatever his father is, that is the employment which the son must follow, to which through life he is bound to adhere, and in which it is his duty to instruct his posterity. This plan would seem, at first view, to secure the advancement of the arts and sciences, and the greater perfection of the trades and manufactures. But it is not so. They are only carried as far as could be expected, without taste and imagination, which flourish only in more congenial climes. Under such oppressive enactments, there is an end to emulation, there is a stop to all skill, ingenuity and improvement, and there is no stimulus to excel even in those branches of industry which the individual may purseu. In England and in China, the humblest peasant, may, by his learning, his genius, his diligence and talents work his way to the greatest honours, and to the highest offices in the state; but the caste of the Hindoo forbids his attempts to rise out of the condition in which he was born; and while trade and commerce have been changing society in Europe, and are now, with the power of steam on their side, propelling it with accelerated speed, society in India has been almost stationary for two thousand years, has withstood all the storms, and changes and revolutions to which it was exposed, and will unquestionably continue the same, till the present combinations be broken to pieces, that, out of the confusion, there may arise a public order more in accordance with freedom, improvement and prosperity.

No doubt, at Calcutta, at Madras, at Bombay, and at some of the large stations in the interior, where numbers of Europeans are collected together, the natives are surmounting their former prejudices. It begins to be understood that caste has been a great barrier to improvement; the manners, the customs and habits of Europeans, and the order of society as existing among them, are producing a salutary influence; and it would only be necessary for the government to adopt a liberal line of policy, to hold out encouragement to genius, to enterprise and to industry, and to introduce into India, all the improvements which are performing such wonders in England, to inflict a blow upon caste from which it will not speedily recover.

But the Capitals are not the country. The towns, the villages and the distant provinces are far behind; and an individual looking at Calcutta, and alleging that the leaven which is working there, is operating, in the same degree, throughout the whole empire, would commit a grievous mistake. But even there general knowledge, the success of the gospel, and new laws and European government are producing similar effects; and let the British authorities lay aside that great partiality which they have invariably shown to the prejudices, the usages, and the extravagant pretensions which prevail in Hindoo society; instead of looking at the natives with pride and hauteur, let the civil and military officers treat them with kindness and condescension; let office and rewards be conferred upon merit, and talent and service and integrity alone; instead of frowning upon the Shoodra in his hut, and scowling the outcast Pariar to a distance and compelling him to prefer his complaint in court, through the medium of another, let them understand that they are men, and that they are deserving of law and justice and right as much as the highest Bramin in the land; let a system of education, on proper principles, and suited to all classes, be established throughout the provinces, and the day must speedily come when the sons of India will vie with those of Britain in the career of civilization, and improvement. The government and all classes of Europeans have it in their power to do much, and while the progress of knowledge and true religion must crown the triumph, education, the press, public opinion, and equitable laws, and measures of amelioration may do a vast deal to hasten and to secure it.

No system could be more the reverse of the gospel, than that of caste, as established by Bramha. According to the letter and the spirit of the Bible, it is our duty to love our neighbour as we do ourselves, to love our enemies, to do good to those who hate us, and to pray for those who despitefully use us and persecute us. While it holds up to reprobation the conduct of the priest and the Levite who, very probably on the ground of caste and their own superiority, looked upon the poor man who had fallen among thieves, and passed him by on the other side; it holds up, as an example to all, the conduct of the good Samaritan who bound up his wounds, and took charge of him. But the spirit and temper which caste generates and maintains in its votaries, are, to leave all, except their own immediate kindred, to starve and perish in their calamities, and to make them unkind and malevolent. A stranger may lie at the door, may writhe in agonies, may die, and become the prey of the jackals or the vultures, before a Hindoo would render him any assistance. To give him a cup of cold water to relieve his thirst, or to administer medicine to him in sickness would be violation of his caste, and would expose a Shoodra to the anathema of his kinsmen. Shortly after our arrival at Bangalore, the roof of our house was under repair; and one of the bricklayers fell from a great height, and was very much injured. In his agonies, the poor man was fainting away, and we called upon his fellow-workmen to run to the well, and fetch some water. Not one of them would stir; and what was the hard-hearted reply? "That man, sir, is not my caste; I cannot touch that man, nor give him water to drink." Hindooism dries up all the human sympathies, and renders its devotees, misanthropes. It is true that the love of fame, and the desire of merit, will occasionally preponderate, and triumph. To dig a well in the desert, to plant a grove or an orchard, to erect a temple, to build a tank, to give presents to the Bramins and alms to the poor, are deeds the most meritorious, and are sure to raise the individual to immortal life and blessedness. But as to real philanthropy, as to the genuine benevolence which the gospel inspires, as to those feelings of compassion and of kindness which are to be found among the poorest classes of our own society, they are scarcely to be found; the system robs the people even of the social affections, inasmuch as it allows them to carry their aged, sick, and infirm parents and relatives to the banks of the Ganges, to stuff their mouths with its soil, and to immerse them in its waters, that their end may be hastened, and they may cease to be a burden.

No institution could be more rigid in its enactments, and more severe in its penalties, than caste. To be turned out of the synagogue among the Jews, was bad; to be under the anathemas of popery, and be exposed to its pains and penalties in the dark ages, was worse; but to be deprived of caste, and to be subject to all the evils which its loss involves, is worst of all. An individual may be wicked, profane, devoid of every good principle, and an abandoned profligate, and yet, as a Hindoo, may enjoy all the privileges of his caste; but the moment that he violates any of its rules, the moment that he would venture to eat and drink with a person of another grade, he exposes himself to the most dreadful denunciations. No person can receive the miscreant into their house, or hold any intercourse with him; every one agrees to cover him with ridicule, contempt and disdain; to be seen with him, would be a crime deserving of reprehension; the woman to whom he was betrothed, would not be allowed to marry him; he is deprived of the protection and immunities to which his caste might have given him a claim; all denounce him as a Pariar, as a Chandala, as the veriest vagabond that ever lived, and his parents, and relatives and friends must be the first to disown him and to shower curses upon his head. No wonder that this system should be regarded as a great barrier to the truth. If the fear of man can bring a snare, well may it operate here. It has, no doubt, kept back thousands from making a profession, who would otherwise have become formalists and hypocrites.

To show how the fear of losing caste operates, I may refer to the case of a brother missionary. He once thought that he had made deep impressions upon the mind of his pundit. So candidly and so meekly did the man appear to drink in the word, that the missionary could not but rejoice. After many professions made by the pundit that he was a Christian in heart, that he believed as firmly in the gospel as any member of the church, and that it was only the fear occasioned by his relatives, which kept him from making the avowal, the missionary pressed upon him the necessity of publicly declaring his attachment to Christ. The man as often tried to evade it, by some dexterous excuse, till on one occasion, he promised that he would, at all risks, receive the ordinance of baptism on the following sabbath. On Saturday evening, he came to the missionary, told him that he was in the greatest difficulties, and knew not what to do; his relatives were so opposed to his baptism, that he did not think his life would be safe; and as to his wife, she had become so frantic that she had thrown herself into a well. The missionary sympathized with him, and replied that it would perhaps, under such circumstances, be as well to defer his profession of Christianity. But some persons in the mission family suspected the truth of his story; went to his house, and found it was all false. The dread of what he would be called to suffer in the loss of caste, and the calamities which it would inflict, there was no doubt, led him to forge this story, and chained him to his heathenism,

But whatever may be the influence which caste exercises over multitudes in keeping them back from an open and a bold avowal of the truth, it visits the weak, the humble and unoffending convert with terrible vengeance. If bonds and imprisonments do not await him, his friends and relatives are sure to cast him out; threats, calumnies, and persecutions attend him at every step; daily is he obliged to take up his cross, to deny himself, and stand prepared to suffer the loss of all things. By the Hindoo law of inheritance, every outcast, forfeits his right to his patrimony; and since every Christian becomes an outcast, he must, on his profession, agree to surrender his claim to all the property which a gracious providence has given him, for his own comfort, and for the good of others.

Of this, Naraputsingh—a convert in Bengal, was a striking instance. During the days of his heathenism, he was able to live like a Nabob, could command his train of servants, and travelled in oriental style. But the moment he submitted to the ordinance of baptism, and embraced the truth, his relatives seized upon his property; he lost, by his profession of the gospel, the sum of eight thousand pounds; he was reduced to absolute poverty, and has laboured, in the service of our society, at the rate of twenty rupees per month.

Many cases of a similar kind have occurred, and have shown how much the natives, whatever may be their caste, have to suffer, when they come out from among the heathen, separate themselves from their idols, and have the boldness to join themselves to the Israel of God. How patiently should we bear with their weaknesses, and their infirmities? How tenderly should we reason with them, and take them by the hand to lead them, like the lambs of the flock, through the terrible wilderness? But what if, instead of being satisfied with the sacrifices they are obliged to make, we should bind burdens upon their shoulders, which, in their infancy, they are not able to bear! What if, instead of being satisfied with their communion among all classes of their brethren at the table of the Lord, we should set up a new test of our own, and compel them to eat and drink with all classes in our own houses! What, if instead of reasoning with them, and winning them over, with love and kindness, to our own views, we should exact from them the same degree of knowledge, and the same measure of Christian experience, as are to be met with among believers at home, and in defect thereof, drive them from the fold, and induce them to think that heathenism, with all its accumulated ills, is better, than such a religion as ours? Will the Lord hold us guiltless? Shall we, on the ground of reason, of revelation, of experience, or of common sense, be justified in such conduct? Most assuredly not. "From this confession," writes an intelligent, an experienced, and a devoted missionary, "the writer would remark, that if great imperfections attend the most enlightened Christians who have, from their very infancy, been trained up in the ways of God; how much more may this be expected to be the case with the first converts from Paganism, who cannot be supposed, in a short time, to divest themselves entirely of the influence of native prejudices, or completely to break the force of former habits?—To object to first converts, because they are less perfect than Christians who have enjoyed greater privileges, discovers great ignorance of human nature, and great inattention to the history of past ages. None but narrow-minded bigots who take up subjects by halves; insipid moralists, swollen with pharisaical pride; and sceptics, in whose eyes religion and vice are mere relative terms, which may be changed and rechanged, according to the tempers and circumstances of mankind,—none but such will sneeringly object to them."*

After an experience of twelve years in the missionary field, I can most cordially agree with such sentiments. There is no one who has a greater abhorrence of caste, than I have; nor is there one who has done more to exterminate it from the minds

* Dr. Milne's Retrospect of the Protestant Mission to China.

and from the conduct of those who have made a profession of Christianity. But to adopt a system that would reduce every convert, whatever might have been his caste when a heathen, to the level of a Pariar, and to the lowest scale in society; to compel the Jews to eat with the Gentiles, or one class of converted Gentiles to eat and drink with another, as a test of religion, is to set up a standard which, I conceive, is unknown to the Bible, and which, if applied in Christian countries, would spread anarchy, disorder, and ruin through our intelligent and prosperous, and long-established churches.

If it is still contended that such a measure is *lawful* to show an abhorrence of caste; I would reply that all things are not *expedient*. Never should such a test be *forced* upon the converts. Are the believers to dine or to sup with the missionaries and with the Pariars in common? then such an entertainment ought surely to be held up as an honour and as a privilege to which they ought to aspire, and not as a criterion of piety. While such civil disabilities and penalties are visited by the government authorities upon Pariars and upon all who eat and drink with them, missionaries ought to encourage the Christians who believe that, in their baptism, they have renounced their caste, and who are so treated by their heathen kinsmen, to take up this heavy cross to please all their brethren; missionaries ought to exert themselves to obtain the repeal of all those enactments which bear so oppressively upon outcasts of every name and every class; and if such a test is absolutely necessary to prove that the converts have abandoned caste, and have reached an indispensable perfection, missionaries ought to be agreed upon this point, and ought to adopt at every station throughout India, the same system, that the grievances of native Christians may be one, their honours and privileges be one, their hopes and fears be one, and their joys and sorrows be one. Show me a native convert who has been baptized and who has communed with his brethren at the table of the Lord, but who has, by such a test, been driven from the fellowship of the faithful; and I will show you a convert whom I would follow as a lost sheep in the wilderness, and whom I would use all the pity and all the love and all the exertion of which I am capable, to find, and to restore, as I feel convinced that, in renouncing his idolatry, and in avowing himself to be a follower of the Lamb, he made greater sacrifices, and endured more trials to prove the sincerity of his faith, than those who have had the temerity to deprive him of the rights and privileges of a disciple.

CHAPTER VIII.

THE LITERATURE OF INDIA.

THE LITERATURE OF THE HINDOOS—SANSCRIT LANGUAGE—SIMILAR TO THE LATIN IN ITS RISE AND DECLINE—NOT THE MOTHER OF THE VERNACULAR TONGUES—EVIDENCE THAT IT IS NOT—THE VEDAS—THE SHASTERS—THE POORANNAS—THE RAMAYANA—HARISCHUNDRA.

In the literature of India, there is, no doubt, a great mass of romance, and absurdity; but not more perhaps than in that of Greece and of Rome. While some have agreed to hold up Indian literature as a model of perfection, as excelling in wit, in eloquence, in poetry, in tragedy, and in all that is agreeable to taste, as well as imagination; others have denounced it as a tissue of extravagant fancies, and pernicious dogmas which have no foundation in fact, and no practical bearing on society. I cannot agree with either of these opinions; and think it may be shown that, amidst a mass of rubbish, there are some facts, some laws, some proverbs, some poetry, some general principles, some philosophy, some grammar and language which are not unworthy the consideration of the scholar and the philosopher.

In all probability, the language in which the greater part of their literature was originally written, was the Sanscrit, and from thence it was, afterwards, transfused into all the vernacular dialects of the empire. But whatever the *original* may have been, one thing is certain, that there is scarcely a book to be found in the one, which has not been written in the other. It is impossible to conceive of a language existing, and arriving at the stage of perfection which the Sanscrit has acquired, without concluding that it must, at one period, have been the language of a people, and have been usefully applied to all the purposes of life. The most probable conjecture is, that it was the language of the Bramins, that they were a race of conquerors who came from the north, that they easily overran and subdued the continent of India, that they engrafted their system of superstition upon the idolatry which they found among the people, and that, as the sons of Brumha, they have retained in their hands, the key of knowledge, and the reins of government.

A great similarity may be traced between the progress and the decline of empire in the East and in the West, at the same periods of time. The Roman power which, in the ages of obscurity, grew up in Latium, swallowed up the adjoining provinces, extended its arms over ancient Europe, tried to amalgamate the customs and the superstitions of the conquered countries with its own, fell a prey to violence in its turn, sank under the weight of its own grandeur and greatness, and, while in the dissolution of the rule which it exercised over the nations, its power was lost; what became of that language of which the Romans were so proud, which they tried to impose upon the conquered provinces, and which was to become universal and be a substitute for all the tongues of the earth? that *language* was expelled from the seat of its nativity, ceased to be the dialect of a people, and was the victim of the dominion to which it aspired. So, and most probably during the same period, the Bramins and the real Hindoos descended in swarms upon the continent of India, spread their despotism and influence among the aboriginal tribes, and established their law, their superstition, and even their language, as far as their power and policy could accomplish it; but one revolution after another annihilated their power, broke up this confederacy, brought them into a closer alliance with the ancient inhabitants, and, whatever may be the hold their superstition had maintained over the empire, their language has almost expired; its students and admirers all speak the vernacular dialect of the provinces in which they reside, and, instead of becoming universal, and taking the place of those which might be deemed inferior, it is the one which is the most likely to sink into oblivion, and to be entirely forgotten.

When we remember the veil which is cast over the earlier history of India, we need not be surprised at the cloud in which the origin of this beautiful language is enveloped, and that all efforts hitherto made for its discovery have failed. As the Sanscrit in the East, so the Latin in the West, is still a distinct language. But were our ancient histories involved in as much romance, and obscurity as those of Hindoosthan, I can easily conceive of a Hindoo arriving in Europe, sitting down to learn German, or French, or English, studying Latin as a learned language which is to afford him great assistance in his work; and what are the questions that would naturally occur to him? What is this Latin? Where did it originate? Was it ever the language of a people? And yet, without the knowledge which we have of the Roman empire, there would be as much difficulty in giving him an answer, as our Orientalists have found in ascertaining the origin of the Sanscrit.

Much as I venerate the names of Sir W. Jones, and Dr. Carey, and other Oriental scholars, I cannot agree with the opinion that the Sanscrit is the parent of all the vernacular languages. To say that it sustains the same relation to the tongues of India, that the Latin does to those of Europe, is perhaps saying too much. As the Italian and the Spanish are more allied to the Latin than are the languages of Celtic origin, so there may be, among the dialects of India, some that are more allied to the Sanscrit, than others. But nothing can be more certain than this, that the Tamul, the Telloogoo, and the Canarese which are the cognate dialects of the peninsula, are of a different family, and have no more connexion with the Sanscrit, than they have with the Persian, or Arabic. In these three languages, there is an ancient and a modern dialect. Nearly all their works are written in poetry, and in the higher tongue, and as we peruse the translations that have been made from the poems of Vyasa and Valmeekee, and all the more ancient classics, the purer does the Canarese, the Tamul, and Telloogoo become; there is scarcely a Sanscrit word to be found; the whole record is in the original language of the country, whereas the modern and vulgar dialects are more replete with Sanscrit terms—a full and convincing proof to my own mind, that the Sanscrit is not the parent of these languages.

All native grammarians too have agreed that these three dialects are radically different from the Sanscrit, and have no dependence upon it whatever, and have therefore divided their words into the respective heads of the language of the land, Sanscrit derivatives, Sanscrit corruptions, and provincial terms. All words expressive of primitive ideas and of such things as are used in the early stages of society; all words denoting the different members of the body, the various kinds of instruments in common use, and the different sorts of cattle; all words describing their food, their dress, their ornaments, their dwelling, their relations in life, and the productions of the ground—belong to the vernacular tongue, while the Sanscrit terms in use belong entirely to law, literature and religion. In addition to this, the conversation of the Bramins, abounds much more with Sanscrit terms, than that of the other classes who speak their own colloquial dialects best, and who, in attempting to use Sanscrit words, often excite the scorn and derision of their more learned superiors. Nor is it unworthy of remark, that the Telloogoo which is spoken by the tribes of the north, is more replete, in the vulgar dialect, with Sanscrit words, than the Tamul and the Canarese which are spoken further to the south, and to the south-west, and since the lower classes of the people are now considered the aborigines of the land, since there is a more intimate alliance between Shin Tamul, and Hulee Canada, and ancient Teloogoo, than there is in the modern dialects, and since the Bramins are considered a race of conquerors who emigrated from the distant north, it would be evident that the dialect nearer to the seat of the aggressors, would be more likely to be affected by the foreign language.

The adoption of such a general principle as that against which I am contending, to account for the division and variety of Eastern languages, is, at first view, very imposing, and has so often been reiterated by the admirers of Sanscrit philology, that scholars have readily taken it for granted; but every European who has studied the vernacular languages, knows that it is destitute of proof. Indeed! it might be contended with equal propriety, that our own language is derived from the Latin, or from the Greek, because a number of their words are incorporated with it, to express many of the technicalities of law, science, and literature; as to contend that these and other vernacular languages were derived from the Sanscrit.

The Vedas are four in number, and are the most ancient, and the most sacred of the Hindoo writings. The Rig—the Yajur—the Sam, and the At-hurwana Vedas are said to have proceeded from the mouth of Brumha, are, therefore, reckoned divine in their origin, and infallible in authority, are esteemed too sacred for the lower classes to hear, and are the books on which the Bramins rely for all their power and pretensions. According to the general belief, they were compiled by Vyasa, and as they do not enjoin any worship to Rama, to Crishnu and to other deities which have long been popular among Hindoos, their antiquity must be very great. But however ancient they may be, they can make no pretensions to divinity. After giving some account of the creation as the work of Brumha, they chiefly consist of prayers to the Supreme Being, to the sun, to the stars and to the elements; and descriptions of various rites, ceremonies, and incantations. The practical parts inculcate their idolatrous duties, advance arguments for their system of mythology, describe the sanguinary chapter in which the sacrifices both animal and human, and the manner in which they are to be offered, are revealed, and give the fearful curses and imprecations which are to be denounced against enemies. In the exercise of their ingenuity to discover resemblances between the true religion, and the Hindoo mythology, some have gone so far as to find in these books, some analogies to the Books of Moses. Because one gives some account of the creation of the world and of man, THAT they imagine corresponds with Genesis. Because another contains laws and ordinances to regulate their worship, *that* is thought to resemble Exodus. Because another has enjoined sacrifices of all kinds and describes minutely the manner in which they are to be offered, *that* is thought to be similar to Leviticus. Because another teaches lessons of morality, and unfolds the blessings and the curses which the priests may pronounce, *that* they maintain must be analogous to Deuteronomy; and since the notion prevails that these Vedas were given by Brumha from Mount Meros, they trace, in this circumstance, the delivery of the law from Mount Sinai. These are, no doubt, strange fancies. But minds of a certain order delight in such researches and in drawing such analogies; it is enough to ordinary minds that they hear of such enquiries and contemplate the results.

Next in importance to the Vedas, the various

Shasters hold a place. In the estimation of the Bramins with whom I have conversed, they have not, as some have asserted, the same claims to divinity as the Vedas. Their rishes and their sages are their authors; but they are not esteemed as inspired, and, should you sweep away the whole circle of their sciences, the Vedas would remain unimpaired, and would be regarded as sacred as before. The Selpee Shaster teaches the science of architecture; the Dhurma Shaster that of law and logic; the Neetie Shaster that of moral philosophy; the Jotee Shaster that of astrology; the Weidya Shaster that of medicine. The sciences are described, are expatiated upon, have the rules by which they are brought into use, are taught in their schools and colleges, and present to the student a formidable array of metaphysics, and of philosophy, and of science falsely so called.

The Poorannas occupy the next place in the Hindoo literature. As mythological poems, they are perhaps the most popular and the most interesting of their writings. The Maha Bharta, and the Bagwuta describe the exploits of Chrishnu; and the Ramayana those of Rama. As it may not be uninteresting to the reader, I shall just give an outline of the latter.

At different times, Bhoodevi or the earth is represented as oppressed with monsters and with demons. Unable any longer to bear their enormities, she enters the presence of Vishnoo, entreats his interposition, and receives a promise that he will be come incarnate and destroy her enemies. Hence so many incarnations. After glancing at the six which have already taken place, in the form of a fish, of a tortoise, of a boar, of a man-lion, of a dwarf and of an ox, Walmeekee proceeds to describe that in the form of Rama who is born as the son of Dhusarutha, king of Oude. His wife is born a princess, and in process of time they are united in marriage. His father Dhusarutha becomes old and infirm, and wishes Rama to take the reins of government into his hands. Rama replies "It cannot be. I have not been born for such a worldly purpose as this. I must call my wife, Seeta, along with me, we must reside, like ascetics, in the desert; and it will presently appear for what purpose I reside amongst men." He does so. They build a hermitage, and spend their time amongst the beasts of the forest. The giant Ravanna—the king of Lunka in Ceylon—the monster with ten heads and as many arms, and to destroy whom, it is the design of the incarnation, hears this intelligence, and is determined, in the struggle, to give Rama as much trouble as he possibly can. Having the power of changing his form, he assumes that of an ascetic, and while Rama is absent from the hermitage, he appears at the door, and intreats Seeta to give him an alms. The moment of bestowing her bounty, upon the traitor, he embraces an opportunity of seizing her, of carrying her off, and putting her in prison. On his return to the hermitage, Rama cannot find his wife, sinks into a sea of grief, utters the most piteous cries, and passes through those deep emotions of sorrow which characterize eastern nations. To assist him in his conflict with the giants, the angels are represented as becoming incarnate in monkeys, and Hunumunta is their leader. Since the latter is worshipped in every town and almost in every village in India, it is evident that he is a deity of no small consequence. Finding Rama in a state of despondency, he becomes his prime-minister, and undertakes to visit Lunka and find out the circumstances of Seeta. He assumes the form of a rat, and pursues his circuitous route, through the houses of the enemy, till he discovers the prison where Seeta is confined. Like a faithful servant, he delivers to her the message of his master, and receives from Seeta her answers in return. After having emerged from the prison, he assumes his proper form, is seen scampering over the walls and the houses, and excites considerable alarm among the giants in Lunka. Whether his visit was an omen of good or of evil they could not understand. At length, they seized him as a prisoner, and brought him to the court of Ravanna to be examined. As they would not give him a seat, but compelled him to stand, he took his tremendous tail and coiled it, as a sailor would a cable, till it rose to such a height as enabled him to sit down on an equality with the throne of Ravanna. In reply to the questions which the king put to him concerning his name, his parentage, his design in visiting Lunka, he gives such clever and ingenious answers, that he sets the whole court in bursts of laughter against their sovereign. Ravanna is frantic with rage, and asks what is to be done with this monkey? Some proposed one thing, some proposed another, but all agreed in the suggestion that as he made such a boast of his tail it ought to be set on fire. Accordingly, all the old clothes, the rags, and paper that are to be found in Lunka, are put in requisition to make a flambeau of this tail. They cover it with tar and pitch and other combustibles, set it on fire, and then liberate the prisoner that they may have a day of frolic. No sooner does Hunumunta regain his liberty than he pursues his race—now through the fields of corn and sets them on fire—then through the farm-yards, and over the hay-ricks and puts *them* in a blaze; then over the walls and through the houses and kindles a flame which is not easily extinguished. Never did such an incendiary visit Lunka before. To save their city from destruction, the giants now pursue him to put out the torch which they had lighted. Hunumunta ascends the tower of a temple and hides himself in its summit, and when he finds it well filled with giants, he throws it down with violence and destroys them all. He makes his escape, and dips his tail in the sea, and returns to Rama. After reporting the exploits of his embassy, they assemble the armies of monkeys, throw a bridge across the sea from the continent to Ceylon, and lay siege to the fortress of Ravanna. The war is commenced, and prodigies of valour are performed on both sides, till Rama kills the monster Ravanna, liberates his wife Seeta, and delivers the earth from the giants whose enormities cause her to groan.

Such is the substance of their Epic Poem the Ramayana; but the poetry, the figures the illustrations, and the descriptions with which it abounds are often interesting and splendid; and while we cannot but deplore that such powers should have been wasted upon such absurdities, we cannot but admire the genius, the spirit, the eloquence, the splendid talents with which its author must have been endowed.

But there is another work which I have read several times, and which though not so renowned as the Ramayana, was always more pleasant, interesting, and useful to me. The history of Harischundra-Raya is almost a counterpart of the history of Job. In the heaven of Indra, there is an assembly of the gods, and moonees, and most meritorious sages. The question arises, "whether there be a righteous prince on the face of the earth?" Vishwamittra asserts that there is not one. He is opposed by Vasishta who declares he knows and he can prove that his disciple Harischundra is a prince in whom there is no fault, that he is a perfect man. In a terrible rage, with a haughty and imperious temper, like a perfect fury, and more in the spirit of Satan than any thing, that I have seen recorded, Vishwamittra declares it is false; challenges his antagonist to the proof; and pledges to lose half of the merit which he has obtained, should he not succeed in showing to gods and to men, that the declaration which Vasishta has made cannot be sustained. Let the gods forsake Harischundra, and let them deliver him into his hands, and he engages to show that this prince is unworthy the praise which has been bestowed upon him, and that he is frail and unrighteous as any of his brethren. Poor Harischundra becomes the victim of this controversy, and is delivered into the hands of this malignant and persecuting sage. The dreadful campaign commences. As though all the power of heaven and earth was committed to this diabolical agent, he assails the virtue of the prince by strong and numerous temptations, and he is foiled in one stratagem, only to commence another that will entwine his victim in his folds, and render him more secure. He reduces him to the most abject poverty, deprives him of his kingdom, drives him from his home and his subjects, covers the road upon which he and his wife and child are to travel, with thorns and briars to lacerate their feet, and make their journey intolerable, compels him to sell his wife and brings trouble and death upon his son. Still the virtue of Harischundra is triumphant. His accuser cannot establish his charge. He makes him a grave-digger, and the prince labours at his occupation with as much diligence and zeal, as when he administered the affairs of state. The mind of man cannot contemplate a more wretched, and pitiable object, than Harischundra in a grave-yard which is described as being hideous, frightful and disgusting as the Gehenna of Judea, or as the Tartarus of Roman mythology. But the prince retains his integrity to the last. His accuser is confounded, and is obliged to confess his defeat. The gods themselves do honour to the virtue of the prince; Vishwamittra loses his stock of merit, and gives it to his antagonist; and Vasishta bequeaths it to Harischundra; and as a triumph to the ordeal through which he has passed, the king is reinstated upon his throne, his queen is restored to him, his son is raised to life, and, as it was with Job, so it was with this eastern prince, his latter end was better than his beginning.

Whatever toil and labour it may cost him, and however dry and uninteresting the study may be, every one who wishes to obtain a knowledge of the native language, must apply to the classics. At first, he may, perhaps, peruse a translation, or a work written by a European with advantage; but if he rests satisfied with this, and with conversation and similar methods, he will never be a scholar, and he cannot expect to advance his own usefulness, and to live to the greatest benefit of others. Nothing is so easy as to obtain a smattering of two or three languages, and to gratify the vanity of the mind, with the name of being a great linguist. But the writer has no sympathy with such childish pretensions. In attempting to gain too much, the student gains comparatively little. Far better that the missionary should give his whole time to *one* language spoken by eight or ten millions of people, and so master it, that he might use it as his own, apply it to all practical purposes, and that he may be rendered a blessing to the multitudes who understand it, than to have a superficial knowledge of *many* and not be able to use any of them with efficiency. It is too much like those who are always learning, and never coming to the knowledge of the truth. Were the life of man to be devoted to such pursuits only, it might be pardonable. But as a missionary only studies language as the means of accomplishing the most glorious end; his energies ought not to be wasted; his short career ought to be improved to the noblest purposes; and his own reputation and fame should be nothing to him, when compared with the interests of humanity, with the prospects of usefulness, and with the glory of God.

CHAPTER IX.

THE SYRIAN CHRISTIANS.

THE SYRIANS LAND ON THE COAST OF MALABAR—THEIR PRIVILEGES UNDER HEATHEN PRINCES, CONTRASTED WITH THE INTOLERANCE OF THE PORTUGUESE—THE VIOLENCE OF THEIR PERSECUTORS—THE EFFECTS OF THESE OPPRESSIONS—A REMNANT LEFT—THE EXERTION OF SIR T. MUNRO FOR THEM—WELCOME THE CHURCH MISSIONARIES—THEIR CONNEXION WITH THE SEE OF ANTIOCH DISSOLVED—ARCHDEACON ROBINSON'S REPORT OF HIS VISIT TO THEM.

ON the coast of Malabar, and among the hills of Malayalla, there exists a colony of Syrians. Whence they came, and how they have contrived to remain a distinct people, seems to be involved in considerable mystery. Some regard them as the disciples of St Thomas who, in his journeys of benevolence, visited the coast of India, established churches among the people, and afterwards fell a martyr to the truth, on the coast of Coromandel. Others imagine them to be a colony of Nestorians who, in the fifth century, fled before the persecuting violence of the second Theodosius, and who, while many of their brethren settled in Persia, and others were driven to various parts of the East, took refuge among the heathen in Malabar. Their colour, their names, their manners and customs, their style of architecture, the use of the Syrian language, the rites and ceremonies used in their worship, and their subjection, in former as well as in modern times, to the see of Antioch, would go far to establish the validity of the latter opinion; while the legendary tales of Romanists appear to be the only support which can be rendered to the former. Under the guidance and direction of their first Bishop Mar Thome, they secured a resting-place in Malayalla, and derived from him the name of St. Thome Christians—a designation which the Portuguese tried to affix to them, on the ground that they must, therefore, belong to the Roman Church, and be submissive to the authority of the pontiff.

At their first settlement, they were successful, history affirms, in making converts to their religion from among the Nairs, and the Bramins; had great honours and privileges conferred upon them by the native princes; have always been esteemed for their truth, their honour, and their integrity of conduct: and were regarded by their sovereigns as the most faithful and courageous in war, and the most quiet and industrious in peace. But the arrival of the Portuguese in the beginning of the sixteenth century, was the signal for anarchy and confusion among this interesting people. At that time their number must have been large, as they reckoned a hundred and ten churches under the Rajahs of Cochin and Travancore. So long as their intercourse, their commerce and their political subjection were confined to idolatrous Hindoos, they lived in peace; veneration and respect fell to their lot; liberty of conscience was fully enjoyed; converts were added to their communion without enkindling any jealousy in the breasts of others; their metropolitans passed from Antioch to India, and returned if they wished to their native country unmolested; the honours and privileges granted to them, by the Peramals, were enjoyed in tranquillity; and the prince who could number most of them among his subjects, was looked to with greatest respect by his neighbours. But the moment that Europeans landed on their shores; the moment that Portuguese Christians—then the rulers of the ocean—established their marts, their factories, and their power in Malabar, the spirit of the West began to blow, in pestilential breezes, over the peaceful abodes of the Syrians. On hearing that such a colony of Christians existed, the Portuguese, asserted dominion over their faith; bribes, intrigues, treachery, and jesuitical arts of all kinds were employed to bring them into subjection to the Roman see; divisions were soon in the camp; commerce was converted into an instrument of temptation and of evil; and the power and influence of the Rajahs were engaged to win them over to a system which their ancestors had learned to despise.

But the Syrians resisted such efforts. They determined to adhere to their primitive faith. The *respect* which they had for the cross was better to them, than the favour of the Virgin, and the long catalogue of saints which adorned the Romish calendar; and they preferred the word and the service of God, to the nostrums and the traditions of men. Still, the craft and the power of the Jesuits were not to be resisted with impunity. In proportion to the steadfastness of the Syrians, the Portuguese became more violent; the thunders of the Vatican rolled in frightful peals, among the hills of Malabar; and the inquisition established at Goa,* was brought to bear upon the stubborn and

* "During the months of November and December," says Dr. Dellon, "I heard every morning the shrieks of the unfortunate victims who were undergoing the question. I remembered to have heard, before I was cast into prison, that the auto-da-fé was generally celebrated on the first Sunday in Advent, because on that day is read in the churches that part of the gospel in which mention was made of the last judgment; and the inquisition pretend by the ceremony to exhibit a lively emblem of that awful event. I was likewise convinced that there were a great number of prisoners, besides myself; the profound silence which reigned within the walls of the building, having enabled me to count the number of doors which were opened at the hours of meals.

On the 11th of January the great bell of the cathedral begun to ring a little before sunrise, which served as a signal to warn the people of Goa to come and behold the august ceremony of the auto-da-fé; and then they made us proceed from the gallery refractory heretics. Whose pen could describe the miseries that followed? The tranquil habitations and peaceful villages of Travancore were converted

one by one. I remarked, as we passed into the great hall, that the inquisitor was sitting at the door with his secretary by him, and that he delivered every prisoner into the hands of a particular person, who is to be his guard to the place of burning. These persons are called parrains or godfathers. My godfather was the commander of a ship. I went forth with him, and as soon as we were in the street I saw that the procession was commenced by the Dominican friars, who have the honour, because Saint Dominic founded the inquisition; these are followed by the prisoners, who walk one after another, each having his godfather by his side, and a lighted taper in his hand. The least guilty are foremost; and as I did not pass for one of them, there were many who took precedence of me. The women were mixed promiscuously with the men. We all walked barefoot, and the sharp stones of the streets of Goa wounded my tender feet and caused the blood to stream, for they made us march through the chief streets of the city, and we were regarded everywhere by an innumerable crowd of people, who had assembled from all parts of India to behold this spectacle, for the inquisition takes care to announce it long before in the most remote parishes. At length we arrived at the church of St. Francis, which was for this time destined for the celebration of the act of faith. On one side of the altar was the grand inquisitor and his counsellors, and on the other the viceroy of Goa and his court. All the prisoners are seated to hear a sermon. I observed that those who wore the horrible carrochas came in last in the procession. One of the Augustine monks ascended the pulpit and preached for a quarter of an hour. The sermon being concluded two readers went up to the pulpit, one after another, and read the sentences of the prisoners. My joy was extreme when I heard that my sentence was not to be burnt, but to be a galley-slave for five years. After the sentences were read they summoned forth those miserable victims who were destined to be immolated by the into scenes of violence, spoliation and fiendish barbarity; the Syrian metropolitans were imprisoned, and transported—one to Lisbon, and the other to Rome, till they submitted to the Pope; all the authority and influence of Portugal, were employed to rouse the Rajah of Cochin to oppress, to imprison, and to persecute his unoffending subjects; and the navigation of the western coast was so arranged, as to prevent all intercourse between India and Antioch, and to deter any bishop from coming to supply the place of the persecuted brethren, and to watch over the interests of the suffering churches.

At length, Menezes—the archbishop of Goa—determined to carry the citadel by storm. After summoning the Syrian priests to a council at Odi-

holy inquisition. The images of the heretics who had died in prison were brought up at the same time, their bones being contained in small chests covered with flames and demons. An officer of the secular tribunal now came forward and seized these unhappy people, after they had each received a slight blow upon the breast from the Alcaide to intimate that they were abandoned. They were then led away to the bank of the river, where the viceroy and his court were assembled, and where the faggots had been prepared the preceding day. As soon as they arrive at this place, the condemned prisoners are asked in what religion they choose to die; and the moment they have replied to this question, the executioner seizes them and binds them to a stake in the midst of the faggots. The day after the execution the portraits of the dead are carried to the church of the Dominicans. The heads only are represented (which are generally very accurately drawn, for the inquisition keeps excellent limners for the purpose) surrounded by flames and demons, and underneath is the name and crime of the person who has been burned.

amper, and laying down the laws to them, with the authority of a judge, as well as a bishop, he consigned all their ancient manuscripts and books to the flames; transferred the bishopric of Angamalee to Cranganore; brought the whole districts of the low country into subjection, and drove their more invincible clans of the mountains to arms to defend their liberties, their religion and their lives. No wonder that when Dr. Kerr, and Dr. Buchanan and the Church missionaries visited them, they found them in a low and a destitute condition! Without Bibles, without instruction, and without suitable ministers, what was to be expected but that they would be depressed in spirit as well as in circumstances, and be prepared to welcome the English and true Christians as their friends and deliverers! Trample upon the liberties of a people; attempt to bend their consciences to your opinions, as well as deprive them of their immunities, and you, no doubt, make them your slaves; but rest assured that retribution slumbers not. If there is not a power on earth to avenge, there is one in heaven; and "Vengeance is mine, saith the Lord! I will repay." The oppressors of these poor Syrians are already humbled, and laid prostrate. The nation that afflicted them, has long been visited with indignation. The system that heaped upon them so many calamities, is shorn of the splendour which it once boasted in the East; and while a long train of judgments await it in every part of the earth, while

Babylon the great will be thrown down from her eminence, like a millstone into the midst of the sea, while heaven and earth will rejoice at her destruction; the poor Christians of Malayala will have their captivity turned again like streams in the south; the Sun of righteousness will yet shine upon them with healing in his wings; and a sabbath of joy and peace, and prosperity will dawn upon their land.

But notwithstanding the persecutions of their enemies, and the oppression which their own princes have learned to inflict upon them, a goodly remnant is left. Sixty or seventy thousand cleave to their ancient faith. Their articles of theology are found to be orthodox, though their calumniators denounced them as heretics. They acknowledge the authority of the word of God, and encourage the use of it among the people. Celibacy is no longer enjoined upon the priests, but marriage is reckoned honourable among them, as amongst the laity. Instead of their worship being confined to the reading of their liturgy in the Syriac—a dead language and one which the congregations could not understand, it is now read in the Malayalim; and the divine ordinance of preaching is diffusing light and freedom, through the minds of their community.

At the time that Sir Thomas Munro was resident at the Court of the Ranee, he exerted himself, in a most commendable manner, on behalf of the Syrians.

He wrote an address full of power and eloquence, to the British government, in their favour; he persuaded the Queen to establish and to endow a college for the education of the Cattanars as the ministers and instructors of the people; and he obtained for many of them places of trust and emolument under the government of Travancore. Through his kind arrangement also, the missionaries of the Church Society were located among the Syrians, and have carried on their labours of love among them for many years. Under the oppressions of their foes, the people were reduced to extremities; their spirits were broken; they became indolent and inactive, and seemed to be lost to society, as well as to the church; the greatest ignorance prevailed among them; and there was no education in the land. But the Lord is giving them a revival in their bondage. As the depositories of the scriptures in the Syriac language for so many ages past, they have now received the Bible published in that tongue, and also in the Malayalim—the vernacular dialect of the people, and under the kind, the superintending and fostering care of so many devoted missionaries, the work of reformation is advancing, and will, I trust continue to advance, till their hills and their dales resound with shouts of praise and gratitude to the Lord our God.

In consequence of the great disorders which were occasioned by the despotism and persecutions of the Portuguese, and in consequence of the poverty into which the people were plunged, and which disqualified them to send messengers to Antioch, and to support their foreign metropolitan in that style which was deemed necessary to his dignity and authority, the Christians in Malabar had for a long series of years, chosen their bishops and metropolitans from among themselves, had submitted to their authority, and had no correspondence with the see of Antioch. But after the establishment of the college in Travancore, and the settlement of English missionaries among them, very considerable interest was created about them in England; great attention was drawn to their state and circumstances; and greater efforts, it was evident, were likely to be made for their emancipation and their prosperity. This intelligence was received in Antioch, and the patriarch whose zeal and regard for his flock in India had slumbered for fifty years, thought it was time to supply the necessities of his diocese. Having appointed a metropolitan and an archdeacon, he sent them to India with full powers to rectify all disorders, and to unite the Syrians in Travancore more closely with their original see. On the arrival of Mar Athanasias and his ramban in Malabar, they commenced a most fierce and alarming conflict with all parties, excommunicating their predecessors, dissolving the marriages which they had celebrated, making alterations in the churches, and conducting themselves with any thing but the humility, and the meekness of Christ.

Their conduct was represented to the Resident, and to the Court of Travancore, as most mischievous, and measures were adopted for their removal; and they were banished the country. Whatever difference of opinion may exist on the propriety of making an appeal to the civil power for their banishment, every Christian must rejoice in the hope that the Syrians of Malayala will no longer be associated with Antioch. The doctrines and the practice of the Maronites seem to be paramount in that patriarchate, and as it is evident, according to accounts received from many parts of the East, that there are no greater enemies to the truth, and to Protestant missions, than the votaries of this sect, we cannot but feel grateful to God that the Syrian Christians are likely to be rescued from their hands. The ecclesiastical authorities chosen in India, seem to have been on the very best terms with the Church missionaries, and wish to co-operate with them in every plan for the removal of evils, and for the spiritual welfare of their people; and should these dear brethren be the means of causing the streams of life and salvation to flow among the hundreds of youth committed to their care, and whom they are called to instruct in the great principles of the gospel; and should many of those youths become the ambassadors of reconciliation, and diffuse these waters of life and immortality among the lukewarm congregations of Syrians, our hearts may ere long be gladdened with the tidings that the wilderness and the solitary are made glad and that the desert rejoices and blossoms as the rose. I cannot better conclude this notice of the Syrian Christians than by an extract from a report given of his visit to them by Archdeacon Robinson in 1830.

"My visit to the society's mission at Cotyam, among the Christians of St. Thomas, was productive of the greatest pleasure; and I beg leave to request the earnest attention of the committee to this most interesting establishment. I had fomerly an opportunity of visiting them in the year 1818, when our intercourse with the venerable church was in its infancy; and since that time, peculiar circumstances have led me to regard them with increasing interest. It was highly gratifying therefore to witness the great progress both of sound learning and religious feeling among the Syrian youth who are destined for holy orders, the great desire for education which has spread throughout the country, and the confidence and affection with which the brethren at Cotyam are regarded generally by both the clergy and laity. The improvement thus produced, especially among the candidates for priesthood, gives us the best ground of hope for the future, and that probably for many years, it must be the object of hope rather than of exultation, of earnest prayer and wise counsel.

"My attention was chiefly directed to the actual state of the college and the degree of proficiency which the pupils have obtained, and I have great pleasure in assuring the committee that the result of my examination was highly satisfactory and most honourable to the Rev. Mr. Doran, to whose judicious superintendence and unremitted instruction it is indebted for its present improved and flourishing condition.

"On May 3, in sixty-four catechist districts, comprising two hundred and forty-four towns and villages, more than two thousand families, consisting of above seven thousand five hundred souls, were under direct Christian instruction; in one hundred and fifty churches, ninety-four smaller houses of prayer, sixty-two schools, a seminary of thirty-six pupils, and a class of preparandi containing about thirty young men, the number of scholars was one thousand four hundred and fifty, of whom one hundred and twelve were girls.

"My principal object, however, was to ascertain the progress of the students in religious knowledge, and I therefore catechised them very carefully in the chapter 1 Corinthians x.; which they read in English and translated verse by verse into Malayalim. The result was highly satisfactory, of course with a very perceptible difference of the younger boys; but in the higher classes there is a knowledge of the doctrines, history and scheme of Divine Revelation, which shows that the main object of the college, their preparation for the church is sedulously kept in view. When I saw *one hundred and three boys* thus educated by one clergyman, in so many different branches of learning almost all of which were totally unknown to them a few years ago, I could not help viewing it as an institution of incalculable value and importance."

CHAPTER X.

THE DANISH MISSIONS.

MISSION TO TRANQUEBAR—EUROPEAN SOCIETY—REGARD FOR THE HEATHEN—TAMUL LANGUAGE—ROMAN CONVERTS—DAILY STUDIES—PECUNIARY EMBARRASSMENTS—CHRISTIAN KNOWLEDGE SOCIETY—LETTER OF GEORGE I.—DEATH OF ZEIGENBALGH—GRUNDLER'S EFFORTS AND DECEASE—HOPES OF THE ENEMY—NATIVE ASSISTANCE—THE EXERTIONS OF EUROPEAN MISSIONARIES — SUCCESS — BAPTISM — ARUNASALAM — SWARTZ —CASTE—BISHOP WILSON—REFORM.

At the time that Asia was laid open to the zeal and enterprise of the western nations, an East India Company was established in Denmark; and some of its citizens tried their fortune at Tranquebar. Though the speculation did not succeed, and the company were obliged to resign their charter into the hands of the sovereign; the factory thus established was maintained by the state; a governor and other subordinate officers were appointed; the undertaking continued to flourish under more powerful auspices; and many of the subjects of Copenhagen became rich, in consequence of their commerce with their settlement on the coast of Coromandel.

Frederick, who reigned at the beginning of the eighteenth century, appears to have been a wise and a benevolent prince, and at the suggestion of Dr. Lutkens, he determined on establishing a mission for the conversion of the heathen at Tranquebar. Though many difficulties arose; Providence evidently favoured the design by raising up two young men, endowed with eminent zeal, piety, self-denial, and devotedness to take the lead in the arduous work. No Christian soldiers were more fitted, by gifts and grace, for their sacred enterprise, than Zeigenbalgh and Plutscho; nor could they be excelled in the spirit with which they entered upon the field.

After their arrival at Tranquebar, discouragements soon attended their steps. Like all Europeans who visited India in those days, their own countrymen were more intent upon making fortunes, than on setting examples of virtue to the heathen. They scorned, they calumniated, they persecuted the missionaries; they hated them for the truth's sake that was in them, and for the testimony which they bore against their works of darkness; and on one occasion, the governor arrested Zeigenbalgh, and confined him four months in prison. Such scandalous conduct would have been little to the missionaries, had it only affected themselves. But alas! it had most injurious effects upon the cause of God among the heathen, and it therefore wounded them the more. The language of the natives, expressed in their bad English, used then to be, "Christian religion, devil religion; Christian much drunk, Christian much do wrong, much beat and much abuse others." "Truly," says an author of that day, "it is a sad sight there, to behold a drunken Christian, and a sober Indian; a temperate Indian, and a Christian given up to his appetite; an Indian that is just and square in his dealings, and a Christian that is overreaching and exorbitant; a laborious Indian and an idle Christian, as if he were born only to fold his hands. O what a sad thing it is for Christians to come short of Indians, even in moralities! come short of those who themselves believe to come short of heaven."

Nor was this all. But these very Danes who ought to have supported the truth, scoffed at Christianity, laughed at the heathen who became anxious about their salvation, and told them often that they were better in their own religion, than to make themselves mean and contemptible by embracing ours. But amidst evil report and good report; troubled on every side, yet not distressed; perplexed, but not in despair; persecuted, but not forsaken; cast down, but not destroyed; always bearing about in their body, the dying of the Lord Jesus; the brethren persevered in their course; they were willing to suffer all things for the *elects'* sake, and continued therefore, to preach the word in season, and out of season. It does one's heart good to record their sentiments amidst the howling of the storm.

"At this rate," say they, "the word of God runs on amain. Our congregation consists of sixty-three persons, and another is to be baptized to-morrow. We hope more will shortly come over; there being a pretty many up and down, who have already received a favourable impression of the Christian religion. There is a blind man in our congregation, endued with a large measure of the spirit of God, who begins to be very serviceable to us in the catechising of others. He has such a holy zeal for Christianity, that every one is astonished at his fervent and affectionate delivery in points of religion. We cannot express what a tender love we bear to our new-planted congregation. Nay our love is arrived in that degree, and our forwardness to serve this nation, has come to that pitch, that we are resolved to live and die with them. I am sure you would wonder, if we should give you an account at large of all the oppositions we have met with hitherto. Yet all these engines set on work by the devil, have only served the more gloriously to display the works of God, and to unite us the nearer to him who is the only support of all the distressed. *Heathens* and *Mahometans* are kind enough to us, notwithstanding we have all along laid open to them, the vanity of their idolatries, and superstitious worship. But those that *pretend* to be Christians and are worse than heathens at the bottom, have shown to us all the spite and the malice they ever could. However, there is a remnant left among them too, that love to be sincerely dealt with."

In commencing their work among the natives, the brethren had many and great difficulties to contend with. A barbarous jargon of Portuguese, spoken by a few of the people, and introduced by the Romanists among them, as the language of perfection, seemed to divide their attention for awhile, and to have withdrawn their minds from that constant and untiring industry which they ought to have given to the Tamul—the dialect spoken throughout the province. They very soon saw the folly of this. The Portuguese and those who spoke this jargon, were not a fraction of the inhabitants. Being chiefly adherents, and proselytes to the church of Rome, they became a great source of vexation, and trouble to the missionaries. As the carnal weapons, and the worldly policy, and the deceitful intrigues, which the Jesuits had used to bring over the people to their Catholic superstition, were still carried on by their priests and their votaries; the natives distrusted the missionaries, and looked upon them as kinsmen of the same family, as labourers at the same craft, and as professors of the same religion with the clergy of Rome. Thousands of poor and wretched beings who had been seduced by various motives, into the pale of Romanism, who had become outcasts, and were abandoned by their friends and relatives, and who, unable to obtain a living, were obliged to beg and to starve, brought a great disgrace upon the Christian name, and added greatly to the prejudices of the heathen against our religion.

The missionaries, therefore, saw it to be to the advantage of their cause to disavow all connexion with the Portuguese party; they gave themselves up entirely and assiduously to the service of the heathen; and they wept and mourned over the *millions* who were perishing in their idolatry and crimes. I hope it will not be found that in Protestant missions, there are some who devote their time and their talents to a few strangers and foreigners in a country, who speak a different language from its aborigines, while they leave the millions of the land to perish forgotten and neglected. If that be the case, they have mistaken their vocation. It is a pity they ever left their native land; indeed, they ought now to abandon their station, since they prevent its being occupied by men whose reason and common sense would induce them to live and to labour that the gospel may be established among the teeming population of the province. What would be thought of a missionary to London, who, finding some few French emigrants in its suburbs, would sit down among them and learn their language to be useful to them, while he neglected the English tongue and with that, the millions who used it, and left them in their delusions and their sins?

But whatever error they at first committed in this respect, Zeigenbalgh and his coadjutor nobly redeemed it. They gave themselves to the study of the Tamul, with an ardour and a devotedness which brought their own reward, and notwithstanding the difficulties they had to surmount, and the very few facilities which they had to assist them, they were soon able to preach to the heathen, in their own tongue, the wonderful works of God. As a sample of his diligence and indefatigable exertion, as an example to the brethren who may be called to follow in his steps, and as a specimen to the Christian church, of the manner in which a missionary has to labour during the first years of his career, I cannot help transcribing the account Zeigenbalgh gives of his daily studies.

"After morning prayer," says he, "I explain the heads of our catechism from six to seven. From seven to eight, I repeat my *Malabarick* vocabulary and the phrases gathered in this language. From eight to twelve, I am entirely employed in reading such Malabar books as I have never read before; a Malabar poet and writer being present at the same time to assist me. The poet is to give me a fuller insight into all the circumstances of each story recorded in the book, and to clear up the more dark and intricate passages of their poems; but the writer is to take down such expressions as I am unacquainted with as yet. At twelve o'clock, I go to dinner, having appointed one to read to me all the while out of the holy Bible. Between one and two, I usually rest a little, the excessive heat of these countries not permitting a man to enter upon serious business immediately after dinner. The hour from two to three, I spend in catechising, and then I fall again to read *Malabar books* till five, when we begin our exercise of piety in our native tongue, for the edification of the Germans residing there. This lasts to six, and from this to seven, we meet for a mutual *conference*, every one giving an account of the management of that particular charge which is committed to his trust, and of the difficulties it is attended with. At the same time we consider, by a joint concurrence of proper *means*, how to remove everything that may retard the work and how to order the whole matter to the best advantage. When this is over, a Malabarian reads to me out of one of their books till eight o'clock; but the choice is made of such books only as are done in a plain and familiar way, the style whereof I endeavour to express in my daily work and conversation. Hence it has happened, that now and then one author has been read a hundred times to me, and has never been laid aside, till I was fully acquainted with every word in particular, and its entire coherence with the rest. By this means, I have considerably improved myself in this language. From eight to nine I am at supper, which being finished I enter upon a short examination both with my children and myself about the things which have happened that day, and then conclude the day's work with singing and prayer."

A few years after the mission was established, the brethren had to contend with pecuniary difficulties. What with a large sum of money that was sent from Denmark, having been lost in the sea near to Tranquebar; what with the amount which was required for their own support, and that of their establishment; what with the funds that were necessary for the maintenance of their charity-schools in which the children were boarded as well as educated; what with the expenses attendant upon their journeys undertaken to preach the gospel, and upon the erection of school-rooms and places of worship, and upon the native teachers, and the writers employed under them in carrying on their labours; it required a very considerable income to meet their expenditure. Nothing, than this, was more distressing to their minds. Sometimes their prospect was most dark and dismal; not a ray of light appeared to dissipate the gloom. But in the most distressing seasons, they trusted in God, and were not disappointed. He raised up friends for them in India; the faithful and benevolent in Denmark and in Germany came to their help; and in 1710, the Society for Promoting Christian Knowledge began to take an interest in their affairs, and since that period has patronised them and encouraged them, and has been the principal means of carrying on the work of God in southern India. Many and great may be the faults of this good society; the spirit and temper of its directors and agents may be very different now from what they were in days that are past; small may be its income, and feeble its efforts when compared with the amount of patronage and wealth and influence which it might command; but as it was the first society in the field, as it was established in an age when no efforts were made by any other denomination to propagate the gospel, as it has numbered among its missionaries some of the most devoted and illustrious of men, and has done a great work which, now while I write of it, makes my heart glad, and reflects an honour upon my country, it is impossible to speak of it but in terms of commendation and gratitude. May its former spirit and labours and success be revived, and may it yet appear a bright luminary to enlighten the world.

As the missionaries had hitherto only been able to translate books and distribute them in the very contracted sphere which such a method would allow, the society in London sent them a printing-press and fount of types, and enabled them to publish the Scriptures and tracts for the edification of the native Christians, and for the conversion of the heathen. This was a measure, which, with the translation of the Scriptures into the Tamul language, contributed greatly to the advancement and prosperity of the mission. The word of the Lord began to run, had free course and was glorified.

Hitherto confined to Tranquebar and its neighbourhood; it now extended to Negapatam, to Trichinopoly, to Tanjore, and to Madras and to the towns and villages in the country. It was about this time that his Majesty George I. wrote a letter of encouragement to the missionaries, and lent his name, his patronage, and his benevolent example to the missionary cause. Not only is it due to the memory of the worthy prince by whom it was dictated and to the missionaries who received it, that it should be recorded in the notice of this mission; but for the sake of the church and the world, and for the sake of those who think it would be low, undignified and disreputable to patronize such an undertaking as the conversion of the heathen, it ought not to be omitted, but should be held up for imitation.

"George, by the grace of God, king of Great Britain, to the Reverend and learned Bartholomew Zeigenbalgh and John Ernest Grundler, missionaries at Tranquebar. Reverend and beloved,—Your letters dated the 20th of January of the present year, were most welcome to us, not only because the work undertaken by you of converting the heathen to the Christian faith doth, by the grace of God, prosper; but also because that in this our kingdom such a laudable zeal for the promotion of the gospel prevails. We pray you may be endued with health and strength of body; that you may long continue to fulfil your ministry with good success, of which, as we shall be rejoiced to hear, so you will always find us ready to succour you in whatever may tend to promote your work and excite your zeal. We assure you of the continuance of our royal favour. George R.

"Given at our palace of Hampton Court, the 23rd of August, A. D. 1717, in the fourth year of our reign."

Happy the prince whose heart was imbued with such sentiments; and happy the kingdom that enjoyed the rule of such a prince! When kings thus become nursing fathers and queens become nursing mothers to the church of God; when princes and peers and governments will consider it their honour, and privilege to extend the kingdom of Christ, and to send ambassadors to the heathen, then the hills of difficulty and of opposition will be compelled to bow; the vast sums that are expended upon armies and navies, and wars, and pageantry will be reserved for the conflicts with the powers of evil, to secure the triumphs of the gospel; monarchs and chieftains and bishops and such dignitaries will once more lead on their faithful and courageous bands—not on a crusade against the Turks and the Infidels—not to rescue the land of Palestine from the hands of the enemy—not to restore the holy sepulchre and to rebuild the waste places of Jerusalem—no; but to drive Satan and all his agents from their dominion upon earth, to rescue perishing souls from the hand of the terrible, and set the captives free, and to gain for Immanuel the conquest of the globe.

Very shortly after this, Zeigenbalgh was removed into the eternal world. As the first Protestant missionary to India; as the founder of that interesting and important station; as a servant of Christ who faithfully served his day and generation and laid the groundwork for the splendid superstructure that was raised to the glory of God, it is impossible now not to mingle our tears and our sorrows with those first converts who wept over his early grave. All Israel mourned for him with a bitter lamentation; the sluices of affection were thrown open, and poured forth the floods of grief and sorrow; while the enemies rejoiced in it as an event that must annihilate the Protestant mission. The converts might well exclaim, "Pity us, pity us, ye friends, for the hand of the Lord hath touched us."

Scarcely had the grave been closed upon Zeigenbalgh, when Grundler was laid low and was reduced to the greatest state of weakness. He was obliged to sit in the pulpit. With strong crying and tears, he was accustomed to beseech the Lord to spare the little flock, not to expose them to the fury and malice of the beasts of prey, by the removal of both their shepherds; but to interpose and spare him till others should arrive to watch over them and to carry on the work. His prayers were heard; Schultze and his coadjutors came to their assistance; and Grundler had the satisfaction of seeing them enter into the field. But his race was finished, and he was soon laid beside his departed friend. Oh!

these Jeremiahs who weep and cry for the abominations that exist in the land; these apostles who travail as, in birth again, till Christ be formed in the hearts of sinners the hope of glory; these faithful missionaries who long to gather in the heathen into the fold, and who watch for souls as those who must give an account; why are they not spared longer in the vineyard? why are they called away when their labours, and their cares and their talents are most required? It is the Lord, let him do what seemeth good in his sight; his ways and his judgments are past finding out! Perhaps to crown them with early reward and to take them away from some evil to come; perhaps to correct some evils which are beginning to germinate among the people, to warn them, and to lead them to greater watchfulness, prayer, and meditation on eternal things; perhaps to prepare the way for the developement of some principle or of some character which might otherwise be concealed; perhaps to confound the enemy and in the hour of their triumph, to annihilate their power; perhaps, but why ask for reasons, why not bow silently and submissively to the divine will? What we know not now, we shall know hereafter.

In their hopes, the enemies were thoroughly disappointed. Schultze and his companions waxed stronger and stronger. Many of those who were most violent in their hostility to the gospel, became obedient to the faith. Instead of four, their schools amounted to twenty-one, and contained at one time five hundred and seventy-five scholars. The whole scriptures were published and gave the greatest delight to converts; Rajanaikeen and Sattiannaden and many more native teachers were raised up and qualified to preach the gospel to their countrymen, to endure with patience and magnanimity, the greatest trials and persecutions, and to convert the most obstinate to the side of the cross. In proportion to the rage and violence with which the Roman Catholics carried on their persecutions, in the same proportion did the word of God become mighty to the pulling down of strong holds. Great numbers flocked from the country to the missionaries to enquire what they must do to be saved. The love and faith and zeal of the converts grew exceedingly, and gave the greatest joy and comfort to all. Instead of regarding themselves the only instruments through whom the work of mercy was to be carried forward, the missionaries saw the necessity of raising up native teachers, of giving them an education suited to their sacred office, and of sending them forth to those parts of the country where they were not as yet permitted to sojourn themselves. Then they led them forth and shewed them how Bramins and antagonists were to be defeated, and how souls were to be won to the Redeemer.

Missionaries have sometimes erred upon this point. Instead of becoming leaders in the conflict, they have thought it should be wholly left to the natives. The missionary who can forsake his native country and dwell among a race of idolaters, without endeavouring to learn their language, and then declaring among them the mercy and grace of God —must be very different in the constitution of his mind, in his views of missionary work, and in his experience in carrying out plans and principles which are peculiar to this undertaking, from those of the writer. He may reside among the natives, may be very diligent and active in giving instructions in a way which he regards very highly himself; but what if he has not zeal and application enough to learn the language of the people; what if the natives never find him in their towns and their villages endeavouring to unfold to them the great mysteries of godliness; what if they only hear that he is the head of a seminary, or the president of a college where the young are taught science and religion; will they not be apt to conclude that he is very lukewarm in his sacred calling, and however important the religion may be, which he has come to propagate, that it is not indispensably necessary to their salvation? But when he remembers that the prophets of old, while they attended to their schools at home, went abroad also to publish to Israel their transgressions, and to call them to repentance and to the service of God; that our blessed Master led forth his disciples to the cities and villages of Judea to proclaim peace and reconciliation, while he privately prepared them for their future work, and instructed them in the mysteries of his kingdom; that the apostles and evangelists watched and prayed and toiled to establish the gospel, while they committed the ministry into the hands of the faithful men, who in their turn might instruct others also; what will be the effects which a missionary will produce upon his catechists and his native teachers, and upon the heathen, when, following such divine examples, and summoning up his self-denial and his zeal, and pouring forth his pity and his compassion to men, though with broken accents and a stammering tongue, and beseeching them, as they have never been before, to be reconciled to God, he stands forth often and delivers the message of his master? The people may not be converted; but the moral impression which is produced, is incalculable. His teachers imbibe a portion of his spirit. It gives a new impulse to every sermon and to every exertion. The enemies are confounded with the simplicity of purpose, and with the disinterested zeal which labours to accomplish it. The heathen see and acknowledge that, while many others come to obtain glory and renown, or wealth and power, the missionary has come to seek for souls, aims at their eternal welfare, and is not satisfied till he gains them for his joy and his crown of rejoicing.

The translation of the Scriptures into the language of the people, and the publication of suitable works for the instruction of all; the establishment of schools in which children were taught the great principles of the gospel; the raising up of native teachers and catechists who would be able to preach Christ crucified, to their countrymen; and the public declaration of the truth by the living voice, and undertaking missionary tours in distant parts; such are the plans which were adopted by Schultze and his coadjutors, by Swartz and his successors, and by all the great and the good men who have laboured in that field. What were the effects with which they were accompanied? A goodly number of converts were added every year to the infant church. The gospel was introduced in many of the large towns in the neighbouring provinces. Schultze, under the sanction of the Society for Promoting Christian Knowledge, established a mission at Madras, and so did Swartz at Trichinopoly and Tanjore. Some of the brethren carried the gospel to Calcutta, and others published it in Cudalore, and Palamcottah. In 1775, there were five branches of the mission. At the various stations, there were thirteen missionaries and more than fifty native assistants; and in the several congregations, there were not fewer than nine hundred and nine new members in that one year.

It is impossible to look back upon such a state of things without gladness of heart. As yet, there was no laxness of principles in the admission of the converts, and if they were allowed to retain their caste, it was in ignorance of its nature and of the effects which it would likely produce in days to come. The brethren appear to have shown great caution and diligence in the preparation of candidates for baptism. There was at first a general system of examination in which the catechumens received instruction from the teachers, during several months, and sometimes for a whole year; then there was a particular inquiry in which their views of divine truth, their Christian experience, and their general conduct underwent an investigation, and it was laid down as a rule, that none should be admitted to baptism who were ignorant of the truths of the gospel, and did not appear sincere in their profession. I cannot here justify the conduct of Mr. Gericke—much as I respect his memory and his virtues; highly as I esteem his Christian simplicity, primitive devotedness and ardent zeal—and greatly as I honour his love to the heathen and the example of benevolence which he gave in leaving all his property £6,000 to the Vepery mission—I cannot justify his conduct in baptizing hundreds of heathen in a day, during his visit to Palamcotah and its neighbourhood, since it must have been evident, on the slightest inquiry, that the people were actuated by the hope of being exempted from public burdens, and were any thing but sincere in their profession. But these were exceptions to the general rule, and the missionaries manifested, in general, as much strictness, according to the views which they entertained, in the admission of members, as we could wish to see.

But while I am an advocate for Christian caution and judgment and impartiality, and would not, in any case, dispense with a knowledge of the gospel, and with sincerity in the candidates for baptism, I cannot agree with those who would look into the heart, who would insist that every motive, and disposition and principle are what they ought to be, and who would demand an assurance that the person is regenerated before the ordinance be administered to him. Where are such views found in the Bible? Were not Ananias and Sapphira, who lied afterwards to the Holy Ghost, and who fell down dead as a judgment upon their guilt, baptized? Was not Simon Magus the magician—the man who afterwards developed ungodly principles, and was found in the gall of bitterness, baptized? Were not many of the Corinthians and Romans and Ephesians who afterwards apostatized and brought dishonour upon the truth, baptized? I frankly confess that I am disposed to regard baptism more as an initiatory ordinance, as a renunciation of heathenism, and an introduction to the gospel economy, as a band of allegiance to the church on the one side, and of obligation and claim to Christian instruction, to privileges and watchful care on the other, rather than as a sealing and saving ordinance. If a heathen be impressed with the truth, understands the leading principles of revelation, and shows a sincere and ardent desire to join the fellowship of the faithful, and is, above all, willing to renounce his caste and submit to all the evils to which this act will expose him; who would forbid water that he should be baptized? No, I would say to him as Philip did to the eunuch "If thou believest with all thine heart, thou mayest." On a profession of his faith, I would baptize him, and would leave all the consequences; and would consider him bound to receive instruction, to attend the ordinances, and act as a disciple of Christ, and myself bound to look after him, to watch over him, and feed him with milk and not with meat, until he was able to bear it.

At Cuddalore, Mr. Hutteman pursued his labours, not without considerable success. Among the fruits of his ministry, there was a Pandaram of the name of Arunasalam whose history is interesting, and shows how the gospel triumphed over the prejudices of the heathen in those days. Originally a man of caste, a student of the learning, philosophy, and mythology of the Hindoos, and a worshipper of the destroyer, he resolved to become a priest of Ishwara, to visit all the celebrated temples, and to wash in the sacred waters of the Ganges. After pursuing his studies for five years, and after being initiated into all the licentious mysteries for which the Lingawantras are distinguished, his eyes were opened to behold the iniquity of such worship, and considered it impossible that a wise, a holy and a just God could ever look, with approbation, upon such disgusting abominations. Such, it appears was his state of mind when he visited Cudalore. Dissatisfied with his own religion, he was prepared to embrace one that so much accorded with his reason, his conscience, and his heart; he found the Redeemer fully qualified to relieve his wants and his miseries, and he embraced his system of mercy. On hearing of his conversion to the truth, the Pandarams belonging to the college at Tarmaburam in the province of Tanjore, addressed to him the following epistle.

"The grace of Sciva the creator, redeemer, and destroyer, be effectual in the soul of Arunasalam. If you inquire into the reasons of our writing this letter to you, know then: You were on a journey to the holy place of Cashy, and behold by the cunning fraud of that arch-enemy, the devil, your great wisdom and understanding have been so blinded, that you were not ashamed to go at Cuddalore, to the low and base nation of Franks and Europeans, who are no better than the Pariars, and that to hear and be instructed in their despicable religion. Oh into what amazement were we thrown on hearing this. The moment we heard it, we met in the Divine presence of the head of the sacred college of Pandarams, and consulted on this event. Indeed we are sunk in an ocean of sorrow. It is needless to write many words on the subject to a man of your understanding. Did you belong to the cursed populace, many words might be necessary. Remember, Arunasalam, your change is like a king turning Pariar. What have you wanted amongst us? Had you not honour and a subsistence sufficient? It is inconceivable what could induce you to bring such a stain on the character of a Pandaram. We must impute this misfortune that has befallen you, to a crime that you have committed against God in some former generation. Consider, Arunasalam, the noble blood of the Tondamar from whence you sprang. You associate yourself to the basest people who eat the flesh of cows and bullocks. Can any wisdom be amongst them? The moment you receive this letter return again to this place; may Sciva give you understanding.

"This is the divine oracle, written at the command of his holiness the head of the Pandarams at Tarmaburam."

To this letter, Arunasalam returned a reply of which the following is an extract.

"The grace of Parabara Wastu, Jehovah the living God, the blessed creator and preserver of the universe, fill the souls of all the Pandarams at Tarmaburam. I have received your letter and read the contents with sincere compassion. Will you know the reason? It is this. You have unaccountably forsaken the living God, the eternal Creator of all that exists, and have given the honour due to him to the creature. You think yourselves wise, though fallen into the most dreadful foolishness. You worship the devil the arch-enemy of all that is good. You give divine honour to men who were born of father and mother, and who during their life have been notorious fornicators, adulterers, rogues and murderers. In your books are related the obscenest facts, where by lust, the fire of Satan, is furiously kindled in an instant. My heart melts within me. I weep over you. Fourteen years have I been witness of your infamous worship in your pagodas; and I am, in my conscience, convinced, that you are on the road that leads directly to hell and eternal ruin. How holy how majestic is God, as described in the sacred books of the Christians! You call them a base and ignorant people, but this is owing to your pride, which cometh from that proud spirit Satan. Come, my dear friends, and worship with me the God who made you. Be not deceived to expiate your sin by the washing and sacrifice of Lingam: the Christians alone have an expiatory sacrifice worthy of God. When I think on your blindness, my heart pities you. You know the integrity of my life; you never heard scandal of me. Could you then think I would renounce the religion of my fathers, without conviction of its falsehood and dreadful tendency? The God of infinite compassion hath delivered me a wretched sinner, out of the captivity of the devil. Your promises of honour and riches touch me not. I have the hopes of an everlasting kingdom: you may also inherit it, if you will repent. I have changed my religion, but not my caste. By becoming a Christian, I did not turn an Englishman: I am still a Tondamar. Never did the priest of this place desire of me, any thing contrary to my caste. Never did he bid me eat cow-flesh, neither have I seen him eat it, or any of the Tamulian Christians, though such a thing in itself is not sinful. Turn to the living God: so writeth Arunasalam, formerly a Pandaram, but now a disciple of the blessed Jesus."

No period could be more unfavourable to the developement of Christian principles, to the maintenance of Christian character, and to the establishment of Christian missions, than was the eighteenth century on the coast of Coromandel. War, anarchy, and disorder desolated the land. The Europeans, intent upon their own interests, and upon empire alone, transferred their hostilities to Asia and mustered their forces to decide the conflict. The native powers, unable to maintain a neutrality, were obliged to declare for the one party or the other; and in the end, became the victims of both. Hyder Ally, urged on by French influence, and at the head of an army more powerful and more brave than any that was ever known in India, descended from the Mysore, laid waste the Carnatic, and the lower countries, beseiged Madras, obliged Cuddalore to capitulate, and threatened Tanjore twice with all the horrors of desolation.

But such seasons produce great men, give scope to their talents, and exhibit them in all their greatness and magnanimity. Amidst these commotions and distresses, Christian Frederick Swartz appeared in the field of missions. It was a curious sight to behold a band of Christian champions trying to establish the gospel of peace, diffusing its holy, and meek and benign and gracious influence over the country, and standing forth as the advocates of harmony, and good will, amidst wars that raged with frightful violence, and amidst nations that were trying to devour one another. But such were the attainments that Mr. Swartz had made in the language; such was the confidence, that his truth, his urbanity and benevolence had inspired in the natives; and such were the respect and admiration which his consistent and Christian deportment had gained for him from princes and the highest authorities in the land, that all regarded him as their friend and benefactor; the Madras government requested him to go to Mysore and become their negotiator with Hyder Ally, and to secure to the country the blessings of peace; and the Rajah of Tanjore, unable at a time of siege to secure any longer the assistance of the Brinjaries and to obtain their confidence through the means of his courtiers, called upon Swartz to interpose, and supplies were immediately obtained; and unable at another time to keep his people from leaving the country, and to prevent the horrors of famine which threatened the community, he entreated Swartz to give them his word, and the men who would neither trust the king, nor his ministers, nor the English, relied upon the promise of the missionary, and the fields were cultivated and brought forth an abundance.

What an example to devoted missionaries, is Father Swartz! I do not regard his talents and acquirements as very extraordinary; but his piety was fervent, his diligence was indefatigable, his labours were incessant, his love to souls was intense. Very deep were his sympathies with the people, and great was the benevolence of his heart. Money had no charms for him, and all that he could obtain, was most cheerfully devoted to the cause of his master. The plunderers of the province were reclaimed by the persuasive tones of his voice, and the heathen learned to put more trust in his word than in that of sovereigns. He liked to hide himself from observation, and escape from the praises of men; but honour attended his steps; he became the friend and companion of princes; the great and powerful courted his alliance; the young learned to lisp his name with fondness, and the old rose to do him service; he gained the confidence and esteem of one heathen Rajah, had another committed to his care, and died in his arms. Great was the respect and esteem that were shown him in life, and greater if possible were those which were rendered to him at death. The mission in which he laboured was constituted his heir. His name is engraven on marble, and many monuments perpetuate his deeds; but they are embalmed in the hearts of his people, and will live, through their means, among generations yet unborn. His name will be held in everlasting remembrance, when the memory of the wicked shall rot.

Nothing in the state of the mission, and in the circumstances of the time, could contribute so much to the prosperity of the gospel, as the long and laborious life of Swartz. Under his wise and judicious management, and through the means of his exertions and example, the mission was extended on all sides, and it has been reckoned that in the days of its greatest prosperity, not fewer than forty thousand members were connected with it; it maintained its vigour for a period of a hundred years, under a succession of agents who seemed to grow in talents, and wisdom, in energy and success in proportion to the demand of its necessities, and amidst outward troubles as numerous and as formidable as any that history can record. But the seeds of evil were sown, and very soon after the close of Swartz's career, began to germinate.

Whatever might be the views of the missionaries about caste, and however ignorant they might be of the evils which it must, in due time, produce, it is unquestionable that, in admitting their converts from Paganism, into the pale of the Christian church, they did not call upon them to renounce this badge of their idolatry. This little leaven was allowed to enter, and it soon leavened the whole lump. This poison was allowed to circulate through the blood of the ecclesiastical body, and the whole head became sick, the whole heart became faint; there was nothing but wounds and bruises and putrefying sores which had not been bound up, nor mollified with ointment. This Upas-tree was allowed to be planted in the garden of the Lord, and while nothing that was sweet, or beautiful could grow under its shade, what were the fruits it produced? Malice, envy, jealousy, pride, ill-will, strifes, hypocrisies, every evil passion and every evil work.

The younger missionaries who came to labour in the vineyard, felt themselves incapable of contending with this evil, and most of the bishops who came to India, and under whose superintendence, the missions were placed, did either not comprehend the magnitude of the disease, or did not know what remedy should be applied to it. Some regarded this caste as only a civil rite, and thought it might therefore be tolerated in connexion with the church in India. A civil rite! yet it was preying upon the vitals of Christianity, and had brought down the black hairs as well as the gray hairs of devoted missionaries with sorrow to the grave. A civil rite! yet the people required the church to be divided into different sections according to their rank, they entered to their seats by different doors, and under the same roof, they worshipped the same God, and could not look but with scorn and contempt upon each other. A civil rite! yet they would not come to the table of the Lord together, would not eat of the same bread, nor drink of the same cup, and would not live in the same village, nor allow the same catechist to enter into their houses to instruct them and their children. A civil rite! yet they consulted Bramins as to fortunate and unfortunate days; Shoodra widows and virgin widows were not allowed to marry again; their wives were treated as slaves; their marriages were celebrated with intemperate feasts, and with processions of tom-toms, music, and all kinds of heathen peculiarities. A civil rite! yet the Bramin looked with disdain upon the Cheitra; the Cheitra, in his turn, despised the Veishya; and the Veishya treated the Shoodra with contempt; and the Shoodra trampled upon the Pariar as a slave; while every diabolical passion and temper were rampant among them. This was caste in *reality*, and well might the missionaries be loud in their complaints against such a system.

But at length, Bishop Wilson came to India. I cannot approve of all the measures which this prelate has adopted to further the interests of Christianity, in Hindosthan; but I rejoice to think that he looked at this monstrous system with decision, and determined to put it down. From his residence at Calcutta, he issued one epistle after another, calling upon the people to abandon such superstitious rites, or to prepare for such Christian discipline as had never been tried before. Afterwards, he visited the churches in the south, and in the midst of the evils which every one must deplore, he declared that, while the greatest consideration should be shown to the prejudices of the old, and those who had grown up in the system, the man who would not abandon caste was no longer to be regarded as a member of the church or congregation, and that the ordinances should no longer be dispensed to him or to his children; and that the catechist who would not relinquish caste, and enjoin its abandonment upon others, was to be deprived of his office and regarded as a heathen man and as a publican.

Such Christian discipline has, no doubt, created a schism in the body; but it is better that there should be a schism, than that the name of Christ should be blasphemed among the heathen; better there should be a schism than that idolators should be able to point to such churches, and instead of saying, "Behold how these Christians love one another," should be able to say, "See how they hate and devour each other."

So long as such evils were allowed to exist,

they were like so many goads in our sides, and thorns in our eyes, as the Philistines were to Israel in Canaan. However much we might frown upon caste and disallow of its existence in our churches, it was impossible to hide from the converts that it was looked upon with favour at Tranquebar and at Tanjore. Greater privileges, more temporal security and protection, lighter trials and crosses, therefore, were thought to attend a profession of Christianity in the older stations, than in the younger. Individuals who had resided in the south for a time and who had enjoyed these advantages were often, in the course of providence, called to visit other mission-stations, and were found to recount the many temporal immunities which the Christian caste enjoyed on the coast of Coromandel, when compared with those of other parts of the country; and such reports were calculated to create discontent and dissatisfaction among the native Christians who are still babes in knowledge and in experience; and make them to sigh for lighter crosses and greater privileges.

But now that this evil is removed and this discipline is enforced what effects are likely to be produced? We hope that the old leaven will be purged out; that primitive Christianity will be revived; that faith and love and peace and all the graces of the spirit will take the place of faction and of strife; and that these churches, instead of being cold and dead, and exerting a baneful influence over others, will repent, will return to their first works, will strengthen the things that remain and are ready to die, and will shed a sacred, a healthful, salutary, reviving spirit over all the Christian societies of India.

CHAPTER XI.

SUCCESS AMONG EUROPEANS.

FORMER CHARACTER OF EUROPEANS IN INDIA—MORAL CHANGE —BRITISH SOLDIERS—LETTERS FROM A SERGEANT—EUROPEAN OFFICERS—BIOGRAPHY OF DEPARTED SAINTS—JUDGE DACRE—MR. CATHCART—GENERAL CHARACTER OF THE BELIEVERS—LIBERALITY OF VIEWS—FEMALE INFLUENCE—WIVES OF MISSIONARIES.

During the first three centuries after the landing of Europeans in India, the natives had a most deplorable specimen of their character and principles. If the Portuguese, the Jesuits, and the whole Catholic party, only fomented intrigues, and cabals to advance their interests, converted the various settlements into so many depôts for spoliation, rapine and empire, and rendered their religion a handmaid to their commerce, their worldly greatness, and their own rapacious designs; the British and the Protestant party threw off every restraint, lived like infidels and heathens, indulged in every species of riot, and disregarded the authority of God and of men. As soon as a young man left his country, it was understood that he left his religion behind him, and whatever might be the education which he had received, and the principles in which he had been trained, he was regarded as an advocate of infidelity and ungodliness. No sooner did he land on the shores of India, than he was surrounded by the votaries of fashion and the world, who would not suffer him to leave their society, till they had initiated him into their system of depravity; till they had made him more the child of the devil, than he was before; till they had compelled him to fight his number of duels, and very probably imbrue his hands in blood. What, in those days, was the representation which was given of our holy religion to the natives of India? It was held up to their view as a religion of revenge, of avarice, of malice; as a religion that encouraged every evil passion, every wicked word, and every ungodly work,—as a religion which gave a licence to its votaries to indulge in the lust of the flesh, the lust of the eye, and the pride of life. When the missionaries went among the heathen to propagate the gospel; what was the reply which they met with? "Why do you come amongst us? Why do you not try to teach and to reform your own countrymen? What! would you have us to adopt such a religion as yours? to abandon the system of our ancestors to become drunkards, and swearers and blasphemers, and adulterers? to call our friend or our neighbour out into the field, and fire at him and murder him?

You tell us that, if we remain heathens, we shall certainly perish; but it is better that we should thus suffer, than adopt such a religion as this." In a word, the natives had the idea that Europeans had no religion at all, and when Mr. Thomas published an advertisement in a Calcutta journal to find a Christian, there was not one to reply.

But those days have passed away; this scene is completely changed; a moral revolution has taken place among our own countrymen in India; and it is now impossible to visit a station of any importance, without meeting with those who are the servants of the living God.

The gospel has become the power and the wisdom of God, to the conversion of many of the poor soldiers. I was travelling for the Missionary Society in Staffordshire; and at one of our public meetings, there was, upon the platform, a minister to whom I had not been previously introduced. In rising to second a resolution, he said he only wished to bear his testimony to-night, to the gracious effects which were produced in India, by the ministry of the missionaries upon our own countrymen there. "Prior to my settlement," said he, "in England, I was pastor of a church and congregation in Scotland. In connexion with that church, there was a poor widow woman who had an only son. Instead of being a comfort to her heart, he grew up a wicked and a profligate lad; he would not listen to the advice, he would not be guided by the counsels, of his mother. At length, he enlisted in the King's Royals and went to join his regiment in Van Diemen's Land. From thence, it sailed to India, and after its arrival in Calcutta, this youth wrote a letter to his mother in which he said that he had not yet met with any of those men whom they called missionaries, and he hoped he never should. This letter increased the grief of his widowed parent, and she could only mourn over, and pray for, such a wild and profligate child. The next letter which he wrote," continued the minister, "was not addressed to his mother; it was written to me. I sent for the poor widow to read to her the intelligence which I had received. On entering the door of my apartment, she exclaimed; 'O sir, is my Thomas still the same reprobate youth that he was before?' 'Sit down,' I replied, 'and you will hear.' The letter stated that his regiment was now located at Bangalore. Induced by some of his companions, he attended at the mission-chapel and heard a missionary preach. The sermon delivered that night became to him the engrafted word which is able to save the soul. 'Tell my mother,' said he, 'that I am now a member of the church at Bangalore; tell her how deeply I mourn over all the sorrow and pain that I have occasioned to her; tell her, if I am never permitted to meet her again upon earth, I hope to meet her in heaven, and spend an eternity with her in celebrating the praises of the Lamb.' I am glad, sir," said the minister, "to meet that missionary on this platform to-night, and hope that he will long be spared to convert many such wanderers to the fold of Christ." My heart was, of course, made glad that I was the instrument, in that dark and distant land, of causing the poor widow's heart at home to sing for joy, and that she was able to say in reference to her child, "O this my son was once dead, but he is alive again, he was once lost, but he is now found.'"

At the time that I left Bangalore, our English church was composed of about forty members, many of whose experience, corresponded with that of this young man. But being a military station, the troops are changed almost every three years, and we are often called upon to bid an adieu to many of our pious and excellent members whom we hope to meet around the throne. A few extracts from letters, written to myself, by a most interesting and devoted sergeant of the 62d, after their arrival at Masulipatam, will show the manner in which the gospel works among the poorer class of our countrymen.

From the time that the regiment left Bangalore till its arrival on the coast, the cholera had raged with terrific fury, and had carried off hundreds of the men; and writing in the name of his brethren, and in allusion to the scenes of danger and of trouble through which they had passed, the sergeant continues:—"We hope to follow your kind advice to us on leaving Bangalore, that we should all unite together, and continue to meet for prayer and praise, and examining the Holy Scriptures. We have much need of these helps, for we are often ready to forget ourselves; these deceitful hearts of ours, are apt to get cold, in the bustle of marching, and in the want of ordinances. One would think when there are so many instances here of the shortness of time, and such numbers of the dead and dying around us from the sickness that has raged, that we should be more particularly watchful to be found in Christ Jesus, and giving all diligence to make our calling and election sure; but although we are professors, and have in some degree forsaken the vanities of the world, there still remains so much corruption within us, that we have many a gloomy hour: but we are determined to hold on, in the strength which is to be found in Christ Jesus, and hope to continue steadfast unto the end, trusting that He who, we hope, has begun the good work in our hearts will perform it until the day of Jesus;—we are weak, but Christ is strong. Remember us in your prayers, that we may be kept by the power of God, through faith unto salvation; that we may be delivered from all the corruptions that there are in the world through lust, and preserved spotless and blameless until the appearing of our Lord and Saviour Jesus Christ, by whose name we are called, and in whose steps we desire, through his grace, to follow. We sincerely hope that God will prosper you, and your beloved family, and that the station where the Lord has placed you, may, through his blessing resting on your labours, prosper and flourish. We shall always remember with gratitude the solemn warnings and instructions we enjoyed under your ministry, and trust they will not be forgotten by us, while we sojourn in this vale of tears, but that, through the aid of God's Holy Spirit, we shall often call them to mind, and bless God for ever bringing us to Bangalore."

In another letter, they describe the happy and triumphant death of sergeant Lyall, a fellow-member, and a most consistent and humble Christian. Seized by the cholera, "he reposed his confidence on the omnipotent arm of the Captain of his salvation, and came off more than conqueror through Him that loved him. When his eyeballs were sinking and the image of death was upon his countenance, a friend approached him, and asked him, whether he were afraid to die? 'No,' replied he, 'depending on Jesus, I am not afraid. The words of Christ are 'Come unto me all ye that labour and are heavy laden, and I will give you rest;' and moreover he declares that none who come to him will be cast out; and shall I not believe his own most precious words? I know that if I were to get what I deserve, there would be no hope for me; but oh, it is a faithful saying, and worthy of all acceptation, that Christ Jesus came into the world to save the chief of sinners.' Those passages of scripture which he had often read, and which particularly rejoiced his heart in the hour of nature's extremity, were those which had an especial bearing on the freeness of gospel mercy through a Redeemer. While he saw his own unworthiness as a hell-deserving sinner; by faith he was enabled to exult in a risen and ascended Saviour. On a friend's remarking that his affliction was mingled with mercy, in the absence of those excruciating cramps which are often the concomitant of cholera, and on his being favoured with the continued use of his senses, of which many, in such circumstances, are often deprived, he replied, 'Yes there is a mixture of mercy in all God's afflictions, and I feel his mercy to me in this. O pray for me that I may be made thankful, and that God may mercifully carry me safe through this dark scene.' A worldly comrade told him to keep up his heart, and that he would soon get better. He rejoined that he saw nothing to tie him to this world, that he was quite willing to part with every thing connected with time, when God saw meet; and his warnings and exhortations to worldly comrades about him were so earnest and solemn, that many, who could not enter into his feelings, said that he was raving. Frequently on being asked the state of his mind, his reply was, 'I am happy.' In his final struggles, a brother in the gospel was making some remarks on the Pilgrim's Progress to a better country, when the dying believer exclaimed, 'At the cross, at the cross! There lies the hope of the sinner.' When his friend was taking leave, he shook him by the hand, and said,

'I trust we shall soon meet again where parting will be no more; my dying words to you are think on the shortness and vanity of time. Farewell!' Thus dear sir we have given you a few particulars of our brother's happy departure from this world of cares and troubles. God grant that we may be enabled to live the life, and die the death of a Christian."

But the success of the gospel, has not been confined to the poor soldiers alone. No. Among those who are high in rank, and station and authority both in the civil and military service, many have become obedient to the faith. Not a few of the youth of our nobility and of our merchants have left the land of their fathers—the land of Christian sabbaths and ministers and sanctuaries—the land of Bibles and ordinances and means of grace; and have gone to that land of idolatry and death, where Satan has his seat and where he reigns triumphant; for what purpose? Has it been to obtain wealth and fortune and worldly aggrandizement; and return to their home to spend it in vice and licentiousness? No. For what purpose then? Has it been to acquire fame and honour and earthly renown, and come back to boast themselves as far superior to their neighbours around them? No. They have gone there to be converted to God, to taste of that mercy which they here despised, to bow to the authority of that Saviour whom they here rejected, and to strengthen the hands and encourage the hearts of those missionaries whom they once contemned.

I was afraid, a few years ago, that Satan would obtain a triumph over us, and was to be permitted to hinder the good work which divine grace had commenced. In consequence of two excellent officers—then residing at Bangalore—having refused to obey the orders of the government, having publicly declared that they would not superintend the erection of an Eedgah to the Mahometans, and having boldly stated that they would rather suffer any thing, than compromise their sacred principles and bring dishonour upon the worthy name by which they were called; the sword of state was suspended over the heads of the believers; the government appealed to the orders and the regulations of the army, and reminded them significantly that pains and penalties could extend to the higher as well as the inferior branches of the service. But these champions of the truth maintained their allegiance to the gospel and determined to "serve God, rather than man." After a time, one officer was ordered to a different station; another was sent to occupy a post where, as a Christian, he would probably be alone; a third was commanded to join his regiment; and thus an attempt was made to break up the noble band who, at Bangalore, were valiant for the truth; and that others might be overawed and deterred from acting in that bold and independent manner which it is the honour and the privilege of a Christian to do. Nothing is better understood in India, than a removal, or a supercession, or an order for a staff-officer to join his regiment, as a mark of disapprobation from the authorities. But what was the effect produced by this persecution on the part of the government? It just resembled the persecution which was raised by Herod against the primitive believers: in proportion as it raged, the word of God, "grew and multiplied." The number of the pious and devoted at Bangalore, was greatly augmented, instead of suffering loss by the measure. The faith and zeal, and boldness of the brethren, scattered up and down through the provinces, began to assume a more energetic and decided character from that period. Wherever these devoted officers went, they forgot not the cause of their master, nor that of mankind. In the absence of chaplains and missionaries, they assembled the people together on the Lord's Day; they read sermons to them and exhorted them to flee from the wrath to come; and one and another was added to their number; and the purpose of Satan was defeated, while glory and honour and praise redounded to the Lord our God.

It is impossible to speak too highly of the zeal, and devotedness of these our Christian countrymen. They are, in reality, primitive believers; instead of regarding their property and their income as their own, many of them regard their possessions as belonging to Christ, and themselves as the stewards of his providence to whom much has been given that they may expend the more upon perishing men. They are the supporters of our schools, the contributors to our benevolent societies, the patrons of our seminaries and colleges, the best and the warmest friends of our missions. At the time it was proposed, that our new chapel should be erected at Bangalore, my esteemed colleague Mr. Reeve, and myself sent forth a circular inviting the contributions of our friends to this object, and in the course of six weeks, no less than five hundred pounds were subscribed; and though the erection cost about a thousand, the amount was nearly obtained by the time that the chapel was opened. In a communication which has lately been received from an esteemed missionary at Chittoor, he states that he proposed to erect a chapel in one of the large towns adjacent, and that he wrote to the excellent collector of the district to obtain a grant of ground for the purpose. But in addition to a grant of ground; what did this devoted and benevolent man enclose to him? A check upon his banker for five hundred pounds with which to erect the chapel.

Joseph Dacre, Esquire, of Chittoor, is now no more, but his memory is blessed. He was one of a thousand. His piety, his compassion to men, and his regard for the divine glory, corresponded with

N 2

the generosity of his heart. Occupying one of the highest and most important stations in the judicial department; his talents, his influence, his property and his time, as far as a regard to his official duties, would permit, were entirely consecrated to the glory of Christ, and to the conversion of the heathen. Much was the calumny and persecution, he endured for the sake of his master; but his record was on high; he remained steadfast and immoveable, always abounding in the work of the Lord. Some, no doubt, tried to impose upon him, and others abused his unsuspecting and ingenuous confidence; but he was a great philanthropist, a benevolent man, and a devoted Christian. His labours were more abundant. A large room in his own house was appropriated as a chapel; there, hundreds of the natives assembled, morning and evening, to worship; and on the Lord's Day, regular services claimed their attention, and directed them to eternal realities; and on such occasions, he was accustomed to pour out his soul, with the greatest fervour and energy, inviting sinners to repentance, and professors to holiness and a preparation for heaven. His exertions were blessed to the conversion of many of our own countrymen; and the heathen will long mention his name with affection and reverence. He was a burning and a shining light, and many had reason to rejoice in his light. By all the wise and the good who knew him, he was loved and honoured in life; and great was the lamentation that was made at his death.

Captain —— lived for some years at Bangalore. In the days of folly and indifference, the world was his portion; he was distinguished for his excesses among the votaries of fashion, and for his courage and daring in the field. But after his conversion to God, his natural talents found a new theatre for action. He became a good soldier of Jesus Christ, and fought valiantly the battles of his Lord. While others were in the valley, he was accustomed to be on the mount, enjoying an assurance of the divine favour. His natural cheerfulness gave a buoyancy to his exertions, and a joyful character to his religion, and set forth a life of faith and godliness in an attractive form. Armed with zeal for the glory of God, and glowing with compassion for sinners, he had always something to say in defence of the truth—something appropriate to the station and the character of those with whom he was brought into contact—something that was useful and profitable to souls. Many both among Europeans, and the natives will remember him as their friend, their benefactor, and their spiritual father. Though many years absent from India, his name is still mentioned with pleasure, and is a sweet savour to numbers. I shall always think, with gratitude and delight, of the services which he rendered to the cause of Christ in that dark land.

May he and his respected partner live long, and be as happy, and as useful in their sphere at home, as in the one which they occupied abroad.

R. Cathcart, Esq. was a young civilian and was a distinguished Christian among his brethren. Descended from pious parents, brought up in the nurture and admonition of the Lord, and early impressed with the great principles of our holy faith, he commenced his career in India like a Christian man, as well as a talented servant of the government. After entering on the duties of his profession, he showed most fully, that zeal and devotedness in the service of Christ, were perfectly compatible with the faithful discharge of public duty. Such was the great satisfaction which he gave to his superiors in office, such was the diligence and activity and zeal with which he laboured in his worldly vocation, and such was the deep impression which his steady and consistent Christian course, made upon those with whom he associated, during his residence at Darwar, that the highest respect was entertained for his character and principles on all sides, and the best testimonials were sent from the government of Bombay to that of Madras, when Mr. Cathcart was transferred to the latter in consequence of his promotion in the service.

"In forwarding this application," writes Mr. Anderson, "which I do with extreme regret, from the value I place on Mr. Cathcart's assistance; I trust I shall not be considered as departing from rule, if

I endeavour to express my appreciation of Mr. Cathcart's services, and declare that I have met no young servant of greater diligence, or possessing in a higher degree those qualities, and those talents which contribute to render their possessor an invaluable and distinguished public servant.

"The Right Honourable the Governor in council will, I full well know, be desirous to do full justice to all servants employed under the government, but lest it should not occur to his lordship in council, I beg it as a personal favour, if I may venture to solicit such, that in communicating to the Madras government the acceptance of Mr. Cathcart's resignation and return to his own presidency, mention may be made of the estimation of his services by those of this presidency under whom he has been immediately employed, and their conviction that wherever employed. it will ever be with honour to himself, with benefit to this government, and usefulness to the public."

Worldly men may sneer at religion, and may affirm that it disqualifies the individual for the ordinary duties of life. But experience shows that the charge is untrue, and that the men who are the most devoted to God, are the most faithful to man. In the Indian service, this is abundantly manifest, and in no case more than in the history of Mr. Cathcart. Where is the individual, devoted to business, wishing to gain the favour of his superiors, aiming at wealth, honour, advancement in rank, and distinction among his peers, who would have wished for a stronger recommendation than this? Yet Mr. Cathcart rose far above worldly considerations; nobler principles animated his bosom; he was more anxious to serve his God and gain his approbation, than to receive the applause of men; these were his ordinary duties, but they were discharged as in the sight of his heavenly Master, and with a view to his glory; in the midst of them all, our young friend was willing to confess that he was a most unprofitable servant, and did nothing but what it was his duty to do; yet this very spirit led him to perform them in a manner the most just, conscientious, honourable and successful.

But if Mr. Cathcart exemplified his religion in his relations to man and to society; what shall I say of his piety and his devotedness to God? All the graces of the spirit shone most conspicuously in him. He studied the example of Christ. His humility, his supreme love to God and to the truth, his regard for the divine glory, his spirituality of mind, his love to the brethren whatever might be their name and denomination, his compassion for perishing souls, his love to peace and his exertions to promote it, and his unbounded liberality—all showed how abundantly his own spirit was refreshed with the waters of life, how much he lived in communion with that Divine Saviour whom he loved, and how largely he enjoyed the grace and comforts of the blessed Spirit. It was like heaven to be in his society. He ripened fast for the glory and happiness into which he entered so early. "The world," said he in a conversation with a friend a short time before his death, "think me a happy man, and I am so. I enjoy a large share of the blessings of life; I have every thing that my heart can wish, and I desire to be thankful. Yet when I think of the glories of the heavenly state, they are so transcendent that the most valuable earthly objects lose their importance, and I desire, with the apostle, to be absent from the body and present with the Lord, convinced that it is far better." Death, he considered, not as an enemy, but as a friend who was to introduce him to the fellowship of the redeemed, and though he was willing to live for the benefit of man, and the advancement of the Divine glory, yet he seemed to regret the days which divided him from his Lord, from heaven, and from the glorified.

On his removal from Salem, a Christian friend thus writes: "We are threatened with a painful dispensation (I call it so) by the expected removal, from this station to Chingleput, of that blessed man of God Mr. Cathcart—the sub-collector. He is one of the most pious gentlemen I was ever acquainted with; nor do I ever expect to see his like on this side the grave. His excellence is that he is perfectly dead to the world, and he is truly eyes to the blind, feet to the lame, and a father to the fatherless. It would astonish you to see in what veneration this young saint is held at Salem by all classes of people, and how they weep at his expected removal from them. Christianity is truly respected here from the light which emanates from this child of God. The Lord bless him wherever he may go, and preserve him blameless to the end. Deadness to the world in a Christian is the most summary method to gain a complete triumph over sin and Satan, which I see exemplified in the life of Mr. Cathcart. His self-denial amazes me, and his fasting and abstinence confound my senses—the grace of God is truly magnified in him."

He lived not unto himself. So heavy were the obligations that he was under to Christ; so great and pressing were the wants and necessities of the world; so short was time, and unimportant its transitory affairs; so near were death, judgment and eternity, that he considered every thing as lost which had not a bearing on the interests of immor tality. Instead, therefore, of making provision for the flesh to fulfil the lusts thereof, he was wont by abstinence, and watchings and prayer, to keep down his body, and bring it into subjection that he might serve God with greater freedom and might have more of his property to consecrate upon the altar. He regarded not his income as his own. It was his to put it out to usury, to give it to the service of the sanctuary, with the full conviction that God would provide for friends and relations, for children and dependents, when a Christian was faithful to the trust committed to him. Acting on these principles, no sooner did he receive his monthly salary, than it was divided among those institutions which stood most in need of his assistance. The missions at Belgaum and at Salem, and others throughout the peninsula, shared largely in his benevolence. Wherever he was, the heathen had an important place in his affections, in his sympathies, in his prayers and in his gifts. He laboured hard to win souls to his Redeemer. What was his delight when he heard of sinners converted to God! Many from among the Hindoos, and from among his countrymen, will he have for his crowns of rejoicing. By his conversations, by his correspondence, by his exertions in distributing tracts and scriptures, and especially by his fervent intercessions, not a few received the intelligence of mercy and were made partakers of saving and converting grace.

He died, as he had lived. Seized with the cholera, and in the midst of strangers, he paid his servants their wages, and in the prospect of dissolution, directed them to that Redeemer who abolished death, "and brought life and immortality to light." His master found him faithful unto death, and then gave him the crown of life. Short was his career upon the earth; but in labour and in usefulness, it was long. May the mantle which he wore, fall on many of his brethren. He is gone; but he is neither dead nor forgotten. His services are lost to the church on earth; but they are consecrated to a purer worship in the sanctuary above; and gathered now to the general assembly and church of the first-born whose names are written in heaven, he will shine, among them, I doubt not, as a star for ever and ever.

Such are a specimen of our Christian brethren in India. Many more there are whose virtues, I could record, and whose praise is in all the churches there; they live in my affectionate remembrance, and neither time, nor distance will deprive me of that esteem in which I hold their names. Time and space would fail me to tell of their number and their devotedness to Christ. In the year 1836, it was reckoned that no fewer than eleven officers in the sappers and miners alone were separated from the world, and were living to the praise of God. Primitive simplicity, indifference to the frowns and smiles of the world, spirituality of mind, disinterested zeal for the divine glory, and commiseration for the perishing Hindoos, are pre-eminent among them, and distinguish them from the rest of the community. They live to Him who loved them and gave himself for them. Like Lot in Sodom, like Abraham and Isaac and Jacob in the land of Canaan; like Daniel and Shadrach and Meshach and Abednego in Babylon, they are witnesses for God, they bear their testimony in favour of the truth, they shine as lights in the midst of a crooked and perverse generation, and as a peculiar people, as a royal priesthood and as a holy nation, they show forth the praises of Him who called them out of darkness into his marvellous light. They are now a blessing to India, instead of a curse. Many of the heathen take knowledge of them that they have been with Jesus; and seeing our religion now as one of faith and piety and love and patience and benevolence, they are induced to consider its claims on their regard, and to abandon a system which can never save.

The religion of these Christian brethren, has hitherto been of a liberal kind. They "have known no man after the flesh." Free from intolerance and bigotry, it has associated them with no denomination in particular; it has rendered them the friends and the supporters of all who love Jesus in sincerity and in truth. More like primitive Christians, than many are in our day, more led and guided by the word of God, than human systems, and living far distant from the lands where party spirit, and national prejudices, produce violent conflicts, they think it essential to brotherly love, harmony, peace and good-will, to bury non-essential points in oblivion, and to seek, by united efforts, the progress of the gospel. Long, I trust, they will continue to stand fast in the liberty wherewith Christ has made them free, and not be entangled by any yoke of bondage. As the servants of God, and as the disciples of Christ, I hope that they will regard themselves as set for the rising of many in India; that they are not there to represent a party dominant, nor a party inferior; that they will continue to regard party distinctions as inimical to the advancement of the truth; and that nothing is more requisite, among idolatrous Hindoos, than to show that Christianity is the same system now that it was in former days—a system which binds all its members together in the bonds of love, and which overlooks all inferior considerations to extend its power, its grace, and its reign over the family of man. Attempts, I know, have already been made to attach them to party, and to use them as partizans, and greater efforts will yet be made to incorporate them with some future movements to establish a legalized system that may embrace Hindoos, as well as Englishmen in its comprehensive folds. But I trust, more enlightened sentiments will rule in their minds, and more reasonable principles operate in their hearts; that they will show the advocates of bigotry a more excellent way, and that, animated by the love which passeth knowledge, and by the love which it begets in the mind, they will direct all their energies to convert Hindoos to the knowledge, and to the service of Christ.

In concluding this chapter, I cannot overlook the influence which our fair countrywomen have had, in effecting this moral change. To advert to the state of Europeans in India, during the last century, it is not again necessary. As in all communities similarly circumstanced, and where few females of character and worth are to be found, the men were very wicked and ungodly, and worse, perhaps, than the heathen around them. But as the number of European females of respectability began to increase, their influence on society was speedily felt; riot and disorder gave way to more upright and honourable conduct; deeds which were formerly committed in open day were reserved for the shade and darkness of night; politeness and gentlemanly behaviour required that, in female society, oaths, curses, and all kinds of indecent language should be laid aside the sabbath which was almost universally profaned, soon began to be more regarded; and the churches which few thought of entering before, were filled with an attentive and respectful audience. Marriage became fashionable, and the relation—if not universally—is generally respected. The influence of such women as the Marchioness of Hastings, Lady William Bentinck, Lady Munro, and other ladies both in the higher and inferior grades of society, has done incalculable good to India and has added greatly to the morality, and real religion of the European community.

But in addition to the general and salutary effect which is thus produced; still greater and more beneficial is the influence which is exercised, when piety and all the graces of the Spirit adorn the female character, and render their dispositions more amiable and their accomplishments more lovely. I have seen, in many instances, how powerful female virtue and excellence have then become in India, and how valuable is their moral worth to the empire. Instead of being confined now to effects of a preventive kind, their pious characters and their consistent example draw many to Christ, to the sanctuary, to the meeting, and to prayer; they allure some to works of benevolence and mercy; they engage others on the side of God and truth, and win them over to be followers of Christ, companions of the faithful, and friends to the heathen. Many whom I have known, have been like angels in their visits to the abodes of men. They have gained the ear and the heart of their female friends, and have impressed their minds; these have brought their husbands to the sanctuary and have allured them into the paths of wisdom and of peace; and these husbands, in their turn, have become valiant for the truth, and have drawn their brother-officers and their friends to the ordinances and to the fellowship of the gospel.

I cannot therefore agree with the opinion, that missionaries should go out unmarried to India. As their wives are pious, devoted, and benevolent, what powerful influence will they exercise in their own families, among Europeans, and over the heathen. Not to speak of the assistance they may render to their husbands in their labours and their difficulties; of the comfort and encouragement which they can yield to them in the days of trial and distress; of the blessings which they may become to female converts and female children in the schools; of the example which they set before all, as wives and mothers and friends, bringing up their children for God, and diffusing peace and happiness around; how do they add to the universal and to the individual influence which is exercised over European society, and promote the general good which must go hand in hand with the conversion of the heathen, and which must have an important bearing upon the prosperity of Hindosthan. On other grounds, I could prove that it is reasonable, expedient, useful, and scriptural; the system of celibacy is too much in accordance with Popery and its priests, and has given rise to many evils disgraceful to the cause of Christ; and as the unmarried are not so highly respected, among the heathen, as the married, it is desirable and necessary that the institution* should be honoured; and that missionaries, in every relation of life, should be examples of all that is pure, lovely and of good report.

* It is not uncommon for a heathen when he hears that the missionary is unmarried to ask if he is a Catholic.

CHAPTER XII.

ON TRANSLATIONS AND ORIGINAL WORKS IN THE VERNACULAR TONGUES.

THE REFORMATION FROM POPERY—THE LATIN LANGUAGE—BISHOP GARDINER—THE EXERTIONS OF THE REFORMERS—VIEWS OF THE FIRST MISSIONARIES—TRANSLATION OF THE SCRIPTURES—OBJECTIONS MADE BY OPPONENTS—THE MADRAS BIBLE SOCIETY—BIBLE THEOLOGY—THE USE WHICH THE NATIVE CHRISTIANS MAKE OF SCRIPTURE—THE DISTRIBUTION OF TRACTS AMONG THE PEOPLE—THEOLOGY ADDRESSED TO HINDOOS.

THE liberty of the press, associated with the dissemination of truth, affords the greatest promise to future exertions. At the revival of literature in Europe, and at the time of the Reformation, nothing had a greater influence in the changes which took place, than the invention of printing and the labours of the press. From the days of the apostles when every man was permitted to hear in his own tongue the wonderful works of God, to the period when Luther and his coadjutors burst asunder the shackles of an ecclesiastical despotism, the use of the Latin—a dead language—had shut up the stores of learning and of theology from the mass of the people.

"During the sixteenth century, and in the reign of Henry the Eighth and Edward the Sixth, a person who did not read Greek and Latin, could read nothing or next to nothing. The Italian was the only modern language which possessed any thing that could be called a literature. All the valuable books then extant in all the vernacular dialects of Europe, would hardly have filled a single shelf."*

Latin was every thing. The mass was performed in Latin; the prayers were read in Latin; sermons were delivered in Latin; conversations between the great and the learned were carried on in Latin; and lectures on subjects of interest, and books of every description were written in Latin. Whatever was delivered in the vernacular tongues was thought to be worthless, vulgar, illiterate and contemptible. In a word, the same method was adopted to support the reigning superstition, which has sustained every other idolatrous system, and which exists to this day in the mythology of China, and of Hindosthan–there was a language which was sacred and another which was profane—a language in which theology and literature and science were wrapt up in mystery, and another that was suited to the common people and to the usual engagements of life—a language through the medium of which alone God ought to be worshipped, and men ought to be prayed for, and another in which it would be a deadly sin to

* Edinburgh Review, cxxxii. p. 10.

write upon, or to converse upon such sacred themes.

Religion, it was said, could not be understood in the vulgar tongue. There were not terms which would properly convey the meaning of theological words, and in the reign of Henry the Eighth, the cruel, the bigoted and infamous Bishop Gardiner had the assurance to propose "that instead of employing English expressions throughout, in the translation of the Scriptures, many Latin words should be preserved, because they contained, as he pretended, such peculiar energy and significance that they had no correspondent terms in the vulgar tongue. The words "ecclesia, pœnitentia, pontifex, contritus, holocausta, sacramentum, elementa, ceremonia, mysterium, presbyter, sacrificium, humilitas, satisfactio, peccatum, gratia, hostia, charitas," &c. were too sacred to be expressed in English. "But as this mixture," remarks the historian, "would have appeared extremely barbarous, and was plainly calculated for no other purpose, than to retain the people in their ancient ignorance, the proposal was rejected."

During the dark ages, then, and while century after century rolled away, the use of a learned and of a universal language had a fair trial; and what was the result of the experiment? To keep the people in the grossest darkness; to bring dishonour and scorn and contempt upon the vernacular dialects; to give a monopoly of science and literature and religion to the favoured few; to rob the community of their civil and religious liberty, and to deprive them of advantages both temporal and spiritual, which, but for such a system, they might have enjoyed for many an age. No wonder that when our reformers, when Luther, Latimer, and Ridley, and Cranmer and Knox began their labours, they used the language of the people. A strange and a foreign tongue, they knew, had kept the masses too long in ignorance, and in slavery; and, determined that their countrymen should hear and read in their own tongues the tidings of salvation, they employed the press to pour forth their thunders against the corruptions of Rome, to publish the gospel of Christ among the multitudes who were ready to perish, and to enrich their native dialects—with what? With translations from the works of the fathers? No. With translations from the mine of classic and ecclesiastical lore? No. But with their own warm thoughts and meditations on the strange theme of mercy to the conversion and the delight of thousands. The non-conformists of the following age, advanced in the same line, and replenished their own tongue with a literature and a theology which is still the boast of our land, and these principles, so much in accordance with reason and with common sense, continued to deepen and to spread, till now the English language is in possession of a mine of religious and intellectual wealth which the Greek and the Latin never knew.

From the moment that Protestant missionaries landed in India and acquired the language of the country, they began to publish grace and salvation to the inhabitants in their vernacular tongues. It was easier, they contended, for the few who had more leisure, had greater facilities, were endowed with ability and talents, and kept such a transcendent object in view as the conversion of the heathen, to learn the language of millions, than for the heathen to learn the language of strangers, or for ambassadors of mercy to accomplish their design through the medium of interpreters. As soon, therefore, as difficulties were overcome, Grammars were written, and Dictionaries were compiled, so as to render the language easier of acquirement to their successors. Numbers of tracts and many treatises on theology were published in a style suited to the capacity and corresponding with the habits and genius of the Hindoos, and now, in some languages, every native teacher has his small library to instruct him, and to open to him the treasures of the gospel. Above all, the sacred scriptures—a book which, written in an Eastern language, is peculiarly adapted to eastern climes, has been translated into almost every tongue, and has been disseminated among the people as the bread and water of life.

Some have found fault with the translations. They tell us that they are ill calculated to give a right view of the divine originals; that such are the false idioms, the barbarous phraseology, and the incorrect style with which they abound, that no native can obtain from them just views of the truth; and that it would be much better to wait till we could give a translation more suited to the taste and understandings of the natives. I wish our translations were as pure as the Hebrew and the Greek; I wish they were free from every blemish in language, in idiom and in style; I wish they were so immaculate that we could point to them and say, "Here, there is nothing human, it is all divine." But have they ever been spoken of, but as *translations*? Have we ever said that, in passing from one language to another, they are not liable to savour of human knowledge and of human instrumentality? Never. But this I will affirm that our Indian translations—those of them which have been made in the provinces where the language is spoken, and by missionaries who have understood the language,—those will stand a comparison with any first translations that have ever been made, and that, in the generations to come, they will be regarded as hallowed attempts to give the revelation of heaven to perishing heathens. Nay more. I shall not withhold, from the people, this fine gold though it should be mixed with some alloy; I shall not hide, from them, this pearl of great price, though it should be soiled; I shall not deprive them of this mine of wisdom, though it should be worked with human hands; I shall not conceal from them this heavenly treasure, this invaluable boon, this sacred directory, though it must still be accompanied with imperfections which are sure to cling to human performances. No. Whatever may be their defects, they contain light and truth enough to illuminate the minds of men, and to guide the feet of the wanderer into the paths of peace and happiness.

In order to render the translations more perfect, no pains, no expense, and no labours are spared. The committee of the Madras Bible Society act, in this department, with an anxiety and a zeal which deserve the highest commendation. No sooner is a translation finished and proposed for their acceptance, than a committee is appointed to give it a searching examination, and a small number of copies comparatively constitute the first edition. As soon as a second edition is proposed, a committee of revision is nominated; every member examines the copy; alterations and improvements are frankly and freely solicited; reasons for any changes which are proposed are expected to be given; and the translator is bound to give to all such opinions his best consideration. I was a member of the Committee for the revision of the Canarese version, and I can bear my testimony to the pains and trouble which are taken, to render the translations what we would wish them to be. They must at first, of necessity, be imperfect. If our own English Bible has passed through six versions, before it has attained the perfection which characterizes the seventh, why should we wonder that our first Indian translations are not yet so perfect and so pure as we should like to see them? But when I think of the amount of good which has been accomplished through their instrumentality both among native Christians, and among the heathen, I cannot but praise the Lord for all the grace and goodness which he has displayed.

Much as we lament that our vernacular literature and theology should be so scanty, yet it has this good effect—that it leads our native believers to study the word of God more freely and more frequently. They are in reality Bible Christians. Their prayers, their conversations, and their experience are full of scripture. They render honour to the truth and their appeal is constantly made to the law and to the testimony. Like the primitive disciples, the babes in Christ there find the sincere milk of the word and grow thereby; the young men find there the strong meat which renders them healthy and vigorous to fight the good fight of faith, and to overcome the wicked one; and the fathers in Christ find there, the grace, the promises, and the consolations which make them flourish like the palm-tree, and grow like the cedar in Lebanon, and which cause them to bring forth fruit in old age, and be fat and flourishing.

The great object which so many wish to accomplish in England, has already been secured in many parts of India. The Bible is the principal class-book in the schools. The minds of the children are imbued with the facts, the doctrines, and the precepts of the scriptures. Instead of being confined to Christian schools, the gospels and the epistles have, among heathen children, supplanted the native classics, and are diffusing the knowledge that maketh wise unto salvation among ignorant and superstitious pagans. To show how the truth enters the minds of the children, and how it is bound up with their affections, their associations and their language, and how it is used in their devotional services, I give the translation of a prayer which I once overheard offered up by a youth, in leading the devotions of others.

"Oh! Holy Lord! Before thee angels bow with veneration, and cast their crowns at thy feet. Thou art clothed with holiness, as with a garment. It is impossible for us to reckon up our sins before thee. Thou didst create our first parents holy, righteous, and happy; but they did that which thou forbadest, and they sunk in a sea of troubles. O Lord on account of their transgressions, we were born in sin, and have grown up workers of iniquity. We might reckon the sand upon the sea-shore, we might number the stars of heaven, but it is impossible for us to reckon our transgressions—a thousand we commit every day, and we deserve thy wrath. But we praise thee for sending our Saviour Jesus Christ. He came and took upon him our nature, and suffered on Calvary, and bore our transgressions, and died to save us from sin, hell and wrath. For all this, O Lord we praise thy name. For his sake pardon all our sins—give us grace to love him, with all our hearts, and soul and strength and mind. As thou didst in former times deliver Israel out of the land of Egypt, and from their dreadful bondage, so do thou set us free from the bondage of Satan, and deliver us from this wicked world, and these evil hearts. O take away our old hearts, and by thy Spirit, put new ones within us. Let us not be like the foolish virgins, who took their lamps, but took no oil with them; but may we be like the wise virgins, and have the oil of grace in our hearts, and be ready to meet the bridegroom, and go into the marriage supper. Let us not resemble the unfaithful servant, who went and hid his talent in the earth, and called his lord a hard man; but may we resemble the faithful servants who received five and ten talents, and may we trade with the same, and receive our Lord's sentence, 'Well done good and faithful servants enter ye into the joy of your Lord.' As thou didst send down, on the day of Pentecost, thy holy Spirit on thy apostles, so send him now down upon us, and give us grace and strength to serve thee. Hast thou not said to us, O Lord, 'Fear not little flock, it is your Father's good pleasure to give you the kingdom?' Bless, O Lord, the poor heathen round about us; as the people of Nineveh heard the voice of thy servant Jonah, and repented over their sins, and covered themselves with sackcloth and ashes, so may these heathens hear the voice of thy servant, and repent over their transgressions and bow down their heads in the dust, and abandon their idols and believe in Christ. For the sake of Christ's death and sufferings; for the sake of the intercession he is making at thy right hand, we beseech thee to hear us, O Lord, Amen."

But this effect is still more strikingly manifest in the experience and in the addresses of our native teachers. Like those of primitive times, they reason with the people out of the scriptures. In their opinion, the word of God is "quick and powerful and sharper than any two-edged sword, piercing to the dividing asunder of the soul and spirit, and of the joints and marrow and proves a discerner of the thoughts and intents of the heart." Its principles, its parables, its descriptions, its illustrations, are used with a power, and grace and a readiness far superior to any thing that we find at home. Do they wish to exhibit the corruption and depravity of man? They point to the character and to the rebellions of Israel, to the parable of the prodigal son, and to the delineations which the apostles have given of the heathen world. Do they describe the wrath which has been revealed from heaven against sin and iniquity? They remind their hearers of the banishment of men from paradise, of the deluge which overwhelmed the world of the ungodly, of the destruction of Sodom and Gomorrah, and of the calamities that descended upon the Egyptians and their king. Would they hold up to the view of the people, the mercy and benevolence of God in providing a Redeemer for the guilty and the lost? They remind them of that creditor who when his debtors had nothing to pay, freely forgave them all; they dwell upon the parable of the good shepherd who watches over the interests of his flock, leads them to the green pastures and makes them lie down beside the still waters, and in order to rescue them from the wolf and the tiger, has given his life for the sheep; they expatiate upon the emancipation of Israel from the thraldom of Egypt, and, from the temporal deliverances wrought out for the people of God in Old-Testament times, they illustrate the strange and wonderful redemption under the New. Do they animate their hearers to holiness, to withstand the temptations of Satan, and to persevere on their journey to heaven? They allude to the parable of the marriage-supper and the guest who was found destitute of the wedding-garment, to the hypocrisy of Judas who was numbered among the twelve, to the tribes who fell in the wilderness and were not permitted to enter into Canaan, and to the expulsion of the Jews from their land, on account of their rejection of Christ, and hold them up to view "as examples for our admonition upon whom the ends of the world are come."

I would be the last to withhold from the Hindoos,

literature and science as profound and as abundant as are to be found in any country of Europe; I would be the last to raise any obstacle to the progress of intellectual advancement, and to the emancipation of the national mind from the error and prejudice and thraldom in which it has been held for ages; but I would not exchange the simplicity of a scriptural and a primitive Christianity for all the knowledge and worldly wisdom which systems of philosophy can bestow. There must unquestionably be a progress in nations as well as in individuals; their science and literature must grow with their growth and strengthen with their strength; when precocity of talents is displayed, the human mind is often so loaded that it is stunted and rendered dwarfish, and nations, by a similar policy, may be injured in their career, instead of advancing, with steady and gradual steps, from youth to manhood, and from manhood to perfect age. I expect to see in India the same religion that grew and flourished in the first ages, more than the religion which exists at present in England; and notwithstanding the vain boasts that are made about our science and our literature, it would perhaps be better for society and better for our religious communities that we had more of our Bible and the spirit of primitive times.

In the provinces of India, the Tract and Bible Societies are handmaids to our missionary work, whose labours and whose success we highly appreciate. What can afford more pleasure to our minds; what can better ensure the prosperity of our toils in the vineyard, than to be able after having proclaimed salvation to the lost, to put into their hands these messages of mercy, or portions of the sacred volume, and to know that they are taken to their homes to be perused in private? I am aware that this source of comfort and joy has been deemed false and spurious, and that as an evidence of success, it has not only been questioned, but has been ridiculed and contemned. At the time that Sultan Categherry was in Scotland and visited the towns as the advocate of the Bible Society, "What," said a minister, "is the use of making such a noise about this man being willing to receive a Bible and that one to receive a Tract? Let me have Tracts and Bibles to distribute, and stand upon the street or in the road to give them gratuitously away, and what individual would refuse the gift? No; every one would know better than this; he could sell it, or make a present of it to his friends, or in some way, turn it to his worldly advantage; why then make a boast about persons being ready to receive such gifts?" Now, this objection might sound well, so long as it is confined to our own country; but it is the veriest sophistry when applied to Turkey, to China, or to Hindosthan. In going amongst an idolatrous people whose prejudices and apprehensions are so easily excited; we are regarded with as much suspicion as the same number of infidels and atheists would be among a Christian community. We bring strange things to their ears; we offer them a religion which, they understand, is to abolish that of their fathers, is to upset the altars of their country, is to hurl their divinities from their seats, is to silence the oracles in whose responses they confide, is to destroy the bond of caste and uproot a system which has hitherto united society together; what fears then, what apprehensions must prevail in hearing our message, and in receiving the books which propagate it? Here the father sometimes may be seen dragging his son away from the assembly; there the mother is pursuing after her daughter and driving her to her home; and now the friend is compelling his relative to shut his ears, and to leave the place of concourse; lest they should be contaminated by the principles of the strangers.

Nor is this all. The Bramins and the priests—the parties most interested in this affair,—pour forth the most fearful anathemas against all who will venture to listen and to read. "If you hear these missionaries," say they, "and receive their books, rely upon it they will bring the plague into your house; your children will die; these strange Shasters will be a serpent to bite you, a poison to destroy you, a curse to rest on you and on your posterity for ever;" what terror, what trembling must seize upon those who are the subjects of such denunciations? what risks do they run, if from worldly motives, they should receive and keep and peruse our tracts and our Scriptures? No man will deprive me of this source of rejoicing. When a people, in spite of such curses as a Bramin can utter, in the face of dangers and difficulties which none but Hindoos can rightly comprehend, and in defiance of prejudices and apprehensions which are apt to upset the strongest mind, will receive our books, will peruse them in private, and will take them from their concealment, and read them occasionally to a friend, I call it a triumph over error and superstition which ought to fill every heart with joy.

As soon as we have declared the message of mercy and reconciliation, and entreated the blessing of the Lord upon the truth which has been proclaimed; we commence our distribution of Scriptures and tracts. Whatever may be the fear and shyness which may be shown by the multitude, as to the reception of the first; the example is no sooner set them, than all are eager to obtain the prize; hundreds carry them to their homes; and numerous and indubitable are the testimonies which we receive that they are well and carefully perused. Many a visitor has come to the mission-house, bringing his bundle of Scriptures and of tracts; and as he unfolds, to our view, the treasures which he has accumulated, we are glad and thankful to see that it is no new coin just come from our mint at Bellary, but that which has been soiled and handled, that which has been put out to usury, and that which has been enriching others as well as their owner. He has brought them; for what purpose? To make his objections to the doctrines which they contain; to enquire further about the wonders of grace which they have brought to his view; and to become acquainted with the teachers who publish this new religion through the land.

Deeply convinced as the writer and many of his friends were that it was essentially necessary to put the heathen and the native Christians in possession of a summary of divine truth, written in a plain and forcible style, he undertook to compose a work in Canarese called "Theology addressed to Hindoos," and has already finished two volumes of it. The following are the subjects which have been treated on, and which are now in a course of circulation among the heathen.

FIRST SERIES.

On the Existence,—the Spirituality,—the Unity,—the Eternity,—the Immutability,—the Omnipresence—the Omniscience,—the Holiness,—the Justice,—the Patience,—the Mercy,—and the Goodness of God.

SECOND SERIES.

On the Creation of Man;—on the Chief End of Man;—on the State of Innocence;—on the Nature of Sin; on the Fall of Man;—on the Immediate Results of Transgression;—on the Universal Depravity of Man;—on Original Sin;—on the Misery of Man in Consequence of his Apostacy.

THIRD SERIES.

On the Covenant of Grace;—on the Mediatorial Office;—on the Person of Christ;—on the Trinity;—on the Divinity of Jesus Christ;—on the Deity of the Holy Spirit;—on the Pro-

phetical Office;—on the Priestly Office;—on the Nature of Atonement;—on the Severity of Christ's Sufferings;—on the Necessity of the Atonement;—on the Testimony of Scripture to the Atonement;—on the Sufficiency of Atonement;—on the Example of Christ.

Some of these subjects, it will be seen are adapted particularly to the heathen, while others are more suited to those who have embraced the truth, as it is in Christ. But as they are all addressed to idolaters, and are specimens to our teachers of the manner in which they should speak to their countrymen, they will all, I trust, be useful in advancing the great object—the glory of God. In treating each subject, the principal objections which the heathen make to Christianity are answered; the strong-holds of idolatry are attacked; principles acknowledged by the Hindoo system, and passages, selected from their own Shasters, in which idolatry is condemned, have been turned against their paganism; the truths are established from reason and Scripture; and a short address, calling upon them to renounce this system of error, to believe in the true God, and to love the Saviour whom he has appointed, closes the whole. Much patience and perseverance, and much strength from above did the author, amidst so many other duties, feel to be necessary, while engaged in thus writing a work in a strange language; but he was greatly encouraged. Year after year, the Religious Tract Society kindly supplied him with paper, and the co-operation of

Tract Societies and many benevolent friends in India, granted him the means of publishing many thousands of these monitors to the heathen.

As the divinity of our Lord, the Deity of the Holy Spirit, and the great doctrine of the atonement are dwelt upon at considerable length, it might appear to some, at first view, to be rather unnecessary and almost unwise. But apart from the great importance which these doctrines possess in themselves, constituting, as they do, the very fundamentals of Christianity, they have already been assailed in India, and the dreadful heresies of Socinianism are trying to find a settlement among the people. While these subjects, must, in every system of truth, hold of necessity a very conspicuous place, it is of essential importance, in a land where the gospel is yet to be established, that the minds of the first converts should be well grounded in the faith, and that the bulwarks of their religion may become impregnable to the assaults of error in such terrible forms.

Many have lamented that the instances have been so few in which the dissemination of the Scriptures and of tracts, have proved successful in the conversion of the heathen. But have not the expectations of such individuals been rather extravagant? It is scarcely to be expected that truth distributed, however rousing and alarming, should produce such immediate and striking effects in India, as we know it often does in our native land. The degraded state of the heathen; the total blindness of their understandings, and the awful depravity of their hearts; the want of those principles in their minds, which enable us to work upon the consciences of our own countrymen, may account, I think, in some measure, for the deficiency of success. The Spirit of God can enlighten the darkest understanding, and impress the most obdurate heart; but his ordinary method now of working upon man is through the medium of his word; and it will not be until there is a degree of religious information—till the seed has been extensively sown, and has, in some degree, taken root in the understanding, that we can hope to witness the same striking effects produced, through the means of alarming representations. It is now with us in India, the season of spring, during which we must sow the seed, and use our best endeavours to cultivate the ground aright, and we must wait, with prayer, and with patience, for the refreshing shower from above to produce the harvest.

CHAPTER XIII.

DIFFERENT DENOMINATIONS.

ALL SECTIONS ENGAGED IN THE STRUGGLE—UNITY AT HOME AND ABROAD—A BLESSING GRANTED TO ALL—ENGLISH ESTABLISHMENT—LETTER FROM BISHOP WILSON—BAPTIST BRETHREN—DIFFICULTIES OF THE INFANT MISSIONS—TRIALS—SUCCESS—CHURCH MISSIONARY SOCIETY—LIBERALITY—TINEVELLY—LIBERTY—WESLEYAN MISSIONS—DISCOURAGEMENTS—MELNUTTAM—A BRAMIN—GREATER EXERTIONS—THE INHERITANCE THE SAME.

On a review of the last fifty years, during which the church has been engaged in this contest with the systems of paganism, it is delightful to see how the missionary spirit has increased, and has spread, from one party to another, like a flame of love, sympathy and zeal. Instead of sect being ranged against sect as in the days of old; instead of Calvinists thundering against Arminians, Baptists against Pædo-Baptists, Presbyterians against Independents, and Episcopalians against them all, and challenging them to defend their respective opinions and maintain the high ground which they had taken, they are now engaged against the common enemy, and are assembling their hosts for the spiritual warfare. Some sections have been slow and reluctant to give up their prejudices and their antiquated notions, and to join with the confederated armies; but I know scarcely one whose opinions may be termed evangelical and whom it is our duty to respect, that continues to stand aloof from the consideration of this great question. Were it left to one tribe of our spiritual Israel to encounter the foe, and to take possession of the land, it must be a hopeless undertaking. But as all the tribes have consecrated themselves to the service, they present a united and a powerful phalanx to fight in the name of the Lord, and to subdue the enemy.

Much do I lament to find, that, at home, the feelings of love, harmony and goodwill are not so triumphant and so prevalent among different parties, as they once were. This is deeply to be deplored. Whatever may be the struggles of party, and whatever may be the efforts of the great adversary to divide and to destroy, it behoves every true Christian to fan the flame of love, to abstain from expressions and from deportment that would injure the heavenly spirit, and to cultivate and promote everywhere the sacred affections which may have been injured.

But if different sects can afford at home to divide upon points of minor importance, it is impossible to do so in India. In the field of battle; among millions of heathen who are prepared to convert every thing to the disadvantage of our cause; and in the presence of principalities and powers, and the rulers of the darkness of this world, and spiritual wickednesses in high places, we dare not disagree but at the expense of our common faith; we feel under the heaviest obligations to stand united against the foe; and instead of turning our arms against each other in the camp, there is every inducement to present a strong and unbroken front in the contest. But from affection more than from fear, we live together as brethren. Love, unanimity, good will, peace and concord rule supreme. The triumph of one, is the triumph of all, and the defeat of one, is the defeat of all. We rejoice with each other, when called to rejoice; we weep with each other, when called to weep. There is no rivalry but that of love, that of bringing souls to Christ, and that of advancing the cause of God, against the confederates of evil. We bear each other's burdens, and so fulfil the law of Christ. In a Christian and especially in a missionary you meet with a brother and a friend. However warm may be the atmosphere at home, it is cold and chilly, when compared with the one abroad; and the distance, the ceremony, the finesse, and ridiculous pretensions sometimes manifested in England, are a perfect contrast to the warmth, the friendship, the sincerity and the generous feeling which prevail in Hindosthan. Every one must feel how delightful it is, to enter a circle where pride and formality are laid aside as unchristian, and mingling with pure and hallowed spirits of a heavenly order, and separated from jarring interests and the grovelling affections of time, to hold intercourse with liberal and superior minds. Then we feel how good and how pleasant it is for brethren to dwell together in unity.

Nor has the divine blessing in India, been confined to one denomination. As though the Lord would show his regard to all his faithful servants, and put bigotry and intolerance to silence, the benediction has rested upon all. Go from the Church Mission station, to that of the Wesleyan, from the Baptist, to that of the London Mission, from the American settlement to that of the General Assembly's and from that to the Christian Knowledge Society's, and you will find that the Shekinah has not rested upon one in particular—all have partaken in the supply of grace and mercy. Though expectations may not have been realized, yet none have been left to complain as forgotten or overlooked. At every station, there will be seen a native church of twenty, or thirty or fifty, or a hundred members who walk in the fear of the Lord, and in the comforts of the Holy Ghost. If there has not been success in one way, there has been in another. Some have had greater prosperity among the young, and the children in the schools have been the source of their joy; others have seen adults converted from among the heathen, and have been permitted to behold them casting their idols to the moles and to the bats. In this mission, the brethren have had many Europeans and Hindoo Britons as the crowns of their rejoicing; and in that one, Mahomedans and Roman Catholics have been led to abandon their superstition and join the number of the faithful. But all have had reason to give glory to the Lord our God for the measure of success with which their labours have been crowned.

My time and space will not allow me to go round and visit all the stations where my dear brethren are engaged, and congratulate them and the Christian public on the testimony which they have borne, and the reward they have received. It might not be expedient to do so, as there are some parts of the field in Bengal and in the Bombay presidencies with which I am but ill acquainted, and though no one would be more disposed to do them justice, than the writer, it would be a very partial view which he could give. But I must be permitted, in a passing notice, to bear my humble testimony to the advancement of their work.

In accordance with the charter of 1813, the English establishment was planted in India, and in the charter of 1833, it was greatly enlarged. It now consists of three bishops, three archdeacons, and between eighty and ninety chaplains. It has chiefly a reference to the instruction and the spiritual welfare of our own countrymen. But long before this system was formed, there were many chaplains who were a blessing to India. The names of Brown and Buchanan, of Martyn and of Corrie will long be revered; they were shepherds who watched for souls as those who must give an account; in their day, they were burning and shining lights and many had reason to rejoice in their light; they lived and died bearing a good testimony to the truth. Some have appeared as their successors in later times, and have shown great boldness in defence of the gospel. While many care little for India, and for the welfare of Zion, others have been men of God, have not feared to declare his whole counsel, have withstood the frowns of the great, and have been a great help unto many. I love them for their work's sake, and the names of some whom I have known and who are now gathered to the assembly of the blessed, I greatly honour, and revere. Whereas it was almost a crime, in former days, to declare the truth in high places; heretical doctrines would now scarcely be tolerated. Nearly all the churches at the presidencies, are filled with pious and evangelical clergymen; and some are to be met with in the provinces, who labour assiduously in their sacred calling, and who endeavour, in addition to their duties among our countrymen, to exercise their influence, their talents, and energies, and sometimes their ministry among perishing heathens. Here and there, a bigot is to be met with, whose spirit and temper are annoying to all. But he is an exception to the general rule; his own party cannot but condemn his conduct; he is only a remnant of a bye-gone age; and all unite in the wish that whether he be a chaplain or an archdeacon, or a bishop, his place was filled by a man more worthy of his station and of his sphere.

In some parts, the work of the Lord prospers under their superintendence. A letter which has just been received from Bishop Wilson addressed to the Earl of Chichester, contains the following very delightful intelligence.

"It appears that between fifty-five and sixty villages are thirsting for the waters of life, in a greater or less degree; they stretch to the north and north-east of Kishnagur, on the Jelingha, to the distance of forty or fifty miles, and to the south-west fifteen or twenty. The numbers described as prepared for baptism—in various measures of course—are betwen 3000, and 3500. The archdeacon assisted himself at the reception of about 500 souls, including women and children, into the Christian church, and there seems the fairest prospect, if we can but enter at the wide and effectual door in time, that not only these 3000, or 4000, but the whole population of the fifty or sixty villages, may receive the Christian faith, and resemble our Christian villages in the time of our Anglo-Saxon forefathers, in the sixth and seventh centuries. Such a glorious scene has never yet been presented to our longing eyes in Bengal! and after making all deductions for over-statements, sanguine hopes, the existence of secular motives, and the instability of large numbers—nay, after allowing for the influence of the temporal relief which was exhibited to the sufferers, Christian and heathen, during one of those inundations to which the sandy banks of the Jelingha are peculiarly liable, and which occurred during the progress of this religious awakening—admitting all this, and as much more as the most timid observer can require, it still appears that a mighty work of divine grace is begun—a work wide and permanent, as we trust—a work marking the finger of God—a work which will demand, and warrant, and repay all our pastoral care, anxiety and labour—a work for which our fathers in India, Brown, Buchanan, Martyn, Thompson and Bishops Corrie, Middleton and Heber would have blessed and praised God, in the loudest strains of gratitude and joy."

Affection and faithfulness will not suffer me to forget the noble band who met in 1792, in Kettering, Northamptonshire, and who dared, amidst the storms that were gathering in Europe, and the indifference and lukewarmness that were so prevalent in the church, to propose a mission to the heathen. Small was the sum which they could then collect for their enterprise, yet their warm hearts kindled a flame which has burned, enlarged and extended to the present day. The names of Fuller and Carey and Pearce and others will long hold a distinguished place in the history of missions, as the originators of the spirit in modern times. To their minds, India, as a sphere, seemed to be recommended by many considerations. The field which it presented, was immense; much of it was already under the sway of Great Britain; the missionaries who embarked in the work, might there possibly be able to support themselves; and Providence seemed to point to the East.

In 1793, Mr. Carey, and Mr. Thomas who had already been twice in Bengal as a surgeon, embarked for India, and after a six months' voyage, arrived in safety at their destination. Sanguine as were their views, and promising as their field appeared, they soon found that the Hindoo superstition was not to be suddenly overthrown; difficulties which many would have deemed insurmountable, obstructed their course; their finances failed; and they had no Christian friends to whom they could unbosom their complaints. But Providence was kind and gracious. A gentleman in the Bengal service offered them the superintendance of some Indigo manufactories at Madnabutty where great numbers of the natives would be under their control, where they would have a large district to perambulate, where they might establish schools for the young, and exercise an extensive influence among the people. As this offer was not only liberal, would not only relieve them from their pecuniary embarrassments, but promised a large field of usefulness, they gladly accepted it. But notwithstanding the opportunities thus afforded; they seemed, for six or seven years to labour in vain; and the seed which was sown, resembled that which falls by the way-side, or on stony ground, or among thorns, it brought forth no fruit.

This should not be considered a matter of great surprise, and reflects no discredit upon the diligence, the faithfulness and zeal of the first missionaries. In Bengal, the ground was entirely uncultivated; the brethren had to bear the burden and heat of the day; Grammars required to be written, and Dictionaries to be compiled; there were no facilities for the acquisition of the language and every thing had to be commenced; no helpers gave their aid in the labour, nor cherished the children in the schools; the Europeans had every thing to attend to; what then could be expected in such circumstances? Most deeply can we sympathise with our brethren amidst their trials and their discouragements, and their complaints. But we have no sympathy with those who would render these complaints the ground of their own triumph. It is an easy matter now for missionaries to land in India and commence their work, and speak of their prosperity. Other men have laboured and their successors have entered into their labours. The fallow ground is broken up; the way of the Lord is prepared; and every year that is added to the nineteenth century, renders India more accessible to the gospel, more prepared, as a vineyard, to bring forth fruit; and more likely to afford satisfaction to the laborious husbandman.

Another important consideration ought not to be here overlooked. In the infancy of our missionary societies, the world, and in too many instances the church too, were arrayed in hostility against them; the expenditure had to be regulated by a small income which was not obtained without difficulty; and the brethren who were sent to the field, were charged to find out means by which the society might be relieved, and the mission be enabled to support itself. Mr. Carey and Mr. Thomas, were under the necessity, as we have seen, to superintend indigo factories that they might be less burdensome to their friends at home; but what a drag was this on their time, their spirits and their sacred calling? If we are engaged in the affairs of the world, it is impossible to avoid being contaminated more or less with its spirit, and it is vain to expect that so much could be done for the heathen. These were the days of trial and of poverty; I am glad that the days of prosperity are come. Most thankful am I, that their successors are no longer called upon to mingle with worldly avocations, to establish boarding-schools and to undertake the office of interpreters, in order to be less expensive to the churches; but that now, the societies being more rich and affluent, they are able to sustain the missionaries and their families without having recourse to such expedients. It was a wretched system. Instead of leading to economy; it proved the bane of some; it was dangerous to the peace of many; it was hurtful to the spirit and piety of all.

In 1799, the mission was increased by the arrival of Mr. Ward, Mr. Marshman, and two other brethren. On their landing at Calcutta, the spirit of the English monopoly began to work. The authorities prohibited them from joining their brethren on British ground. All Mr. Carey's efforts were in vain to obtain permission for their settlement in the neigbourhood of Malda. If they remained not in Serampore, they must leave the country. They preferred the former, and as the Providence of God seemed to direct them in this choice, Mr. Carey, though at great loss, gave up his connexion with the factory and joined the mission at Serampore. This arrangement was overruled for good. At this station, they had the protection of the Danish government; greater liberty was enjoyed to prosecute the objects of their mission; their facilities for translating and for printing the Scriptures were greatly increased; a larger neighbourhood was afforded them, on which to bestow their labour; and though nothing but a dire necessity led them to adopt this expedient, it turned out, in the end, more useful for the prosperity of the cause. It was about this time that they came to the resolution that no one should pursue any employment for his own private benefit; but that the amount which was, in one way or other, obtained, should be thrown into a common fund for the interests of the mission. This was very noble and generous; but it ultimately gave rise to much trouble and perplexity; to a breach between the Serampore missionaries and the society at home; to serious discussions and to a long separation of love and effort and interest, which did no good to any party. But in proportion as we were grieved to see brethren once divided, do we now rejoice and give God praise that they are again united in love; that Serampore is incorporated with the Baptist Society; and that parent and children now appear a large, and happy and prosperous family, to the Christian and the heathen world.

In consequence of their residence at Serampore, one great object which the missionaries were led to pursue, was the translation of the Scriptures into the dialects of the heathen. No design could be more grand and magnificent, than that of giving to the nations of India, in their own tongues, the Revelation of Heaven. The design was worthy of that nobility of spirit which has always characterized the operations of our Baptist friends in the East; and though many of these first versions have been superseded by those which have been made by other missionaries residing in the different countries, and more intimately acquainted with the respective languages; yet the resolution gave an importance to the object, and a stimulus to accomplish it, which they would not otherwise have obtained, and have induced the churches, the Bible Society, and missionaries to lend their energies, with greater diligence and perseverance, to the consummation of this great work. First translations, under the most auspicious circumstances, must be defective; what surprise, then, need we feel that those versions made at a time when the facilities were few, and disadvantages were many, should give way to others which, though made under happier auspices, must, in their turn, yield to those which will be rendered more perfect?

As the missionaries had toiled so long without any apparent success, they became more fervent in prayer; they dwelt more upon the great doctrines of the cross in their message to the heathen; the Spirit of God seemed to rest upon them and enabled them to wait upon God. They did not wait long. As Mr. Thomas was a surgeon, and often engaged in his profession to render it subservient to the truth, he was called to attend a Hindoo named Crishna who had dislocated his arm. In setting it, Mr. Thomas directed him to the balm of Gilead and the Physician who is there. As the man had heard the gospel before, he now felt that he was a sinner, and cried and sobbed aloud. A neighbour of the name of Gokool was present and heard what the missionary said, and had his mind impressed in favour of the gospel. A few days after, both Crishna and Gokool came to the mission-house, conversed unreservedly with the missionaries, sat down to table with them, and partook of a repast. "Brother Thomas," writes Mr. Ward, "has waited fifteen years and has thrown very much time away on deceitful characters; brother Carey has waited till hope of his own success has almost expired; and after all, God has done it, with perfect ease. Thus the door of faith is opened to the gentiles; who shall shut it? The chain of caste is broken; who shall mend it?" That very evening also, Crishna's wife and her sister stood forth before the church, and publicly avowed their attachment to Christ and their determination to obey him. Who, on reading this statement, does not rejoice in such a testimony of success, and acknowledge it to be of the Lord? After labouring so many years, and watching with anxiety and prayer and tears for the fruit, who does not see here, as the brethren did in the South-Sea Islands, that the work is to be accomplished, not by might, nor by power, but by the Spirit of the Lord? From that time, God prospered them. One convert was added to the church after another; native teachers were raised up to preach the gospel among their countrymen; tracts were distributed and became the means of quickening dead souls; new translations issued from the press; churches were formed from among the heathen;

station after station was established; and amidst good report and evil report, the word of the Lord continued to run, had free course and was glorified, till the little one has become a thousand, and many have been added to the Lord.

After the charter of 1813 had granted us liberty to go to India, the Church Missionary Society entered upon that field, and has established settlements both in Bengal and in the Peninsula. Besides its mission in Travancore, it has missions at Cochin, at Mayaveram, at Madras, at Palamcottah, and at other stations both in eastern and western India. Whether it was the catholic spirit of its founders, or the peculiar circumstances of the times, or the benevolent nature of the work in which it was to be engaged, the Church Society was, from its establishment, endued with a liberality of spirit which has endeared it to other denominations, as well as to its own. If we refer to its directors and its exertions at home, these have always been in harmony with that good will, that Christian affection, that disinterested benevolence and that kind conciliating temper which renders it easy and pleasant to co-operate with other bodies in carrying on the work, and which gains the approbation and the esteem of all. If we refer to its operations abroad, there have been many evidences that, in past days, its directors and friends sought not their own, but the things that are Jesus Christ's, and showed that, provided the kingdom of grace was advanced, it mattered little to them, how it was done. When they heard of the state and circumstances of the poor Syrians, they hurried to their help, and have done what they could to raise them from their state of humiliation. When they could not find, in their own communion, agents to go to the heathen, and carry the gospel under their own banner, Lutherans, and Germans were received into fellowship instead of Calvinists and Englishmen, and were sent forth with the understanding that, on points of difference, they were to enjoy Christian liberty. When, in some parts of India, they had not agents to establish schools and to carry on a system of instruction for the young, they granted money to others to carry forward their own plans, and have done much by their influence and encouragement to promote the interests of male and female education; and when, a few years ago, they were unable to find a sufficient number of missionaries in their own communion to send forth to spheres of labour, they made overtures, I understand, to the Wesleyan body, that if the latter would find the men, they would provide the means and support them. In all this, there is a spirit of liberality and Christian benevolence which I love and admire. It breathes much of that lovely temper which characterized the apostle of the Gentiles when he said "So that Christ is preached, I do rejoice; yea, and will rejoice." May this spirit continue to distinguish their proceedings in the future, as it has done in the past, and may no root of bitterness spring up to trouble them.

To say nothing of the success which has crowned the efforts of their missionaries at Madras, and at other stations, Tinnevelly has long been a scene of spiritual prosperity. Through the exertions of Mr. Rhenius and his coadjutors, and the blessing of the Spirit upon the word, what idol temples overthrown! what heathen villages brought under moral culture and influence! what numbers of idolaters brought to profess the Christian name! what rents made in the kingdom of Satan! what churches formed, and schools established, and souls gathered into the fold of the great Shepherd! In less than fourteen years, one hundred and twenty native teachers were raised up, and prepared to labour under the auspices of the mission; two hundred and sixty small towns and villages were constantly visited by the messengers of peace and salvation; and ten thousand natives were either baptized or brought under a course of instruction. Well might the society at home, as Christians did everywhere, rejoice in these triumphs of grace. Long has this mission been cherished in its growing prosperity by its friends and supporters; with gratitude to God, the achievements of the cross in Tinnevelly were often held forth, to the Christian public, in the reports and in the journals of the committee; and many a time was the zeal, the perseverance, and the devotedness of Mr. Rhenius dwelt upon with commendation and delight. Most deservedly so. While gratitude was rendered to the great Author of these triumphs, it was due to his servants that their labours and success should be recorded. What surprise and grief were occasioned throughout the Madras presidency when it was known that *Indian bigotry* had so far triumphed, as to create a rupture between Mr. Rhenius and the Church Missionary Society—a rupture which was not likely to be healed, and which might seriously injure the advancement of the work of God? There was not a friend of the society, nor of the Redeemer who did not most deeply deplore it, and felt that the man who had *occasioned* this separation, had inflicted a heavier blow upon the "church and her handmaids," than he could ever heal. But for *this bigotry*, we should never have heard of the "green book" nor of the calamities which have befallen the Tinnevelly mission. May all these breaches be healed, and may the vine which has there been planted, survive the storm, and continue to grow till it fills the land.

I cannot but bear a most honourable testimony to that excellent and devoted missionary who has now gone to his rest and his reward. Mr. Rhenius was an able and a faithful missionary of the cross. His memory will long be cherished by all who knew him, and though every one will be ready to acknowledge that he had his faults like other men, yet he lived and laboured under the smile of his Master, and counted not his life dear unto himself that he might finish the ministry which he had received from him.

Most earnestly and affectionately do I entreat the society to consider well the state of its missionaries in India. If the evil to which I have alluded, is not attended to, it will grow, and will blast the prospects and the promises of prosperity. Some years ago, a writer in the Missionary Register in alluding to this subject, said "We want a new canon for the East Indies, and another for the West." If the missions in connexion with the Church of England, wish for peace, and growing usefulness, this is absolutely necessary. Without some modification of the present system, there will always be jarring interests, and a heavy drag will hinder the best and most judicious efforts. More liberty is required, by the missionaries, to think and act for themselves, and to carry on their labours among the heathen. So long as they must be subject to the bishop of the diocese, to a corresponding committee, and to the directors at home, it is difficult to know whose opinion they should abide by; their energies must be cramped, and their success endangered; and discouragement must render their greatest exertions feeble and powerless. Whatever may be the claims of dignitaries and of others, the missionaries themselves who labour in the field, and who are brought into contact with the trials and the encouragements of the enterprise, must be the best judges of the plans to be pursued, and of the mode in which they should be carried into effect.

I write these things in love. I feel the highest regard for the Church Missionary Society and wish it great prosperity. Many of its devoted missionaries, I have known, and their memory is dear to me. With not a few, I have taken sweet counsel, and we have gone to the house of God in company. On their behalf, and on behalf of their usefulness, I plead for more Christian liberty, and for an extension of privileges, in order that they may enjoy a spiritual freedom in their work; that they may be less fettered by rites and ceremonies which are more suited to a Christian country, than a heathen people; and that they may enjoy, and fully improve those opportunities which are daily afforded in such a country as India.

For twenty years past, the Wesleyan Missionary Society, has had establishments in the Peninsula. At Madras, and Bangalore; at Negapatam and Melnuttam, the missionaries have laboured with great zeal, diligence, and success. Afflictions, deaths, and removals to England, have often reduced the number of the chosen band, have weakened the hands of those who were left behind, and have sometimes dispirited them in their attacks upon the lines of the enemy. But whatever have been their trials and discouragements, they have still kept possession of the field. The history of their mission to India, may be taken as a specimen of the whole. At first, the struggle was almost for existence. The few had to toil, and pray, and weep amidst trials, disappointment, discomfiture and despondency. The attempt was regarded at home as a failure. While the notes of victory would have secured support, plaudits, reinforcements, and materials for carrying on the war, the missionaries could only announce the strength of the foe, the difficulties of the campaign, the ravages which death was making in their own ranks, and the necessity there was for greater exertions, and larger supplies. Patience and perseverance became nearly exhausted. Had it not been for the noble band who continued in the field, and urged on the battle, the retreat must have been sounded, and victory have been declared for the enemy. But faith and hope at length prevailed; the signals of Providence became more certain and evident; tokens of success began to scatter the clouds of unbelief, and despondency; wide and effectual doors were thrown open for the entrance of the truth; fresh courage was infused into the friends at home as well as the forces abroad, until coldness and indifference have been put to shame and a new system of operations, more commensurate with the immensity of the field, has been determined on.

Such has been the experience of almost every mission to India. I like to record this progress—

through a course of trial and of disappointment—from weakness to strength, from unbelief to confidence, from defeat to triumph, from indifference to determined exertion, because it is the work of the Lord, it is success granted to patience and perseverance, it is the seal of Providence to the faithfulness of his servants.

In the year 1831, the Wesleyan brethren were invited to take the village of Melnuttam under their pastoral care and superintendence. Partly Romanists and partly heathen, its inhabitants were anxious to renounce their false systems, to investigate the truth, and to become acquainted with a religion more suited to their peace, comfort and happiness. The assistant who went to visit them, brought back a good report of the land, and the missionary was permitted, on a subsequent call, to see that the people were anxious to receive instruction, that numbers assembled morning and evening to read the Scriptures and to worship, and that a school was established for the education of the children. On his visit to this village, Mr. Bourne was enabled to give a favourable report of the people. Having had some experience in missionary work, his expectations were moderate. It was impossible to expect that a few poor and uneducated husbandmen could obtain those correct views of divine truth, that sound experience, and that high Christian character which others, under more favourable auspices, could lay claim to. But taking into consideration their short period of trial, the fewness of their advantages, and the opportunities which they had enjoyed since they were brought under the care of the mission, their improvement in scriptural knowledge, in their outward deportment and in their anxiety about salvation far exceeded his most sanguine expectations. No circumstance delighted him so much as the attention which was paid to the Lord's-day, among this simple-hearted people. Like a Sabbath in England, the morning was still, calm, and tranquil; every implement of industry was laid aside; a general cessation from ordinary business, was perceptible; and at the hour of prayer, all repaired, in clean apparel, to the building which served as a temple to Jehovah. Twice during the day, the sacrifices of prayer and of praise were presented upon the altar, and the gospel was proclaimed to the poor outcasts who were just emerging to the light of day. For the erection of a chapel, a large piece of ground was purchased by a few native Christians, subscriptions were obtained from Europeans, and a commodious sanctuary was built and opened for the service of the true God. So favourable was the state of that people, and so evident was the blessing of God, and the tokens of prosperity, that Melnuttam has long been occupied as a principal station, and the sound of salvation is bursting forth from it upon the districts around.

In November 1835, a very interesting event happened at Madras, in connexion with the Wesleyan mission at Royapettah. A Bramin, determined to renounce his caste and his heathenism, and all for Christ, was received into the church by the ordinance of baptism. For some time previous, he had been receiving instruction at Royapettah; the circumstances of his history were peculiar; the intelligence was circulated through the native community, and excited great interest among the tribe to which he belonged; some said he was a hypocrite, and others said he was distant from his family and had nothing to give up. But amidst scorn and contempt, the convert remained unshaken, and on the day of his baptism, determined to take up his cross and follow his Lord.

After the missionary had read suitable portions of the sacred Scriptures, the Bramin stated that he came from the capital of Travancore with three associates on a pilgrimage to Cashy;* that on reaching Madura, one of the party was taken ill, and died; that he and his two companions were greatly distressed at this circumstance, but they performed all the usual ceremonies, and having burnt the body, and thrown the ashes into the river, proceeded on their journey; that they passed through Tanjore, Trichinopoly and other holy places on their way to Madras; that in the south of India, he had conversed with Christian teachers, and heard some tracts read on his journey; but when he came to the presidency, he wished for more in-

* Benares.

formation on the subjects contained in the holy Scriptures; that he was directed to the Rev. Mr. Carver at Royapettah where he was received into the institution, was instructed more fully in the Christian religion, and determined to embrace the faith of Jesus; and that his former companions had remonstrated with him in vain, had left him in anger, and had proceeded themselves to Cashy.

The first Sunday in Advent was fixed for his baptism, and when the minister came to that part of the service "Dost thou renounce the devil and all his works?" he answered, "I renounce them all;" and immediately took his Braminical cord from his neck, and gave it to the minister, who gave him, in return, a copy of the sacred Scriptures. The convert then offered up a solemn and earnest prayer to that Saviour who alone can protect and preserve his servants to life eternal. One simultaneous ejaculatory prayer seemed to be sent forth to God, by a deeply affected audience, that he would crown the ordinance with his blessing.*

No missionaries could be more active and zealous, than our Wesleyan brethren. But the system of changing from one district to another, and which prevails at home, is not found to answer in heathen lands. So long as the missions are situated in the

* "Wesley Abraham died last night at half-past ten o'clock. His last moments were marked by strong confidence in God. He rejoiced in the prospect of heaven, and fell asleep in Jesus without a struggle.—R. CARVER. *Saturday*, 8th *July*, 1837."

same province, and where the same language prevails, the plan may not be so objectionable, though, then, the removal of a missionary from his sphere of labour, must be attended with serious inconveniences; but when there is a difference of language, the change must be incompatible with growing success. Experience has, I rather think, already applied a remedy to this case, and should changes continue, they will be confined to the district where the same language is spoken.

But notwithstanding the labours and trials, through which our brethren have been called to pass, and the zeal and diligence and prosperity with which they have carried on their work, the Wesleyan board have scarcely been satisfied with the results of their mission to India. Their approbation and encouragement are made to depend too much upon success. This is not right. The Lord likes to try the faith and the patience of his people sometimes; and brings them through fire and water into a wealthy place; and though we must fight and labour and pray in darkness and in doubt, yet he will bring forth our righteousness as the light, and our judgment as the noonday. Some years ago, they established a mission under promising circumstances at Calcutta, but as the success did not correspond with the hopes that were entertained, it was soon abandoned, and the brethren were appointed to spheres that were considered more promising. This was not giving Bengal a fair trial.

When the obstacles of a campaign are to be overcome, or when a citadel is to be taken by storm, our Wesleyan friends are found valiant and admirable in leading on the charge, or in ascending the breach; their zeal and valour and intrepidity carry every thing before them, and the triumph is sure. But to carry on a regular siege; to spend months and years in destroying the walls, in the erection of batteries, in starving the enemy to a surrender; to endure the toils and fatigues which the preparation may require, before the attack is made, are achievements which they would rather leave to others; their perseverance is put to the test; their patience fails them; and they prefer the open field and a raging conflict, to a contest with the calamities and the dangers of a siege. In this sacred cause, therefore, their missions to the West Indies, and to some parts of Africa, have always been more in favour at home, than their mission to India. In the former case, there is no language to learn; the people are prepared by oppressions to welcome the gospel, and the attack is at once successful. But in the latter, the difficulties of language must be surmounted; the prejudices and superstitions of the people are deeply rooted; plans adopted, and once very promising are obliged to be abandoned; disappointment is added to trial, and to affliction, till the hearts of the bravest are ready to fail them and labour seems to be vain. These things, however, must be expected in India; we must lay our account to meet them once and again;

and according to the nature of the field which is to be cultivated, we must prepare the instruments with which we are to work, and we must exercise the principles and dispositions which will be most required.

I may be permitted to express my regret and sorrow at the discouraging views which the Wesleyan Committee have taken of their affairs in the East, because I know well that there is little occasion for them; many of their missionaries I number among my dearest friends, and I can testify to the zeal and diligence and industry with which they labour in the vineyard of their Lord; and I know how much these views prevailing at home, are calculated to discourage and enervate their agents abroad. If I am correctly informed, it became, a few years ago, a serious question with the Committee whether they ought not to abandon their mission to India. I congratulate them, and the Christian and heathen world, that better counsels have prevailed, and that instead of announcing a surrender, they have sent and are determined to send more reinforcements to the field, and that India is henceforth to receive from the Committee that attention, those resources, and that encouragement which its urgent necessities demand. In the Mysore especially—that province which is so dear to my own heart, I rejoice that so many missionaries are to be planted, and so many stations established. Among three millions of inhabitants, there is abundance of room for us all. There is no occasion that

Ephraim should envy Judah, or that Judah should vex Ephraim. So that the land is possessed, it matters little what are the lots which fall to the different tribes. Most gladly do we welcome you to the field and to the conflict. Like the tribes of Reuben and of Gad and the half-tribe of Manasseh; our inheritance may be on this side of the river; here, may be our towns and our villages, our vineyards and orchards, our fields and flocks, our wives and families, our congregations and our sanctuaries; and it may be yours to cross the Jordan and take possession of the land promised to our fathers. But there is not a time that your troops will surround a Jericho, and when at the sound of the rams' horns, its high and imperious walls will tumble to the ground, but we too will send forth our notes of rejoicing; there is not a time when, in consequence of an Achan being in the camp, your armies will suffer a defeat from the men of Ai, and will be driven back, in discomfiture, to their tents, but we will mourn with you in the hour of trial; and there is not a time when, at the command of our Joshua, the sun will stand still upon Gibeon, and the moon in the valley of Ajalon, till you have trampled upon the necks of your enemies, and have obtained possession of the land, but we will join you in songs of praise and gratitude to the God of Israel. In the name of the Lord, let us set up our banners, and let us go up boldly and courageously, for the Lord hath delivered our enemies into our hands.

CHAPTER XIV.

ON THE TAMUL MISSIONS.

THE FIELD OF OPERATION—OCCUPIED BY VARIOUS PARTIES—THE TAMUL CHRISTIANS—APPEARANCE OF MADRAS—ITS CLIMATE—MR. LOVELESS—MR. KNILL—MR. TRAVELLER—MR. NICHOLSON—DUTIES OF THE MISSIONARIES—MR. BILDERBECK—PURSEWAUKUM—TRIPASORE—MR. SMITH—A REVIVAL—COMBACONUM—THE COUNTRY—ESTABLISHMENT OF THE MISSION—NATIVE TEACHER—MR. CRISP—DIFFICULTIES—PROGRESS—SEATS OF IDOLATRY.

In the largest division of Southern India, the Tamul language almost universally prevails. Draw a line across the peninsula from Madras on the Coromandel coast, to Cananore on the coast of Malabar; descend on the one side, or on the other, to Cape Comorin; and you have an immense tract of country in which this tongue is spoken by almost every tribe, in various provinces, on the hills and in the plains, on the coast and in the interior. Religion seems to have followed in the steps of commerce, since the ports that were earliest opened to the latter, admitted most freely the ambassadors of the former. As Tranquebar, Madras, and Negapatam on the coast of Coromandel; and as Telicherry, Cochin, and Quilon on that of Malabar were stations of great importance to Europeans in trade, the missionaries of the cross began their career under the protection of their governments; advanced from thence into the interior as opportunities were offered, rendered the large towns in their march so many posts of attack on the surrounding districts, and spread the influence of Christianity over numbers of the people. For spiritual privileges, for missionary zeal and enterprise, for the light and liberty which prevail, this spacious territory may well be styled the Goshen of India. As the Tamul was the first language which the missionaries learned—the first in which they preached the gospel to the people—the first in which the Scriptures were translated, exertions were made and success was obtained among the heathen; so it was the first which afforded greater facilities to successors; Grammars and Dictionaries, and Christian books were already prepared; the difficulties to be encountered in the prosecution of the work were less numerous and more easily overcome; and the provinces just beyond the existing missionary stations, presented an inviting field for Christian settlements. All these were most auspicious circumstances in favour of the south, while the aspect of the north was still bleak, cold, and forbidding.

The Danes had laboured long and successfully, and had established their missions, on permanent ground, before an English monopoly could venture to dispute their claim to the vineyard; and no sooner was that barrier removed, than one society seemed to vie with another in occupying stations which were more in the neighbourhood of cultivated grounds, and where there were greater facilities in learning and in using the language. Instead of seeking for new and untried fields in the north—fields that are equally good and accessible to the spiritual husbandman—fields that are teeming with finer, nobler, and superior races of men—fields where no sower has yet been to cast in the seed, where no reaper has been to gather the fruits, and where the enemy maintains his dominion undisputed and undisturbed; the societies have agreed to cultivate the south and lavish their strength and their efforts upon its inhabitants. It is a delightful sight to behold Danish missionaries and Americans; Churchmen and Dissenters; Lutheran Germans and Wesleyan Methodists; Presbyterians and American Baptists all labouring to promote the welfare of this people. The field is large enough; long may they toil and strive without envy, and jealousy, and contend earnestly for the faith which was once delivered to the saints. It was, perhaps, the intention of Providence that the south should become the field of experiment—that the objections and the scandals of the enemy should there be exposed—and that it should there be made manifest to every one that India so long insulted and contemned, was capable of bringing forth the fruits of righteousness, and of yielding praise and glory to God.

Happy Tamulians! so many privileges have been in store for you. Societies at home and agents abroad are anxious for your conversion. The lines have fallen to you in pleasant places, and you have a goodly heritage. Your brethren in the north will look to you for an example of all that is wise and good and benevolent. Improve, I entreat you, your privileges. It is almost time that you were supporting your own pastors, and giving the gospel to your neighbours and to your friends. You cannot be allowed much longer to eat the fat and to drink the sweet, while your kinsmen are ready to perish for want. In the regions beyond you, there are millions who are panting for the truth, and we shall look to you to send them some of the blessings which have so long been your portion.

MADRAS.

This town is the largest of the Carnatic, is the presidency of Fort St. George, and is the capital of southern India. As viewed from the roads, it presents a splendid sight. On the north side, there is little to interest, except the remains of the old wall, the village of Royapooram, and the sandy beach upon whose banks the foaming surf dashes with imposing grandeur. In the centre, are long ranges of magnificent buildings, raised upon arches, adorned with colonnades to the upper stories, and stuccoed by the beautiful chunam made from shells. On the south side, is seen the Fort of St. George, which withstood many an attack in the struggle for supremacy, and is rendered strong by its vicinity to the sea, and by its bulwarks on the land side. A parade, resembling the one at Brighton, extends along the beach, appears all alive with the crowds of natives during the day, and is to Europeans a most refreshing and agreeable drive in the evening. But with all its advantages for trade and commerce, and with its power and acquisitions as a British settlement, Madras is but an indifferent situation for a capital. So tremendous is the surf that rolls upon the beach, that the landing is often dangerous in the highest degree, and during the north-east monsoon, the flag-staff is hoisted from the beginning of October to the end of November, to warn vessels that it is unsafe to remain in the roads. A few years ago, it was proposed to transfer the seat of government to Bangalore where its situation would unquestionably be more central, where the despatches from England, via the Red Sea and Bombay, would be received as early as at Madras, and where health and comfort would be more secured to all the officers belonging to the different departments of the state.

As to climate, Madras is dry, and more salubrious than Bengal. In January, the thermometer stands lowest at 70°, and in July, the highest is

91°. But the prevalence of the hot winds* in the summer months, makes it almost resemble a furnace, and were it not for the sea-breeze in the afternoon, the largeness of the houses, the use of cascus mats, hung round the verandas and kept constantly wet, and other means adopted to cool the atmosphere, it would be almost intolerable. The natives inhabit Blacktown, and are reckoned three hundred thousand. The Europeans generally reside in their garden-houses in the neighbourhood, and enjoy more of the free air, and better grounds for exercise, than the town can afford.

In 1805, Madras was occupied as a station of the London Missionary Society. Mr. Loveless, its first agent, was a very pious, simple-hearted, and devoted man. His labours were chiefly directed to the Indo-Britains, and to Europeans, and many of them yet remember the simplicity, the honesty of purpose, the affection and faithfulness with which he preached the gospel. He bore his testimony in the day when it would have been reckoned a crime for any English missionary to make efforts to convert the heathen to Christ, and when it was almost as necessary to order his speech aright in India, as it was for our brethren in the West in the days of slavery. Such was the love of his heart; such was his meek and humble deportment; such was the respect with which he was regarded by all

* While the hot winds are blowing, the skin of the face is often blistered, the chairs and tables crack, and glasses are broken.

ranks of the community, that his ministry was always well attended. In 1810, a spacious and elegant chapel was built for the mission in Black Town. Two free-schools—one for boys and the other for girls, descendants of Europeans—were established and liberally supported; and every benevolent object which Mr. Loveless proposed, was sure to be responded to in a manner grateful to his heart. Though he did not labour among the natives, and though his talents were called into exercise in a different sphere; yet no one could be more useful in removing European prejudice, in conciliating all classes to the great object of his mission; in establishing Missionary, Bible, and Tract Societies; and in preparing the way for those who were likely to combat and to overcome the idolatries of the natives.

In 1816, the mission was strengthened by the arrival of Mr. Knill. His boldness in the gospel, his zeal for the Divine glory and compassion to souls, his solemn and fervent addresses, arrested the attention of the people. Great anxiety and concern were excited in the minds of many. Some individuals were savingly impressed, and one young man, after a course of study, became a missionary. Great was the grief that was felt and expressed when indisposition obliged Mr. Knill to proceed first to Travancore for change, and ultimately to England. India has still a warm place in his heart, and his name is still dear to many in India.

Mr. Traveller next joined the mission. At this period, the inhabitants of Pursewaukum were destitute of the means of grace, and an opening appeared among them for the introduction of the gospel. Mr. Traveller exerted himself very commendably to erect a new chapel, obtained subscriptions for it, and built a very handsome edifice in which much good has been done.

The next missionary who entered into this field was Mr. Nicholson. He was a good man. His time was chiefly devoted to the study of the language; very considerable was the progress which he made in the acquisition of the Tamul, during the short time that he was permitted to study it; and he panted to preach to the heathen the glad tidings of mercy. But inscrutable are the ways of Providence. The cholera raged, seized him as one of its victims, and removed him into the invisible world. Amidst the agonies that he endured, he was heard to exclaim "Heaven after this! heaven after this!" I have stood upon his grave, dropt a tear over his early departure, and have thought of the honour which is in reserve for those who are faithful unto death, and who fall with their face towards the foe.

On our arrival in May 1824, the mission was under the care and superintendence of Mr. Crisp and Mr. Massie who joined it—the former in 1822, and the latter in 1823; and these dear brethren met us on the beach, gave us a hearty welcome, and entertained us very kindly during our stay at Madras. What with the departure of Mr. Loveless to England; the death of Mr. Nicholson and of Mrs. Massie; and some other adverse circumstances, the missionaries were discouraged. Some who ought to have been a comfort to them, had grieved their spirits, and much as they desired to give themselves up to the heathen, they were in the trammels which others had prepared for them. The labours of their predecessors were attended with this disadvantage, that they were almost entirely confined to Europeans and to Indo-Britons; and the services thus established laid the junior brethren under a kind of obligation to carry them on. What was very suitable at the commencement of the mission was now, in consequence of the general liberty that was granted, and the many doors of usefulness opened among the heathen, rather a hinderance to those active and energetic exertions which the state of the population required. The brethren felt these things, yet it was difficult to find a remedy. Three English services a week; pastoral visits among the people; so many meetings of different societies to attend, and the business which they consequently bring along with them, were sufficient in such a climate, to fill the hands of any man. It is impossible, with all these things to attend to, that any time can be given to the heathen, and these have been some of the disadvantages with which the Madras mission has had to contend.

But notwithstanding these obstacles, the brethren continued to pray and to labour for the conversion of the heathen. Nothing but the greatest zeal, diligence, and faithfulness could have enabled them to rescue time from the services to which I have alluded, in order to consecrate it to native preaching, to missionary tours, to the superintendence of native schools, and to the distribution of tracts and Scriptures. In the year 1827, the Madras District Committee was formed, and at its recommendation, the brethren divided the mission into two districts. Mr. Crisp had charge of the eastern, and Mr. Taylor superintended the western, and both had occasional help from Mr. Traveller who, though not then connected with the society, continued to take an interest in the work, and assisted, as far as in his power, the various measures which were adopted for its progress.

Henceforth, more was done for the heathen. The brethren both spoke the Tamul with great propriety and fluency. Six hundred children were under a course of instruction in their native schools, and the greatest pains were taken to render their education, Christian in its character. Preaching stations were established where the gospel was regularly and faithfully published, and divine truth was widely circulated in a variety of ways. The number of members united to the church in both districts, was thirty-five, many of whom gave great delight to the brethren by the fervour and solemnity with which they conducted their prayer-meetings, and by the spirit of compassion which they displayed for the heathen.

About this period, two young men gave themselves to the Lord. Their history is intimately associated with the Madras mission, and cannot, therefore, be overlooked. Mr. Nimmo was already engaged as an assistant missionary, and after labouring for many years in this capacity, and proving himself to be a workman that needeth not to be ashamed, was ordained in 1837, and is now the missionary at Combaconum. I give the history of Mr. Bilderbeck in as concise a form as possible.

He was born in Madras and of Roman Catholic parents. Early instructed in the forms and ceremonies of popery, and educated in the Jesuit College of Pondicherry, he was attached to that communion, never saw a Bible during his whole residence in the institution, and grew up in false principles, and in strong prejudices against the Protestant faith. After the death of his parents and of a valued uncle with whom he lived at Madras, his education fell into the hands of Protestants, and he was placed under the care of our missionary Mr. Nicholson. Now, the prejudices of his early life were called into exercise. Determined upon adhering to *that* religion in which his parents had died, he was unwilling to study the sacred Scriptures, and to attend to those religious exercises, which the missionary reckoned of the first importance. But this feeling was overcome. The death of Mr. Nicholson made a serious impression upon his mind. He was remarkably struck with the composure, the joy and holy serenity which were manifested by the missionary in the prospect of dissolution; and resolved to investigate the religion which could produce such effects, before he rejected it as unworthy of notice.

After this event, Mr. Bilderbeck was placed under the care of Mr. Crisp, whom he regards as his spiritual father, and whose kind instructions were rendered a blessing to him. "I soon," says he, "suspected the errors of my former sentiments, and began freely to search the Scriptures for myself, till I was led to the conviction that *popery was a practical libel upon that sacred religion which was established by Christ and his apostles!* I found that the Romish priests could give me no satisfaction, and that they could do no more than abound in unwarrantable threats. I felt it, therefore, to be my duty, from the honest convictions of judgment, and the force of truth, to leave their church, and to embrace and defend Protestantism, as that which was most in accordance with the word of God. Some of the priests told me, on one occasion, that if I took upon myself to read and interpret the English Bible, I and my Bible would most assuredly go to hell! Others said that, if I persisted in acting contrary to the authority of the church that gave me birth, I should die with an ulcer in my throat! My decided renunciation of popery soon exposed me to no little personal trial. The smiles of my friends, which I had once valued, were now forfeited; those who cheerfully received me at home, no longer gave me a welcome reception, and the root of bitterness sprang up to disturb our peace and harmony."

After another residence in Pondicherry, and considerable declension in the ways of God, Mr. Bilderbeck was induced to return to Madras Under the ministry of Mr. Crisp, his early impressions were renewed. He was brought to feel the enormity of his guilt and the necessity of an interest in Christ; he obtained peace and joy in believing; the services of the Sabbath became delightful to him; he was made useful to others, joined the church in 1828, and after visiting England, was ordained to the missionary work. He is now the very zealous, laborious and successful missionary at Chittoor.

In 1829, Mr. Crisp removed to Combaconum, and Mr. Smith joined the mission at Madras. A native congregation, established by Mr. Taylor, at Pursewaukum, was considerably increased; several converts, giving evidence of a work of grace in their hearts, were baptized in the name of Jesus; and some who were already the subjects of grace, seem to have been gathered to the assembly of the blessed. In reference to one of these, Mr. Taylor writes: "The aged native teacher Trichelroy departed this life, last November, in the hope and consolations of the gospel; of which, for many years, to the best of my knowledge, he had been a bold, zealous, faithful, and among his fellow-Christians, and the heathen, a popular preacher. His views of divine truth became clearer in his latter days; and his letters written to me, in the native language, while he was at a distance from Madras, breathed the high and holy spirit of one prepared for heaven. I avow my firm hope and belief that he will be found among the first-fruits of the Madras mission from among the natives, in the eternal world."

Tripasore, as a branch of the western district, was now an interesting station. Joel the native teacher, laboured among the heathen, and much good, through the instrumentality of a pious sergeant, was done among the European pensioners. After some years of usefulness, and of considerable exertion to promote the glory of God, the latter was removed into the invisible state, and in 1831, Mr. Taylor thus laments his departure: "Mr. Ince was the deacon of the church and indeed its father. I could not do justice to this worthy individual in the limited space of such a report as this, and I must therefore make the attempt in some other form. But death found him well prepared. In his own words, 'the enemy had no power,' and at almost the last moment, his language was, 'I know in whom I have believed.' I was at the place during four days of his last illness. He never gave utterance to a word of doubt or fear. On my coming away, he took solemn leave of me. His death occurred four days afterwards on the 21st October. Besides other persons, he was followed to the grave by the children of the free-school, members of the congregation, and those of the English and native churches; the latter of whom, I understand, sang alternate verses of hymns, as the procession moved along—an arrangement entirely local and spontaneous. Such an attendance was the greatest honour the departed could receive. Had not divine Providence raised him up to be a burning and a shining light in that place, my attention would probably not have been attracted to it, nor would the chapel, the congregation and churches have existed. May his example be a blessing; and his death be followed with salutary consequences to survivors."

A native church being now established in Pursewaukum, and giving comfort and joy to its pastor, I cannot help transcribing the account which Mr. Taylor gives of it in 1831. "Since October 1830, the number of members admitted to the church is thirteen; some candidates have of necessity been rejected. We have been under the painful obligation of dismissing two members who joined at the commencement, and one member is at present under suspension with hopeful indications of recovery. Two members have died during the year; both aged females. After deducting cases of every kind, the number at present in full communion, remains thirty-eight, among whom there are some very excellent and pious people, and perhaps a few of whom I ought not to speak with positive certainty, but of whom I hope the very best. The *Lord's Supper* is administered once in two months. The communion-table is placed in front of the pulpit; a few sit on seats on either hand, and the greater proportion on the floor-mat in front; the emblems are given by the minister to the deacons, and they go round with them to each member. A collection is made afterwards, appropriated strictly to widows or poor of the church. We are not troubled with any distinctions or differences about *caste;* the Lord's Supper, rightly distributed, is a caste-breaking institution. Individuals who value their caste more than their Saviour will of course keep aloof from us; discovering that we make it no point of attention or even remark. It has pleased God, as I humbly trust, to make these occasions, seasons of peculiar refreshing and of spiritual blessings. I have seen more of the wisdom of our divine Lord in the appointment of the two great ordinances of his church; and discovered more of their power and utility, than I could possibly have done, had I not had such a native flock to watch over in the Lord." Since November 1834, the charge of this district has devolved upon Mr. Drew, whose reports of the native church and congregation are encouraging, and will I trust, continue to be so, that his heart may be made glad, that this little one may become a thousand, and that from this, as from a centre, the blessings of salvation may emanate to the heathen around.

In the eastern district, Mr Smith laboured with zeal, diligence and success. Some young men under his care have been raised up for the work of the ministry, and to this department, he has lately given much of his time and attention and has met with encouraging prosperity. A revival which has lately taken place in the English church, has called forth gratitude and praise from the brethren, and has encouraged them to persevere in the work of the Lord. Some of the American missionaries who had witnessed similar seasons in their native land, and who, upon their voyage to India, were the instruments of exciting a revival on board the ship in which they sailed, joined with our own missionaries in seeking the salvation of men. After a striking sermon delivered by Dr. Scudder to the young on the first Sabbath of 1837, all those who were inclined to separate from the world and give themselves to Christ, were invited to the vestry. Nearly thirty persons responded to the call; a solemn hymn on judgment, was sung, and some showed by their expressions of grief, and of decision, that the Lord was among them.

"The impressions of that night," says Mr. Smith, "were not transitory. They continue to this day, and several individuals, having given satisfactory evidences of conversion, have subsequently joined the cnurch. The excitement has subsided; but there is yet a goodly number who are regarded as promising candidates for Christian fellowship. Though this spirit of religious inquiry prevailed among the young, it was not restricted to them, since we could point out instances in which parents and children sat on the same form as catechumens of the church of Christ; and those to whom reference is made are now all admitted to communion. Should the disclosures of eternity prove that only ten or twelve souls were brought to Christ on the occasion referred to, it will be a subject to angels and glorified spirits, of unceasing thanksgiving and praise. To give a tangible idea of the results which have arisen from the recent outpouring of the Spirit, it may be observed that, irrespective of a considerable number in Blacktown, and in the Fort who may be regarded as candidates, about twenty-five members, have been added to the church during the last twelve months, and the greater portion of these have been admitted since the beginning of January 1837.

One of the most interesting aspects in which

this revival can be regarded is, its probable bearing on the propagation of religion among the native community. We have substantial reason for the belief that some of our East Indian youths, whose attention has lately been directed to the things that belong to their peace, will rise up as heralds of salvation to the perishing heathen; and we have the satisfaction to state, that a considerable number of the catechists, readers, school-masters and members of the different missions in this city have formed, on their own responsibility, a voluntary association for prayer and other useful objects. From all we can hear of their exertions, we have reason to calculate on good results. We trust the time is not far distant, when we shall hear of the word of God having free course and being glorified by the spontaneous agency of native Christians, and when multitudes of converts shall go forth among their countrymen, and successfully declare the unsearchable riches of Christ."

COMBACONUM

Is in the province of Tanjore, and was, in former days, the capital of the Chola dynasties. This race is now extinct; but notwithstanding the various corruptions which the word has undergone, their name is still preserved in the one which is given to the whole coast—that of *Coromandel;* and in native manuscripts, the sovereign is still denominated the Cholia Rajah. The province is exceedingly rich, and has always been regarded as the garden and granary of the Carnatic. The Cavery rising among the hills of Coorg, forming the island of Seringapatam, passing through the Mysore, dashing with tremendous violence over the rocks and through the jungles of Sciva Samudram, and watering and enriching in its course the province of Coimbatoor, divides into two branches near to Trichinopoly, and while the northern stream is permitted, under the name of the Colleroon, to run waste into the sea, the southern, retaining the name of Cavery and prevented by immense mounds from joining its sister current, is led into a great variety of channels to irrigate the province, spreads on every side abundant fertility, and renders a paradise of a country which would otherwise remain a barren waste.

As the Mahommedans never occupied the territory, nor obtained permanent establishments in it; Hindooism has been preserved in considerable splendour; the Pagodas retain their ancient endowments and the Bramins luxuriate in wealth. There is scarcely a village in which there is not a temple to be found, whose massive tower and heavy structure remain as monuments of their architecture, whose revenues support hundreds of idolatrous priests, and to whose shrines, numbers of pilgrims hurry to pay their devotions. As the government grants an allowance of forty thousand pagodas a year for the support of the smaller temples, the Bramins are not only the principal holders of the land, but they are said to be exceedingly loyal to the British authority under whose reign they enjoy so much protection, and so many advantages.

Combaconum is especially the grand emporium of idolatry. Its tanks, its shrines, and its temples are numerous and imposing, and among its forty thousand inhabitants, the Bramins occupy a great proportion of its soil, and enjoy a large share of its revenues and its riches.

The mission was established in this heathen city by Mr. Mead in 1825. His health having failed in Travancore, he resorted to Combaconum for change, found the climate very beneficial, and returned, in 1827, to his former station. The claims of Combaconum, were taken into consideration at the first meeting of the Madras District Committee, and as Mr. Crisp expressed a wish to occupy the station, the mission was renewed in 1829. During the interval, several readers had laboured in the field, and were found diligent and active on Mr. Crisp's arrival. The following extract from the journal of one of the readers will give some idea of the simplicity with which the native brethren proceed in their work.

"Discoursing with a bazaar-man on the heinous sin of idolatry, telling him that all men are sinners, and that the rites and ceremonies of the heathen, would not take away sin, he seemed to listen with very little interest and asked me a number of vain questions. I offered him a tract, but he declined to receive it, saying, that he had no time to read. After leaving this place, I fell in with several people who, to my surprise, listened with great attention. One asked, how sins were to be pardoned. I, of course, spoke of the Lamb of God which taketh away the sins of the world ; a woman likewise was very attentive. It was an interesting meeting to me, and I hope to them. I left them with an earnest exhortation to embrace the gospel, which had been explained to them, observing that the time past was long enough for them to have remained in darkness.

"As the schoolmaster of Karupoor was reciting the poems of an ancient monk on the vanity of the world, and on the misery of those who seek it in preference to the eternal God, I explained to him that we are by nature ignorant of our Heavenly Father; and though we might hear or read good moral instruction, yet our corrupt nature is averse to follow it, and that the Holy Christ must renew our minds by his grace. I exhorted him and his family to embrace the gospel. 'Hereafter,' said he, 'this must be done.'"

On the settlement of Mr. Crisp, there were, he found, some schools established, and a commencement was made; it remained to him to reform and to consolidate, and to adopt measures to secure future prosperity. As Combaconum is so much in the neighbourhood of the old stations where caste has been allowed, the evil soon began to germinate and to grow among those who made a profession of the gospel. At the formation of the church, thirteen members joined in the communion; but as they were all Soodras, it was impossible to ascertain whether they would stand the test of sitting to eat and to drink at the table of the Lord with their outcast brethren who might be called into the fellowship of the faith. "I have ever felt," says Mr. Crisp, "that the evil is one which ought to be resisted, and have often remonstrated against it. The more I see of its tendency, the more thoroughly am I convinced that every lawful means must be used to put a stop to it; but there is much difficulty in deciding how the object can be accomplished. We are plain and decided in our declarations on the subject both in private and from the pulpit; and I am humbly determined, to the best of my ability, to labour to convince the Christians around us that caste is as heathenish in its tendency as in its origin. I have been surprised and grieved that some who, in other respects, manifest what appear to be the fruits of the Spirit, are still so tenacious of this distinction, and so susceptible of offence whenever the subject is touched upon. I very much fear that caste has had a baneful influence upon our welfare as a church; that it has imperceptibly stunted the growth of those Christian graces which might otherwise have appeared vigorous, flourishing and influential; and that we shall never see much of the life and power of religion among the Christians nor realize any extended success among the heathen, till this offence is removed."

As the truth advances, this will be a source of grief and trouble to every faithful missionary. If the Soodras give up their caste and sit down in peace and harmony with the Pariars, then in attempting to avoid one evil, we shall find that we have fallen into another. The outcasts are not satisfied; envy, jealousy and suspicion are always at work; it would require the hand of wisdom and experience, as Mr. Crisp justly shows, instead of that of fancy and presumption to intermeddle with such questions; and while the renunciation of caste must prove a very strong and decided test of sincerity to the higher classes, it is a great pity but that one of similar power could be applied to test the principles of the Pariars. By his Christianity, the former has every thing to lose; the latter every thing to gain.

On the resumption of the mission, the congregation did not exceed forty, but in 1833, it amounted, old and young, to one hundred and forty; it assumed a settled and steady appearance, and became thus a source of encouragement to the missionary who had watched its progress from such a small beginning. Mr. Nimmo had now joined the mission as an assistant, and in 1835, the attention of the brethren was directed to a large Catholic village where the people wished to renounce superstition, and place themselves under their care and superintendence. The distance of the spot, and some other circumstances caused them at first to hesitate, lest insincerity and worldly motives should be mixed up with the proposition. But as these did not appear, the place was visited, a school was established, services were commenced, and many regularly attended on the means of grace.

"The spirit of persecution soon began to manifest itself in a trying manner. The house of one of the people was burned down, and we have reason to believe it was the work of an incendiary although of that there is no positive proof. The head-man of the village, exerted himself to persuade both Catholics and heathens to take their children from the school and succeeded in a very great degree. The Lord may see this 'fan' to be needful, in order to prevent the chaff from accumulating as it has done in most places where all has been quiet and peaceful." After Mr. Nimmo had visited the village in August, his report is very encouraging. "They are but a small band in the midst of hundreds of Roman Catholics, and they do indeed adorn the doctrine of God their Saviour in all things. They are making great advances not only in divine knowledge, but, I hope, also in piety and in love to the Saviour. The Lord seems to be opening a wide door here. The Roman Catholics do not now manifest the same aversion and prejudice which they used to do; but calmly hear the truth when declared, and some of them even acknowledge its goodness. Some of the principal men among them have expressed a wish to join us, but they want more faith and true Christian courage. The school here is doing better, than before, and the Romans who were some time ago opposed to it, are now commencing to send their children."

Some instances, among the children in the schools, have encouraged the brethren not a little. "The Lord has been pleased of late to grant us one instance which appears to be a case of real conversion among these young objects of our care. A boy who was formerly in one of the schools has professed his faith in Christ, his abhorrence of idolatry, and his determination to renounce it. He has steadfastly and perseveringly refused to place on his forehead the mark of idolatry, and he has, in consequence, endured very severe and cruel treatment from his friends. Hoping to put a stop to his progress, they took him away from town and he is now seldom seen by any of us. Without being in an undue measure elated by this solitary instance, it is not too much to regard it as a gracious testimony of the Lord's approval, and an illustration of what he can do, on a larger scale, and of what we may expect he will do for us eventually, if we faint not."

"A girl in the female school has afforded us much reason for hoping that she had received the grace of God in truth, and that she has died in the faith of Christ. She had been formerly in the female school at Mayaveram, and removed here in November last, with her mother. Her general conduct was exceedingly correct and pleasing, and she always paid great attention to the lessons which were taught her, and the explanation given of them; but it was not till after her death, that I became fully acquainted with what had been her character. In a land where the blasting influence of heathen associations is perpetually felt, we cannot but rejoice if we see any indications of youthful piety, or observe the fruits of the Spirit to be in any measure produced. Thus have we had in the male and female departments of our schools, something over which to rejoice as the work of the Lord among us."

It is thus that the work is advancing. It has been a question whether such stations as Combaconum, where Braminical influence is so powerful, and where idolatry is set forth to captivate the people in such fascinating charms, are the best for missionary enterprise. But whatever might be the decision which reason and experience would make on this point, it is delightful to think that, at a station where Satan has his seat, where the head-quarters of idolatry are fixed, where prejudice and superstition so much prevail, and where the Bramins are so numerous and so inveterate, an altar is erected to the living God; there are a few who fear his name, and maintain his worship; the captives are rescued from the hands of the terrible, and some of the young and of the old give glory to Immanuel.

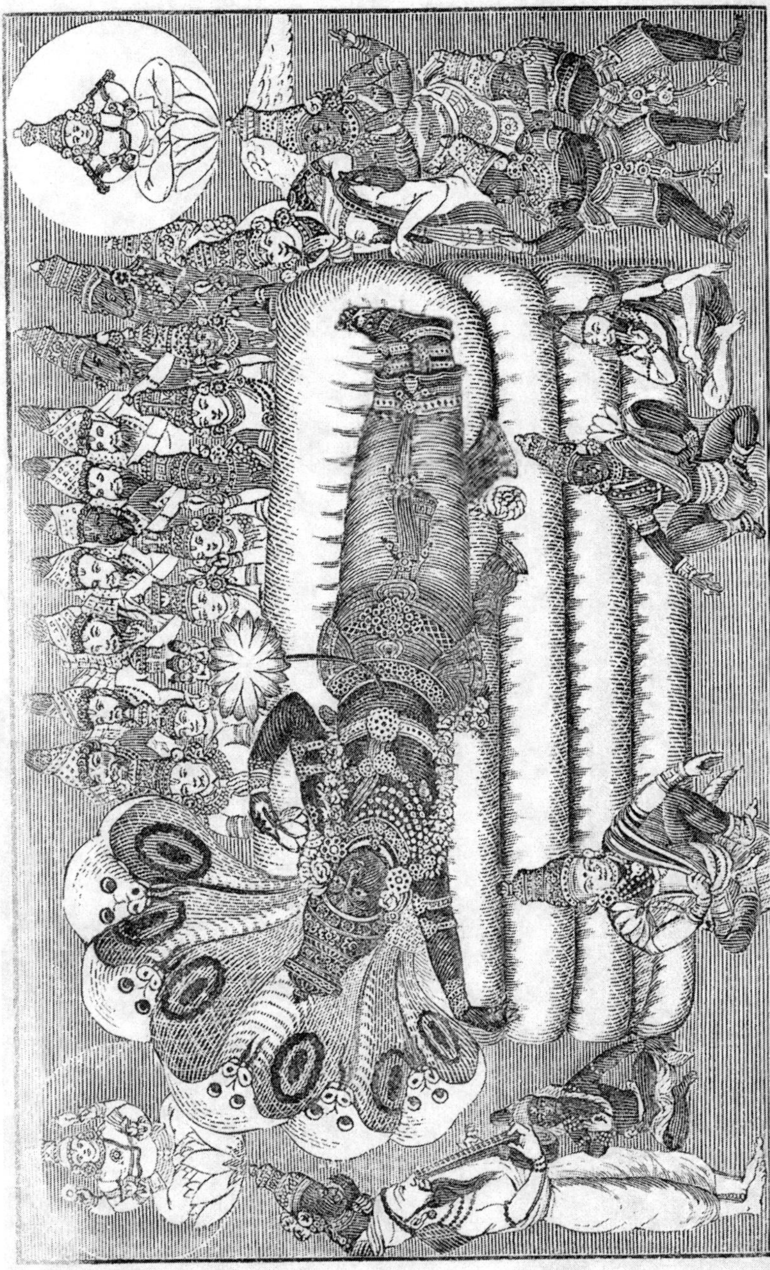

CHAPTER XV.

TRAVANCORE.

SCENERY—THE PROVINCE—THE MISSION ESTABLISHED—MR. RINGLETAUBE—MR. MEAD—ADVANCEMENT OF THE TRUTH—A CHRISTIAN VILLAGE—NATIVE TEACHER—READERS—SEMINARY—SCHOOLS—TRACT SOCIETY—ADDRESSES—QUILON—THE CLIMATE—A NATIVE CONVERT—TRIALS AND DEATHS—MR. THOMPSON—SUCCESS—SCHOOLS.

In the south-western extremity of the peninsula, and not far distant from Cape Comorin, is the province of Travancore. Forty miles in breadth and a hundred and forty in length; divided from Tinevelly by a range of lofty hills on the east, bounded on the north by the territory of the Cochin Rajah, and on the south and west by the sea, it is thought to contain about a million and a half of inhabitants; but that number may be its amount in its best and most prosperous days. Nature has done every thing to render it a happy and delightful land. The diversity of hill and dale, its mountains covered with forests, and its valleys crowned with an almost perpetual verdure, render its scenery often enchanting and sublime. The waters rush from the hills, and descending through the plains, cover them with abundance. Pepper, cardamums, cassia, frankincense, and aromatic gums grow spontaneously in its woods. Its superior soil, its favourable climate, and its seasonable rains enable it to dispense with those reservoirs upon which cultivation, throughout India, so much depends.

Not having been subject, for any length of time, to the Mahommedan powers, and enjoying peace and tranquillity under its native rulers, Travancore is characterized, like the coast of Malabar, by the Hindoo habits, manners and customs, in greater perfection, than most parts of the country. The system of the Bramins has been paramount here, as well as through the rest of India; but the descendants of those Mahommedans who came fromArabia totraffick in Malabar are very numerous; the Christian edifices are, in some parts, so many that a traveller would be ready to imagine that he was in a Christian land; and the Syrians, long resident and long oppressed, form a strong and independent colony. The Rajah of Travancore has long been tributary to British rule. While the supreme government, is a security against all foreign aggression; has been the means of putting an end to those feudal and perpetual quarrels which existed among the petty rajahs; and has thus given greater peace, order and happiness to the people; the maintenance of a subsidiary force in the district has often been attended with the greatest evils. The prince or his minister relying upon British protection, have often imposed taxes upon the people which they have not been able to bear; the poor ryots have been driven to desperation; the fertile and beautiful provinces which were a paradise even in war, have been converted into a desolate wilderness by the oppressions which have reigned in the days of peace; and the British troops have sometimes been called out to quell insurrections which misrule has raised, and have been obliged to appear as the supporters of tyranny and bad government. A good deal of this, has occurred in Travancore. In 1799, an additional tax laid upon pepper, caused a rebellion in the province, and was obliged to be repealed, before the insurgents could be brought to obedience. Under the last treaty, the Dewan * superseded the authority of his master; his conduct became hostile to the British power, and in 1809, he ventured to oppose our influence with an army. His design was speedily defeated; and the whole country was brought into subjection; but since that time, the British troops have been employed in expeditions, and in actions, through Travancore, which have ill accorded with their own notions of liberty and justice and beneficent rule.

The mission to Travancore, was established in 1806. Mr. Ringletaube laboured among the peo-

* The Prime Minister.

ple with diligence and success for many years—now travelling through the country to propagate the gospel, and then residing at Mylaudy to train up the young in the knowledge of God and to direct the old to salvation and to heaven; at one time distributing tracts and portions of the Scriptures among the heathen, and at another dispensing the ordinances to those who had already believed, till he had erected chapels in seven villages, had baptized hundreds of the people, had collected them into congregations, and laboured among them with testimonies of divine approbation. In 1818, the late Sir Thomas Munro, while resident at the court of the Ranee, makes honourable allusion to his labours. "The small Protestant community formed by Mr. Ringletaube in the south of Travancore, although still in a state of infancy, is extremely respected. Its neophytes are called the Vadahars or Persons of the Book, and it receives more proselytes than all the other sects of Christianity in Travancore."

Mr. and Mrs. Mead arrived at the station in 1816, and began their missionary career; and as Mr. Knill's health had failed at Madras, he tried the effect of this more salubrious climate; but after beholding a few marks of the grace and mercy which the Lord had in reserve for that people, and after laying the foundation of a house of prayer, he was obliged to return to England. Mr. and Mrs. Mault joined the mission in 1819. Did space permit, it would be pleasant to trace the progress of the work from that period to the present time; to watch the indications of providence by which wide and effectual doors have been opened for the gospel; to witness the people, in hundreds, abandoning their idols, throwing down the temples and the altars erected to demons, and calling upon the missionaries to instruct them in the truth; to look at the courage and the fortitude with which many have endured persecution from their kinsmen and their neighbours; and to see how the natives who have renounced their heathenism to worship the God of Israel, have increased in number from eight and nine hundred to as many thousands, and the congregations from ten or twelve to a hundred. But I leave this to some who may have more time to enlarge than I have, and would just glance at a few points which are of interest to missionaries and to the Christian world.

Let the reader fancy himself among the hills of Travancore. It is a sabbath in the month of December—when neither snow, nor frost make their appearance, but when the land has been refreshed with its rains and its nullas, and all nature is ready to sing for joy. Let us enter this Christian village, to worship and to see the order which prevails. No din of labour is to be heard; the song of the drunkard rends not the air; nor is the lascivious dance rendered to demons; all is hushed to quietness and repose, because the inhabitants have begun to remember the sabbath-day to keep it holy. Look at the Christian sanctuary;—it occupies the spot where their heathen temple stood, and some of its stones were used in its erection. Behold the worshippers going to the service; they are all sober, clean, decently attired, and their looks and their manners are far better than their dress. Let us go with them to prayer. The house is full and the spirit of devotion rests upon the audience. They sing no longer the praises of Vishnoo; they celebrate now the praises of the Lamb: they bow no longer at the shrine of the evil spirit; they send forth their supplications to the God of Israel: they listen no longer to their Vedas and their Shasters; they hear now the words of eternal truth. Who is that individual in his snowy mantle and is declaring with such energy and zeal and affection and faithfulness, the gospel of God? That is the reader of Mylaudy. While he was yet a youth, some of his neighbours went to offer sacrifice to a celebrated idol near Tanjore; they were introduced to the missionaries, and heard from their lips the tidings of mercy, and received books to peruse at home and to increase their divine knowledge. Such was the impression which this visit made upon them, that, on their return, they threw away their idols, and commenced the worship of the living God, and when they heard of Mr. Ringletaube, they invited him to their village to instruct them in the truth. This youth and his parents were then numbered among those who made a profession of Christianity. But though he was baptized, though he became a member of the church, a schoolmaster, and was employed as a reader; yet he acknowledges that his heart was hardened, that he indulged in sin, that he resembled a man walking in the dark and likely to tread upon serpents, though he saw no danger, and that he made a sinful use of the ordinances to soothe his conscience, and to preserve him from fear. But by the grace of God, he was led to meditate upon such passages as these, "Thou that teachest another, teachest thou not thyself?" "Thou hypocrite! cast out the beam out of thine own eye, and then shalt thou see clearly to take out the mote that is in thy brother's eye; and that servant who knew his Lord's will and did it not, will be beaten with many stripes." Such passages filled him with alarm, led him to repentance and deep humiliation of soul; showed him the necessity of a mighty Redeemer, and, enabled by faith to trust in Jesus, he obtained a good hope through grace of the glory that is to be revealed. He is now a truly devoted man; a judicious and prudent assistant upon whom the missionaries can always depend. What a change is produced upon him? and what a change has the village in which he labours, undergone? On his arrival at Mylaudy, he found the hearts of some though they professed Christianity, as hard as stones; but a considerable improvement is visible among the old people, while a few individuals show that they "are washed and justified and sanctified in the name of Jesus and by the Spirit of our God." Sixteen persons who were members of that congregation, are either regularly or occasionally engaged in making known the truths of the Bible to their countrymen!

Unable to meet the wants of the people, and to propagate the gospel as extensively as they wished by their own exertions, the missionaries soon perceived the necessity of employing the natives to assist them in their work. At first, their chief business was to read the Scriptures in the villages, and thus bring the word of God as a testimony against the works of darkness; but as the readers gained more Christian knowledge, gave evidences of piety, became more bold in their labours, they were allowed to give a reason, to those who asked them, of the hope that was in them with meekness and fear. The example of one operated upon many; the brethren met them occasionally to give them instruction, and to hear their reports; they were furnished with answers to the objections which the heathen were accustomed to make; their gifts and graces increased as well as their number; and though the missionaries are very far from considering their congregations as composed of true Christians, yet it is a delightful sight to see so many who are no longer heathens, but enquirers after the truth. If these be the first fruits; what will be the harvest? But what is the remuneration which these readers or native teachers receive? They are paid at the rate of ten pounds per annum—a sum which does not equal the wages of a common servant in other parts of India. Now this amount may keep them alive among the poor in Travancore; but is it right, expedient or honourable, that the salary of a teacher should be fixed at the lowest possible grade? Is it likely that persons of character, respectability, and talents will accept of an office which, however honourable in itself, yields only a pittance to its most zealous and most laborious agents? Is it not calculated to lessen the influence of the teachers among the people, and to injure their usefulness, and to furnish a very bad precedent to the converts when they begin to support their own pastors? I know well that it does so in other parts of the country. Nothing is more common than when a friend comes from a distance, and calls upon a Hindoo, that he treats his kinsman or his acquaintance with kindness and generosity; how then must it sink the teachers in the estimation of their countrymen, when they find that they are the only parties, holding a respectable situation, who are unable to show to others the common marks of civility and kindness? But to pass by the contrast which it is impossible to help drawing between these teachers, and the Cattanars among the Syrians in the same district, who are paid at the rate of twenty or thirty pounds a year, as recommended by Mr. Bailey; so small a salary can only be allowed them, on the supposition that they are a very inferior class of teachers; and it is right the religious public should understand that this amount will scarcely suit the circumstances of any station in India except Travancore; and that if the benevolent wish to support men whose character, piety, talents and usefulness will elevate them above mediocrity in every way, they must abandon the ten-pound system, and afford to their representatives in heathen lands, the means of living in comfort, and in respectability among their own people. As I am a great advocate for native agency, my brother missionaries must pardon these remarks, and attribute them to my anxiety to see our native brethren raised to a higher scale of intelligence, character and usefulness.

But the brethren soon foresaw that it would not be prudent to depend upon adult converts alone, for a supply of readers and teachers. To meet the wants of their congregations, they perceived the necessity of establishing a seminary to prepare native youths for the ministerial work. Many were supported, received a religious education, gave evidence of their devotedness, and went into the villages to hold forth the word of life that others may rejoice in the day of Christ. It is from this nursery that they have been able to fill up their vacant spheres with those who, from their superior education, their general intelligence, and their studious and active habits, have been better qualified, for their work, than their predecessors. No hours can be too precious, no care can be too assiduous, no exertions can be too many, and no sums too large, to be devoted to those infant institutions which, in India, have for their object the education of native preachers. Nothing would be more unreasonable, than to expect that the people who are just emerging from paganism, or that youths who have been trained up in a heathen land, amongst idolatrous customs and associations, should be on an equality with Europeans in energy, in piety, in acquirements, and in exertions. There will be men who will rise above their neighbours, and excel all their competitors in the race; but these will be exceptions to the general rule. Whatever may be the part of the heathen world in which they dwell, the first race of teachers will not, in the midst of heathens, come up to that high standard which we should wish them to reach; and it can only be through a long course of discipline and experience that they will advance to greater steadfastness, and more daring enterprise. But a beginning must be made, and what cannot be accomplished in the first, we must hope to witness in the second generation; and when I think of what has already been done in Travancore, and of what the present system promises to accomplish, I am surprised that more vigorous efforts are not made at every station to train up an efficient native ministry. Too much at present ought not to be expected.

The perfectionists will look and wait long before they see their expectations realized. The natives are mere infants, and they are exposed to many temptations and difficulties with which Europeans are unacquainted. They will fall once, and again, but they ought not, on that account, to be abandoned. Means should be taken to restore them; and when they are humbled, and perceive the many evils to which their corruptions expose them, they will become more watchful, more prayerful, and more useful than before; and perhaps in a different sphere of labour, they may become a comfort to the church, and blessings to the heathen. Some native teachers whom I could name, have gone through a course of trial and of discipline similar to this, and are now strong and vigorous in grace, and very useful in converting idolaters to Christ.

In labouring to convert the old, our brethren have not been unmindful of the young. In their schools, there are more than three thousand children, all of whom are receiving a religious education, are under the tuition of masters many of whom appear to have received the truth in the love of it, and are growing up better prepared to value the gospel and to embrace it, than their fathers. It is impossible to calculate the amount of good which must arise from such schools scattered through the province. What prejudices are overcome! what ignorance is dissipated! what evils are prevented! what good principles and good habits, are, in many cases, secured! what a work of preparation for future success is advancing!

On a review of this mission, every one must rejoice at the number of missionaries who have lately accompanied Mr. Mead to strengthen and to confirm the labours of the brethren. What can be done by three or four Europeans in such a field? As yet, it is evident that much confidence cannot be reposed in the readers as a body; and the missionaries state frankly that, instead of attending to the duties of forming the people into churches and building them up in faith and in holiness, their visits extend little further than to the catechumens and enquirers. Let us hope that the late supply will relieve the brethren from some of their arduous duties, and will permit them to form the converts into churches, and to dispense among them the ordinances, the regular attendance upon which must in every country be of essential service to the interests of the gospel. Among a people, some of whom have endured the greatest persecutions for the sake of the gospel, and are bold and courageous in their profession, I am surprised that none of the native teachers have been selected as the most wise and devoted and useful, and set apart to the office of Evangelists. I am aware that this is a subject which requires great care and consideration; but it is one which must be attended to, which the interests of the church demands, and which, according to the laws of the New Testament, it would be sinful to overlook. If it be a duty to lay hands suddenly on no man; so it is also a duty to commit the things which we have heard to faithful men, that they may teach others also, and may dispense all the ordinances of Christ.

It is delightful to perceive that the Christians in Travancore, have begun to show their love to the Redeemer and to his cause, and afford the hope that they will one day support their own ministers, and extend the gospel to the regions beyond them. Nothing is of greater importance among new converts, than to lay down this as a principle—not only to show their compassion to others—not only to afford evidence of their sincerity and of their attachment to the Redeemer—but to promote their own spiritual good, and to keep alive all the mercy and benevolence of Christianity in their hearts. A native Tract and Bible Society have existed for some years. Their anniversaries are sometimes attended by 1000 people. More than £120 have been collected during the year for the publication of tracts; and their meetings are often the most animating and delightful. It may be well to conclude this notice, by a few extracts from their speeches on such an occasion. The reader Palmer rose and said, "Some of the women connected with my congregation though incapable of reading, have committed to memory the substance of many of our tracts, and go from house to house to teach others what they have thus learned. One of them, on a certain day, as she was going on this errand, met with a sorcerer who, she was aware, had come for the purpose of deceiving the people. She looked steadfastly at him and said, 'Tell me the truth; are you not come hither for the sake of gain, to deceive these people, and thus to ruin their souls and your own?' At which he was very angry, and threatened to destroy her by his incantations if she attempted again to address him in such language. To this, she answered that it was out of his power to injure her by his charms; for the God in whom she believed was mighty to save. Again he abused and threatened her; but was unable to intimidate her. Many of the heathen who witnessed the courage of this Christian woman, who dared to defy the power of the magician, are beginning to despise these men who, for ages, have been such a curse to the country."

The reader Balm said, "Our tracts are circulated among all classes; and among the poor they are doing good; for many of that class have seen the evil of idolatry, and have lately joined this and other congregations, who were principally excited to this step by the truths they have learned from our tracts. One instance is so pleasing and so much to the purpose that I am persuaded the relation of it, will gladden the hearts of all present. Some months ago, as I was returning after the labours of the sabbath, from a neighbouring village, I met a Pandarum in my way, who was dressed in the usual style of that fraternity; and as he approached me, he appeared from his gait and demeanour, to think himself some great one. I accosted him; and observing that he returned the salutation, I ventured to ask him who he was and where he was going. He candidly told me he was a Pandarum of the sect of "the Eight Letters," and that he was going to teach his religion, for by that he obtained his living. I spoke to him of the necessity of repentance towards God; but he soon interrupted me by answering that he possessed one of our books. On asking him whether he had read it and what it contained, he observed, 'That he who would enjoy the felicity of heaven, must esteem the world and all its glory, as less than nothing and vanity.' To this and other truths, he declared his assent, at which my heart was filled with joy and I could not refrain from exclaiming, 'Who can tell the amount of good our books are doing?' After some further conversation, I invited him to Nagercoil, where he shortly after paid us a visit, and received a fresh supply of books, by the perusal of which and other instruction, his profiting soon appeared to all men. He is now appointed an assistant reader, and is diligently employed in teaching others the way of salvation."

QUILON

Is situated on the Malabar coast, and belongs to the province of Travancore. As a place of trade, it has been the resort of all nations; its traffic consists of pepper, cardamums, cotton and various other articles of merchandise; good rice, pine-apples and bannanas are abundant; and fish of all kinds are caught on the coast. It was here, that the Archbishop of Goa first opened his conference with the Syrian Christians, and compelled so many of them to embrace the tenets of the Romish church, and it is reckoned that, besides the three congregations in Quilon, there are seventy-five, belonging to the Roman Catholics between this, and Cape Comorin. In consequence of the commerce which is carried on with various parts, and of the cantonment which once existed, there are many who speak Tamul, Portuguese and Hindosthanee, but the Malayalim is the vernacular language, and the one, of course, which the missionaries have studied and in which they instruct the people.

The mission was established in 1821. Notwithstanding the reported salubrity of the climate, the health of the first missionaries completely failed. Mr. Smith was very soon obliged to return to England, and Mr. Crow continued to labour and to suffer as long as there was any hope that his life would be spared, and that his talents could be employed with any advantage to India. But short and trying as was his career, it was not without comfort and usefulness. In bidding an adieu to the scene of his labours, he was enabled to write the following account of Poonyan—a gun Lascar in the Company's service—a man whom

I well know, who was afterwards a member of the church at Bangalore, and whose conduct was always Christian, consistent, and creditable to the profession which he made.

"From his own account," says Mr. Crow, "it appears that by reading a book some years ago, in the Tamul language which was translated or composed by a missionary, he was faintly impressed with the folly of idolatry and had ever since relaxed in his attention to its rites. This impression seems to have been considerably strengthened by the perusal of a tract given to him when passing through Nagercoil about six months prior to his coming to me. Though convinced of the absurdity of idolatry, I found him but slightly impressed with a sense of sin, totally ignorant of the way of salvation, and cleaving to his own obedience as the ground of acceptance before God. His progress in Christian knowledge was remarkably rapid, and he shortly appeared to have obtained a clear and consistent view of the way of a sinner's reconciliation to God. The doctrine of the atonement always seemed most to interest and affect his heart. The feeling and earnestness he evinced, and the regularity of his attendance at the Mission-house, appeared to indicate sincerity, while as far as I could ascertain, he had nothing to expect from becoming a Christian, except the scorn and reproaches of his comrades. I procured for him a New Testament, which he usually made his companion, and on looking at it, on one occasion, he said with a countenance of joy, 'I could feed on it,' signifying the high value which he placed upon it.

"As it had always been my custom in my interviews with him, to dwell upon important truths, he had scarcely had his attention at all directed to non-essential things; but early in the morning of the day on which he was to be baptized, he came to me to inquire whether it was not necessary, before he received baptism, to cut off his long hair, to take out his ear-rings, and his child's nose-jewel, and to strip himself of other heathen ornaments. I referred him to the passage in Corinthians, 'Doth not even nature itself teach you that if a man have long hair, it is a shame to him,' and to the one in Peter, 'Whose adorning let it not be that outward adorning of plaiting the hair, and of wearing of gold, or of putting on of apparel; but let it be the hidden man of the heart, in that which is not corruptible, even the ornament of a meek and quiet spirit which is, in the sight of God, of great price;' and these passages seemed to have their full and immediate effect upon him. He hastened home, cut off his hair, stripped himself and his child of every jewel, and in a short time returned with his wife and infant, anxious to testify his adherence to the cause of truth and piety. By those who are acquainted with the superstitious attachment of the heathens here to their jewels, long hair and other ornaments, this circumstance, though in itself trivial, will be considered indicative of a determination to renounce every vestige of heathenism."

The convert thus described was always steady, adorned the gospel, gave the greatest satisfaction to his commanding officer, and was zealous among his friends and his comrades to propagate the truth. Both his wife and his mother were afterwards baptized at Bangalore, and while they remained with us, we had great joy in seeing this family walking in the road to Zion.

Mr. and Mrs. Thompson arrived at the station in 1827, and Mr. and Mrs. Harris joined them in 1831. The same afflictions and trials came heavy and fast upon these dear brethren as they came upon their predecessors. Mr. and Mrs. Thompson were soon obliged to remove to the Neilgherries, and though Mrs. Thompson rallied for a time, her constitution was undermined. She was under the necessity of returning to her native land, and was soon removed into the eternal world. The life of Mr. Harris was soon despaired of, and he reached the shores of England only to die. Mr. Thompson remained at the station, and his health has been restored; but it is a question of serious import—a question of humanity and benevolence—and a question which deserves to be seriously considered by the agents and the directors of our missionary societies, how long a station that has proved so fatal, ought to be occupied. Whether after missionaries of various constitutions and temperaments have fallen victims to disease and to death, more ought to be exposed to the danger; whether it would not be more in harmony with the gospel, to regard such visitations as signs of Providence, and remove to a locality where their health, as well as their usefulness may be preserved. I would not have Quilon condemned and abandoned without decisive evidence; but while thousands and millions are spiritually perishing in countries where the health and the life of the missionary would be secure, it appears to me unaccountable, and demanding more plain and satisfactory reasons than enthusiasm would supply, that such stations should be kept up as Sierra Leone, which has only proved an hospital for the sick, and a grave for dying missionaries, and which is celebrated not so much for the few whom it retains, as that it has allowed one or another to escape alive. Quilon will not, I trust, be known in missionary annals, as an aceldama, or a grave. Let it have a fair trial; but if it should prove in the future what it has been in the past, remove, I would say, the seat of the mission to a more salubrious climate, and supply by East Indians, or by natives whose country it is, the necessities of the population. More attention ought certainly to be given to this subject. Where is the use of exposing Europeans to unhealthy climates, when natives and others would remain uninjured? I am happy in being able to quote, on such a point, the views of Sir Thomas Munro. "Seringapatam is itself extremely unhealthy; and we are not sure that Holligall is favourable to the European constitution. It is therefore desirable for this cause alone, even if there were no other, that natives who are less liable to suffer from the climate, should be employed, instead of Europeans. Should this experiment, in the present instance, prove successful, as I am confident it will, the employment of native judges may then, by degrees, be extended to some other remote and unhealthy districts, such as Soondah, and in time to every place where their services may be useful."

Amidsts such trials and sufferings, what could be expected? Yet the labours of the brethren have prospered. A suitable chapel has been obtained; many schools have been established, in which a Christian education is given, and contained in 1831, no fewer than 512 children, of whom 142 were girls; many readers endeavoured to propagate the gospel; and some in the midst of trials and persecutions, have dared to acknowledge Christ, and have maintained their profession with great satisfaction to all. As to idolatry itself, Mr. Thompson remarks in 1835, "I have reason to be fully assured that if the people were only protected from their head men, who, without the sanction of the government, levy contributions forcibly upon them, as a source of gain to themselves, after defraying the expenses of their superstitions, that idolatry would die of itself, as it regards the public observ

MISSION PREMISES AT QUILON

1 Assistant's House. 2 Printing Office. 3. Mission House. 4. Girls' School. 5. Church. 6, 7. Readers' Houses 8. Boys' School

ance of it. The people in this village express their expectation that next year nothing will be done to honour their stone god. The schoolmaster at Kalloorvilley has, with another proprietor of a joint pagoda renounced, by a formal deed, his connexion with it, and left it to the only remaining shareholder. When a Hindoo gives up property, or when the proprietors of temples, deem them not worth holding, something is evidently going on."

A seminary has also been established for the education of the young, with the hope that some from among them may arise to praise the Lord. The question of caste seemed for a time to stand as a barrier against its progress; but as prejudice has given way, and knowledge has increased, the objection has been removed, and Mr. Thompson alluding to it says, "From the seminary, three youths have been sent out during the year to take charge of schools; one having been sent at the request of the head men of the place, has a good school; the others have not been able to collect so many children; but I confidently anticipate their exercising a more efficient influence in promoting a solid education, and that they will be able to collect a greater number to enjoy its benefits. At present, ten youths are under instruction, besides several day-scholars. The eldest have acquired a very considerable knowledge of divine things, and promise well at a future period to be useful labourers with us. Three instances have been mentioned of children being the means of directing their parents' attention to Christianity, and where the reading of heathen legends in the evening, has given place to the children reading the word of God. Some months ago, we were invited to commence a school in Paroor—a very large village, and to send a person who was capable of teaching the people and their children *Christianity*. This is the first case in which the head men of a village have united in such a request. One of the seminary youths was sent as schoolmaster, and there seems a decided inclination to learn. In one house, the worship of the true God is established.

CHAPTER XVI.

ON THE TAMUL MISSIONS.

SALEM—CHEVEROI HILLS—MR. HENRY CRISP—HIS LABOURS AND DEATH—MR. WALTON—SCHOOLMASTERS—VISITS TO MARKETS—THE NATIVE CHURCH—ITINERARIES—COIMBATOOR—NEILGHERRIES—INHABITANTS OF THE HILLS—IDOLATRY IN THE PLAINS—MR. ADDIS—EDUCATION—A READING-ROOM—CONVERTS—CHITTOOR—THE FATHER OF THE MISSION—MR. JENNINGS—DIFFICULTIES—DEATH OF MR. DACRE—DEATH OF MR. JENNINGS—MR. BILDERBECK—BRANCH STATIONS.

SALEM

Is the principal town of the Baramhal district. It contains about 60,000 inhabitants, and the province more than a million. As it is situate on a plain, and on the descent of the Ghauts to the south, the climate is hot and dry; the trees, except around the villages, are comparatively few; and the face of the country, in the hot season, looks barren and uninteresting, though the soil is good and productive. In descending from the Mysore, every thing here appears diminutive; the fowls are not larger than bantams; the eggs resemble those of pigeons; the goats and sheep and cattle of all kinds are remarkably small; and the human race seem to partake of the dwarfish character which is thus impressed upon the whole animate creation. Not many miles from Salem, the Cheveroi hills tower amid the clouds. In the village of Guntoor, half-way up the ascent, their inhabitants are seen to most advantage. There are about thirty cabins, and the people are shepherds. I have not seen any human beings so wild, and so much on a level with the beasts of the forest. Their houses are built neither of brick, nor stone, nor clay. But bamboos in a circular form, are stuck into the ground, and the roof covered with thatch, gives the dwellings the appearance of a large cage. About a cubit of space is left between the inner and outer row of bamboos, that the poor children may have liberty to crawl round, and then, as the floor inside is elevated, the rains which must descend from the hills with great violence, run off in this outer path, and leave the interior dry; and the inmates say it is enough that their dwellings resemble those of their sheep and their goats. Indeed! vulgar report affirms that these people live on such good terms with the savage tribes of the woods, that when the mother goes out to her toil, she leaves her infant in charge of the tiger. Such a report, false and ridiculous as it is, shows the estimation in which these people are held by their more civilized brethren.

In some parts of the ascent, the roads are so bad,

and often so steep, that you pant, and blow, stand still and sit down, and wish for the top a hundred times before you reach it; and when you have actually gained the summit, your joy is unbounded that you have got over this hill of difficulty. The climate is as cold, I think, as Bangalore; some Europeans who have lived much here, maintain that it is scarcely inferior to the Neilgherries; and it is certainly a perfect contrast to that of the plains. Here and there, you behold a few cabins worse perhaps than those of Guntoor, and these form a village, and the people carry them hither and thither with as much ease apparently, as a company of gipsies do their tents in England. But the soil is very excellent and the views fine. The large orchards are beautiful, and produce immense quantities of fruit. One plantation of coffee is reckoned the best in the country. Oranges grow in abundance, and where patience and industry are shown, the hills richly repay the farmer and the landlord.

In 1820, the Cheveroi Mountains were highly recommended, and being so near to the presidency, many Europeans hurried away to take advantage of a region which seemed prepared for the restoration of health, and which formed such an agreeable asylum, from the rigour of the hot season. Many houses were built, and the climate promised well for a time; but the residents, escaped from the hot atmosphere of Madras, indulged in greater exposures, than prudence would sanction. The heavy dews which continue for hours in the morning, were rather courted, than shunned. Fevers began to rage and to cut down the visitors, and regions which, with prudent care and management, might have been turned to account, were speedily deserted and denounced as the most fatal. The Europeans residing in the district were not so frightened by the panic, since they often dwell there, and find the air very cooling and invigorating.

The principal collector and magistrate of Salem, had long expressed a wish to have a missionary settled at the station. In the year 1827, the deputation visited the spot, and deeming it a very appropriate field, recommended to the district committee that, it should, if possible, be occupied; and Mr. Henry Crisp became the first missionary to the Baramhal. No one could be more devoted, more zealous in the cause of his master, more indefatigable in the attainment of the language, and more laborious in exertion to advance the interests of the heathen. Assisted by Isaac David—a bold, energetic, and zealous native preacher from Bangalore—he spared no pains to diffuse the savour of the Redeemer's name in every place. Very soon, the dark cloud began to lower upon his path; death entered his dwelling, and removed his partner into the invisible world; and he was left to mourn. But these afflictions, while they no doubt wounded his tender spirit, seemed to render him more assiduous and more diligent in his sacred calling. He laboured while it was yet day, fully persuaded that the night cometh when no man can work. A chapel was erected in a position as well adapted for arresting the attention of the traveller, as for meeting the wants of Christian worshippers. By his visit to the villages, by his conversations, and by his public addresses to the heathen, he made a deep impression in favour of the truth; he had the honour of baptizing some to whom the gospel had become the power of God unto salvation; and I cannot now but express my fears that he fell an early victim to his zeal and his anxieties in this sacred cause. His sun went down while it was yet day; but in its setting, it threw a radiance around, that cheered and delighted all who knew him. At the request of the district committee, I visited the mission in 1832, and as we approached the station, it was delightful to hear from the natives such a pleasing testimony borne to the diligence and to the faithfulness of our departed friend. While at Salem, I had the pleasure of baptizing one who had long been an inquirer under his ministry. He lies by the side of his beloved and excellent wife, and I could not help shedding the tears of sorrow over their early tomb.

In the beginning of 1832, Mr. Walton removed from Bellary, and took charge of the station; in the latter end of the same year, he was ordained at Bangalore, and returned to Salem to carry on his labours.

The mission which, under his predecessor, gave

so much promise, has continued to prosper. In 1834, the schools were nine in number, and contained three hundred and fifty-one scholars. As they are conducted on Christian principles, large measures of Divine knowledge are communicated to the children; the lessons which are learned at school are, in some instances, carried to their friends and relatives at home, and excite, among some, considerable fear and alarm, and lead others to inquiry and consideration. One promising boy was removed from the school, because he had argued with his parents that their heathen Gooroos were blind guides, and Jesus Christ was the true one. Another interesting youth threw down the idol which they had in their field, in order to convince his mother and his grandfather that the gods which they were worshipping could do them no harm. His relations became alarmed, and were afraid that some heavy calamity would befal him from the anger of the idol; but the boy urged them not to be uneasy, as nothing of a disastrous nature would happen to him; and as this turned out to be true, it has shaken the confidence which they had in gods of their own making. Though this boy is taken from school, he often comes to see the missionary and receives books which he attentively reads.

Similar effects are produced upon some of the schoolmasters. In 1834, there died a master who was a Mahommedan, and who during the last two years of his life, had been regarded as a serious inquirer. "As soon," says Mr. Walton, "as his death was made known, I went, and found near the pillow on which he had reclined his head, the Gospel of Mark, and the Book of Psalms, a portion of which he had read, a little before he was summoned into the presence of the Judge of all." On the mind of another Mahommedan schoolmaster, impressions seem to have been made; he is seriously inquiring and is in the habit of privately studying the Scriptures. His daughter was lately attacked with a dangerous illness, and having no hopes of her recovery, he came to the missionary and said, "The only hope I have is in the Lord Jesus Christ; He who by one word cured so many diseases and wrought so many wonderful miracles, can heal my daughter. Pray for her that she may be restored to health." To hear one of the followers of the false prophet entreat the prayers of the people of God on behalf of his afflicted child, and that too with an earnestness and solemnity which were truly pleasing; to behold him suffering much opposition and obloquy in consequence of his attachment to Christianity, has animated and encouraged the missionary greatly in his work. Such instances are calculated to show that the good seed of the word is taking root in the minds of the heathen; there may be hundreds more of such cases which are now unknown, and which may remain a secret, till the judgment-day will disclose them; and as there were seven thousand in Israel who, unknown to the prophet, had not bowed the knee to the image of Baal; so it is possible, that, unknown to many missionaries, there may be numbers who no longer serve the gods of their ancestors, but who worship the God of Israel.

Within a few miles of Salem, in every direction, there are many spots where weekly markets are held, and where the people assemble in thousands to carry on their commerce. Mr. Walton and the native teachers have made it their business to attend at such places and disseminate, among the crowds, the knowledge of God. On such occasions, books have been distributed to those who are able to read; long discussions have been carried on; many inquirers have sought after the new religion; and not a few have acknowledged that they have come to the market as much to hear about the new way, as to attend to their worldly interests. As I know that great good has often resulted from such visits, I am disposed to advocate the attendance of missionaries at such scenes, more than at their public festivals. At the latter, the people are mad upon their idols; the guilty passions of their nature are brought into violent exercise; the sight of the idols—the procession of the cars—the influence of the Bramins—the crowds exciting each other to frenzy—and all the abominable ceremonies which are celebrated both in public and private, disqualify the people for giving any thing like serious attention to the truth; and though the missionary, it is true, bears his testimony against their idolatry, it is a time when all their prejudices are most violent, and when there is not only the least hope of doing them good, but a danger of exciting within them passions which will be called up on other occasions when we might do them service. At the former, they are set upon their trade and upon their avarice, it is true; but they are better prepared, than at the festival, to listen to the truth; they are looking for novelty and for something to interest, as well as for gain; many attend who have no object whatever in view, and are pleased with listening to a European preaching in their language; and when they carry to their homes the books which, in their spite, they might have torn to pieces at the festival, there is some hope that they will be read, and do them some good.

The native church is composed of thirty-two members whose walk and conversation afford comfort to the missionary. The congregation which may be denominated Christian amounts, on an average, to one hundred and fifty persons. A Christian village has been established, and affords protection, and good neighbourhood to sixteen families who might otherwise be obliged to live among the heathen, and suffer much from their society and their example. Schools have been established at some of the adjacent towns, and constitute a district for visitation and for exertion. The native teachers advance steadily in their work and give promise of further usefulness, and animated by the example of the missionary, often journey and labour to diffuse, through the province, the name of Christ. In reference to one of these tours, Mr. Walton says, "After preaching and distributing tracts, we returned to the choultry, when a respectable merchant entreated us with great importunity to come to his house, offered to provide us with refreshment and lights, and to invite his friends to come and hear more about that Saviour Jesus Christ. We gladly accepted his invitation, and followed him to the house, where we found a large assembly collected, the lamps lit up, and mats and carpets spread for our accommodation. We were supplied with milk, and other refreshments, after which our host went into another room and brought out a copy of Luke's Gospel which he had received two years ago. 'The thing I want you to do is,' said he, 'to read and to explain to me this book, for I declare before all I have no faith in any of my gods!' We shortly became so intensely engaged, and the attention of our hearers was so riveted to the important subjects now offered for their serious consideration, that the midnight hour passed, and the first crowing of the cock informed us it was three o'clock in the morning, when the merchant's brother and the females of his house began to be alarmed lest their relative should forsake the religion of his forefathers and become a Christian.

They called out to him to dismiss the unwelcome visitors, and not to act so foolishly in condemning their gods and speaking in favour of a strange religion. 'What harm have I done,' said he, 'in speaking the truth? Christ's religion is the true religion, and if you wish to discard me, you are welcome to do so. I shall join the Christians for they are in the right way.' When we were about to leave the house, our host gave us a general invitation, whenever we came to Racheepooram, to lodge with him, and not to mind what the people do or say. 'I will no longer,' said he, 'be a slave to the wicked gods whom I have so long served.'"

COIMBATOOR

Is the capital of the province which has also received this designation. As it adjoins that of Salem, the climate in the plains is much the same as in that district. The Cavery and the Bhowannee are turned into numerous channels to fertilize the land. The earths are in many places impregnated with saline qualities. Large quantities of salt-petre are collected, and exported to foreign markets. The ore from which they make the best steel, is not only to be found in this and in the Salem district, but instead of having to dig for it, they gather it, in the greatest abundance, upon the face of the hills. Much of the soil is cultivated in garden-ground, and the capily* and the yata† are brought into active and diligent operation, since this kind of cultivation makes a small piece of ground so productive that it supports many persons, and yields a high rent to the landlord.

In this district, are the Neilgherry hills, and perhaps the reader may not deem me out of order in giving a passing description of them. After you have crossed the Cavery, in a round basket-boat, which is covered with leather; and have advanced into the district of Coimbatoor, the Neilgherries are seen in the distance; blue mountains, they, in reality, appear; and as you scale one elevation after another, you seem as far from their base as before. The Canarese language is met with at the bottom of the hills. As soon as you have crossed a small stream, two peons. armed with firelocks, announce themselves as a guard of honour to conduct gentle-

* The Capily is an apparatus used often for drawing water, and consists of a pulley fixed at the top of the well, a rope to which a large bucket is attached, and is worked by two oxen.

† This is another method of raising water in India. The well is circular; on one side of it a large upright post is planted in the ground, and in a mortise which is made at the top of the post, a very long pole is transversely fixed, and acts as a lever. One of the gardeners stands over the well, and holding a long pole which is fixed to the lever, sends down the bucket into the well, while another stands at the top of the lever, and steps backwards and forwards to assist his neighbour in raising or in lowering the bucket.

men through the thick jungle, five miles to the ascent. This part is infested with elephants. The old road is greatly worn and very steep; but the new one which is now completed, exceeds every thing that has been seen, and those who have made it, deserve well of the present generation and of posterity. It is almost impossible to describe the sensations that you feel in advancing to the summit, and in drawing near to Conoor; but the gentle zephyrs remind you of home, and are reviving beyond any thing that you have felt in India. In many parts of the road,the declivity is frightful; the chasm is sublime; and the dashing torrents roll like thunder, echoing through the range. At Conoor, we met with some of the aborigines who are styled Budugavaroo. They all spoke Canarese, and though it is not pure, but mixed with Tamul words which they have derived from some of the camp followers, it is evident that it is their original language. On reaching the top, a scene opens upon you the like of which you have not probably seen before; the hills are beautiful, circular in their form, undulating, and like so many waves rising in majesty upon each other in the days of storm, covered with verdure, and possessing a fine soil for cultivation, intersected with valleys through which runs the meandering stream, and in which the thick wood forms a recess for the wild dog, the bear and the tiger. To Ootacamund, the road is enchanting; all hill and dale; here and there, a lovely spot of cultivation; the air cold and invigorating; and the rural villages giving variety to the scene, till you reach the mountain of Dodabetta, and as you wind round his lofty summit, the cantonement bursts full upon your view; the Gothic church, stately mansions and pretty cottages adorning the brow of the hills, render the landscape picturesque and magnificent. It is impossible not to be pleased with this settlement. As you look at it upon all sides, it would be difficult for pen or pencil to do justice to the splendid scene. The waters of the lake sparkle below; on the left, the towering Dodabetta raises its head among the clouds; another and more distant range, bounds your prospect upon the right, and receive, like the western hills, the last rays of the setting sun; on every hand, are beautiful and undulating hills covered with verdure, and intersected with wood and stream; here the handsome dwelling, and there the rural cottage give beauty and variety to the view—all forming the lovely valley of Ootocamund. Take a ride over these charming grounds: the white strawberry and the blackberry grow in profusion at your feet; the swallows fly about the lake; the larks mount into the air, and make it resound with their enchanting music; you fancy that you breathe again the atmosphere of Europe; the daisy and many other English flowers yield their agreeable fragrance; and you could almost imagine that you are ranging among the wild heather on the mountains of Caledonia. On one side, you have an extensive view of the plains of Coimbatoor, and on the other, you look far down upon the Mysore dominions.

The Budugavaroo are the aborigines of these hills, and the Todavaroo are their priests. The latter live in seclusion. Infanticide, I am afraid, prevails among them, since every woman is allowed to have a plurality of husbands, reigns among them as a queen, and treats them almost as her slaves. While the plains around them abound with the insignia of heathenism, the inhabitants of the hills have neither idol, nor temple. The Todavaroo are graziers, and possess large herds of buffaloes, while the Budugavaroo are cultivators of the soil, and live by the labour of their hands. When the English made their appearance among them, they were, it is said, perfectly ignorant of the use of money; but Europeans were so generous that they gave them presents whenever they came to visit them, and they have become so avaricious that nothing is thought of now but "filthy lucre;" you cannot stop one of them upon the road to speak to him, but he is sure to make his salam, and ask for a present.

As the hills are so healthy and invigorating, it would be a very desirable object to have a Canarese mission established; to constitute it a sanatory station for our missions in southern India; to have a large house in which a family or two from the plains might be accommodated in case of ill health obliging them to remove from the stations, and that they might thus give a trial to the Neilgherries before undertaking a voyage to Europe. At present, supplies are obtained with great difficulty, and the charges to visitors are enormous, and do not differ materially from the expences of a voyage; but a resident family would be able to provide with greater economy, and could reduce the amount to all parties. As there is a considerable town, and the inhabitants are greatly on the increase, it might be rendered a most interesting sphere. From east to west, the length of the hills is about forty miles, and from north to south, their breadth varies from fifteen to twenty-five. Many of the plants resemble those of Europe, and the grounds and gardens abound with English fruits and vegetables. Their height is reckoned at 8,500 feet above the level of the sea, and the glass, in the months of December and January, often falls below the freezing point.

I have said that the plains around are full of idols, and one cannot but observe the difference which exists between the external aspect of the superstition in this district, and that in other parts of the country. As you approach the temples, you are struck with the number of horses and of other animals made of clay, burned in the furnace, and ranged in order, as the stud of the divinity. In the open court of the pagoda, there is a range of large figures of a similar kind on each side, forming a line through which the votary must pass in approaching to the seat of the idol, armed with clubs and spears and a variety of warlike implements, and bearing, many of them, evident marks of having been engaged in conflict. What is the meaning of all this military display? When a person is in affliction, or is under a calamity, or exposed to danger, he makes a vow to his idol that, should he interpose and rescue him, he will make him a present of a steed, or of a protector; and these guards of honour in front and these rows of horses behind, are the pledges of their sincerity and devotion. What a train of absurdities make up the system of heathenism!

The town of Coimbatoor is in the centre of the province. It contains about twenty thousand people, while the district numbers about a million. In the days of war, it was often the theatre of tumult, siege, capture, and devastation; in the days of peace, it is the mart of trade and commerce. Tobacco, cotton, both raw and spun, thread, cloth, sugar, capsicums, onions and other productions are among the articles which are exported, and which give employment and prosperity to the population.

The mission was established here in 1830, and Mr. Addis, after being ordained in Travancore, settled among the people. During the few years of its existence, it has received a very promising measure of success. At first, prejudices were strong; schools were established, but the parents removed their children before they could receive any thing like an education; the heathen, in some cases, disturbed the worship, and showed their enmity to the gospel; and many who seemed promising for a time, returned to their idolatry. But one obstacle has been surmounted after another, and the people begin to estimate the labours, and kindness and anxieties of the missionary.

In attempting to improve upon the native mode of education, Mr. Addis has introduced the British and Foreign System into the schools. Experience has taught him that it works well. It promotes the rapid improvement and good order of the scholars; it grounds them well in what they have attained, since they cannot pass into another class, until they have made good progress in the one which ranks before it; and it acts as a check to the deception and indolence of the schoolmasters, and impels the children onward by emulation, more than by coercion. The number of schools under this system were twelve, and contain between six and seven hundred children. They are, in reality, Christian schools, and the teachers seem to take an interest in their instruction and advancement. As cotton is extensively cultivated, the parents find it more to their worldly advantage to employ their daughters at an early age in spinning it, and obtaining something for their living, than in sending them to school; but as a female boarding-school has now been established, the girls will be supported, and will be able to learn more fully and more rapidly the doctrines of salvation.

In 1835, sixty-eight of the children belonged to Bible classes; seventy-five learned the Scripture lessons; fifty had made considerable progress in Tamul arithmetic and writing; and all have committed several Scripture catechisms to memory. "I am often," says Mr. Addis, "surprised at the attainments of the boys when I think of the number of holidays, and other difficulties which obstruct their progress; the amount of their Scripture knowledge, and their answers on difficult points often astonish me. The utility of our mission-schools, and their superiority to those of the heathen, appear to be very extensively appreciated, and prejudice to them is now very rarely found. The schoolmasters and Bible classes also, now allow me to offer up a prayer to God for his blessing previous to our customary reading of the Scriptures together, and our holding our weekly catechetical service; which, when contrasted with their former strong prejudice, is a subject of much pleasure."

Among the children was an interesting girl about nine years of age who had given encouragement in this department. She loved and practised secret prayer, and evinced a desire to walk strictly according to Christian rule, and exhorted others so to do. She would often be found reading Christian books to her aged heathen grandmother, and simply explaining them, and sometimes she prevailed upon the old woman to join her in prayer. Surely this instance ought to stimulate exertions among the young. No system of education can be more wretched, than that which prevails in India. Every plan should be adopted, that the prejudices of the people will admit of, to improve it; public examinations before the Europeans of the station, must have a very stimulating effect both upon parents and upon children; the substitution of the Scriptures, of Christian lessons and of catechisms for heathen fables, must be a triumph which every exertion should be made to obtain; and in proportion as such systems will prevail, we may expect that the rising generation will be wiser and better than their fathers. If such a system does not convert them, it will prepare them to appreciate the truth and to receive it. But while I am a great advocate for extensive and universal education, it will not be made so subservient to our cause as it ought to become, except we are able to bring home the truth to the consciences of the children, to take them aside occasionally and speak to them freely and unreservedly upon their eternal interests; and the only objection which I can see to schools being so large and so numerous, is that the whole time is obliged to be spent in the mechanical department, instead of devoting a portion of it to higher objects. To impress the mind, and to convert a soul; what important concerns are these!

Another plan which Mr. Addis has adopted, and which promises to be useful, is the establishment, in the centre of the town, of a reading-room where he converses with enquirers, gives away tracts and Scriptures, and enters into discussions with the more bold and superstitious. As it would be incompatible with the health, comfort, and even life of a missionary to dwell in the midst of a native town, the mission-houses are usually situated in the neighbourhood; and such a plan as this must give greater publicity to his object, and must facilitate his intercourse with strangers. Such a place was once opened at Bangalore, and excited great interest. A large board was prepared; suitable passages of Scripture in the native language, written upon paper, were pasted upon it; and it was hung up in the verandah of the shop to arrest the attention of spectators. At first, numbers of the people continued to read them; but after two or three days, a great sensation was produced. Heathens and Mahommedans and Catholics became much irritated. An individual posted a paper on the other side of the Bazar, containing much abusive language, and calling upon the Cutwall to examine this board, and put an end to these mischievous attempts to insult his gods. Two peons were sent from the Police-office to apprehend the accused, and bring it, as a delinquent, to trial and to justice; but strict as the examination was, nothing could be proved against it. It was remanded to prison for the night, where about forty persons had the opportunity of learning its message. Next day, it was again brought into court, and was examined before many learned natives; its innocence was substantiated; it was set at liberty, and was restored again to its public station.

Every plan that can excite attention, that will rouse the apathy and dulness of the natives, and that will lead the ignorant to inquire after the truth, ought to be adopted, and committed to the blessing of Him whose servants we are. "Several instances have occurred," remarks Mr Addis, "of people from remote distances, coming to seek for books, for instruction, &c., and on one occasion very lately, seven respectable men in authority from distant talooks applied for Scriptures and tracts, who had seen some in the hands of others; but it appears they were so valued by their owners that they would not give them even for perusal, and referred the visitors to the mission-house to seek copies for themselves. On their application, I gave them a moderate supply which they thankfully received, wrapped them carefully in cloths and carried them away with such apparent joy, as would have gladdened the hearts of those who contribute of their worldly substance for such purposes."

Two native teachers who accompanied Mr. Addis to Coimbatoor soon left him, and returned to their own country. But the missionary has been diligent in preparing others to assist him, and can now speak of twelve who are anxious to spread the knowledge of the truth. They take long journeys to distribute the bread of life, and often receive encouragement and assistance in their work. Among the thirteen members of whom the church is composed, it may be well to select a few instances of their experience. In the month of March 1832, Mr. Addis baptized the first heathen who, at that station, abandoned his idolatry. After a probation of eight months, the missionary was fully persuaded that the man had indeed been taught by the Holy Spirit, and was become, in all respects, "a new creature." Very desirous to make a public profession of his faith, he boldly did so before a large assembly and before several of his relations, and much to the pleasure and encouragement of the missionary. He soon became as zealous a Christian, as he had hitherto been a heathen. His wife and son were induced regularly to attend with him on the means of grace, and some of his opposers ceased to molest him; nay, several of them, through his forbearance and Christian deportment, were led to attend family prayer at his house. In 1834, a government peon who had been, for some time, under instruction, and was regular in his attendance at the ordinances, was called to endure, from an aged father and other heathen relatives, a great fight of afflictions, on account of his attachment to Christ; but he was enabled to witness a good confession, before them all, and endeavoured, to the extent of his ability, to make known to others the precious Saviour whom he had found. After a service of eight years in the employment of the government, he gave up his appointment, to serve the mission and the cause of Christ at a considerable pecuniary loss to himself.

Such instances are cheering in this infant mission. May these only be the first-fruits of an abundant harvest! The foundation seems to be laid; the mission is shortly to be strengthened by a European coadjutor; and should the schools be well superintended, and means adopted to impress the minds of the children; and should the native teachers—well educated, and carefully superintended in their labours—prove themselves workmen that will not need to be ashamed, we may look for a growing and a gracious work in the province of Coimbatoor.

CHITTOOR

Is situate at the bottom of the eastern Ghauts, and on one of the principal roads leading from Madras to Bangalore. The climate is very warm, as it suffers from the hot winds of the Carnatic, and is surrounded with small hills whose reflected heat is very great. If any thing could be a recompence for this inconvenience, it is the beauty of the surrounding country, the fruitfulness of the gardens, and the boldness of the scenery. In the distance, the Ghauts rise in grandeur and magnificence, and scatter the showers in heavy torrents over the province, and as Palmanair is only one night's run from

Chittoor, the residents often retreat, during the hot months, to that salubrious station, and live in greater comfort and enjoyment upon the hills.

Till the time that the Chittoor Pollams * fell, by treaty, into the hands of the British, they were under the authority of Pollegars, who rendered tribute to the Nabob of Arcot. But amidst the commotions into which the country was thrown, the chiefs became refractory and turbulent, and a military force was sent against them in 1804. Two of them surrendered at discretion; but the others were driven into the jungles, and their forts demolished. In 1805, fixed rents were allotted to the lands of each cultivator, tranquillity was restored, and the settlement greatly increased the revenue.

Chittoor is famous for its delicious mangoes † which are sent to all parts of the country. The gardens abound with plantains, guavas, cocoa-nuts, limes, oranges, pine-apples, and other eastern fruits. The European houses are large, elevated, airy, commodious, and well suited to the climate. As it is constituted a civil station where the collector, judges, and authorities reside, there is an excellent court-house, jails, and all necessary provisions for the administration of justice. The majority of those who are accustomed to hear the word of God,

* Small districts under the dominion of a chief called Pollegar.

† In 1824, the cholera was attributed to the eating of this fruit.

come from the distant districts to settle their law-suits, and to transact other public business; some are connected with the convicts in the jail, and many are the relatives of those who fill respectable offices under government. The population is comparatively small, and is composed of Mahommedans, Telloogoos, and Tamulians who act as merchants, farmers, and mechanics.

Among the judges who were at Chittoor, Mr. Dacre was a most pious, active, zealous, and persevering Christian. Not only did he direct his own countrymen to the Redeemer, but overflowing with pity and compassion to the heathen, he established schools for their children; a large room in his own house was consecrated to the use of native Christians as a sanctuary; he preached to the assemblies with great fervour of spirit, and lavished his fortune upon the support of institutions which had the good of the heathen in view. To the number of three or four hundred, the natives who made a profession of Christianity were collected under his auspices at Chittoor. His house was always open for Protestant missionaries when they passed that way, and during their residence, they were accustomed to examine candidates for baptism, to preach to the people, to catechize the children in the schools, and to baptize those who were deemed qualified to make a profession. Mr. Dacre had not only often expressed a wish that a missionary might be settled among them, and take the people under his care and management; but as there were many reasons to urge the claim, the London Missionary Society appointed Mr. Jennings to the station in 1827.

The missionaries who had paid occasional visits to Chittoor, had, of course, very few opportunities of becoming acquainted with the native Christians, and had to depend on the evidence of catechists and of others for the estimate which they formed of candidates for baptism and the Lord's Supper. A church was formed, consisting of seventy members, and the best hopes were entertained that they were holy and consistent characters. But Mr. Jennings soon found that many of them were deceivers, and were actuated by any motives but those of love to the Redeemer and his cause. Instead of sifting them, and trying to separate the chaff from the wheat, he thought it best to dissolve the church, and to form one, if possible, of different materials. Some have thought that this step was rash and precipitate, that, as a young missionary, who did not yet understand their language, and was but ill acquainted with the habits and customs of the people, he should have exercised more caution, and patience, before he resorted to such severe discipline. The professors were loud in their complaints, and whatever may be thought of the measure, it seemed, for a time, to defeat his usefulness.

Many of the customs which prevailed at the old stations in the south, had crept into the congregation. Great trouble arose from the existence of caste. To show to the multitude that whatever estimate others might put upon such distinctions, they were not to be found in his theology, Mr. Dacre invited a number of the poorer native brethren to his table to partake with him. But this plan, instead of allaying the disorder, rendered it worse. The parties grew in their pride and self-importance, invited Mr. Dacre to eat and drink in their houses in return, and because he would not sit down with them, they contended that *caste* had as much dominion over him, as over others.* In passing through Chittoor once, I was requested by the assistant missionary there to marry a couple in the afternoon. As the marriage parties did not come at the hour appointed, and I was engaged to dine with a gentleman at a specified time, I was obliged to leave before they made their appearance. We had just sat down to dinner, when a note arrived from Mr. Nimmo, stating that there was likely to be

* Mr. Dacre took one wrong step. Whether it was to show his abhorrence of caste, or with the hope of being more useful to the people, he married a native female. Divines talked of her being a Christian, and philosophers reasoned that colour could be no objection. But Mr. Dacre lived to regret the match which he made. His wife was neither a friend, nor companion to him. Highly polished in his manners, and very agreeable in his person, he was fitted to move in the highest circles of society, while the education, the customs, and the mental habits of his wife were entirely dissimilar to his own, and unfitted her for associating with Europeans. The union was formed unadvisedly; experience has shown that it was neither a happy, nor a useful one.

a cabal in the chapel, that the people had come, and were so incensed at the missionary having left before the marriage was performed, that he was afraid of their violence, and entreating me to come immediately. I had not been accustomed to such storms of passion, and thought that, as they had kept me waiting an hour for them, it was but right they should manifest more patience in waiting for me. After dinner, I went to the chapel, and found them assembled, and more composed; I rebuked them sharply for their inconsistent and unchristian conduct, and as I understood that they were in the habit of using heathen formalities at their weddings, I entreated them to abandon such customs, and to act as Christians ought to do among an idolatrous people. But it was of no use. On my return to the house of my friend, I passed them in my Palankeen, and they were marching in a procession with their music, as heathens are accustomed to do.

The existence of such evils among them at a period subsequent to the days of Mr. Jennings, shows that the old leaven was at work, and might justify the missionary in adopting the severe measures which he deemed it necessary to employ.

In the beginning of 1828, Mr. Dacre was removed into the invisible world, and ended a career of devotedness and benevolence which few are permitted to run. He died in peace. As the father and founder of the Chittoor mission, he deserves a place among the best friends to the heathen world. Such was his philanthropy, and such was the estimate in which he was held by the natives, that, on the evening of the day on which he died, there was such a burst of weeping and wailing and almost of despair, as were enough to melt the stoutest heart. Their friend and protector was gone, and the natives were inconsolable.

After the decease of Mr. Dacre, Mr. Jennings continued to struggle with the evils which existed in the mission, and some progress was made in reducing the confused elements to some order. A large piece of ground, and a Bungalow which had been erected on it, were granted, by Judge Waters, as mission premises; more than two thousand rupees were collected for the erection of a chapel; and a very neat and commodious sanctuary was built and opened for native service in the beginning of 1831. The schools were five in number; the progress of the children was good; and a scriptural system of education was pursued with success. At the native services, the attendance was increasing, and some gave evidence that they were, in reality, the children of God. But it would have required a veteran to have coped with the difficulties, instead of a young and inexperienced missionary. Possessed of a very delicate mind, and a weak constitution of body; subject to depression in a debilitating climate; thrown upon the troubled waters of strife, while his piety, his talents, and his persuasive address would have rendered him a popular preacher at home, Mr. Jennings was ill calculated to sustain the shock which he had already received, and to contend with the evils which gathered round him. He had applied to the directors in England for permission to remove from a sphere where his spirit had been wounded and where his missionary prospects were still so gloomy, and that request had been most readily and affectionately complied with. A pressing invitation had been sent more than once from Bangalore, entreating him to resort to its more salubrious climate, and arrangements were making either to go there, or to the south. But it was too late. The seeds of disease had long been sown in his delicate frame; the liver was disordered; and admidst the lamentations of relatives and friends and the sorrows of the church, he sank into an early grave. I have paid a visit to his tomb. On a black marble slab which the hands of affection and friendship raised to his memory, there is engraven the following epitaph:—

Sacred

TO THE MEMORY OF

THE REV. ROBERT JENNINGS,

MISSIONARY TO CHITTOOR,

FROM THE LONDON MISSIONARY SOCIETY,

WHO DEPARTED THIS LIFE

JUNE 1, 1831, AGED 34 YEARS.

THIS MONUMENT IS ERECTED BY THE EUROPEAN SOCIETY AT CHITTOOR AMONG WHOM HE LABOURED.

HIS PIETY, WORTH AND TALENTS, NEED NO MEMORIAL TO IMMEDIATE SURVIVORS. BUT THE COMING AGE MAY REGARD WITH INTEREST THE GRAVE OF ONE OF THE EARLIER EVANGELISTS IN THIS AT PRESENT HEATHEN LAND.

Affection would detain me here to dwell upon the virtues of my departed friend. While goodness, natural gifts, personal address, and great eloquence would have rendered him an ornament to the ministry at home, he preferred the missionary work, and consecrated all to the service of the heathen. His race was very short. But many remember his prayers, his exertions and his conversations with satisfaction and delight.* A widow and an only child were left to mourn his loss.

As we passed through Chittoor in the end of 1831, the mission was under the care of Mr. Nimmo, an assistant missionary from Madras, and was, on the whole, well managed, and in a promising state. The congregation was large and attentive; the singing, to instruct them in which Mr. Jennings had taken great pains, was delightful and was conducted

* Among these persons, was the Rajah of Punganore. He was as good a specimen as I have met with of a Hindoo gentleman. In passing his bungalow one evening where he had been entertaining some of his friends from Chittoor, the author, Mrs. Campbell and their little son received a very kind and pressing invitation from the Rajah to stay and take tea with him. He was smoking his hooka which perfumed the room. His dress was half European, but the tea-table was spread in oriental style. The reception which he gave to his guests, was most hospitable, and his album in which the author wrote, bore ample testimony to his kindness and liberality. He was greatly delighted in conversing in Canarese; took our son upon his knee, and loaded him with sweetmeats at our departure. Mr. and Mrs. Jennings spent some time at the Rajah's palace. Let us hope that their social intercourse was useful to him, and that their prayers were heard in heaven on his behalf.

entirely by the natives; and Mr. Nimmo preached with great zeal, unction and simplicity. We were very much pleased with the manner in which our Sabbath was spent.

On my next visit in December 1835, Mr. Bilderbeck had taken the superintendence of the station, and since that period, it has remained under his control. After the measures that were adopted by Mr. Jennings, and the discipline which has been maintained by his successors, to purge and to purify the Christian professors at Chittoor, it is pleasing to know that so many families still remain at the station, and are now improved in their character, deportment, and circumstances. The changes which they have undergone are striking to those who know what they were in former days. Though real religion is dormant, and very little spirituality is to be seen, yet there are many evidences of improvement. Once, it seemed as though mendicity was the only plan by which they obtained their livelihood; now they labour with their own hands, and provide for their own households. Once, the missionary was daily called upon to settle their quarrels and disputes; now, they settle them among themselves, or learn to forgive those who offend them. Once, they could scarcely be brought to the sanctuary upon the sabbath, though they were visited on Saturday to secure their attendance, and again on Monday to know the reason of their absence; now, they come voluntarily to the house of God, and in greater numbers, though these visits are discontinued. Once, there were none who could express themselves with propriety in prayer, and none who were either inclined or qualified to join in the communion; now there are a few who can pray with fervour, unction and freedom, and some who meet around the table to celebrate the death of their Lord.

Among the godly few, there was a female named Martha—who, since the formation of the mission, had conducted herself with the greatest credit to her profession, and with entire satisfaction to all the missionaries. During 1836, she was called away from the church on earth, to the church in heaven. I saw her on her bed of languishing as I passed through Chittoor on my way to Madras. Like a light in a dark place, Martha's piety and Christian conduct shone forth amidst a crooked and a perverse generation. The constancy of her faith, the meekness of her temper, the ardour of her love, and the consistency of her deportment formed a striking contrast to the general darkness, apathy and worldly-mindedness of other professors, and her firmness and Christian conduct were often the means of cheering the missionary amidst trials and mental depression. Her illness was not long, but her agonies were excruciating. Nevertheless, her patience, her resignation to the Divine will, and the strength of her faith seemed to grow as her sufferings increased; while her spirituality of mind, and her preparation for heaven, made it manifest that the hour of her departure was at hand. In her case, tribulation worked patience, and patience experience, and experience hope—a hope that made her not ashamed, and which brightened as she drew nearer to the confines of eternity. At the age of sixty-five, she was gathered, like a shock of corn fully ripe, to the blessed, and finished her course with joy. Her property which consisted of two small houses, and some jewels which she had never worn, since she became a Christian, she bequeathed as a thank-offering to that society from which she had received so many benefits. "Blessed are the dead who die in the Lord!"

As Chittoor is but a small town when compared with many around it, Mr. Bilderbeck determined to visit the large ones, and if possible, establish branches of the mission in them all. He could not but mourn over the thousands who, in Palamanair, Arcot, Arnee, Wallajapettah and Vellore, were perishing in their heathenism. After a visit to view the ground, and witness the condition of the people, he determined on a course of operations. He obtained native teachers, established them in the towns and superintended their exertions. As a city containing a large and respectable population; as a position more central for the head-quarters of the mission, and whence the truth would be likely to find its way to Nellore, Masulipatam, and Hydrabad; as a station more adjacent to the famous Conjeveram, Cholinger and Old Arcot, and from whence, the out-stations of the society, might be well overlooked, Wallajapettah has been esteemed, by Mr. Bilderbeck, as admirably located, and as affording the greatest facilities to carry on the work. A spot of ground most advantageously situated, and near the gate of Wallajapettah, has been procured by the kindness of the collector; the plan and estimate of suitable buildings, consisting of a mission-house, a place of worship, a school-room, and a dwelling for a teacher with all necessary out-houses, was prepared by an officer of the engineers; a sum of money adequate to cover all the expenses has been received from a valued and a generous friend; and the workmen are proceeding as fast, as circumstances will admit, with the erection. Most likely Mr. Bilderbeck will take up his residence at this town, while Mr. Leach who has just sailed for Madras, will be located at Chittoor. A line of stations may thus be established which may be well superintended, and which will connect the Carnatic with the Mysore and with Madras. This is the right plan of consolidating missions. It is not necessary that all the European missionaries be congregated together in one town; but that they should be so near as to co-operate with one another, and that in case of necessity they should be able to render assistance, and that one part of the plan of operations, should render all due and necessary support to the other, till the whole of the fortifications are completed, till the breach is made, and till a bold and simultaneous attack can be carried on against the bulwarks of the enemy.

CHAPTER XVII.

THE TELLOOGOO MISSIONS.

TELLOOGOO COUNTRIES—MULTITUDE OF THE PEOPLE—SPIRITUAL CONDITION—PAST NEGLECT—CLAIMS OF TELINGANA—ARGUMENTS TO EFFORT—VIZAGAPATAM—CRAN AND DESGRANGES—A TELLOOGOO BRAMIN—DEATH OF MR. CRAN—DEATH OF DESGRANGES—LABOURS OF THE BRETHREN—DHERNA—A PAGAN PRIEST—SHOCKING MURDER—TRANSLATION—DEATH OF MR. DAWSON—POOROOSHOODUM—MISSION RENEWED.

THE Telloogoo language is reckoned the Italian of the East. Such is its beauty, its sweetness and fulness, that it has stamped peculiar interest upon the people and the country where it prevails. It is spoken in the northern circars, and in many neighbouring provinces, embracing that immense range of country which stretches along the Bay of Bengal, almost from Madras to Orissa; in the ancient kingdom of Andhra, as well as in Ganjam and in Hydrabad. Deducting a million of Mahommedans who may be found scattered over its provinces, the Telloogoo is the vernacular language of nine millions of Hindoos, and prevails over an area of 200,000 square miles.

This extensive dominion is divided into the

collectorates of Ganjam, Chicacole, Rajamundry, Masulipatam, Guntoor, Cuddapah, the Northern Carnatic, and Hydrabad. It is watered by the Crishna, the Godavery, and other inferior streams, and has been, in former times, a granary to the Carnatic during the north-east monsoon, as Tanjore was reckoned in the south-west. Golchonda is renowned for its diamond mines; Rajamundry for its large teak forests which grow on the banks of the Godavery; Masulipatam for its calicoes and its palampores; Chicacole for its muslins, and Berhampore for its silks.

The Teloogoo people are a superior race of men, high in their caste, noble and independent in their bearing, and have often withstood the despotism of their oppressors with the sword. What is most remarkable about this intelligent race and their country, is that their spiritual interests have been almost entirely overlooked by the Christian world. With the exception of the missions to Vizagapatam, and to Cuddapah, no efforts have been made to emancipate this race from their spiritual thraldom. The brethren of the Church, of the Wesleyan, of the Baptist, and of the American societies have never gone to proclaim, in their sweet, and mellifluous language, the tidings of grace.

Nine millions of people, on the coast of Coromandel, perishing in their heathenism! who will account for this strange neglect? If their country was situate in the wilds of Tartary, or near the mountain of Thibet where few Europeans have travelled, and where war and anarchy are still liable to prevail, our amazement would not be justified; but the territories are our own; the ships to and from Bengal pass along their coast; their ports are open to our commerce; and they contribute to the wealth of England. But perhaps the provinces, it may be said, are not so well prepared to receive the truth; perhaps the tokens of divine Providence are less obvious, and the opportunities to carry on the work are less numerous, than in other parts. Why, since 1802, the most of these districts have been under British rule and protection; our own countrymen are the judges, the magistrates and the collectors to manage their civil and political affairs; and all the large towns and villages present to the benevolent mind, as many advantages as any new field of labour could enjoy. But the path, it may be objected, is comparatively untrodden, and the country untried; the missions which have already been established, have not been crowned with that eminent success which would encourage others; and the facilities to labour are very inferior when compared with other spheres. What! Is it not a greater honour, then, to cultivate a field upon which others have bestowed no labour? Have not Cuddapah and Vizagapatam met with as much success, as we could expect from the money and labour bestowed upon them? Have not tracts and other works in divinity been published, and the Scriptures been translated and printed in the language, and are now waiting for labourers to distribute them among the people?

Ah! the truth is, no one has taken the trouble to describe the miseries and the destitution of this interesting race; no man of Andhra, nor of Telingana has been seen in our churches, and at our mission boards, crying "Come over and help us;" every one of the dear brethren who led the van, and who prayed and wept and toiled in this field, repose in the silence of the tomb, and they can no longer lift up their voice to invite the Christian soldier to battle and to victory. But though no advocate should appear to plead her cause; though the world should visit her only to drain her of her riches, and to grant her no adequate favours in return; and though the church should not feel for her miseries, and should send no ambassadors to direct her children to glory and to heaven; yet the country of the Andhras is consecrated ground; the dust of a Cran, and Desgranges, of a Pritchet, a Gordon and a Dawson, is precious in the sight of the Lord; the tears which they shed, the prayers which they offered, and the labours in which they toiled will not be forgotten, but will come into remembrance before him; and Telingana will yet become as renowned for her Christianity, as she is for her classical associations, and for the beauty and grandeur of her scenery.

If I had a voice that would reach the humane and benevolent in Christian lands; that would be listened to in the palaces of the great and in the hamlets of the poor; that would arouse the efforts of those great societies which have the best interests of the heathen world at heart; with what language would I advocate her cause? I would describe her beautiful hills and dales as reverberating—not with the song of praise and thanksgiving—not with the voice of joy and comfort and salvation—but with the clangour of arms to rob her of her liberty, with the shouts that accompany idolatrous feasts, and sanguinary rites to render them palatable, and with the wailings of the infant, the widow, and the oppressed who are slain to propitiate their monstrous deities. I would tell them of plains and provinces—not trodden by those feet which are beautiful upon the mountains,—not replenished with harvests of glory and honour to the Lord our God,—but watered with the blood of the slain, laid waste by the famine, the plague, the pestilence and the sword; and swept, time after time, as with the besom of destruction, till their sepulchres were too small for the number of their dead, and till their rivers became putrid with the carcases of the multitude. I would remind them of towns, villages and dwellings where grief and sorrow are without a comforter, where slavery reigns without an indignant voice lifted up against it, where a worse than an Egyptian darkness rests upon the minds and the prospects of the people, and where the poor perish without a vision and without a hope. No. It would perhaps be better to bury all these temporal plagues and calamities in oblivion. It would perhaps be better to lift up the veil that conceals the past from our view, and point to the many generations who have fallen in the wilderness, and have never been permitted to enter into a Canaan of rest. It would perhaps be better to look into the invisible world, and behold their rich, and their famous, and their mighty men lifting up their eyes in torments, calling for a drop of water to cool their tongues, and entreating an Abraham to send a Lazarus, to their father's house, to warn their brethren lest they also should come into their place of torment. It would perhaps be better to spread their state of destitution before the Lord, to lay their cries, their tears, their sorrows and their miseries upon his altar, to plead fervently with him to pity, and to send them deliverance; and since devils triumph in their captivity, and men disregard their delusions and their crimes, and Christians will not help them in their time of need,—to call upon him to plead their cause, and interpose to grant them salvation.

VIZAGAPATAM

Is a large town of the northern Circars. Situate upon the sea-coast, it is reckoned a healthy, dry and invigorating climate. The mission was established in 1805. Whatever might be the motives by which the Indian government were actuated, they permitted the brethren to settle here, and to carry on their operations, at a distance from the seat of authority. Cran and Desgranges were the first missionaries. Very devoted to their work, they entered upon a new sphere of labour with great zeal and determination. Though they had studied Tamul for a time at Tranquebar, yet on their arrival at Vizagapatam, they saw it was useless to them, and, instead of devoting their time and attention to the few Tamulians whom they might find acting as servants to the Europeans, they gave themselves to the Telloogoo, with an industry and a zeal which soon surmounted every obstacle. One great inducement with them to settle in the Circars, was that they might not interfere with any missions already established. So important did their situation appear to them, that they soon earnestly entreated the directors to send missionaries to their assistance Besides that in the town where they resided, there were 20,000 inhabitants, perishing for lack of knowledge ; besides that, on every side, there were numbers of large towns and villages where thousands of the heathen lived in the grossest superstition, and claimed their pity and compassion, the station which they occupied was the most favourable for branching out into every part of the Circars. There was an abundance of room. Hundreds of miles to the right and the left, presented fields where many might labour with freedom, and where there would be no brethren to complain that they interfered with their mission. "Would to God," say the missionaries, "that all the ministers in our native land, the students at the different seminaries, and the religious public could see what we see, and hear what we hear! Then, every man bowing down to a stock or to a stone would prove a new argument to come over and help us. The horrid noise of thousands of idolaters at the celebration of their festivals, would sound like thunder in their ears, 'Haste, haste to the help of the Lord against the mighty.' And those who could not themselves come, would have the number and the ardour of their addresses to the throne of grace, increased a hundred fold."

In learning the language, and in the translation of the Scriptures, the brethren were greatly assisted by a Bramin who bore the evidence of genuine conversion, and of whom they entertained the highest opinion. He had served as an accountant in Tippoo's service, and after his death, was engaged in a similar employment by an English officer. Desirous of obtaining eternal happiness, he was advised by a senior Bramin to repeat a certain "muntrum" *four thousand times.* This task he not only undertook, but performed it with every laborious ceremony, and every rigorous penance which could render it meritorious. But deriving no comfort from such superstitious exertions, he resolved to return to his family and live as before. On his way home, he met with a Roman Catholic who gave him two Christian books which he perused, and which led him to further enquiries after this new religion. He was recommended to a Romish priest who required him to go home and return again with his wife. He obeyed the mandate; but his friends were exceedingly alarmed at his intention of becoming a Christian, and entreated him not to bring a reproach upon his *caste*. But whatever might be their arguments, they had no effect upon him; he declared that he preferred the salvation of his soul, to all worldly good, and as his wife would not accompany him, he left her behind. The priest still hesitated to receive him as a convert; but when he offered to give up his Braminical cord, and to cut off his long hair, and thus surrender his badges of caste, the priest instructed him, baptized him, and gave him the name of Anundarayer.

After this, he was sent by the priest to Pondicherry where he sustained many disappointments; but he had the pleasure of meeting with his wife who had suffered much from her relatives, and resolved at length to join her husband. Having heard that there were large congregations at Tranquebar; that there were masters and schools of another order; that the Scriptures were translated into Tamul and other books were published; that in the church, there were no images, against the use of which he had always protested among the Catholics, he proceeded to that station. At first, the missionaries at Tranquebar were suspicious of him; but after repeated conversations, and after a residence among them of some months they were satisfied of his sincerity, and admitted him to the table of the Lord. Very attentive to all their religious exercises, and diligent especially in the study of the Bible which, to him, was a book perfectly new, he began to make translations from the Tamul into the Telloogoo—his own native language, and one that he wrote with the greatest eloquence and propriety. As he preferred being engaged in the service of the church to any secular employment, he was recommended to the brethren at Vizagapatam, and was engaged by them as a teacher, and as an assistant in the translation of the Scriptures. One gentleman wrote of him, "Whatever the Lord requires of his followers, he has really performed. He has left wife, mother, brother, sister, his estate, and other advantages that were offered him, and has taken upon him all the reproaches to which a Bramin must submit in losing his *caste*, and has been beaten by some of the heathen to whom he has declared Christianity. Still he bears the marks of their violence upon his forehead; but he has declined complaining of it, and bore it patiently."

Shortly after his arrival at Vizagapatam, he went, for three months, on a missionary tour, to the southward, and preached, during that time, to great numbers who heard him gladly. About three months after, his wife was baptized, and joined to the number of believers. "I am happy," writes one of the brethren, "to say that she increases in divine knowledge, and that her conversation is as becometh the gospel. In short, she is an ornament to her profession, and is under the daily tuition of Mrs. Desgranges." These were very cheering and encouraging circumstances; the hearts of the brethren seemed full of joy and praise. But a dark cloud gathered over the mission and their delight was soon turned into sadness. Mr. Cran had gained a considerable knowledge of the language, and was entering upon a career of usefulness, when death removed him into the world of spirits. This mournful event was a heavy stroke to the mission and a severe affliction to those members of it who were left behind. In deep distress, and worn down with disease, he undertook a missionary tour for change of air, and with the hope of being useful. Travelling among the heathen, holding forth Christ to their view, and bearing a good testimony to the power of the gospel, he died in his work, and from labours upon earth, he entered into the rest of heaven. Who can read the following extracts from his letters without painful emotions?

"CHITTERPORE, December 17, 1808.

"I hope you will assist me to adore the God of all grace for recovering me so far, when I assure you that in leaving Chicacole, I did not expect to reach this place. I even expected to die, before

I got to the encampment God orders all things, and to him be all praise! I have had much conversation with the natives; at least once or twice every day; and sometimes with considerable numbers of both sexes. In short, I have spent many pleasant hours with them, and found many of them desirous to hear more of the gospel. Travelling among the natives, and proclaiming the good news of salvation is certainly delightful work!"

"CHITTERPORE, December 21, 1808.

"You will be happy to hear that my health is much improved. We are not destitute of friends even in this remote corner; and I am heartily glad that I undertook the trip, on many accounts; but you must visit this place and the surrounding country. I wish the brethren—(alluding to Gordon and Lee)—were arrived that we might have an opportunity of travelling among the natives."

Such were the last letters that he addressed to Mr. Desgranges. Sixteen days after this, he died in the Lord, and was committed to the dust at Chicacole. His character, his zeal, his devotedness, his experience and his labours, reflected the highest credit upon the gospel and upon the work in which he was engaged. His decease was sensibly felt, and caused the deepest sorrow among the little band at Vizagapatam. Had health and time and complicated labours permitted, his surviving colleague intended to have drawn up a memoir of his departed friend. But one trouble rapidly followed another, and the last enemy speedily renewed his attack upon the infant establishment.

As Mr. Desgranges was now left alone, he was in labours more abundant. There were sources of joy and comfort; but his mind was much distressed with the darkness and idolatry around him. In addition to a feeling mind, to a heart that bled over the guilt and woes of others, and to a conscience that was alive to all the responsibilities of his sacred office and his important trust, his liver was sadly affected, and tended to give a gloomy and melancholy tinge to the moral scenery with which he was surrounded. The brethren Gordon and Lee just arrived in time to witness his last efforts for the perishing heathen, to see how he travailed as in birth again till Christ was formed in their hearts the hope of glory, and to testify how he wept, and prayed and laboured in the service of his master. He died on the 12th of July 1810. Mr. Gordon was so ill that he was forbidden to attend him. Mrs. Desgranges was lying seriously ill in an adjoining chamber, and a few hours before his death, she was obliged to be carried through his room, to another house. As she was passing, he bade a final adieu to her, and to his children—and such a parting scene has seldom been witnessed in a heathen land! The concerns of the mission were much upon his mind; more especially the translation of the Scriptures, "But," said he, "the Lord can carry that on without me; so that my life is not necessary on that account." Poor Anundarayer was much affected. He burst into tears, and pressing the hands of his dying father to his lips, he kissed them and asked if his mind was fixed on Christ. The dying missionary replied in the affirmative. "Will you pray to Jesus," said the teacher, "to give us his blessing?" Mr. Desgranges then put his hands on the Bramin's head and prayed for some time. Many natives surrounded his bed and wept; they were all constrained to say "He was a good man."

Such was the end of Mr. Desgranges' short, but useful and brilliant career. As long as he lived, he determined to know nothing among men, save Jesus Christ and him crucified. His soul longed for the conversion of the heathen by whom he was surrounded. To learn their language, his exertions were most indefatigable, and to convert them to God, he reasoned with the Bramins, collected the villagers, and addressed them often on the great doctrines of salvation. Not only did he labour with the greatest zeal and assiduity to translate the Scriptures, but he used the most strenuous efforts to disperse copies of the Gospel through the country. In the course of translation, he had just finished the Gospel of Luke, when he was obliged to abandon the good work in which his whole soul was engaged. He lived to see a church formed at the station, and about three months before his death, he administered the ordinance, with great solemnity, to the few members who assembled together.

Mr. Gordon and Mr. Lee, joined by Mr. Pritchet, carried on the work which had thus been commenced. Mr. Lee, afterwards, tried to establish a mission at Ganjam; but ill health, and affliction in his family, obliged him to abandon his post and to return to his native country, and the station has never since been occupied. The Brethren—Gordon and Pritchet—both gave themselves to the study of the language, and to the work from which their devoted predecessor had been removed. They established schools for the young; they preached to the English and other residents; and they often accompanied the teachers to the villages to publish salvation, and to distribute the messengers of grace. In these excursions of benevolence, their minds were often deeply affected with the cruelties of heathenism, and, at the very period when some in England were violently contending that the system was a mild, and genial, and harmless superstition, they received awful demonstration that it was one of the most cruel and barbarous that Satan ever succeeded in establishing upon earth.

Amongst the customs of the Hindoos, there is one which is called "Dherna." If a man demands satisfaction from his neighbour for some grievous offence; if a creditor determines to pursue extreme measures with his debtor to obtain what is due to him; if a relative has been cheated by another out of his patrimony or his rights, and wishes to exact them from him; they respectively take the poignard or a cup of poison in their hand, and knowing that the offending party is at home, they sit down at his door in Dherna. That moment, the defendant within is considered as under arrest. He cannot touch food, so long as his accuser continues to fast; and should he not come to terms, but drive, by his obstinacy, the plaintiff to despair, and allow him to use the dagger, or drink the poison, his blood rests upon his head. This may be termed their *ordeal*—their mode of demanding satisfaction—their system of duelling—their *dernier resort*.

At the village of Pannabaka, there was a priestly Bramin who had lately come from Bellary, and had undertaken to attend upon the idol of the place. His was the privilege to levy contributions on the inhabitants for his support. A householder who had, for a time, given him a halfpenny a day, refused to continue his allowance; and though the priest insisted upon the payment, he remained inflexible. The priest then threatened that unless he received the amount, he would cut out his own tongue, and the householder would have to answer for giving him such a provocation. Incensed at the obstinacy of his opponent, he whetted his knife, and cut off the tip of his tongue. He bled profusely, and his tongue swelled to a prodigious size. The pains which he endured only served to render him more desperate, and he declared he would bring his whole family, and sit in dherna, till he should obtain a sum sufficient to make a feast to his god. The householder was not to be intimidated, and remained as obstinate as the Bramin. The priest, his wife, and his four sons sat down, and kept their position at the door of the defendant; but during the second night, the female was bit by a snake, and died in the morning. This event exasperated the priest; he increased his demand; and as the village had remained neutral in the affair, he now laid a tax upon all its inhabitants. As he had not only sustained a personal injury; but had lost his wife while standing up for the rights of his order, and for the honour of his god, nothing less would satisfy him now, than a sum adequate to meet the expenses of the funeral, and to make a feast to propitiate the deity who was offended by such daring sacrilege. Till these demands were met, he resolved to keep his station, and to retain the corpse of his wife unburied at the door of the house. As the people of the village rejected his claim, he then threatened that, in order to be avenged upon them, he would first kill his four children, and then put an end to his own existence. It was the act of a Bramin; it might be viewed by Hindoos as a pardonable offence; it was done in honour of his god; it was occasioned by the obstinacy of the people; it was a sacrifice that, according to a monstrous mythology, would meet with a future and a bountiful reward; its helpless victims were to be raised to life again by the divinity whose honour it was done to vindicate; but it is not ours to make apologies: we have only to record the fact, that this priest,—this worshipper of Sceva—this monster—this raging fury took his knife, laid hold of three of his children, and severed their heads from their bodies. It was not enough! His eldest son tried to make his escape; but this murderous father allured him back, and promised that, prior to his own self-destruction, he only wished to embrace him, and bid him farewell. Thus invited back by the soft whispers of love, he returned, but the moment that he came within the grasp of the murderer, he laid him prostrate as another victim at the shrine of superstition and revenge. His attempt to dispatch himself, ended in making a dreadful wound in the back of his neck.

"On my arrival," writes Mr. Pritchet, "I went to the spot where the deed occurred, followed by the greater part of the inhabitants. It had been enclosed by the people, and covered over with branches of trees, and before the entrance was placed a heap of thorns. At my request, they removed the thorns, and I entered in, and beheld a spectacle truly horrible. The people had suffered the remains of the murdered to lie just as they found them, and here lay all exposed the skulls and hair and bones of the four children—the remains of the mother were covered over with the clothes she had on—the skulls and bones were quite bare, lying among the rings and beads and such like marks of superstition as they wore."

Such, it may be said, are only solitary instances. It would not be right to quote such deeds to bring opprobrium upon a whole people; any more than it would be just to appeal to the horrid murders in England, as a specimen of our own customs. But the cases are utterly dissimilar. The inhabitants of Pannabaka stood by, and saw the horrid deed performed; they seemed, afterwards, to be amused, and highly delighted at the bravery of the act; they expressed their resentment at one individual, and at the police-officer who called upon them to interfere to prevent it; and there can be no question that if this priest had been restored to his liberty, and his horrid altar again, they would have received him with enthusiasm, and revered him as a saint of superior sanctity. In a village some miles distant from the spot, the people no sooner heard of this murder, than they left their employment, and proceeded to Pannabaka with every demonstration of joy; and after a few days, they returned saying, "The children are not indeed restored to life; but why are they not? It is entirely owing to the inhabitants who have not made a feast which would cost 2000 rupees, to propitiate the favour of the god—a feast which the priest had declared to be necessary."

While they bore their testimony against such deeds of darkness, Mr. Gordon and Mr. Pritchet gave much of their time and attention to the translation of the Scriptures into Teloogoo. The New Testament translated by the latter has long been printed and circulated over the country; but the translation which was made by the former, of the Old Testament, has lain, for many years, in the rooms of the Madras Bible Society. Why? Is it because they are unwilling to publish it? No. Is it because it is not worthy the toil and trouble and expense which have been lavished upon it already? No. But because its author is no more; and because there are not agents whose piety and talents and attainments in the language would qualify them to revise it, and superintend the work in passing through the press. Such a state of things, will, I trust, soon find a remedy, and that a committee of revision, qualified to undertake the task, will be formed, and will not rest till the whole Bible is given to this neglected and interesting people.

Mr. Dawson—the last of the senior missionaries—died on the 14th of August, 1832. During the last years of his life, and those of Mr. Gordon, the brethren were much distressed at the want of success. Among the Europeans and among the Indo-Britons, prosperity had often attended their exertions, and the church had sometimes, in numbers and in piety, revived their drooping spirits. But among the heathen, their cry often was, "Lord, who hath believed our report? and to whom has the arm of the Lord been revealed?" Still "in the morning they sowed their seed, and in the evening they withheld not their hand, as they knew not which should prosper, this or that, or whether both should be alike good." They watered it often with their tears, and prayed fervently for the heavenly rain to render it fruitful. But they died without beholding the joy of harvest.

Scarcely, however, had Mr. Dawson been committed to the dust, when an event occurred which would have gladdened his heart. Religious tracts and portions of the Scriptures had been disseminated far and wide through the Circars. One of these tracts had fallen into the hands of a heathen, whose conversion I will now describe.

In Hindosthan, there is a class of men whose numbers are yearly increasing, and whose character and circumstances are of the most peculiar and interesting kind. Dissatisfied with their heathenism, they are enquirers after the truth. Nothing in the Vedas and the Shasters; nothing in the wisdom and instructions which their Gooroos can give; nothing in the sacrifices, the austerities, and the penances which the ascetics can perform; nothing in Mahommedanism and other false systems, can give them rest and peace. They ardently long to drink at the fountain of truth, and obtain emancipation from sin and delusion. Such a character was Poorooshudum. As a Hindoo, he was descended from respectable parents, and could boast of his high caste, and his attainments in learning In the days of his youth, he praised Vishnoo, and prostrated himself in religious adoration to the sun. But advanced to manhood, all the acts of his childhood were contemptible as religious observances. To obtain happiness and peace, he read the Ramayana, the Bagwuta, and other Pooranas; he visited Jugernaut, and many sacred temples of Hindoo superstition; he submitted to penances, and was obedient to priests who deceived him; he prostrated himself before vast numbers of Byragees, washed their feet, drank of the water in which they had bathed, placed the dust of their feet upon his head, and partook of their leavings as sacred food; he determined to become a Jogee himself, learned to contract his limbs, cultivated the acquaintance of devotees, composed hymns in honour of his spiritual guides, and used ablutions and practised austerities. But it was all vain. Nothing could give him peace, nor deliver him from the fear and apprehensions that haunted him.

While his mind was in this state, and he was seeking the satisfaction which Christianity alone can give, a heathen boy put a Teloogoo tract into his hand. Though at first, he could not understand it, he recurred to it again; he studied it; and saw plainly that his former ways were all a deception, that he was a guilty and a condemned transgressor, that his heathenism, and his books were all useless inventions, and that there was another and a better way to peace and to immortality. Two more tracts fell into his hands, and strengthened him in the belief of the Son of God, as the Saviour of men, and he longed to become acquainted with Europeans or with missionaries that they might instruct him in the truth.

In 1833, a tract was given him entitled "The True Way of Salvation." On reading this monitor, the perplexity of his mind was dispelled; his doubts were scattered to the winds; the true light shone upon his spirit; he found the pearl of great price, and it was better to him than thousands of gold and silver. A prayer which the tract contained, he committed to memory, and used it every day; and under the emotions of first love; what did this converted heathen do? He debated with his friends and relatives on the great concerns of eternity, and held forth Jesus Christ to their view; he despatched a representation of his ardent wishes to the missionaries at Berhampore; he continued to hold fast the truth amid the difficulties and obstacles which were thrown in his path; he travelled first to Vizagapatam where he found some Christian friends who fed him with the milk of the word, gave him some books and encouraged him to go on his way rejoicing; and when he found no missionaries there, he started for Cuttack, and travelled a distance of more than two hundred miles to join the people of God, and be numbered among the faithful.

He has laboured, with great acceptance, as a native teacher, at Vizagapatam. His fervid zeal, and the excellent and commanding talents which he possesses as a preacher, enable him to make an impression wherever he goes. He has suffered the greatest persecutions from his friends and relatives; but he rejoices that he is counted worthy to suffer shame for the sake of his Lord. Such is the ardour of his mind, such his compassion for souls, that he has no time for study; the word of the Lord seems like a fire in his bones as it was in those of Jeremiah, so that he cannot remain in the house, nor in the city, but must be ranging through the villages and through the district, warning men to flee from the wrath to come, and to embrace that Saviour whom he has found. May the Lord watch over him, and keep him by his mighty power, through faith unto salvation.*

After the mission had been left destitute of labourers and of assistance for nearly three years, Mr. Gordon—the son of our late missionary,—succeeded his father at his station and in his labours; and at the end of the same year 1835, Mr. Porter

* "We have received satisfactory intelligence of the continued steadfastness of Poorooshudum, the young man who was converted about three years ago in the neighbourhood of Chicacole; and we have the pleasure to state that he has been recently made the means, in the hands of God, of bringing another Brahmin, in the Goomsoor district to the knowledge of the truth."—*Madras Missionary Register.*

"In Jan. 1836, Poorooshudum had the happiness of persuading his wife and child to relinquish their friends, kindred, and country, in order to join him; after a good deal of persecution on the part of his relatives, this was effected; and after examination into her views and character, she was baptized by the Rev. A. Sutton at Cuttack."—*M. D. C. Report.*

entered upon his missionary career. In the establishment of schools, in preaching the gospel, and in spreading the good news throughout the Circars, they have shown a commendable zeal and diligence. The first Protestant chapel was erected, and was opened for native and English services in 1836. The English church and congregation are good, and the native services in town and country are encouraging. During the days of famine, many poor, starving children were admitted into the schools, and are receiving a Christian education under the care of the missionaries; and many, from among them, it is to be hoped, will arise to praise the Lord, and be a blessing to the heathen.

Such is a short review of our mission to Vizagapatam. The burden of the Lord is laid upon the junior brethren. They labour in a sphere where many tears have been shed, where importunate prayers have been offered, where great exertions, and personal sacrifices have been made, and where many lives have been offered upon the missionary altar. May these considerations not discourage them, but cheer them on in their sacred career, and may the Spirit of the Lord speedily descend, and render fruitful the seed which has been committed to the ground, that those who have sown and those who reap may in the end rejoice together.

CHAPTER XVIII.

CUDDAPAH.

BIJANAGUR—CEDED DISTRICTS—PRODUCTIONS OF THE SOIL—CUDDAPAH—MR. HOWELL—ASPECT OF THE MISSION—NEW CHAPEL—CHRISTIAN VILLAGE—CONSPIRACY—MURDER OF MR. MACDONALD—DELIVERANCE—LETTER—ENQUIRERS—CATHOLIC BAPTISM—PROTESTANT BAPTISM.

THE Balaghaut ceded districts are divided into two collectorates—those of Cuddapah and Bellary. Balaghaut stands in opposition to Payenghaut—the former signifying the region above, and the other the territory below, the Ghauts. From the Crishna to the southern boundary of the Mysore, the mountains rise, both on the eastern and the western side, like tremendous walls, supporting the table-land, and elevating these terraced plains into an empire of health, beauty, and fertility. Of this immense and lofty region, the ceded districts are that part which the British Government acquired by treaty in 1800. In ancient times, they formed a part of the kingdom of Carnata; and in modern days, a part of the illustrious empire of Bijanagur—whose capital was once styled the city of science, and then the city of victory. At the height of its power, this kingdom comprehended the whole of the Carnatic both above and below the Ghauts; and the Chola, the Chera, and the Pandian dynasties were obliged to submit to its authority. But the four Mahommedan kings of the Deccan conspired against it, defeated its prince in battle, sacked and plundered its capital, and put an end to the power and the glory of the royal house. It became tributary to the Moguls, was afterwards subdued by Hyder and Tippoo, and then fell into the hands of the British, after the treaty of Mysore.

During the period that war and anarchy raged in the peninsula, these districts were the theatre of rapine, treachery and oppression. Lawless banditti ransacked and plundered the towns and villages, and set all order and government at defiance. At the time when they were ceded to the British, they were in the most deplorable state; the annual revenue was constantly on the decline; an army was always in the field and required the whole of the collection to support it; and the Nizam seems to have handed the territory over to our government, because it was so unmanageable and expensive. But no sooner were the districts placed under the control and management of Colonel Munro, than they began to prosper. Such were the principles on which he conducted the government, that the province was soon reduced to a state of peace and order; the people were protected and made happy; the revenue increased, though the tax was greatly reduced; and when wolves ceased to prey upon the sheep, the shepherd that watched over their interests, was loved and honoured.

Some parts of the districts, may, from their locality, be dry and unhealthy; but the climate, in general, is salubrious and invigorating. They contain two millions of inhabitants. Their principal towns are Adoni, Bellary, Bijanagur, Ghooty, Cuddapah, Harponhully, and Gurrumcondah.

Sugar and jagerry are manufactured to some extent; large quantities of indigo are grown and exported; but the soil is black, and, like many other parts of India, is admirably suited to the production of cotton. It is reckoned that in these districts alone, there are three million acres of waste lands which were once cultivated and fruitful, and which, instead of being covered with forests and jungle that would require to be cleared, are now fit for the husbandman, for the seed and the harvest. If encouragement were given to the growth of cotton, there is no doubt that it might be imported to England as good in quality, and as large in quantities, as can be brought from America. Why, then, should not the productions of our own territories be patronized? Why prefer the article that is raised by the hands of slaves, and sold for the interest of slave-holders, to the article which can be grown by freemen, and sold by the enemies of slavery? Why not turn the current of our trade from a channel that is impure, into one that is clear and healthful, and thus compel the Americans to abolish slavery, or seek a new market for their goods?

Cuddapah is the capital of the eastern district, The climate is dry and very hot. Being a civil station, and a large town containing 60,000 inhabitants, and a place of great resort, it had many claims as a field for missionary exertion. Having acted for some time as an assistant missionary at Bellary, and as a superintendent of schools, Mr. Howell was prepared to occupy a distinct sphere of labour, and settled here in December 1822. The Europeans at the station gave him a kind reception. He continued to labour among the heathen, and as his labours were crowned with a promising measure of success, he was ordained at Madras in 1824. Without ordination in India, a missionary occupies no peculiar station in society. He does not take rank among Europeans, where rank is so much attended to; nor do the natives esteem him so highly, since their Gooroos set an inestimable value upon their induction into office, and teach their votaries to do the same. However trifling may be the importance which some attach to this rite, it is expedient that all Europeans who go as missionaries to India, and all who are recognized there as ministers of Christ, should be publicly set apart, and receive the approbation of their brethren.

In 1824. the mission began to assume a new

MISSION PREMISES AT CUDDAPAH,

1. Christian Village. 2. 3. Paper Manufactory. 4. School House. 5. Mission House. 6. Chapel.

aspect. Hitherto, Mr. Howell had preached the gospel in his own house; a few families used to meet together on the Sabbath to receive instruction; and the truth was regularly proclaimed among the heathen; but no church was formed, and no regular congregation could be said to exist. As many natives followed Judge Waters from Chittoor, these and the people who were accustomed to assemble, formed a respectable congregation, and they met in a bungalow which this generous friend had given up for the purpose. At this very time also, many of the heathen who had heard the gospel, and had long been undecided, no longer halted between two opinions, but came forward, renounced idolatry, and declared openly their attachment to the truth. The congregation thus formed were viewed as nominal professors only, while those who gave evidence of real piety were formed into a church, and ten members celebrated the death of the Redeemer.

The want of a chapel was felt in 1825; and Mr. Howell obtained subscriptions upon the spot, and throughout the presidency, and erected a sanctuary where the natives have assembled, and worshipped the living God. A proposition was made, at the same time, to establish a Christian village. On a piece of ground well adapted for the purpose, many houses have been built, and 150 persons located. To prevent sloth and idleness, all are engaged to labour. Some of the people are agriculturists and cultivate the mission-ground; a paper-mill was established and has given employment to others. Many work at their trades, and all contrive by diligence and industry to obtain their livelihood. Mr. Howell does not seem to regard all these natives, as decided Christians. But they profess to have abandoned their idolatry; they wish to be instructed in the great doctrines of revelation; they are willing to surrender their caste, their good name, and their respectability among their heathen neighbours for Christ; and lest they should be exposed to the malice and persecutions of enemies, they have taken up their abode in this city of refuge. While they attend the ordinances, one and another of the enquirers understand and value the gospel, and are baptized; sometimes the baptized are impressed, and show more evident marks of faith and repentance, and they are admitted into the communion of the faithful; and as the believers grow in knowledge and in grace, and in ability to be useful to others, they are selected to be schoolmasters, readers, or native teachers. There is something very natural, reasonable, and scriptural in this.

But many who wish well to Zion, are doubtful of the propriety of this system. There is such a liability, they contend, in the natives to be influenced by worldly motives, that it would be better to allow all professors to fight the battle among their own people. No doubt, there must be failures. Hindoos will take advantage of kind and generous plans, as well as Europeans. Whatever may be the discipline, and whatever the circumstances, hypocrites and formalists will be found in every church and in every congregation. Notwithstanding all the assiduity he can exercise, Mr. Howell acknowledges that some families became so incorrigible, that he was obliged to expel them from the village. But adopt what plan you please, there will be objections to it, and hindrances will arise to its accomplishment. Should all be condemned, and executed, because traitors are found in the camp? So long as the people manifest a wish to understand the gospel; so long as they conduct themselves with sobriety and steadiness, and docility; so long as they show good-will, and love to Christianity as the system by which they hope to be saved; so long we would cherish them and instruct them; the plan must be beneficial; opportunities of usefulness must be great; prayer and painstaking may do any thing; and should the parents not become decided Christians, their children are under our authority and care; and this residence in the village and this public separation from heathenism, give us a hold upon their offspring, which we should attempt in vain to obtain under any other circumstances.

In 1832, when so many plots were formed, throughout the peninsula, by the Mahommedans, to destroy the British power, the mission at Cuddapah was threatened with destruction. During the celebration of the Mahorrum, a dead pig was found in a mosque, and was, no doubt, placed there by some disaffected Mussulman to exasperate his people against the Christians, and against the government. The native believers were immediately accused as the authors of this deed, and report basely stated that it was done at Mr. Howell's suggestion. To assemble and to arouse the mob, the nagara or the great drum was procured, and was beaten for three hours without intermission. The Mahommedans both old and young assembled from all quarters of the town and from the neighbourhood; and on hearing this wicked report, swore vengeance against Mr. Howell and against the Christians, The fire of their enthusiasm burst into a flame, the Patans joined with the adherents of the mosque in their rebellious enterprise; and inspired with rage and exasperating themselves and their associates to deeds of blood, their bands advanced upon the mission-house to execute their murderous designs. As soon as the intelligence of the riot, and of the base intentions of the multitude, were known at the magistrate's cutcherry, Mr. Macdonald—the sub-collector, and a gentleman whom all respected for his intelligence, and for his zeal in the public service,—rushed to the spot unarmed, with the hope that, by his powers of persuasion, he would bring the multitude to reason, or keep them at bay till the arrival of the troops. But the moment he began to address them, they cut him down, imbrued their hands in his blood, and were triumphing over him as the first victim of their rage, when the appearance of the troops put them to flight, and put an end to their malevolent intentions. A slow and tardy execution of the law delivered seven of these insurgents to the gallows; but a retributive justice will pursue many more of them, as the abettors of this horrid murder. What a gracious interposition of Providence was this, on behalf of Mr. Howell, his family, and the Christians! Had the mob been permitted to reach his house, the whole defenceless flock must have fallen a sacrifice to their fury. Well might the Christians say, "God has arisen to judge his cause; the crafty counsel of the wicked has come to nought, and now their faces are covered with shame! The Lord our God has done great things for us; we will take the cup of salvation, and pay our vows unto the Most High!"

As Cuddapah is a civil station, crowds of natives assemble, from various parts of the district to settle their affairs and to obtain law and justice. Many of them come, as inquirers to the mission-house, and carry away with them some of the grapes of Eschol. A native sergeant, had lately obtained a tract, and under the burden of his sins, and seeking rest to his spirit, had addressed a letter to Mr. Howell, from which I give a few extracts.

"To the Rev. Mr. Howell in Cuddapah, I make prostration. My history is as follows:—I am a naigue in the 34th regiment, and belong to the Alla-golla caste; my name is Sarapully Venkatapa.

I now offer up my soul and body to the Lord Jesus Christ who is ever merciful; and, receiving him as my father, priest, and judge, the weight of my sins, I lay upon his cross. Such as are righteous and partakers of the grace of God; such as make known God the Father and his Son Jesus Christ, labouring with joy in this world, and making known, with humility and singleness of mind, the grace of God to the blind, insane, ignorant, and foolish who, like myself, are on the road to everlasting fire, I esteem as fathers and brethren. It will give me great pleasure to hear of your peace and comfort of mind. In spiritual things, I am as a child, and I will therefore make known to you my sins which are become so grievous to me. Pray for me to one God the Father, to keep and help me. My transgressions are so great and many, that the intermediate space between heaven and earth cannot contain them. I am not able to save myself; it is for you alone to point out the way in which I am to be saved.

"In 1834, a Bramin came from Budrachellum on his way to Benares, with his idols, to which he offered so many praises and prayers, as to astonish the sepoys of the regiment, in consequence of which they honoured him not a little. I also believed in him and became one of his disciples. The initiation into his fellowship cost me sixty rupees, and in return for this sum, he taught me a muntrum, the purport of which is, that if a person once says 'Rama, Rama,' he benefits by it, as much as if he prayed to God a thousand times. He told me also to plant the tulsi * and to worship it daily, and to confide my soul and body at his feet, and by so doing, all my desires would be fully obtained. From Benares, he returned in 1835, when I washed his feet and drank part of the water and poured the rest upon my head. I presented flowers and sandal, and worshipped his feet, telling him that, according to his request, I had planted the tulsi, at which he appeared glad, and felt satisfied with this act of my devotion. He then taught me the Rama,† teerta-muntrum, telling me that he revealed it, from the regard which he had to me! but that, properly speaking, none should be taught the muntrum, unless he had followed and served him twelve years; on this account, I was obliged to give him some more money!

"One of your tracts now came into my possession. As the Bramin saw me reading it often, he desired me not to look at it; but by reading it attentively, I have become acquainted with the way of life, so as to make me desire to become a Christian. Though a sinner, I have now one favour to ask of you. Be not prejudiced against me, because I am so great a transgressor. Listen to my petition with kindness,—that is that you would favour me with a Bible and Testament, that I may understand the

* A fragrant plant, sacred to Vishnoo.

† The prayer used at the time when the water is drunk in which an idol, sacred stone, or a Bramin has been bathed.

truth from it, as there are none here to teach me the way properly, or to expound the doctrines of Christianity as I could wish. You must also give me a book which would instruct me in the way of praising God. You must also explain the nature of baptism to me, as I cannot obtain leave to come to you.

"I have left off the worship of idols, have renounced my caste, have ceased to put the mark on my forehead, and no longer offer any worship to the Bramin who taught me the muntrums. The sepoys of the battalion are all against me; they shun my company and call me an apostate, a pariar, and a fool. The women also mock and persecute me; but the Bramin more especially! I have no one to look to for support; but I trust in God the Father and in his Son Jesus Christ alone, who gave his life for us and who is full of compassion. You must also be kind to me, and as Christ came to save sinners, you must teach me the way to be saved. As I cannot read and write well, I have written this to the best of my ability; you must forgive the many mistakes which are in it. You are my father and my brother; I have trusted in you; do not forget my request. You must teach me how to pray and explain to me the doctrine of baptism, in such a manner as I may understand it. I beg to send you my salutation, and my love to the brethren; when you write, let me know them by name."

Who can read this letter without feeling deeply affected with its contents? Are not the heathen crying out "Come over and help us?" What Christian does not feel that he is bound, by the most sacred obligations, to make every exertion, to use every means, and to submit to every sacrifice, to send the gospel to those who are in such an interesting state?

In the church of Cuddapah, there are only twenty-three members; but many more have been baptized, and are under instruction. Among the latter, was a Roman Catholic who has been led, by the perusal of the tract "Andrew Dunn" in Tamul, to abjure the errors of Popery, and has remained steadfast to his determination, notwithstanding the persecutions which he has suffered from his friends and relatives in the cantonment. He requested the missionary to baptize him as a proof of his sincerity, and because the Roman Catholics baptized him with oil, salt, and spittle, contrary to the word of God. From this circumstance and after what they have heard from the native Vedabodacum, a few others have expressed a wish to be re-baptized. This is a question which has long been agitated and discussed in India. Some have contended that as the reformers, in their separation from the church of Rome, were not baptized again; and that as those who at home abjure its dominion, are only called upon to make a public recantation of its errors, it cannot be necessary that a different method should be pursued in Hindosthan.

But, are such examples, it may be replied, to be considered infallible authorities? As to the reformers, they could not, with propriety, have baptized one another, since they all left the Romish communion, and their protest against the system was so loud, so solemn, and so determined, that it required not the celebration of any rite, to add to its strength and its publicity. In latter days, the Romish superstition, has been regarded, in England, with a charity which can scarcely be justified, and few measures have been adopted either to protest against its enormities, or to rescue its votaries from the thraldom. But however modified may be the system at home, it is as bad as paganism in India; and however charitably we may be disposed to look at it here, we are bound to regard it as idolatry there. Within its pale, there may be a few who are the subjects of Messiah; but, as a system, it is, in reality, a cruel superstition, it is a vile apostacy, it is the mystery of iniquity, it is the abominations of the earth. Why, then, should we regard any of its rites as valid, especially when they are performed in an unscriptural, and heathenish manner? To test his sincerity, and to make a public renunciation of this idolatry, I would certainly require every Roman Catholic, as much as every Hindoo and Mahommedan to be baptized.

CHAPTER XIX.

THE CANARESE MISSIONS.

THE CANARESE COUNTRIES—THEIR PRESENT CONDITION—ROMAN CATHOLICS—COORG—PROTESTANT EFFORT REQUIRED—BELLARY—SETTLEMENT OF MR. HANDS—SERINGAPATAM—LABOURS AMONG EUROPEANS—REVIVALS—MISSION-HOUSE—FREE SCHOOL—ENGLISH SCHOOL—TRANSLATION OF THE SCRIPTURES—MISSION-TOURS—HUMPEE—HEATHEN CARS.

The countries in which the Canarese language is spoken, are very extensive and populous. Stretching from the Crishna on the north, to the descent of the Ghauts on the south, and comprehending the whole of the table-land, the ancient kingdom of Carnata unquestionably derived its name from the language, or gave to the language its name, as it was there universally spoken. In addition to the province of Canara below the western Ghauts, the inhabitants of the Wynaud, of Coorg, of Bellary, of Harponhully, of Darwar, of Beejapoor, of Bednore, and of many other districts speak this fine language, and wait to receive the gospel through its medium. In 1824, it was reckoned that eight or nine millions of people spoke the Canarese, and since that period, the number must have greatly increased.

But except at Bangalore, at Bellary, at Belgaum, and latterly at Mangalore, no missions have been established in these interesting provinces. Like the Telloogoo countries, they have been deplorably neglected. As a division of the empire, a more healthy, well-watered, beautiful, and interesting one, there does not exist. It is rich in minerals, in spices, in forests, in all kinds of cultivation, and its boundless resources await the time when a wise and enlightened government, or when enterprising companies will undertake to draw forth its stores and riches which are only concealed from view, by the apathy and the indolence of the people. But as yet, the Sun of righteousness has scarcely arisen upon it, with healing under his wings. Its races of men—more strong and athletic in body, more bold and vigorous in mind, more determined in war, and more simple in their manners, than any perhaps in the peninsula,—are still sitting in darkness and in the region of the shadow of death. To-day, they are as open to the truth, to the exertions of the philanthropist and the missionary, to an attack from the champions of the cross, as they ever were, in former times, to the fury of the lawless banditti, and the oppressions of the usurping Polygars. But what has been done to rescue them from the hands of the wicked one?—Alas! the enemy still keeps possession of the land; superstition slays its thousands and its tens of thousands; and the present life is only a stage from which they are passing, in thousands and in millions, to everlasting woe.

Lying on the south side of the Crishna, these provinces were not, till a late period, brought under the power and the oppressions of the Mogul governments. Independent princes continued to rule over them. The manners, the customs, the habits, and the religion of the people remained, more than in the northern districts, peculiarly Hindoo; and though Hyder and his son brought them into subjection, yet his dynasty was too short to produce many remarkable changes.

But if the Canarese escaped more than others, the fury of the Mahommedans, they did not escape the invasion of the Portuguese and the Popish party. Constituting Goa upon the western coast, their head-quarters; the priests poured forth like locusts upon these rich and fertile territories. No intrigues, no bribes, no acts of conciliation and no denunciations were wanting, to convert the Hindoos to their superstition. The plans which they are reported as having used at first, were worthy of the men and of the system. Some of the natives who had either submitted to their authority, or who were hirelings for pay, were sent into different parts of the country to prepare the way of the crafty and the ambitious ecclesiastics. As though the ambassadors were entirely ignorant of their own commission, and of the design which their employers had in view, they assumed the habit and the character of prophets. To excite the curiosity of the people, to rivet their attention, and to fill them with astonishment and expectation, they foretold that great and important changes were at hand—that holy Bramins would very soon come from the West—that a new system of religion would speedily be established—that the gods of the country had sent them to make this announcement—that in dreams, in visions and in oracles, they had become acquainted with these tidings, and warned the people that when the time came that these predictions would be fulfilled, to submit to these messengers, otherwise the most dreadful calamities would ensue. The prophets passed on, but their predictions were not forgotten; the people waited with anxiety and expectation for the accomplishment; and after a time, the holy Bramins arrived; the country was filled with surprise; numbers flocked to listen to the oracles; the predictions of the prophets were realized; and, while the western priesthood were not very scrupulous, in judging of the parties to whom they administered the initiatory rite of their religion, hundreds and thousands were baptized into the Church of Rome. Craft, imposture, and intrigue were more successful with the many, than truth, fidelity and compassion would have been.

Throughout these territories, many thousands

acknowledge the supremacy of the man of sin; but are they better than heathens? Are they more righteous and more spiritual? Are they a greater blessing to society, and a benefit to their race, than idolaters? By no means. Not far distant from Bangalore, there are two popish villages which, in the estimation of the natives, are exact counterparts of Sodom and Gomorrah; and I cannot, therefore, regard the spread of this system as at all beneficial, except as it tends to loosen the regard of heathens to a superstition which has so long held them in subjection, and which every change must, in some measure, affect.

A few years only have elapsed, since the province of Coorg fell into the hands of the British government. Its inhabitants were thought to be eminently prepared for the reception of the truth. The chains of caste which bind Hindoos to their superstitions, were there thought to be weak and powerless. Schools were established, and gave the people the greatest delight. The Commissioner who was appointed, by the government, to superintend its political affairs, was reckoned a devoted and an enterprising man. After his arrival in Coorg, he applied to various quarters to obtain a Protestant missionary; but where was he to be found? Instead of establishing new missions, the old stations required to be strengthened and to be reinforced.* "Well!" said the Commissioner,

* As this opportunity was not embraced, I am very sorry to

"if you will not give me a Protestant, I shall obtain Roman Catholics, since it is better that the people should be initiated into a false system of Christianity, than be allowed to remain in their heathenish ignorance and superstition." Very soon, three Roman Catholic missionaries presented themselves to his view; grants of money were obtained, from the government, to erect a chapel, and to support their establishments in Coorg; and they were sent into that province to take possession of it, after it was offered to Protestants, but which Protestants wanted the men, the means, and the spirit to occupy. I cannot allude to this fact, without almost feeling ashamed of my country, and of the religion which I profess. What! Will the votaries of superstition be more active and zealous in the propagation of error, than the true and faithful disciples of Christ in the propagation of the truth? Will the missionaries of the Vatican, be more numerous and stand better prepared to take advantage of openings and opportunities, than the devoted ambassadors of the Son of God? Will the mere crucifix operate more powerfully upon its devotees, to rouse them to labours, to exertions and sacrifices, than the real cross of the Redeemer? Forbid it, ye adherents of the Protestant faith! Forbid it, ye believers in the Chris-

find that now, when the Wesleyan missionaries have proposed to settle in Coorg, some political considerations have arisen to prevent them.

tianity of the Bible! Forbid it, ye directors of missionary societies! Forbid it, ye servants and ministers of the Most High God! Such an event has occurred once; never, I hope, will it be allowed to happen again? No. I trust that many who peruse these pages, will be glad to follow their Redeemer in his career of devotedness, self-denial, sacrifice and suffering; that many, instead of wrapping their talents in a napkin, or burying them in the earth, will henceforth put them out to usury, will give them to the service of the sanctuary, that the gospel may be sent to those who are ready to perish, and that we may not be chargeable with the blood of souls; and that many, hitherto indifferent and unconcerned about the salvation of the heathen, will hereafter manifest the spirit of primitive times, will bring their hundreds and their thousands to the service of Immanuel, and while some are willing to be in perils of waters, and in perils of robbers, in perils on the sea and perils on the land, in perils in the city, and perils in the wilderness, to carry the glad tidings of mercy to perishing sinners, will make the greatest sacrifices at home, and will use their utmost exertions to save the heathen nations from sinking into woe.

BELLARY

Is the capital of the western collectorate of the ceded districts. Situate on a plain in the midst of a hilly region, it is dry and sultry, but very salubrious. The clouds often intercept the rays of the sun, as they do in the Mysore. A tremendous rock* rises out of the plain, and overshadows the native town. Like other hills in India, it was well fortified, and was often the arena of conflict in former days. The fort still remains, is rendered strong by nature and by art, and is the residence of the British infantry; while the cantonment, where the native battalions are located, is about two miles distant, and is perhaps more cool and healthy. The soil is black, and is well adapted for the growth of cotton. The trees are comparatively few, but tanks of water here and there diversify the scenery.

As Bellary is in the ancient province of Bijanagur, and in the neighbourhood of its capital, it became the seat of a Polygar, after the destruction of that empire. During the period of the Rayeels, this prince held, under them, the office of Dewan, and acquired several Zemindaries. His descendants paid tribute to the sovereigns of Bejapoor, and then to Aurungzebe. Bellary was subdued and taken by Hyder, and the Polygar made his escape. His race is now extinct; but many pretenders have set up their claim to his power and dignity, one of whom, I recollect, was a prisoner on the hill-fort in 1829.

* Such is the heat which this rock often acquires during the day, that it has given rise to the report, that you might roast a beef-steak on the top of it at twelve o'clock at night.

After much discussion with the Madras government, Mr. Hands was allowed to proceed to the interior, and arrived at Bellary in May 1810. His original appointment by the Directors at home, was to Seringapatam; but as the Mysore province was under the authority of a native Rajah, and many other political considerations might prevent his missionary exertions, the Madras Executive would not grant him permission to proceed to that famous city. Whatever might be the disappointment to Mr. Hands and to the Directors in this affair, we cannot regard it now but as a gracious arrangement of Providence. However large and populous Seringapatam might be, and however interesting as a sphere of labour, during the usurpation of Hyder and his son, it is a most unhealthy station, and scarcely a person can sleep within its walls, without catching a very malignant fever. On the fall of the Mahommedan dynasty, it ceased to be the capital of the country; the court and the seat of government were removed to Mysore; the troops, the arsenal, and the public works which gave it importance for a time, have long since been planted in other quarters; the city of the Bahaudars, once so illustrious, has sunk into ruin and insignificance, and is a striking example of the speedy rise, and the sudden overthrow of empires, capitals and dynasties in the East.

Had the original appointment, therefore, been carried out, and Mr. Hands been located in Seringapatam, disappointment must have attended his steps; the effects of the climate upon health and life must have been disastrous; and after passing through a series of calamities, the mission must have been removed to a different seat. But as a station, Bellary has been tolerably healthy; many conveniences have there been enjoyed from the beginning; the authorities have been kind, liberal, and attentive to the wishes of the brethren, and to the interests of the work; and a better situation could not perhaps have been found than this, for the establishment of the first Canarese mission.

Under the greatest disadvantages, our missionary brother commenced the study of the Canarese. Neither grammar, nor dictionary, nor vocabulary, nor any other books could be found to render him any assistance; and the best pundit whom he could procure, was a common schoolmaster. In the Canarese language, there was no lack of such books as those alluded to; but they could neither be obtained, nor rendered available to Europeans at the time. But industry and perseverance can surmount obstacles, and often supply the place of facilities. By conversations with the natives, and mingling freely with them and listening to their colloquial intercourse, Mr. Hands gained so much knowledge of the language, as to be able to make a commencement; he formed a grammar for his own use; he wrote out an extensive vocabulary; he translated Dr. Watts's Catechisms into Canarese, and began his translation of the Scriptures; and in 1812, he was enabled so to speak in the name of his Master that many of the people in the mission-house, in the school-room, and in the bazars, heard from his lips the glad tidings of mercy. If you wish, it is said, to master a subject, write upon it. In the absence of other means, this was the plan that the missionary adopted, and by which he obtained a correct and extensive acquaintance with the Canarese.

At the time when the Bellary mission was established, there was no chaplain, nor place of Christian worship; religion seemed to be almost forgotten; except by the British standard waving on the hill-fort, and some variation of the amusements and the military duties of the day, the sabbath was scarcely to be distinguished from the other days of the week; and no real Christians were to be met with. Very shortly after his arrival, Mr. Hands was requested, by some persons, to commence a sabbath morning service; the collector kindly granted the use of his cutcherry for the purpose; public worship was commenced and regularly continued till the appointment of a chaplain in 1812. An occasional service was established at the garrison hospital; and on sabbath evenings, the people regularly assembled for worship at the mission-house.

These labours, among the Europeans, were not in vain. Though some could not endure the plain and faithful declaration of the gospel, others received the truth in the love of it, forsook the paths of unrighteousness, and gave themselves up to the Lord. On the 4th of June 1812, twenty-seven persons, having given evidence of the sincerity of their faith, were formed into a Christian church, and on the next sabbath evening,* sat down together at the table of the Lord, to commemorate his dying love, and to testify publicly their allegiance to him. This was, to all, a memorable service, a season of refreshing, and an earnest of greater and better things.

Similar effusions of the Spirit were renewed in the history of the Bellary mission. In the year 1816, and after the mission was strengthened by the arrival of Mr. and Mrs. Reeve, a revival took place among the soldiers of the 84th regiment. It was commenced by the labours of the pious and devoted chaplain†—the Rev. Mr. Smyth of Trichinopoly; and while the regiment was in camp, the Lord was

* At the mission stations, the Lord's supper is usually celebrated by the Europeans, after the evening service.

† Mr. Smyth was a most devoted servant of God, and a liberal-minded Christian. Often had he sat at the door of Black Town Chapel of a Sabbath evening, to hear Mr. Loveless. His piety, his evangelical sentiments and liberal views, prevented, there can be no doubt, his advancement in the service; his claims were overlooked; and he was removed from one station to another, only to serve the interests of others, or to gratify the caprice of authorities. But he looked for higher honours, and a better reward. His excellent widow has always been a fellow-helper to the truth, and has done much to advance the cause of God, by her decision of character, and her Christian benevolence.

pleased to bless the exertions of a pious soldier to the conversion of several. After their arrival at Bellary, a great number attended the ministry of the brethren in the fort, and some were awakened, and they hoped truly converted to God. In the beginning of October, twenty-four were received into the church, two more in December, and six more the following church-meeting. The Spirit of the Lord appeared to be in the midst of them, and great grace rested upon them all.

It was well for India, and well for the interests of our missions that such men as Mr. Hands were selected to begin the work. His kind and conciliatory manners won the favour of all classes, and reconciled them to the support of the truth. About a year after the mission was established at Bellary, the government acted with great liberality in granting a valuable piece of ground, very eligibly situated, for mission purposes. A mission-house was commenced and was afterwards completed, which does the greatest credit to those who superintended it. Unlike to the great majority of European houses in India, it is a most substantial building, has an upper story, is lofty, airy, and well suited to health and comfort, but not more so than the climate would require. The garden-grounds around it are extensive and productive, and form such a capacious area between the house and the town, as to allow of a free circulation of air, and of sufficient space for exercise. At the entrance to the compound, there is a school-room on one side, and a very handsome, and substantial chapel on the other.

But notwithstanding the largeness and the eligibility of the premises, the mission-house was unquestionably erected on the old principle, that all the mission-families should be accommodated, and should live together in harmony and peace. When did reason, or providence or scripture sanction and countenance such an arrangement? God has divided men into families, and has shown that love and unanimity are best secured when they dwell in separate habitations; what then could lead to the adoption of such a plan in the prosecution of modern missions? I believe the families at Bellary have always lived on the most friendly terms with each other; but what has given rise to ill-will, strifes, and dissensions, at various stations which I could name? The disregard of this division which Providence has made, and the vain attempt to bring into a closer union, elements which, so long as we are upon earth and in a state of imperfection, will work better when separate, and at a distance.

At a very early period, the education of the young began to receive the care and superintendence of the missionary. As there were many destitute children—descendants of Europeans whose parents were either dead, or who had deserted their offspring, a free-school was established, and has always been liberally supported by the European residents. What confers more than usual interest and importance upon this institution, is that more than a thousand children, comparatively destitute, have received instruction both moral and religious; that great numbers have been clothed, boarded and lodged in the school; that many, who would otherwise have grown up in ignorance, and lived in poverty, have become valuable and respectable members of society; and that there are not a few who, there is reason to believe, have not only been saved by it from temporal ruin, but have been brought into the way that leads to life eternal.

After heathen prejudices had subsided, and the people saw more the value of giving an education to their children, the brethren established schools both in town and country, and gave, to thousands of Hindoo youth, instruction in the principles of Christianity. In 1813, many respectable natives expressed a desire that their children should be taught the English language. For this purpose, a school was commenced in the mission-garden. About twenty of the most promising boys were selected from the Canarese and Teloogoo schools, and began their education in English. Much personal labour was bestowed upon them by the missionaries. The progress of the majority afforded considerable satisfaction, and a superior education was afforded to them, with the hope that they might thus be trained to become schoolmasters, and assistants in the mission. But the brethren were greatly disappointed. As soon as these youths had acquired a sufficient knowledge of the English to qualify them as copyists in public offices, they all left the school, though some of them were offered a small salary to remain. This seminary was continued four or five years, but since it was only attended with much expense and loss of time, and continued to baffle the hopes which the brethren entertained, it was given up. Such has been the experience of the missionaries at other stations, as well as at Bellary, in reference to English schools. The youths added but little to their actual stock of knowledge while engaged in study; their being taught to read and to write English, only put them in the way of advancing their worldly interests; many of them obtained good situations, and some of them appeared grateful for the advantages which they had enjoyed; but no gracious effects were visible, and none did any thing to advance the interests of the mission.

On the arrival of Mr. Reeve in 1816, he entered warmly into all departments of the work. As soon as he obtained a knowledge of the language, he joined Mr. Hands in the translation of the Scriptures. The New Testament had long been under the care, and diligent supervision of the senior missionary, and now, the Old Testament was divided between them—Mr. Reeve taking the historical books, and Mr. Hands the Psalms and the Prophets. After bestowing great labour, prayer, and pains upon them, the whole were brought to a conclusion in 1827, and the first version of the Scriptures in Canarese, has long been published, and put in circulation among the people. It would not be doing justice to these dear brethren to pass by this great work in silence. The names of warriors and statesmen are associated with the kingdoms of the world which must speedily pass away; but the names of those who have translated the Scriptures into such a language, will be associated with the growing empire of Immanuel. Any translation of the Bible into a strange and heathen dialect must deserve well of posterity, and be a blessing to numbers of our race; what then shall I say when I think on the care, the patience, the prayer and the diligence which have been expended upon this work, and which brought it to an auspicious conclusion? Other versions, no doubt, will be made by successors into the Canarese, and the time may come when kings and princes, dissatisfied with the present, may order the wise and the learned of their age to unite their powers to produce a better; but it will be as great an honour to rank with a Tindal and a Coverdale, as with any of the forty-seven who can lay claim to a part of our present English translation.

The brethren at Bellary, have always been in the habit of taking long mission-tours, to preach the gospel, and to distribute the word of life among the distant parts of the province. But an annual visit has usually been paid to Bijanagur—the desolate capital of the Hindoo dynasty, and which has received, in modern times, the name of Humpee.

From the top of a pagoda on a high hill, and with the help of a telescope, the brethren viewed the extensive scene of desolation—the ruins of palaces, pagodas, mosques and other public buildings, the architecture of which appears to have been of a superior kind. When in its glory, the city must have covered a vast extent of ground. After the defeat of its king in battle by the allied princes of the Deccan, the victors, are said, to have spent five months in plundering it, although its inhabitants had employed 1550 elephants in carrying off money and jewels to the amount of one hundred millions of gold, besides the royal chair which was used only on state-days, and whose value could not be estimated.

Whether it be a tribute of honour to the departed glory of the Hindoo government, or whether it be the reverence paid to the superior sanctity of the royal city, the Humpee festival is celebrated with great pomp and splendour; thousands of people crowd from distant parts to pay their devotions at the shrine; and idolatry is sometimes seen in all its weakness, and in its sure indications of approaching decay.

In April 1835, Mr. Paine, accompanied by Samuel Flavel, and the teacher Burder, attended the festival. The crowds were immense, and during the greater part of every day, the brethren were zealously employed in preaching the gospel to the multitudes. When the ponderous cars were to be drawn, and the thousands had assembled to show their attachment to the idols, what a strange scene was exhibited! The gathering blackness of the heavens, the repeated flashes of lightning, and the peals of distant thunder were the sure indications of an approaching storm. Scarcely were the votaries of paganism yoked into the service, and had begun their vile drudgery, when in consequence of the rain, the multitudes rushed to the places of shelter which they had provided for themselves, deserted their gods, and left them to sustain alone the fury of the elements. As the rains were heavy, and the soil was loose and miry, the wheels of the larger car sank into the ground so far, as to render it impossible that any exertions could remove it, that day, from the spot where it had been forsaken. On the following day, attempts were made, but to no purpose. Since the Bramins claim to themselves the exclusive privilege of drawing the smaller car, that performed its accustomed journey—a circumstance which can excite no surprise, when it is remembered that their craft was in danger, that they are the interested parties, that it behoved them, on such an emergency, to give an example of zeal and of energy to the people, and that their united strength was called into action.

The example, however, was almost lost upon the populace. Less zealous in the service of their divinities, the crowds, notwithstanding all the constraint that was used to impress them into the service, could only move the larger car a few yards. Messengers were now despatched to the Rajah of Annagoondy, entreating his aid on behalf of the helpless deities. No sooner did he obey the summons, and attended by his shabby retinue came to the ground, than the whole force was concentrated, immense levers were applied to the wheels, and an elephant was employed to give the first impetus to the huge vehicle. Amidst the clapping of hands, the shouts of the female spectators, and discharge of fire-arms, the car advanced with difficulty a few paces; but the efforts of the many relaxed; the ground became more impassable; and the exhausted strength of the few who were zealous in the cause compelled them to give up the attempt as hopeless.

As the visitors were beginning to withdraw, all the anxieties of the priests were directed to the restoration of the car to its place. The avenues to the valley were instantly closed; none were permitted to depart till the idol was restored to the temple; necessity was called upon to display the superiority of its strength, to that of idolatrous zeal; the efforts of the multitudes were united to serve themselves rather than their idols; and with some difficulty, the car was restored to the shrine. Nothing could more strikingly illustrate the delusion of these worshippers, than the circumstances here recorded. The brethren took advantage of this scene, to show the idolaters the folly of their religion, to convince them that it was impossible such divinities could save, and to beseech them to follow out the convictions of their own minds, and to abandon the gods who are lifeless. Some of the hearers allowed the truth of the appeals, and were constrained to confess that there were signs which indicated the downfall of their system, and that it would not be long before car-feasts would cease to be observed.

Long had the brethren laboured without seeing the heathen converted—*the kind of success* which they most desired, and which is most cheering to the mind. But in 1821, a Canarese man—named Goorapah, and his daughter—Nagama, became the first-fruits of Bellary to Christ. Before he heard of the Redeemer, this venerable old man had abandoned, it appears, the worship of idols, and was gradually prepared for the reception of the truth. He endeavoured to persuade his family to imitate his example, and suffered, on that account, much ridicule and abuse. His arguments led his daughter, Nagama, to reflect upon the subject, and brought her eventually to hear one of the missionaries preach. After her first visit, she came again and again, till divine light beamed upon her mind, and she saw herself a guilty sinner, and was enabled to embrace the Saviour. As she formerly lived in very iniquitous practices, the gospel was more triumphant in her conversion. No sooner did she perceive that these sins were ruinous to her soul, and inconsistent with a profession of our holy religion, than she relinquished them, and became blameless and consistent in her deportment. Taking into consideration, the few advantages which she possessed for moral culture, and spiritual improvement, she made rapid advances in divine knowledge; her mind rose far above mediocrity; and her self-abasement and acquaintance with her own heart, were very conspicuous.

Her father Goorapah, became obedient to the faith about the same time, and both were admitted into the church on the same evening. "The ordinance was administered during the weekly lecture. Brother Chambers preached to the people, and at the close, the two candidates who had been accustomed to bow down to senseless idols, came forward, and in the presence of the congregation, knelt down, we trust, in humble adoration before the true and living God, while brother Hands dispensed to them the solemn rite of baptism. It was an impressive scene. Many appeared deeply affected, and some wept. Our souls rejoiced, and we felt constrained to look forward for the complete accomplishment of divine prophecy in this benighted part of the world."

Shortly after this, Nagama's younger sister embraced the truth, and was baptized with her two children. Then, the mind of the old mother was impressed, and after her conduct and conversation had afforded evidence, for some time, that her heart was changed, she was numbered among the disciples. Thus, the whole family was incorporated into the Christian church, and continued to afford the brethren great satisfaction. In 1823, Nagama was removed into the eternal world, and upon her death-bed, as well as during her life, gave a most delightful testimony to the power of the gospel. Her end was very happy and produced a most powerful impression on the minds of many. Old Goorapah died in 1829, when Mr. Reeve was at the station. In writing upon his decease, Mr. Reeve says, "it was only two or three days prior to dissolution, that we had any certain indications of the near approach of death. Every time that I visited him, I was struck with his patience, his calmness, composure and resignation. On his being asked, if it were the will of God to call him now from time into eternity, whether he was prepared for his great change, he replied 'I hope so; I am very anxious to go, and see the Lord Jesus Christ who loved me so much as to come into the world, and shed his blood for me on the cross, that my sins might be pardoned.' When at another time, the question was asked, 'Is your mind still fixed on the Saviour?' he answered, 'Certainly, my dear teacher, it is; I am waiting for him,' and as to the grounds of his hope, he said, 'I expect to be saved only through the merits of Jesus Christ.' When referring to the situation of his family after his removal, he observed, 'If they continue to seek that

Holy God who is on their side, they will have no occasion to be afraid.' At another time, he said, 'I thank God my mind is happy. I have only another day to spend on earth, then I shall be released from all sicknesses and pains, and enter into that blessed place where all sorrows will be for ever done away.' Shortly after this, he ceased to be mortal, and we trust that he will at last be found included in the number of those who are redeemed from among all nations. During the seven years that have passed away since his baptism, his conduct has been, as far as I can learn, quite unimpeachable. When not prevented by the infirmities of old age, he has been uniform and regular in his attendance upon public ordinances, and in his performance of domestic worship. He could neither write, nor read. At family prayer, one of his grandsons used to read the Scriptures, after which the venerable old man, in a simple and humble manner, would present appropriate petitions to the throne of Grace."

One of his grandsons, is the native teacher—William Burder at Bellary; and the other, John Bogue, died in 1830. In reference to the latter, Mr. Reid writes, "This is the fourth member of that highly-favoured family who has been rescued from the thraldom of Satan's most galling yoke,—who has received the truth in love—who has embraced the profession of the Christian religion, and having given satisfactory evidence of the sincerity of that profession, has died rejoicing in the hope of acceptance with God, through the merits and righteousness of Christ alone. Our hearts have been cheered by this interesting event, and we would bless God and take courage."

But this notice of Bellary must be brought to a close. To continue it, there is no want of materials which interest the writer and which would abundantly gratify the reader. The history of those devoted men who have been converted there, and who are now labouring at other stations to convert the heathen; the journeys of benevolence which the brethren have undertaken, and the conversations they have held with the votaries of paganism; the printing-press—that mighty engine which has been pouring forth its thousands of remonstrances among the natives, under the active and vigilant superintendance of Mr. Paine; the exertions of Samuel Flavel, and the prosperity of the native church; the zealous and indefatigable efforts of Mr. Reid, and the success of the orphan-school; the blessing that has crowned the Bible and Tract Societies—all these would afford interesting points of discussion, and would show that much has been already accomplished, and that a larger work of preparation has been going on for a future harvest, when the Spirit is poured down from on high. But the space which other and important subjects will yet require, prevent me from dwelling so long and so fully upon each mission, as I should otherwise like to do. May brethren who are so dear to me, long have life and health to carry on their labours, and may labours so great, and important, meet with a Divine reward.

CHAPTER XX.

BELGAUM.

BELGAUM—PROVINCE OF BEJAPORE—MAHRATTAS—MR. JOSEPH TAYLOR—ESTABLISHMENT OF THE MISSION—CONVERSION OF BRAMINS—DARWAR—MR. BEYNON—MISSIONARY TOURS—HEATHEN FESTIVAL—CHURCH AND CONGREGATION—THE DECCAN.

BELGAUM is in the province of Bejapoor, on the north side of the Tumbhoodra, and in the territories lately occupied by the Mahrattas. Three hundred and fifty miles in length, and two hundred in breadth, are reckoned the average extent of the country, and notwithstanding the war and anarchy which have perpetually reigned, it is calculated to contain about seven millions of inhabitants. The western districts are mountainous especially in the neighbourhood of the Ghauts, while, in the eastern, the province is level, salubrious, and watered by the Crishna, the Beemah, the Tumbhoodra and other streams. The principal towns are Poonah, Darwar, Bejapoor, Sattarah, Merritch, Punderpoor, Hubley, and Shawpore. On the fall of the Bhamanee dynasty, the Deccan was divided into the kingdoms of Bejapoor, Golconda, Berar, Ahmednagur and Beder.

At Bejapore, the dynasty of Adil Shah existed for nearly two centuries; Amungzebe conquered it, and rendered it tributary to Delhi; and the nominal authority of the Moguls was triumphant for a time. But the rise of the Mahratta power, was almost contemporary with the downfall of the Shahs. It was impossible that the weak and effeminate armies of the emperor, could contend with the fierce and daring troops of the marauders. The battle of Paniput in which their army was cut to pieces, only humbled the Mahrattas for a moment. The successors of Sevajee scoured the Deccan, and converted the best and most fruitful fields into a wilderness. For nearly a century, they were a scourge to the empire. War, rapine, anarchy and devastation attended their march. Now their cavalry rushed to plunder, and were nothing but banditti to ravage and destroy; then, under a more organized form of government, their armies took the field to burn cities and to depopulate countries; but their rule was, throughout the whole, a desolating tempest tearing up all the foundations of the social system; overturning the bulwarks of peace, and liberty, and public order; driving the natives from their towns and their abodes to the dens* and caves of the

* The "*Wulsa*" is the flight of the inhabitants from a town, on the approach of an enemy. No sooner do they hear

mountains; and rendering property, commerce, life, and all temporal blessings, insecure. But at length, this frightful system was brought to an end. The Mahratta confederacy was broken, the British arms were victorious, the Pindarries were annihilated, and Bejapore and the whole Deccan were restored to order and security.

Still the marks of the scourge are visible on all sides, and it will be long before this province is restored to that state of prosperity which its climate, its fertility, and its resources ought to command. After the last Mahratta campaign, Belgaum was chosen as the most healthy station for the cantonment of the troops. It was formerly under the Madras presidency, but is now under that of Bombay. Most salubrious and invigorating, the climate enables the brethren to carry on their operations with greater spirit and perseverance, than in many other parts.

The mission was established in 1820. Mr. Joseph Taylor who had laboured long and diligently with Mr. Hands at Bellary, as an assistant missionary, was proposing to settle in a different sphere, and had his views directed to some of the large towns in

that an army is advancing, than they collect together their jewels, their gold and silver, and their most valuable articles of every kind; decamp from the city; take refuge among the hills; and continue to live there till the storm is past. Such is the confidence which the natives have always had in the British power, that the "*wulsa*" has not been resorted to on the approach of an English army.

the district. While still undecided as to the direction of Providence, Sir Theophilus Pritzler—then commanding the Deccan division of the army—wrote to the brethren at Bellary, requesting that a missionary, if possible, should be sent to Belgaum, promising to afford him his patronage and support, pointing out the facilities to exertions among the heathen, and wishing his services among the troops under his command. Mr. Taylor went to supply. The general and many officers gave him a kind reception. As great anxiety prevailed among the European soldiers to receive instruction, a thatched building was erected, sufficient to accommodate a hundred persons, and the attendance was so great that many were obliged to stand during the service. Among the heathen population, a wide field presented itself at Shawpore, at Belgaum, and in the neighbourhood; and the path of duty appeared plain to the missionary to settle there, in preference to any other place.

The expectations thus raised have not been disappointed. Mr. Taylor settled there, and the blessing of the Lord was soon evident. Not only were the labours among the Europeans rendered effectual to the conversion of many; but became eminently subservient to the mission cause—more so perhaps than if the work had been commenced, and carried on for a similar period, under other circumstances. Indeed! Mr. Taylor is of opinion that no missionary would have been allowed, at that time, to settle in the district, except under these peculiar arrangements. When the intimations of Providence for the establishment of a mission, are quite evident, it is an incumbent duty, if possible, to occupy the ground. If the climate is salubrious, the station central, the opportunities of usefulness promising, the population great, many indications of Providence propitious, and above all, adverse circumstances which may have hitherto prevented the introduction of the truth, be removed, the station ought to be occupied till a missionary can arrive from England, or till some other arrangements can be made. From a want of men, and from an inability to seize the favourable moment, some promising fields of labour have been shut against the gospel, and political or other considerations have arisen afterwards, to prevent the establishment being formed.

The first fruits of the Belgaum mission appeared in the conversion of two Bramins and a Rajpoot who, in order to avoid the threats and violence of their relatives, were baptized at Bombay. No sooner did they return to Belgaum, than the storm burst upon their heads; the most furious persecution was raised against them; and the efforts of the missionaries in Shawpore were scorned and despised. To escape from the evils, the Rajpoot and one of the Bramins took to flight. The former, it appears, never returned; but the latter came back to the fold, and lamented his fear and timidity. As his deportment was becoming the gospel, he was employed as a master in a village-school, where his conduct gave great satisfaction to the missionary, because it showed that he was attentive to his duties, instructed the children in the truth, gained the confidence of the parents, and evinced a conciliating and Christian temper.

The Bramin convert Dhondapah, who remained steadfast during the whole of the persecution, held on his way, and continued to grow in knowledge, in grace and holiness. While there could be no doubt of his sincerity and devotedness to the Saviour, the missionary had to regret that he did not possess an aptitude to teach, and that he was therefore incapable of advocating publicly the cause which he had espoused. But his conduct spoke loudly. Such was his self-denial; his suitable demeanour under losses, persecution and contempt; his great humility, simplicity, and deadness to the world, that they were most pleasingly conspicuous to all, attracted the notice of his countrymen, and produced upon them an impression in favour of Christianity.

After labouring many years at Darwar, and in other places connected with the mission, Dhondapah resided some time with a Christian friend at Bombay, and about three years ago, had left the presidency to return to Belgaum. But he has never been heard of. The missionaries are apprehensive that he is not alive; and conclude that he must either have died in some place where he was unknown, or had fallen into the hands of the murderous Thugs, who, for an article of the smallest value, would not hesitate to assassinate him. Devapah, his companion in baptism, was employed for several years in teaching the prisoners in the jail at Darwar; but the school there has been discontinued by the judge, and the German missionaries who have lately occupied that field, have kindly taken him under their fostering care. He is now employed in communicating the knowledge of salvation to the heathen there, and in the surrounding villages. The brethren report well of his Christian character and prospects of usefulness. It is thus that while not many wise men after the flesh, not many mighty and not many noble are called, and while God chooses the weak things of the world to confound the mighty, and the foolish things of the world to confound the wise; some even of the priests believe, and render glory to the truth.

Having resided for some years, with very delicate health, and with no prospect of recovery, at Bellary, Mr. Beynon joined the mission at Belgaum in 1828, and has not only been remarkably well, but has pursued his course with great acceptance and usefulness. I cannot but think that this is a subject which deserves more consideration, than it has yet received. At some of the stations in India, the health of the missionary is at once attacked, and fails; but it is not right to conclude that another province would not be more conducive to health and comfort. Mr. Beynon is not the only case which might be alluded to. While there are such provinces as the Mysore, Bejapore, and Travancore, where there is labour for a hundred missionaries; why should not these climates be tried, and new missions be formed to meet the exigency? I am far from thinking that a missionary should, on account of every trifle, leave the station to which he is appointed. No. Every real Christian would dread this, and must see the necessity there is for concentration of effort, instead of dividing our strength and weakening all our positions. But the loss of health is an exception to the general rule, and every one must see that it is better a missionary should occupy any part of the field, than be under the necessity of abandoning the work. Mr. Beynon thought so, and he has been able to study and to labour much at Belgaum. He has translated the "Pilgrim's Progress" into Canarese. It was published by Mr. Cathcart, and is one of the few books which, translated from the English, is admirably suited to an Eastern population, and is likely to be the means of doing good.

In the pursuit of their great object, the brethren have undertaken long missionary tours among the heathen. As Darwar was once considered a branch of their mission, their visits to that town were frequent, and their exertions many. Their labours in the jail have often been accompanied with considerable success, and some, there is reason

TORTURES INFLICTED AT A HINDOO FESTIVAL.

to hope, who have suffered the last penalty of the law, have, like the thief upon the cross, been prepared to enter into paradise. On one occasion, they met daily, for two weeks, large congregations assembled at the Mutt * of a Lingum priest who was going through one of their Pooranas. The opportunity was embraced to point out the manifest absurdities and contradictions in their books, and to communicate the way of mercy. The word was heard with attention by many, and with astonishment by others. One individual who attempted to oppose, and who manifested angry feelings, was silenced by the priest; books were readily accepted, and it was evident from allusions made and from questions proposed afterwards, that they had been read, and some knowledge of their leading truths acquired. During 1837, Mr. Beynon visited the Yellamma Jatra and witnessed the most horrible and revolting scenes. The first remark which a native convert made, on beholding them was, "Come, let us flee; this is Sodom and Gomorrah." "A great number of people," says Mr. Beynon, "underwent the swinging torture. They were suspended by hooks thrust through the tendons of the back, or of the leg. The latter mode of suspension appeared much more painful than the former, as they could only endure it for a short time. I can hardly describe my feelings, at first, in the midst of such abominations. But however pained, I felt it

* A place of devotion.

to be my bounden duty to lift up my voice against the atrocities of the place. Many appeared to feel and acknowledge the force of what I said. Some fell at my feet, lamenting what they had done, and saying they had done it in ignorance; others said they would not discharge the vows which they had taken upon them. Most of the devotees were of the Shoodra caste, and a few Bramins among them contrived to discharge their vows by proxy."

I am happy to find that the government has relinquished the revenue which it derived from this festival; and it would be well that it had nothing to do with it. In consequence of some disagreement between the Poojaries who are Shoodras, and the Koolkurnees who are Bramins, about the division of the fees; government has appointed four Bramins as trustees to collect, and take charge of the offerings. The Poojaries are dissatisfied with this arrangement, and say that they have a claim to all and receive nothing. The impression produced on the minds of the people, is that the fees are collected by the authority of government.

Soloman, and Jonas—native teachers from Bangalore, labour with diligence and assiduity, with great satisfaction to the missionaries, and with a pleasing measure of success. The members of the church are about twenty in number. On Sabbath morning, the congregation amounts to about a hundred, composed of the members of the church, children connected with the mission, and strangers, both heathen and Roman Catholics. In the course of 1837, there were five persons baptized and received into the church—a Mussulman and his wife, two Roman Catholics, and one heathen. As the Mahommedans have hitherto been the most determined enemies of our missions in India, it is very pleasing to hear, at this station and at the other, that some are renouncing their enmity, and their delusion, and are taking upon them the reproach of Christ. Many are surprised that more attempts are not made on behalf of the Mahommedans. But it is not strange. Could all the Mussulmen of India, be collected into one district, then, their claims would be manifest, and would be attended to. But they are only a fraction of the population; they are, like the Jews, scattered up and down over the provinces; they speak a dialect different from the Hindoos; and it is only here and there that a missionary can find an opportunity of addressing them, even should he understand their language.

What a splendid field for missionary enterprise, does the province of Bejapore, and the adjoining kingdoms of the Deccan present to our view! In that immense tract of territory which lies between the Nerbudda and the Crishna, stretching from the river Hoogly to the western coast, and which might well be termed the centre of India, what large and populous districts unvisited by the light of the gospel! Irrespective of the northern Circars, and the Telloogoo countries to which allusion has already been made, there cannot be less, in the different kingdoms of the Deccan, than twenty-five millions of souls. The Gonds, the Ooriayas, the Mahrattas, the Mahommedans, the Canarese are a multitude of tribes, and peoples and tongues. With the exception of a Baptist mission in Orrissa, a Scottish mission in the Concan, and our own mission at Belgaum, nothing has yet been done to teach and to evangelize these races of men. Sunk in idolatry, delusion, and crime, they perish not in hundreds, nor in thousands, but in millions at the shrine of evil. Satan rules over the territories with an unlimited sway, he riots in the number of his victims and the value of his spoils, he hopes to render his reign there immortal, and has increased, to a thousand fold, the exactions of his despotism. Weep, my soul, over these dark places of the earth; take a right estimate of the calamities to which these tribes are subject, and the greater evils to which they are exposed; and though thy efforts should be worthless and thy tears unavailing, try to rouse the Christian world to sympathy and commiseration, and continue to hold the arm of the Almighty, till Satan is driven from his strong-holds, and till these nations are emancipated from his thraldom.

CHAPTER XXI.

THE MYSORE.

DESCRIPTION OF THE MYSORE—FACE OF THE PROVINCE—HISTORICAL RECOLLECTIONS—INHABITANTS—CUSTOMS RESEMBLING THOSE OF JUDEA—CANARESE LANGUAGE—THE EXPOSITION OF THE SHASTERS—PREPARATION FOR THE GOSPEL—ANCIENT TIMES—HYDER ALI—MAHOMMEDAN METHOD OF CONVERSION—THE CONTRAST FAVOURABLE TO CHRISTIANITY.

THE Mysore country occupies the great proportion of that elevated table-land which stretches across the Peninsula of India, from the eastern to the western Ghauts. In its extent, it is larger than Scotland, and contains about three millions of inhabitants. Elevated 3000 feet above the level of the sea, very picturesque in its scenery and salubrious in its climate, it abounds with all the freshness and fragrance and variety of European gardens. The height of the land collects the clouds into a canopy over our heads, so as to prevent the rays of the sun from exercising that withering influence over us, which they do in the Carnatic and in the lower parts of the country. It enjoys the former and the latter rain. Scarcely any thing can exceed the beauty of its landscapes, the richness of its soil, and the abundance of its harvests. Rice, ragee, mustard, gram, and every kind of Indian grain are among the productions of its fields. Excellent potatoes, cabbage, carrots, turnips, beet-root, cauliflower, cucumbers and other sorts of European vegetables grow in the gardens, and some of them are exported to all parts of the country. The peach, the apple, the pear, the plum, the strawberry, the vine and the pomegranate, as well as the plantain, the orange, the mangoe, the guava and the pine-apple, are the fruits which, in their different seasons, adorn the table, and afford, to the desert, a refreshing and beautiful variety. The flowers too are charming, and though on the plains, they have beauty without any fragrance, they possess both on the table-land; and the rose, the violet, the mignionette, the geranium, and such like English blossoms, as well as those that are native, are gathered, are formed into splendid boquets, and send their perfumes through the mansions. In the estimation of the Christian natives, the country is the land of Canaan—the land that flows with milk and with honey. The God of Providence has rendered it a pleasant and delightsome province. "He waters the ridges thereof abundantly, and settles the furrows thereof; He makes it soft with showers and blesses the springing thereof; He crowns the year with his goodness and his paths drop fatness. They drop upon the pastures of the wilderness; and the little hills rejoice upon every side. The pastures are clothed with flocks; the valleys also are covered over with corn; they shout for joy and also sing."

In some respects, the face of the country is very peculiar. Now and then, the line of road leads, for miles, through a valley where rocks are piled upon rocks in wild confusion on either side, and appear as though some volcanic eruption had thrown them up in gigantic masses, and in fantastic forms. Tremendous hills may be seen rising out of the surrounding plain, and have usually been fortified as strong towers against the approach of the enemy. Nundidroog, Ramgurry, and Sevendroog are of this description, and were, in former times, reckoned invulnerable. Ten miles in circumference at the base, and a mile in height, some of them are seen at a great distance and are covered with forests, while others are less in dimensions and are scarcely any thing but naked rock. Sevendroog, because of its destructive atmosphere, has been termed "the hill of death." As a place of banishment for criminals, it was famous for its horrors in the Mahommedan reigns; many of the Europeans both officers and privates who were taken in battle, were imprisoned upon its summit, and had they not, by our own army, been speedily delivered, they must, such is the badness of the water, and the impurity of the air, have inevitably fallen a prey to its baneful influence, since very few are able to survive many days.

At the same time, the country abounds with historical recollections. From east to west, it is all classic ground. There is scarcely a hill, or a dale, scarcely a town, or a village which has not been the theatre of some desperate battle, or some chivalrous exploit. The names of Hyder Ali, and his son Tippoo Sultan; the siege of Sevendroog, and the capture of Seringapatam; the victories obtained by a Wellesley and a Cornwallis, have rendered it illustrious in the history of British India. Bangalore may be termed its European capital; it is the head-quarters of its army, and the seat of the government.

The inhabitants of the Mysore are among the bravest, and the most powerful that are to be found in India. No armies proved so formidable to the British in their progress to empire, as those of Hyder, and they were generally composed of as great a number of these Hindoos as of Mussulmen. As far as their superstitions will allow, their habits, their manners, and their national enthusiasm partake very much of the character of the Scottish Highlanders. Proud of their descent, clannish in their associations, independent in their spirit, faithful to their chiefs in the hour of danger, hostile to oppression and despotism in every form, they plant their standard in the earth; they rally round it at the sound of the pipe, the tom-tom and the war-song; they swear fidelity to each other and vengeance to their foes; they draw their scimitars and employ their daggers, till death and destruction are awarded to their enemies, and till freedom and prosperity are rendered secure. Their glens and mountains once resounded with deeds of patriotism; they followed their chieftain to avenge his wrongs, and reposed under his shadow in the days of peace; their martial exploits are still celebrated in the verses of song, and inspire the old and the young with the spirit and courage of their sires.

The manners and the customs of the people are characterized by the simplicity of eastern climes. In passing through the Mysore, you might almost fancy yourselves in the land of Judea under the reign of its kings. "Two women are there seen grinding at the mill," and preparing the grain for the use of the family. Both morning and evening, the maidens, carrying their pitchers upon their heads, flock in bands to the well, to draw water, and return often with joy and gladness. The husbandmen "sow beside all waters, and send forth the feet of the ox;" in the thrashing-floor, the oxen are seen treading out the corn; the winnower, with the fan in his hand, thoroughly purges his floor; the chaff is carried away with the wind; and thus the grain is prepared to be gathered into the garner —a large pit concealed in the field. At other times, the heavens over their heads are as brass, and the earth under their feet is as iron; the clouds of locusts are beheld devouring the herbage of the ground, and the foliage of the trees; the famine rages in the city; young children ask for bread, and no man breaketh it unto them; and they that are slain with the sword, are reckoned better than they that be slain with hunger.

In the wilderness, the shepherds are seen tending their flocks by day, and watching over them by night. Here and there, you meet with heaps of stones, raised as a memorial of some desperate struggle or some deed of horror. Then, you come to a pillar which has been set up to commemorate the conflict of a shepherd with a tiger, in defence of his flock, and both of whom have been found dead upon the spot; and wherever the body is, there are the eagles found gathered together. The merchants, and the money-changers are seen sitting in the market-place. The elders sit at the gates of the city to administer justice, and to decide on cases of complaint. The publicans sit at the receipt of custom, and collect the taxes upon articles as the traders pass by. The traveller lodges all night in the streets, and as their beds usually consist of nothing but a black blanket, or a mattress, it is easy to understand how the man who was cured could take up his bed and walk. Their garments are, generally, white; they gird up their loins for the journey and for the toil; they put off their shoes from their feet, and leave them at the door of their houses and temples as a mark of respect. Like the Nazarites, the Canarese shave not the head till the vow is performed; they bring the strangers into the house, and give them water to wash their feet; and in the annual worship of their implements, they sacrifice to their own net, and burn incense to their own drag. In their schools, the pupils sit at the feet of their Gamaliels; they learn to write with the finger on the ground; they take an iron pen, and write upon the broad leaves of the palm, and the cajan; and their prophets pass through the city, proclaiming tidings of good or of evil as may best serve their worldly purpose. Long before the marriage is celebrated, the female is betrothed to her husband; the nuptial ceremony is performed at night; the parties take their torches and have vessels full of oil, as a supply to their lights; they sit down in rows to partake of the feast; and the children of the bride-chamber mourn not while the bridegroom is with them, but when the day comes that he is obliged to depart, they mourn and weep. In their seasons of sorrow, Rachel is often seen weeping for her children and refusing to be comforted, because they are not; the bereaved and distressed beat upon their breasts, rend their garments, throw the dust into the air, and send forth, in deafening shouts, their wailings and lamentations; the minstrels visit the houses of mourning and the people join them in their noise; they carry their dead upon a bier, and the friends and relatives of the deceased, follow, with bitter cries and tears. Their groves, their burning grounds, and their high-places, remind us of the valley of Hinnom, of Aceldama, of Bethel and of Dan. From these customs, which correspond so much with those of Judea, and which bear such a resemblance to those that are peculiar to Hindosthan, it must be evident that, of all the books, which could be translated into their language, the Bible must be the most appropriate, and the best adapted to the people. Its phraseology, its figures and illustrations, its addresses, and modes of expression are all eastern, find their way most readily to every heart, and almost exactly correspond with the language which Hindoos would use. Whatever, then, may be their darkness and their degradation; however full their land may be, as Palestine was often of old, of heathen temples, of priests, of idols, of sacrifices and abominations, let us rejoice that so many of their customs coincide with those of the Bible, and that they are thus so far prepared to read, in their "own tongue, the wonderful works of God."

The Canarese is the language of the country, and the calculation is, that it is spoken by not fewer than nine millions of people. Circular in its character; sweet and mellifluous in its sound; highly-finished in its style and structure; renowned for its richness and antiquity, it will stand a comparison with any eastern tongue; it is well adapted to convey all kinds of knowledge—human and divine; it abounds with eastern figures, illustrations, and turns of thought, and would but ill receive into its lexicon, the harsher sounds and the colder style of a western dialect. Instead of resembling the Chinese, which being monosyllabic, will, it is said, scarcely admit of any rhetorical appeals, the Canarese is the vehicle of the most impassioned eloquence, now filling the hearers with rapture, and then plunging them into the deepest grief. What with the beauty and richness of its poetry, and the power of expression and variety of style which may be infused into its prose; what with the simplicity and vigour of its diction, and the grace and energy of its elocution, the pundits or learned Bramins, produce the most powerful effects upon their people. Two and two in company, they pass from city to city and from village to village, to expound their mythology, and to instruct their votaries in the errors and superstitions of their fathers. Under the shade of a banyan-tree, or in the porch of a temple, or in some public place of resort, they collect the crowds to hear them; the senior pundit takes out his Ramayana or his Bharta, and reads a stanza of poetry; the junior, sitting by his side, raises his voice into a sweet and agreeable chant, and pours forth his torrents of eloquence, while the people are rivetted to the spot, listen with the most profound attention, are now convulsed with laughter at some dexterous exploit, and then thrilled with horror at some dreadful calamity. At the close, and indeed sometimes during the service, a collection is made to carry on the strangers to another city. In this habit so customary, and so popular among the Canarese, who does not see an admirable preparative for the declaration of the gospel? The people who are accustomed to listen, with attention and with pleasure, to their own pundits while they expatiate upon error, are prepared to listen to the messengers of peace. The habit is one. Curiosity may induce some; and hope of amusement may attract others, to the place where the missionary expounds the gospel of his Lord; but this habit—this fondness for public lecture alone, can account for the numbers which I have seen standing and sometimes sitting in circles around us, and instead of listening for a moment and then hurrying away, detaining them, in attentive and patient audience for an hour, to the message of mercy. A European, it is true, will always command a larger congregation, than a native, and will receive more respect in consequence of his being a foreigner; but I would rather stand in the street, or in the market-place of any town in the Mysore, and call upon its inhabitants to repent and live, than I would stand in any of the villages and towns of Great Britain, and preach to the people. In the latter case, I might remain unheeded, or peradventure might be ill-used, or be taken before the magistrate as a disturber of the peace; but in the former, the people would receive me with kindness and respect, would give me an attentive audience, would thank me for my visit, and would probably entreat me to come again.

In the past history of the Mysore, there is something which renders the country a peculiarly important and interesting sphere for missionary enterprize. During the days of chivalry, the province was divided into so many dukedoms or principalities. Every chieftain had his fort, or his castle, which he maintained as his stronghold, and his extent of territory over which he ruled. His subjects were little better than vassals whom he professed to protect from the enemy without, but whom he led forth, as occasion required, against his neighbours in power, in order to obtain greater dominion and influence in the state. Dissentions sprang up on every side. The whole country was only an immense camp, where one commander watched the movements of his antagonist, and stood prepared to take advantage of every weakness and every infirmity—*a camp* where feuds, and rebellions and conspiracies and wars and massacres continually raged—*a camp* where one poligar fought with another to subvert his power, and to rise on his ashes, to superior greatness, rank and station in the empire. In those days, Hyder Ally—a man who could never write his own name—entered the service of the Rajah of the Mysore Proper. Bold, powerful, valiant, ambitious and enterprising, he very soon rose from the rank of a non-commissioned officer to that of a captain, from a captain to that of a general—from a general to that of commander of the forces, and, in the name of the rajah, he led forth his troops to battle and to victory; he subdued one prince after another, and added their territories to his own, and then he usurped the throne which he had promised to support, and he wore the crown which he had trodden in the dust.

As professors of the Mahommedan faith, Hyder and his son Tippoo were true Mussulmen, and carried on a system of the most fearful persecution against the Hindoos to bring them into subjection to the Koran. The country became Mahommedan in its laws, in its government, in its public functionaries, and in its religion. At first, bribes were held out to the converts, and offices of trust and emolument were offered to them in exchange for their superstition. But when money could not accomplish the object, then, power was at hand to enforce the demand. In the villages around Bangalore, there are still some to be met with, who had their ears cut off, or their noses slit, or were maimed in some bodily member, because they would not submit to the rite of circumcision. Hundreds and thousands were compelled to become Mahommedans by force, and were transported from the Mysore to the provinces below the Ghauts, while crowds of poor people were transported from Malabar to the Mysore, and were obliged to become Mahommedans in their turn. In a special manner, the demon of persecution raged against the Braminical tribe, and raised the shout of execration. As one of them was passing the palace one day, humming or whistling a tune, Hyder commanded the man to be brought before him. "Where, sir," said the Behauder, "do you expect to go when you die?" "I hope," replied the Bramin, "to go to Veicoonta,"—that is, the heaven of Vishnoo. "Send the fellow away to Veicoonta immediately," was the command of the despot, and the poor man was covered from head to foot with sky-rockets, and was blown up into the air. The very same system of cruel and atrocious barbarity which was carried on to propagate their religion, was also adopted to maintain their power and dominion in the empire. Whenever the treasury was empty, whenever a war was to be carried on against the English, whenever their friends and their allies were to be served, then the rack, or the wheel, or the stone were put in requisition, and spread through the city and through the country weeping and wailing and woe. So dreadful were the atrocities which Hyder inflicted upon this people, that there is still a tradition existing among them, that when he died and required a grave, mother earth refused to give it to him; the ground would not yield to the instrument; and they were obliged to erect a tomb for him above the ground. In the remembrance of such atrocities as these; in the recollection of a rule which embittered their existence, which expatriated them from their country, which tore them from their friends and families, made them Mahommedans by force, and brought upon them so many curses and so many calamities; what is the high and the vantage ground upon which missionaries stand when they go among such a people to publish the gospel of the meek and lowly Jesus? If they saw us with carnal weapons attempting to coerce them into obedience to the faith; if they found us enjoying the support and the patronage of the government, and trying to convert them by the power of laws and of penalties; then we should be on a level with their Mahommedan rulers. But no. The sword of the spirit is the only weapon which they have seen in our hands. Our Bibles, our tracts, our sermons, and the establishment of schools are the only ammunition which we have used. The weapons of our warfare have not been carnal; but mighty through God, to the pulling down of strongholds. The law of kindness, they know, has been upon our lips, and compassion and benevolence have been the ruling principles in our hearts. Our word among them has dropped like the dew—like the dew upon the tender herb. In the meekness, the patience, the love, the peace, the gentleness, and all the holy dipositions which the gospel inspires, what a contrast have they to the lust and the brutality of their Mahommedan rulers? And while the religion of Jesus diffuses a mild and a beneficent influence over the government under which they live; while it gives a tone of truth, of honour and of honesty to all the rules and regulations of the empire; while it makes their officers peace, and their exacters righteousness; while it gives them peace for war, and order for confusion, and every blessing instead of every curse, is not the country that is in such a state well prepared to receive the gospel of Jesus, and qualified to judge that our religion is divine, that it has descended from heaven, and that it is suited to the wants and miseries of men? Such is the state of the Mysore—a more important and interesting sphere of missionary labour there is not, in the opinion of the writer, to be found on the face of the earth.

CHAPTER XXII.

BANGALORE.

THE ESTABLISHMENT OF THE MISSION—LOCALITY OF HOUSES—PREACHING IN ENGLISH—FIRST CHAPEL—SAMUEL FLAVEL—THE ARRIVAL OF THE AUTHOR—CANARESE INSTRUCTORS—THE CONVERSION OF TWO BRAMINS—PERSECUTIONS—DECLENSION—BACKSLIDERS RESTORED—DAY-SCHOOLS—SEMINARY.

In 1820, the Rev. Messrs. Laidler and Forbes arrived at Bangalore, and began their missionary labours. As the Mysore was new and untried ground, they soon had many obstacles to contend with. To overcome the difficulties of the language, and to be more in the vicinity of the native town, Mr. Forbes settled in the fort; while Mr. Laidler chose a residence in the cantonment,—both thinking probably, as the writer does, that a camp situated a short distance from the enemy, may be as effectual in reducing the citadel, as one placed immediately under the walls.

Some have contended that a residence, located among the people, and in the heart of the native pettah, must be the most eligible for a mission-house. I cannot agree with this opinion. Such a site is attended with many disadvantages. If a residence at home, in an impure and a heated atmosphere, be considered unhealthy and dangerous, what shall we say of one in such a town as Bangalore, where the people are crowded together in narrow streets, where the mission-house must be surrounded by low, dense and thickly-populated buildings, where a thousand causes give rise to pestilential vapours, and where mosquitoes,* insects, and vermin of all kinds are incessant in their annoyance? The very best climate and situation in India are only tolerable to foreigners; where, then, is the use of choosing those which must inevitably impair the health, and shorten the life, when one in a more salubrious locality would be equally adapted to usefulness?

Such a residence, it may be argued, is necessary, that the natives may see the effects of Christianity, and have a living exemplification of its truths in the mission families. Would, I reply, that there was perfection upon the earth, and that heathens and others could always be led to estimate aright the holy and consistent conduct of the faithful. But it is not so. Look at the case of our Lord Jesus. Though he was holy, harmless, undefiled, and separate from sinners; though he went about doing good, and was perfect in all his principles,

* The mosquitoe is a small fly about the size of a gnat, whose bite is tormenting, especially to Europeans.

his words and his actions, yet the people said he had a devil; he was reputed to be a man gluttonous, a wine-bibber—a friend of publicans and sinners. It is impossible for missionaries and their associates to be perfect; inheritors of the same depraved nature as others, they are frail, infirm and fallible men; circumstances will often occur which, however trifling in themselves, and however easily accounted for by other Christians, the heathen would be likely to construe into objections against the truth. So long as human nature remains vile and corrupt, men will turn aside from all the good that may be visible in Christians, and will try to accumulate all that is evil, and fasten upon the latter, to extenuate their own wickedness, and to render the truth offensive to others. But more than this. While the exemplifications of the gospel, are thus constantly before the heathen, they are calculated to exasperate the evil passions of men; hatred to the system of purity is increased; the people cannot bear the light, because their deeds are evil; the prophets who are always testifying against sin, and prophesying evil concerning its votaries, become the objects of detestation; and the light which might be tolerated when seen in the distance, and in chastened splendour, becomes hateful by its glare, and its unchanging collision with the prejudices, and the evil habits and customs of paganism. But when the mission-house is situated a short distance from the town; when the family is known only as the centre of love, peace, joy and benevolence; when the missionary comes among the people with his hands full of blessings, to distribute portions of the Scriptures and tracts, to preach the gospel, to examine the schools, and to spend hours of the day in works of piety and benevolence, then the evils which are likely to arise from a perpetual collision are avoided, and all the good of a constant residence, is secured. After twelve years spent among Hindoos, and after seeing mission-houses situated in different positions, such are the views which the writer has been led to form upon the subject. Every locality will have its disadvantages; but of all others, *that*, in the midst of a dense and heathen population, in a noisy and crowded street, in a position where you must be constantly brought into contact with idolaters as neighbours, as merchants, as visitors, as rulers, and often as enemies, is to me, the most disagreeable, and the most useless.

But whatever situation be the best for a mission-house, our dear brethren could not have occupied one, among the heathen, had they desired it. The pettah of Bangalore was then under the sway of a native rajah, and the fort and the cantonment were the only spots under British government, and the only localities left for the missionaries to choose.

During the period of learning the language, our brethren deemed it right to turn their labours to account among our own countrymen. As there are generally two European regiments stationed at Bangalore, there was a wide field open for doing good amongst a class whose example and whose influence have often been so pernicious among the heathen. Mr. Forbes preached often in his own house in the fort, and so did Mr. Laidler in the cantonment. But the numbers who attended and the good that was done, led to the determination of erecting a chapel for the service. A grant of ground was obtained by Major Mackworth; subscriptions were raised upon the spot; and a sanctuary was built and opened in 1821. Though, in its appearance and style of architecture, it would be deemed, by the world, a very humble, and unassuming erection; yet it was rendered illustrious by the light which it diffused, and the blessings which were scattered around it. During the period that it stood, it was hallowed ground; it was consecrated by prayer; it became the residence of the shekinah. After it was opened, the labours of Mr. Laidler were very prosperous in the conversion of souls; the church was established; and much good was done in the name of Jesus. The author may be excused for his partiality to that Bethel. As the sphere of his early labours, as the spot where his children were consecrated to God, as the birth-place of many immortal souls, and as the house where the Lord was often seen in his glory, it is endeared to him by a thousand recollections. One storm seemed to burst over it after another; but still the divine glory overshadowed the mercy-seat. While the sacrifice offered upon Calvary for the remission of sins was held up to view as sufficient for pardon and for peace; and while the incense of prayer ascended in clouds to the throne of mercy, the divine blessing rested upon the congregation; the assemblies listened, with deep and hallowed interest, to the publication of the truth; many who came to the station thoughtless and the votaries of the world, returned to their own spheres, deeply impressed, and determined to surrender themselves to God in covenant; and the times of communion were often, seasons of refreshing from the presence of the Lord. As one regiment left the station to be succeeded by another, the sanctuary seemed, for a time, almost deserted, and its former worshippers were scattered over the plains. But the little band gradually increased; the story of redeeming love was accompanied by the heavenly influence; and anew the chapel was crowded by those who were seeking after salvation.

By some, it has been a matter of complaint that missionaries should devote any of their time to English preaching. But I have little sympathy with such an opinion. It may be so frequent, as to engross the time which ought to be consecrated to the heathen, and then it is to be deprecated. But a service on Sabbath evening, and that often divided among brethren, cannot materially interfere with the native work; it refreshes the spirit; it is calculated, amidst difficulties and discouragements among the heathen, to animate the missionary; it draws forth the sympathy, the prayers and the exertions of other believers to the undertaking; it unites the members of the mission families together, and leads them to take more interest in the advancement of the truth.

Shortly after the establishment of the mission, Mr. Laidler engaged Samuel Flavel, recommended by a Christian friend in Mysore, first as schoolmaster, and then as native teacher. It will be gratifying to my own feelings, as well as interesting, I trust, to the reader, to give a brief account of this brother in Christ. In the days of his heathenism, Samuel was engaged in the service of European gentlemen whose profession led them to travel much through the country. As he journeyed one day, he sat down to rest himself under a tree, and there found a copy of the gospels in Tamul. No sooner did he begin to read the book, than it completely engrossed his attention; his heart was greatly affected, and yielded a full assent to its declaration. From that period, he became very anxious to see the preachers of the gospel, to be associated with the body of the faithful, and to read and understand more of that book which unfolded the mind of his Lord. Providence directed his steps to Seringapatam, and though, at that time, he met with a few Christians there who could speak English only, and from whom he could derive but little profit, yet it was a stage on the road in which the Lord was leading him. He purchased a New Testament and two tracts called "True Wisdom," and "Short Prayers."

Thus equipped, the young disciple continued his journeys with his master, and visited Poona, Bombay, and Cananore; but wherever he went, he tried to find out Christians, to enlighten the few with whom he had intercourse, and often suffered persecution from the power and the tyranny of the Roman Catholics. On the return of his master and his family to the Madras presidency, they settled at Mysore. As he could find no brethren there, he prayed earnestly to the Lord that he would raise up a few to associate with him, and by his conversations with some, by the reading of the word of God to others, and by attending a little chapel which he had erected, and in which a few were accustomed to meet, the number increased to fifteen, and grace and mercy were multiplied to them all.

But this was too much for the Roman Catholics to behold, without being stirred up to strife and jealousy; and they therefore resolved to keep down this little Protestant band by violence and persecution. In December, 1819, they threw a shower of stones upon the chapel in which Samuel and his friends were assembled, seized upon John, Alexander, Paul and many others of the Catholics who had united with the brethren, taunted them with having become Protestants, tied their arms with ropes, kicked them, and beat them with their sandals.

This violent outrage was brought to the notice of

Mr. Cole, who was then Resident at the court of the rajah. Protection and liberty were promised to the Protestant party, and the Catholics were threatened with banishment from the country, should they continue their molestations. In this state of mind, enquiring after the truth, and willing to suffer the loss of all things that he might win Christ, the zealous convert purchased books, established a charity-school, erected a small place of worship in Mysore, tried, in all places, to bring heathens to the knowledge of Christ, and meekly and patiently suffered reproaches and persecution for the sake of the truth. He continued to hold fellowship with the few brethren at Seringapatam, and looked to them for counsel and advice; and as they were anxious that one of the missionaries lately arrived at Bangalore, should settle among them, they sent over Samuel with an intimation to that effect in November 1820. Mr. Laidler was struck with his appearance, and after making enquiries of the friends in Seringapatam, he invited him, as schoolmaster to Bangalore.

Thus was he brought into connexion with the mission, and prepared for the work which his Lord has given him to perform. He soon began to address the natives, and his word became the power and wisdom of God to the salvation of many. Through his instrumentality, a congregation was raised; and a church was formed, and he was ordained as pastor over it. He is a remarkably striking and interesting preacher. As he stands up to address his countrymen, there is an energy, an unction, and a seriousness of manner which are well calculated to arrest attention; his audience listen to him with great interest and concern; and heathens are often compelled to weep under his warnings and his representations of the Gospel.

On the arrival of the author and his wife in June 1824, he attended the native service upon the first Sabbath morning. It was delightful to hear a converted heathen address his countrymen with so much fluency and earnestness, as Samuel did. It was refreshing to see the assembly listening with attention to the word of life, and to witness two from among them receiving the ordinance of baptism. But it was a greater source of joy and gratitude, still, to sit down at the table of the Lord, and commemorate his death, with twenty who were once idolaters, now no longer heirs of wrath, but children of the living God, and to see them give evidence of their conversion to Christ. Long shall I remember the feelings which I then experienced, and heartily did I wish that those who pray for the cause, and support its interests at home, could have witnessed such a scene. Nor did Samuel stand alone; two other youths endued, there was reason to hope, with fervent piety, laboured assiduously, as far as their ability extended, and led us to entertain the expectation that there would soon go forth a host of warriors to fight the battles of the Lord, and to warn their countrymen of the danger and destruction to which they were exposed.

After our settlement at Bangalore, the author gave his time and attention almost entirely to the Canarese. As he plainly perceived that it was impossible for a missionary to be useful, without an extensive knowledge of the vernacular language; there was scarcely a day, except the Sabbath, during the first year of his residence in the Mysore, that he did not spend seven or eight hours in trying to acquire it. If this period is not improved for the purpose, it is generally found that the missionary, unable to surmount the difficulties, gives way to despondency and does not use the language at all, or is satisfied with a very superficial knowledge of it. But when this period is employed, with zeal, with perseverance and with industry, to the attainment of this object, the student generally triumphs; the obstacles are surmounted; the future progress becomes easy and delightful; and the missionary not only finds the road to the heart, but enjoys a privilege which enables him to move with freedom and usefulness among the people. I allude to this subject only to stimulate my brethren, and to discuss a few points of interest and importance.

It has generally been thought that the native languages are better learned from Hindoo pundits, than from European instructors. I cannot agree to this. My own experience is exactly the reverse. A Hindoo moonshee does not comprehend the difficulties of the European pupil. From his very infancy, he has been accustomed to pronounce the letters and the words of his language without thought, and his organs of speech are so formed to their enunciation, that he would find it very difficult to pronounce them in a different way. It is not so with the European. He has never heard such sounds before; he is ignorant of the manner in which he should use his organs to pronounce them; and the native cannot direct him, since he comprehends not his perplexities. But the European having overcome all these obstacles, is able to direct the pupil in a moment; will not, as the native is disposed to do, rather than run the risk of offending his patron, connive at his mistakes and blunders; and points out, to his special notice, those peculiarities in idiom, in style, in syntax, and in other parts of grammar, which have given most trouble to himself.

But if, in addition to a European teacher, the missionary could spend some months in England, receiving these and similar elementary instructions, it would be of the greatest importance. The Indian climate soon begins to make inroads upon his constitution; the studies which he is obliged to pursue in obtaining the language are more severe and trying, than any future or past exercises of mind; in his native land, all his strength, intensity of application, and best energies could be brought to bear upon the subject; and a dominion over the intricacies of the language at home, and in his own climate, would enable him to enter, with the greatest facility, and power and acceptance, in the province where he might be called to labour, and would, at all events, break the force of that intense application which, in India, is perhaps more injurious to the constitution, than the climate, or the more active duties of his sphere.

In 1825, two Bramins came to Bangalore, and after a time of serious enquiry, received the ordinance of baptism. Alexander and Rufus were superior, intelligent, and interesting men. Brothers according to the flesh; they now became brethren according to the spirit, and companions in trial and adversity. Alexander had long been feeling after the Lord that if possible he might find him; had met with Samuel Flavel at Mysore in 1819, and received a portion of the Scriptures from him, though the latter was then in his noviciate; and had tried what Popery could do for a wounded spirit. But after wandering long, and finding no rest in any of the systems which superstition could propose, he and his brother came to Bangalore to find the missionaries. Long, serious, and interesting were the discussions which they had with Samuel, and with the brethren. On the day of their baptism, they took the Braminical cords from their necks, and gave them into the hands of the native teacher, and parted with all the insignia of heathenism to show their attachment to Christianity. It was ani nterest ing sight to witness two of the sons of Brumha—once proud and haughty—once the objects of divine reverence and worship, receiving the ordinance of baptism from the hands of one whom they were taught to consider as unclean, an outcast, and the off-scouring of the earth. Nothing could be more humiliating than this to the proud spirit of man, nor could better attest their renunciation of caste, and their determination to be the Lord's. What scorn! what violence and rage! what malice and indignity! what shame, imprecations and revengeful passions were created among their tribe and their family, as soon as they received this intelligence. Exasperated beyond all endurance, the Bramins went to the home of the converts, called upon their parents and relatives to disown them as their children, and to give proper testimony that they consigned them to infamy and degradation for ever. Afraid of the consequences to themselves on the one hand, and enraged at the disgrace brought upon their family by this act of their children on the other, the parents mourned for their sons, as the Hindoos are accustomed to do for the dead; they performed for them the funeral rites which are usual amongst the Bramins, and sent a Chandala, after the ceremonies were ended, to inform their sons that, since they had embraced the Pariah religion, they were committed to the infamy of outcasts, and were never more to regard their father's house as their home, nor to represent themselves as relatives to their family.

This intelligence was a heavy trial to the converts. But through evil report and good report, they determined to persevere. Two or three times, they visited their native village, with the hope of softening the asperity of those feelings which their profession of Christianity had awakened in the minds of their parents, and of obtaining those persons in marriage to whom they were betrothed, and with whom they still considered themselves bound in honour to form, if possible, a matrimonial alliance. But it was of no use; their friends were not to be reconciled. On their first visit, Braminical vigilance was awake, and their relatives left them to silent scorn, and to bitter contempt; and though they remained some days in the village and in the neighbourhood, no relative would venture to speak to them. On their second visit, the head man of the village, their parents, their sister and friends came to the choultry where the party were assembled, to give vent to their spleen and their vengeance. Some were weeping bitterly; others were cursing Samuel Flavel; the mother of the converts, in a fit of frenzy, rolled herself upon the ground; then, covered the teacher with mud, and tossed the dust into the air, invoking the most frightful imprecations upon him, as the author of this mischief, and as the cause of all the shame, and grief which had come upon her and her family. On a third and a fourth visit, their friends manifested the most poignant grief and sorrow, entreating the converts to abandon their new religion; offering to make all exertions to restore them to their caste and privileges again; and promising to grant them their betrothed in marriage, and every comfort which it was in their power to bestow. But these allurements were presented in vain. The converts were enabled to stand fast in the liberty wherewith Christ had made them free, and were resolved not to be again entangled in the yoke of bondage.

For a time, Alexander and Rufus continued to run well, but unmindful of the depravity of their hearts, and the power of corruption, they were led astray. The men who surrendered every thing for Christ, who withstood the calumnies of their enemies, and the persecutions of their friends, and who remained unmoved amidst the tears and solicitations of their dearest relatives, fell before the power of temptations, and were overcome by the corruptions that are in the world through lust. Alexander forsook the mission, and was unknown and unheard of, for a period; but he afterwards came to Bangalore, and was employed as a moonshee by the writer. Still he did not seem comfortable, and suddenly decamped from the station, and was found at Bellary. His career became more humble and consistent. Amidst some infirmities that continued to cleave to him, he rendered considerable assistance to the missionaries; was a bold and eloquent advocate of the truth; and grew in a conformity to his divine Lord, as his end, unknown to him and to others, was rapidly advancing. In the month of March, 1831, he accompanied the missionaries to attend the festival at Humpee. At the first stage upon the road, he was seized with cholera, and died in five hours. His end was calm and peaceful. His humble deportment, his spirituality of mind, his fervent zeal for the Divine glory, the unction and importunity of his prayers, his entire renunciation of all dependence upon his own merits, and simple reliance upon Christ, gave to all around him the assurance that he died in the Lord, and joined the innumerable company and church of the first-born.

The history of Rufus is perhaps more affecting. and more humbling, than that of Alexander. After he fell into sin, he renounced his profession ot Christianity, wore the marks of superstition, and went to great lengths in the service of the flesh and wickedness. As though he would make atonement for the crime which he had committed in forsaking the religion of his fathers, he determined to become an ascetic, to practice austerities, to go on a pilgrimage to Benares, and to pass through every kind of suffering that he might propitiate the favour of Vishnu. With these views, he had travelled four hundred miles, and was enduring the most dreadful poverty and sufferings, when he came to himself and exclaimed, "What a fool I am! I am trying to obtain peace and rest to my soul in delusions and lies. When I was a Christian, I experienced true joy, comfort, and happiness; but I am now in reality the poor prodigal, and am living upon the husks that the swine do eat. Is there not bread enough in my father's house and to spare; why then should I perish here with hunger? I will arise and go to my father, and will say to him, 'Father, I have sinned against heaven and in thy sight, and am not worthy to be called one of thy sons, only make me as a hired servant.'" In spirit and in truth, he returned to his Father and was numbered among the repenting prodigals. He came back to Bangalore. I have never seen a Hindoo so humbled, so contrite, and so deeply affected with a sense of sin. He lay at the foot of the cross. He confessed, before all, his iniquities, and manifested that godly sorrow that worketh repentance to salvation. Since that period, he has maintained a very consistent deportment. He is a powerful and impressive speaker; and I have often been pleased and edified with his addresses. He is now in the capacity of moonshee to Mr. Hands at Bangalore, and his future course will I trust evince that he is a servant of the Most High God.

From the history of Alexander and Rufus, there have arisen some questions which have always appeared of considerable importance to myself, and which may perhaps have arrested the attention of others. Not only did they renounce their caste at baptism,; but they ate and drank in common with the Pariah Christians.* Unable to obtain the females in marriage to whom they were betrothed, Alexander was wedded to a Pariah Christian, and Rufus to a Shoodra one. But is it necessary, at the present juncture, to arouse all the prejudices of their Hindoo countrymen? Nothing, in the estimation of their own people, could be more infamous than this social intercourse, and these marriage alliances. What bearing had these circumstances on the declension of the converts, and on their course of backsliding? To this important fact, I can bear testimony, that this levelling system completely ruined their usefulness. Wherever the intelligence was known, that they had formed such connexions, the people would not listen to them; they were shunned and despised as the most degraded of their kind; when Shoodra teachers, and even Pariah teachers themselves have been heard with pleasure, the Bramin converts have been scorned and execrated. Leaving, therefore, the contempt and the persecutions which the converts have to endure, out of the question, is it wise and prudent, on the ground of usefulness, to awaken the very worst prejudices of the heathen, to adopt a system which is of no real utility to the truth and to religion, and instead of elevating the lower classes in the social scale, to bring down the highest

* I do not use this term as one of reproach, but for the sake of distinction.

to a level with those who *are there esteemed* the very dregs of society?

At the commencement of the mission, five day-schools were established, and were tolerably well attended. But Mr. Laidler soon perceived that there were many impediments to prevent the gracious effects which were so much desired. The children were often irregular in their attendance; heathen teachers were the only persons who could be found as schoolmasters; the greatest objections were made to the use of Christian books; what good the children might receive during the day, was neutralized by heathen example and influence on their return to their home in the evening; the parents, insensible themselves to the benefits of education, were indifferent whether their children made progress or not; and as soon as they could employ them in any way to their worldly advantage, the field, or the service, was reckoned superior to the school.

These obstacles soon convinced the missionary that a different system must be adopted, and he therefore resolved to try the method of boarding-schools, that the children might reside upon his own premises, that they might be withdrawn from the influence and example of their heathen parents and neighbours, that they might be entirely under Christian care and superintendence, and might be brought up in the nurture and admonition of the Lord. All who were thus educated, would be likely to receive Christian instruction, and be initiated into the great doctrines of our holy religion. A school for boys, and another for girls, were established, therefore, on these principles, and were found much more useful, and promised more encouragement, than the others.

From some youths who sprung out of the boys' school, and from others who were converted when more advanced, the seminary was established with the view of raising up native teachers to propagate the gospel. On Mr. Laidler's departure for England, there were fourteen or fifteen students of different ages, talents, and acquirements; but as Tamul was for the most part their vernacular language, and it was thought they would be more useful, and would render more efficient assistance to the brethren in a Tamul country, they were appointed to labour at other stations. While two remained at Bangalore, Samuel and two students went to Bellary; Isaac and two more were sent to Salem; two laboured at Madras, two at Chittoor, two at Belgaum, and several at other missions in the peninsula. Some of these have entered into their rest; but others still remain at their stations, to assist the missionaries, and to carry on the work of the Lord.

CHAPTER XXIII.

BANGALORE.

CANARESE BOARDING-SCHOOL—HEATHEN OBJECTIONS—EFFECTS UPON THE CHILDREN—SERMON OF MOSES—INFLUENCE UPON RELATIVES—CHRISTIAN VILLAGE—ARRIVAL OF MR. REEVE—NATIVE CONGREGATIONS — MR. TURNBULL — NEW CHAPEL — NATIVE TEACHERS—ADJACENT TOWNS—TRIALS AND AFFLICTIONS—POWER OF THE BRAMINS—REVOLUTION—BRITISH COMMISSION—THE CLAIMS OF THE MYSORE.

In the year 1825, the Canarese boarding-school was established. Hitherto, the efforts of this kind were chiefly confined to Tamul children; it was now thought desirable to extend them to the Canarese, whose difference of language, and whose claims as the inhabitants of the Mysore, seemed to require special and indefatigable exertions. As soon as the plan was proposed to the community, our own countrymen raised objections against it. "How absurd," said they, "is it to imagine that the Canarese people, who plume themselves upon their caste, will give up their children to your care and superintendence, will allow them to reside and to eat and drink upon your premises, and will suffer them to be instructed in the truths of Christianity!

It is a perfect delusion. You may obtain as many subscriptions as you please, but we foretel that the scheme will certainly fail."

On the other hand, the Canarese Bramins and priests sent forth their denunciations against their own people. "Venture," said they, "to send one of your children to such a school, and depend upon it, the wrath and vengeance of the gods will be upon you; your eyes will drop out; you will fall down dead upon the street; the cholera will enter into your houses and destroy you and your children. As to these missionaries, they only wish to get hold of your sons and daughters, to transport them to England. If any of your children are found in such a seminary, our anathemas will rest upon you, and upon them for ever."

But, notwithstanding this hostility of our countrymen on the one side, and these terrible denunciations of the priests upon the other, many Canarese parents were found who gave up their children to our care; the school was established; in the name of our God, we set up our banners; one difficulty after another was surmounted; and after a time, it pleased Jehovah to give his blessing to this institution. As we were in the habit of calling the children aside to converse freely with them on the great concerns of immortality, to pray with them and for them, and to bring the truth home to their consciences; the tears might be seen starting into their eyes, and running down their sable cheeks; their hearts sometimes became too full to render answers to our enquiries; the Spirit of the Lord seemed to be operating upon their minds; already well acquainted with the great truths of revelation, they were now beginning to feel their inestimable value and sweetness; and under a deep sense of their guilt and unworthiness, and the suitability of the Redeemer and his salvation to their wants and miseries, some of these dear children came boldly forward, and gave themselves up to the Lord. In the face of opposition, and of sacrifices which they would be called upon to make, they said to all around them, "Choose ye this day whom you will serve; as for us, we will serve the God of Israel."

It may perhaps be interesting to allude to one or two instances in which these children manifested gracious dispositions, and their attachment to the truth. Obliged on one occasion to remove from the mission-house in which we lived, that some repairs might be effected on the roof, and to reside in another at a considerable distance, and where there would be few persons likely to render us aid in an hour of need, we determined to call along with us, a native Christian widow, with her four children, and we assigned them a small house on the premises in which they might reside. As I was taking exercise in front of the house one evening, I thought that I heard the sound of psalmody. "What!" said I to myself, "is it possible that there is some Christian family in this neighbourhood, unknown to me, and that they are now celebrating the praises of God in their domestic worship?" I passed down through the premises that I might ascertain the fact; and in the door of the small house which we had assigned to this Christian widow, there stood her elder boy, about ten years of age. The child had read the Scriptures; he was now singing a hymn in which the other members of the family joined; I saw him go down upon his knees, and heard him offer up, as the leader of their domestic devotions, a very suitable and fervent prayer to the God of salvation. He prayed for himself, for his mother and brother and sisters, for the children in the school, for the missionaries, for the perishing heathen around, and for the prosperity of Christ's kingdom throughout the world. I was greatly delighted with what I saw and heard that night, and could not but exclaim, "Lord! out of the mouths of babes and sucklings, thou hast ordained and perfected praise!"

About to return to my native land, I determined to visit the out-stations connected with the mission. In passing on to Begoor, one of the native teachers came up to me, and said, "Sir, as you are soon to leave us and return to England, perhaps you would like to hear Moses give an address to the people to-day." "What!" I replied, "has Moses begun to address the heathen? I was aware that he was a promising lad, that he was endowed with very good gifts, and talents; I hoped also that he was under a gracious influence; but as he had only been three years in the school, it had not entered my mind that he had ventured to speak to public assemblies." "O yes, sir, replied the teacher, when we go alone to the villages, Moses often gives an address to the congregation." "Well," I said, "I shall endeavour to hear Moses to-day." After we had preached the gospel fully to that interesting people, I saw Moses standing upon my right hand, and I said to him, "Well, Moses, would you like to give an address to the assembly to-day?" "If you please, sir," he modestly replied, "I shall endeavour to do so." He stood forth. There was an idol in the place; it was an image of Ganesa—the god of wisdom. He directed the attention of the people to this idol. "Now," said he, "look to that divinity. It has eyes, but it sees not; it has ears, but it hears not; it has a mouth, but it speaks not; it has hands, but it handles not; it has feet, but it walks not. If you wish to show it, to the admiration of the people, you must employ a porter to bear it upon his shoulders; it is impossible that it can do any thing to assist itself. I should like to know what this idol has ever done for you, in return for all the favours which you confer upon it? You daily place food before it, that it may eat, and water, that it may drink; you give it plantains and cocoa-nuts to please it; you put garlands of flowers around its neck to adorn it; sometimes you make it a present of a suit of clothes; then, on the days of the festival, you place it on the shoulders of a porter, and you cause it to be carried round the streets and lanes of the town, to receive the worship and adorations of the multitude; but what has this idol ever done for you, in return for such favours as these? Why? If you keep a little dog in your house, and give him a portion of rice day after day, that dog will return your kindness with gratitude; it will leap with joy on your approach; it will bark at the advance of a stranger; it will endeavour to protect you from your enemies; but what has this idol ever done for you, as a return for the honour and the offerings which you daily grant to it? No. It cannot do you any good, and I am sure it cannot do you any harm." After he had thus exposed the folly of worshipping idols of wood and stone, he directed them to the living and true God; he showed them that they were sinners of the race of Adam, and exposed to the curse of a broken law; he directed them to the Saviour whom God had raised up for their deliverance; he called upon them to repent of their transgressions, to believe in the Redeemer, to abandon their idolatry and to live. It was a discourse so well delivered, so simple and impressive, so suitable to the wants and circumstances of the people, that I could not but feel grateful to God. Moses has lately been married to an excellent young woman,* who was trained up in

* In connexion with these boarding-schools both Tamul and Canarese, there were classes of females under the care of our

our girls' school, and is now engaged in preaching the gospel to his countrymen.

I rejoice to hear that orphan-schools are now established at so many stations, and that they have become the refuge for such numbers of children, during the horrible famines that have prevailed. Whether these asylums, or schools composed of children whose parents are alive, will be more productive of good to our missions, is a question which time alone will decide. The latter, when they become pious, are likely to have more influence and to receive greater respect among the heathen, than the former. From our Canarese school at Bangalore, there arose John, Timothy, Elisha, Josiah, Noah, and several more—youths of great promise —youths who were diligent in study, fervent in spirit, and anxious for the welfare of men—and youths who will yet, I trust, be great blessings to India. No sooner did they feel the importance of the truth, than they began to reason with others. Allowed occasionally to visit their homes, and spend a day with their friends, they embraced the opportunities to argue with them upon the absurdity of heathenism, and the truth of Christianity, and upon the necessity of renouncing their idols and of giving themselves

respective partners. Many of the adult females learned to read the Scriptures with great propriety, and were useful to others; many of the girls trained to piety and good works have become the wives of our teachers both at Bangalore and distant stations, and are blessings to many in their respective spheres.

to the Lord. Their relatives could not but admit the force of their reasoning. "At the establishment," said they, "of this school, the Bramins foretold the most fearful calamities to us and to our children; but which of them has been realized? Instead of our sons growing up wild, reprobate, disobedient, and ignorant as those of our neighbours, they are wise, learned, respectable, and likely to become an honour to their families. There must be something in this religion very different from our own, to produce such effects." They resolved to attend at the chapel: sermons suited to their capacities were delivered; some of their minds were impressed; and not a few joined themselves to the church of God, and professed to be his people.

It was this circumstance which gave rise to what has been called a Christian village, consisting of a few houses in a beautiful locality, and inhabited by families who had renounced their idolatry, and made a profession of the Christian religion. Behind our school-room, and adjoining the mission compound, there was a piece of ground considerable in its dimensions, cultivated by heathen gardeners, and admirably suited to missionary purposes. Some of its occupants had removed from their premises; others died and left their leases to children who had already found another inheritance; and all agreed to offer their leases to the missionary for a trifling consideration. A covenant, sanctioned by the native authorities, was made, and after a time, a pious officer obtained a grant of the ground from the European commissioners, and made it over to the writer, to be appropriated to the Christian natives. I cannot revert to that interesting spot, without peculiar emotions. Shaded by large trees, and secluded almost entirely from observation, one house after another was added to the number, and no one would have fancied the nursery was there, till their ears, at the dawn, were greeted by the voice of psalmody, or in the evening, by the sweet sound of prayer. The parents, the brothers and sisters, the relatives and friends of our young men, began to claim alliance with the God of salvation. Other parents, allured by their advice and example, placed their children under our care, and came themselves and said, "We will go with you, for the Lord is among you, and he has spoken good concerning you. Only give us a house to reside in, and we will take up our abode under your protection; this is the way to heaven, and we will walk in it; our friends are mad against us, at the mere proposal, and the priests already fulminate their rage; but we must go with you, and our children will become wise and good and happy." Eight of these families resided, at first, in the village, and daily received instruction in the principles of our religion. Some of them lived by keeping cattle, others by working at the anvil; some were gardeners and others were day-labourers; but one great object was to see that they were all employed.

During my residence in India, the people conducted themselves in a very becoming and satisfactory manner. Quiet, industrious, willing to learn, patient in suffering, and attentive to the ordinances, they added greatly to my comfort while labouring alone. Some of them who were employed in the building of our new chapel, showed commendable zeal in setting forward the work. When they came to reside under the care of the mission, I laid them under no conditions, nor engagements, except to attend the means of grace, and listen with attention to the truth; constraint there was none; baptism was set forth as an ordinance which should be administered to those only who believe, which none but anxious enquirers and the subjects of grace could receive, without being guilty of sin and hypocrisy, and which was intended to disassociate them from heathenism, and connect them with the church of God. The teachers and the missionary often went from house to house; and with simplicity and affection, directed the people to their state as sinners, to Jesus as the only Redeemer, and to regeneration, to faith, and to a life of holy obedience as the only suitable preparation for another world. Their objections, their enquiries, their convictions, and the impressions made on their minds were all taken account of, and whenever they began to think, and to take an interest in the great salvation, we could not but rejoice over them. Still they were mere children in knowledge, in Christian experience, in stability and in attention to divine things; and it was only necessary that they should be neglected for a time, that instead of being watched over and prayed with, and daily instructed in the truth, they should be left to the weaknesses of their own minds, and to the corruptions of their hearts, then the weeds of prejudice would be sure to germinate, Satan must enter to deceive and to destroy, and caste was only necessary as a watch-word to scatter the sheep and drive them from the fold.

In 1827, Mr. and Mrs. Reeve joined the mission. Long shall I remember the communion of spirit, the goodwill and unanimity, the love and peace which were enjoyed by both the mission families during the period that we laboured together. In addition to the general interest, and the active duties which called for Mr. Reeve's talents and exertions in the affairs of the station, he undertook the great work of compiling a Dictionary in Canarese. The first part of it, comprising the English and Carnataca was finished at Bellary, and the other part, embracing the Carnataca and English was pursued with great zeal and industry, and brought to a successful termination at Bangalore. It is a very elaborate work, and must render the acquisition of the language much easier to students and to missionaries in future days. While in various departments, we were separate in interest and enterprise, we preached alternately in English and Canarese—the services which were conducted in the chapel on the Lord's day. The Canarese and the Tamul people long continued to worship together. The difference of language would seem necessarily to imply a division of the people; but their union answered some most important purposes. Such are the evils which spring to real religion from caste, that any system which would tend to destroy them, ought to be adopted. As the Tamul Christians were generally Pariars, and the Canarese were Shoodras, there was a constant desire on the part of the former to level all distinctions, and on the part of the latter to maintain their superiority. But their mixing together in one congregation; their sitting on the same benches; their forming one church; their listening to the native teachers both Tamul and Canarese; and their having the ordinances administered in one way, at the same time, and to all indiscriminately—all tended to destroy their attachment to caste and to promote, among them, union and goodwill. When I left the station, there were about forty natives in church-fellowship; but as the Tamul people are only foreigners, the number is liable to fluctuations. Though subject to many infirmities, the Christians were humble and devoted, walked worthy of their high vocation, and brought forth fruit unto God.

Mr. Turnbull—long a member of our church, and a pious, active young Christian—became a candidate for missionary labour in 1830. His improvement in the languages to which his attention was directed, and in the theological studies which he pursued, was very commendable ; and he promised to be a useful missionary. Born in England, and yet brought up in India, his constitution was assimilated to the climate, and he seemed to bear exposure to the heat and to the sun, without suffering any inconvenience. His Christian meekness, humility, benevolence, and modesty were very remarkable, and appeared to qualify him for successful labours among the heathen. That he might enjoy the advantages of an English education, his parents agreed to bear all the expense of sending him to this country, and of pursuing his course of study in one of our theological seminaries. The directors of the society kindly received him, and he studied for three years at Homerton College. He was ordained in 1836, and returned to Bangalore to devote his life to missionary labour, replenished, as we thought, with energy both of body and of mind, richly endowed with zeal and with the spirit of his Master, and promising in his future career to endure hardness, as a good soldier of Jesus Christ. But alas! how have our hopes been disappointed. Scarcely had he entered upon his work, when disease laid him low, and after a long season of trial and suffering, has consigned him to the grave in a foreign land. He died at Sydney, in the full hope of immortality. His excellent widow assures us that his thoughts ruminated to the last on the work of the Lord in India, and in New South Wales. How mysterious are the ways of Providence!

As our old chapel stood so often in need of repair, and required so much expense to support it against the weather; my esteemed colleague, Mr. Reeve, and myself drew up an address towards the end of 1833, and circulated it among the friends of religion at Bangalore, and throughout the peninsula. The kind and liberal manner in which our proposal was responded to, reflected the highest honour on their liberality, and their Christian profession. Eight hundred and seventy-five pounds were required to finish the building, but it was all paid, as soon as the chapel was opened. It would be injudicious here to mention names; but in addition to their pecuniary contributions, some assisted us with their advice and co-operation; others kindly furnished us with the loan of implements and similar articles necessary for carrying forward the work; and some did not withhold, when they were required, their gratuitous and laborious exertions. The chapel is a very commodious building. On the outside, it is, exclusive of the portico, about eighty-five feet long, and forty-six broad, since two vestries, one for the minister, and the other for prayer-meetings, add to its extent, and greatly to its convenience. A row of pilasters on each side, and a portico, extend-

MISSION CHAPEL AT BANGALORE.

MISSION CHAPEL AT RAMAKALCHOKE NEAR CALCUTTA

ing the whole breadth of the building, give it a bold, and handsome appearance. Inside, it is spacious, and will contain between three and four hundred people. The roof is lofty, is composed of three arches running the length of the chapel, and is supported by a row of Saxon arches which rest upon two piers on either side. The whole is regarded as an elegant piece of architecture, and all parties seemed to unite in expressing the greatest satisfaction with the manner in which the work was executed. The foundation is black stone and chunam; the structure brick and chunam; and the roof is fine chunam and Syrian tubes, strengthened with rows of brick. As Bangalore is a very large and important station, and is likely to become the centre of the Mysore mission, it was necessary that we should have a more substantial and commodious building, than our old chapel—one in which the whole of our Christian community, as they increase, might assemble to praise the Lord. Should things proceed in their ordinary course, the present one will, I hope, last for ages to come: may the converts of future days find it a house of prayer, a sanctuary in which the gospel will be faithfully preached, and a dwelling-place for the shekinah!

So prejudicial to health are the heat and insalubrity of the climate; so great are the difficulties with which European missionaries have to contend; and so vast are the multitudes upon which the truth is to operate, that it would be unwise in the highest degree to depend upon Europe alone for the conversion of India to Christ. Impressed with this conviction, the missionaries, from the commencement of the work, saw the necessity of raising up native preachers, and of giving them a suitable education to proclaim the tidings of mercy. Many, through the blessing of God upon our labours, have been trained at Bangalore. Scarcely a station in the peninsula has been more highly honoured in this respect. Jacob, Joseph, Alexander, Joshua, and others have entered into rest; but such was their Christian experience while they lived, and such was the testimony which they bore to the truth on their death-beds, that I have no doubt they stand in the presence of God, and celebrate the praises of the Lamb. There labour now at different stations, as well as in the Mysore, many who are not only well instructed in the gospel, but who are able to teach others also,—many who are workmen that need not to be ashamed, rightly dividing the word of truth—many who have been very useful in converting heathens to God. Instead of dwelling upon the number, the talents, and the labours of those whom I left behind at Bangalore, and who have still a warm place in my affections, my prayers, and my hopes, let the reports from the Chittoor, from Bellary, from Salem, from Vizagapatam and Belgaum bear witness to the diligence and zeal, and success of those who have gone from the station, and are labouring for the good of souls. I speak not now of those who know only a little of Christianity, and go forth to propagate that portion unto others; I speak not now of those who are little better than heathens, and are, therefore, very ill qualified to advocate the truth; but I speak of men who are mighty in the scriptures, who are endowed with the gifts and graces of the Spirit, and who when they stand up among the priests and the champions of heathenism, are able to expose the absurdities of their system, and put its best supporters to silence and to shame.

Well, it may be said, if such teachers are to be found in India, and can be raised up among idolaters, where is the use of calling upon the sons and daughters of Britain, to forsake their country, their kindred and their homes, to publish in foreign lands the gospel of God? No; I reply, whatever may be the character, the talents and acquirements of our native teachers, they will not be a substitute for your lack of service at this hour of the day. Take a battalion of seapoys alone, and send them forth on a campaign where their march is opposed, or command them to storm a citadel where they are exposed to toil, to danger, and to destruction; and what would be the consequence? Such is the influence which a long course of oppression and of despotism has had upon their race that the Hindoos are timid and cowardly in the extreme, and the probability is that, in the hour of trial, they would turn their backs upon the enemy and flee. But let that same battalion be under the command of British officers; let them be led on to battle, and animated in the struggle by the bravery and the courage and example of our countrymen, and they advance to the action with courage,—they ascend the breach in triumph, and they march through scenes of carnage and of death to victory. Our native teachers partake of the character of their countrymen. Though they are Christians, and though many of them declare the gospel with courage and with boldness, yet standing alone, they would make but a feeble assault upon the strongholds of the enemy, and a heartless stand in the day of trial and calamity. No. They want the spirits of the West to be their leaders to battle and to victory; they require the children of freedom "to teach their hands to war and their fingers to fight;" and in their present state, they demand British missionaries not only to give them wisdom and understanding—not only to instruct them in science and philosophy and religion—not only to establish seminaries for their advancement in knowledge and in grace; but to support them in the day of trial—to animate them, by a noble example, in their attacks on the bulwarks of Satan—and to go before them, if it be necessary, to the breach, to the prison, or to the grave!

In the course of providence, some of the native teachers seemed more prepared than others, to act for themselves, and, at a distance from the superintendence of the missionaries, it was thought they might be able to carry on the work of the Lord. This experiment, it is evident, ought to be made as early as possible, at every missionary station. Many disadvantages will unquestionably attend our first attempts. Numbers will likely prove unfaithful. Some, having little principle to support them amidst the dazzling splendour of their former idolatry, may be led to connive at the crimes, and the absurdities of superstition; others, afraid of the shafts of calumny and ridicule, and supported by no one whose faith and courage would keep them steady, may be led to compromise the truth, and to remain silent when they should cry aloud; and many more, at a distance from the eye of watchful vigilance, may sink down into indolent repose, or fall into sin, and forfeit their right to the sacred appointment. But how are these evils to be remedied? Not surely by putting off the trial to some future period, nor by waiting till we obtain those in whom we can place implicit confidence. Such individuals will only be obtained by perseverance in this system, and by gradually raising the character of the teachers. I am reasoning now—not on the ground that miracles will be wrought in our favour—but on the ground that truth will advance in the way it has usually done, under the dispensation of the Spirit. The trial must be made, and the sooner the better; it is as well to meet the difficulty now, as a hundred years hence. Failure must be experienced; but as our teachers increase in number and in talents, our standard of character must be raised; a strict discipline must be observed; ejection from office must become, in every case, the award of the unfaithful; greater confidence and higher privileges must become the recompense of the zealous and the good; and thus, through the blessing of the Most High, will our confidence in their fidelity be increased, and the surrounding districts be blessed with a faithful and laborious ministry.

The question of settling the native teachers in the adjoining towns, is one which might easily have been disposed of, on British territory. But we lived in an independent province, and were under the government of a heathen rajah, and had the power, and the violence of the Bramins to encounter. The question, therefore, with us, was one of peculiar importance and difficulty. Whether the public functionaries on the spot would regard the appeal; whether we should be obliged to apply to the court at Mysore; and whether the Bramins would not exert all their power and craft to injure us, and defeat our purpose, were questions involved in doubt, and were urged as objections to the effort. But in the strength of God, I determined to make the attempt. I wrote a letter to the Fouzdar of Bangalore. Regarding expediency and worldly policy as unworthy in such a cause, and having always found a plain, bold, and honest avowal of our design, the most likely to succeed among heathens, as well as among Christians, I told him faithfully the object which we had in view; I had nothing to conceal; I wished our teachers to be allowed to settle in the neighbouring towns, on the same principles upon which heathens and Mahommedans and Roman Catholics were permitted, that they might establish schools, preach the gospel to the inhabitants, and range monthly through a certain district to distribute tracts and portions of the Scriptures. I requested that a piece of ground might be rented to them upon which they might erect a house, as it was not likely that heathens would let houses to them. This letter was committed to the hands of our teacher Jacob, to carry and to deliver to the Fouzdar. In the evening he returned, stating there was no answer. "Well! Jacob," I said, "you must continue to go daily to the cutchery; sit down in dherna upon the Fouzdar; act the part of the importunate widow in the gospel; and we will give ourselves to fervent prayer that God, who can turn the rivers of water, would influence the heart of this man, and induce him to give us a favourable reply. For six weeks did this bold, generous and devoted teacher continue to go, and sit down in the presence of the Fouzdar, reminding him that he had brought a letter, and waited for a reply! At length, faith and prayer and importunity triumphed. One morning, Jacob brought me three letters stamped with the government seal, and addressed to the Subedars of three towns. On this authority, Jacob was admitted into Begoor, David into Kingeree, and Joseph carried his epistle and gave it to the Subedar of Yelevunkum. But he was a Bramin, and a determined enemy to the truth. To evade the order of the Fouzdar, he called his underlings in office around him, paraded with them the streets of the town, and called upon them to say whether there was a spot of ground which could be given to this man for the erection of a house. Their testimony was loud and violent in the negative, and Joseph was not permitted to enter the town. But before the end of the year, the government was changed; that Bramin was driven from his office; a more kind and benevolent man received the appointment; Joseph returned to Yelevunkum, and on the ground of the Fouzdar's letter, was permitted to erect a house, and to labour in peace till the day of his death. I thanked God for this triumph—not merely because the teachers were suffered to reside in these towns; but because we had succeeded in establishing the general principle, that they had an equal right to settle there with heathens, Mahomedans and Roman Catholics; that their profession of Christianity ought not to subject them to civil loss, degradation and penalty; and that the towns and villages, throughout the province, might henceforth be occupied without a doubt, or a question being raised.

Never was such a hot season, for the number of deaths, and the amount of sickness, known at Bangalore, as that of 1833. In both European regiments, the cholera raged with frightful violence, and as many as a hundred of our countrymen were committed to the silence of the tomb; while the Bazar, the town of Bangalore, and the adjacent villages felt, in a similar manner, the scourge and the indignation of the Lord. I have already stated that three of the native teachers were located in the neighbouring towns. In the middle of the night, and while I was labouring under a severe affliction, David came in and told me, that he had been to Yelavunkum to see his brother Joseph, who was very ill with cholera; that he had scarcely arrived there when a message came from Kingeree to tell him, that his wife was ill with the same disease; that he had left Joseph a little better, and was hurrying to his home, and begged me to allow three of the students to accompany him, and they would return in the morning, should she be restored. I willingly complied with his request, knowing well how little the assistance would be, which the heathen would afford him in this season of distress.

The morning came, and brought the melancholy tidings that this poor teacher's companion was no more. As the people in the village would render them no assistance, all the Canarese Christians went out from Bangalore, and carried their sister to her long home. David was plunged in grief, but was supported by the conviction that she had departed to be with Christ, which is far better. Bathsheba—that was the name she received at her baptism,—was disposed, after the conversion of her husband, to hold to the idols of her fathers, and remain a heathen, and gave David a great deal of trouble. But after they came to reside in our compound, her prejudices gave way; she began to attend the sanctuary; and what with the conversations of others, and the declaration of the truth and the example of those around, she was convinced that this was the true way to heaven, renounced her idolatry, and declared her faith in the Redeemer by receiving the ordinance of baptism. With grateful emotions, I remember the day when I administered the rite to her and her infant offspring, and admitted them into the visible church. After this, she was often catechised, and instructed, and she grew in the knowledge of God and of his Son. Still, while they remained at Bangalore, David often complained of the violence of her temper. But after they went to Kingeree, what a change did she undergo, and how well did she attend to the charge they both received, on going to reside in a heathen village! Let the simple testimony of her husband, who was not disposed to praise her when she acted contrary to his wishes, and to the Gospel of Christ, speak for her now:—"After our arrival, sir, she could scarcely speak, but I knew what was in her heart, and am convinced that she died believing in Jesus. From the day we went to live in Kingeree, what a change has been manifest in that woman! She, who was so obstinate and perverse and unmanageable before, became meek and humble and docile as a child. She always remembered we were Christians in a heathen village, and in word and in deed she bore testimony against their idolatry. Notwithstanding their insults and calumnies, and opprobrious epithets, she would not answer again, but bore them all with patience and forbearance. Such was the example that she gave in favour of Christ, that the people admired it, and often confessed 'her conduct is good, she is an upright woman, this is their religion.' She gave me the greatest help among these heathen; she was always ready for our prayers and our religious exercises, and took delight in them. Now she is gone, and I am convinced that she died trusting in God, and believing in Christ, and I have no doubt but she is now in heaven." Such was the account which David gave of his departed wife, and very often, I now remember, did he describe this change to me on my visits to the village, and when he has conversed with me at Bangalore; and I have as often rejoiced with him in the grace which God had thus bestowed on her. She rests in peace, and is numbered now I trust among the living in the new Jerusalem.

But this was not all. Scarcely had the believers

returned from the interment of their Christian sister, when a messenger announced the sad intelligence that Joseph was dead at Yelevunkum; and the faithful few, though tired and worn out with their former journey, had to proceed directly to this village, to carry another of their companions to the tomb. Though he had many errors—errors that could easily be traced to his heathen education,—yet I trust that Joseph was a good man, a true disciple of Jesus, and as far as he was acquainted with the truth, a faithful teacher to others. His wife, who was the only person with him when he died, mentions that he departed, calling upon his God and Saviour, and charging her to go and live in the Christian village, and not to return to her people; and as no one in the town would render them any assistance, we may justly reason that he bore a faithful testimony against their idolatry and in favour of the truth as it is in Jesus. Such is a brief history of Joseph and his sister-in-law. They were among the first-fruits of the Mysore to Christ, and may we not indulge the hope that they will be found among the number of those who will come from the East, and sit down with Abraham and Isaac and Jacob in the kingdom of heaven, while many of the children will be cast out? It may be some answer to the enemies of missions to say that they were persons who, in their ignorance and idolatry, gloried in their superiority of caste, but who learned, in their estimate of the truth, to count this and all other things but loss for the excellency of the knowledge of Jesus Christ their Lord.

During the first ten years of the mission, we had to contend with many and complicated difficulties. An independent rajah ruled over the province. A very weak, yet generous and kind-hearted prince, he was by no means ill disposed towards the settlement of missionaries in his kingdom; and had he been under better counsellors, might have rendered us some assistance. But in an evil hour, he surrendered the power of his government into the hands of the priesthood His prime-minister was a Bramin, the treasurer and all the secretaries of state were Bramins, the governor of every district, the judge upon the bench, and the magistrate in the city, were Bramins. Every office, from the highest to the lowest, where power was to be obtained, and money was to be accumulated, was in the hands of the oligarchy. I should not find fault with this as a mere political arrangement, since the Bramins are the most intelligent, and best educated class of the community. But when their power is turned into oppression, and when they occupy their offices only to prostitute them to purposes of evil, and to heap calamities upon the people, then "God will arise, and will plead the cause of the poor and needy!"

While this administration lasted, the missionaries, it

is true, were permitted to travel through the country, and preach the gospel without molestation; but sometimes we were forbidden to proclaim it in the streets and lanes of the city; and no sooner did we attempt to establish a school, to obtain a piece of ground for the erection of a chapel, and to enter the strong-hold of idolatry, than the power of the executive was exerted against us, and our defeat was sure. Many a time did we pray that God would interpose, that he would give these rulers a better spirit, or remove them from office, and that he would open a wide and effectual door for the entrance of the gospel.

Little did we expect that our wishes were so early to be realized; but in 1830, so dreadful had the oppressions of the Bramins become, that a change in the government was rendered inevitable. So mad, infuriated, and reckless was the career of injustice, that the poor natives represented themselves as in the jaws of the tiger; their cattle was not safe upon their fields; their jewels were torn from the necks of their wives and their children; their houses were stripped of their goods; and every thing was seized to gratify the avarice and the rapacity of their oppressors.

But the night of justice and of vengeance came. Almost without concert, the agricultural population rose like one man against the government. In their fury, they hanged twenty of these Bramins upon trees, and as no one would venture to cut them down, their bodies were allowed to remain till they were devoured by the birds and the beasts of prey; the very name of Bramin became an execration; the oppressor was hunted like a wild beast on the top of his mountains, and was obliged to flee into Bangalore as into a city of refuge.

Determined in their resistance to despotism, the people could not be put down. The Resident at the court of the Rajah, was obliged to report to the supreme government, that the Mysore was in a state of anarchy, that the authority of the ruling prince was at an end, and that, except the British power took charge of the province, public order could not be restored. A commission was immediately appointed, and out of eight gentlemen of whom it is composed, the majority are, I believe, pious, devoted and excellent men,—who wish the spiritual, as well as the temporal welfare of the natives.

In a remarkable manner, the power of the Bramins was overthrown; the whole country was opened to the gospel, and to the ambassadors of reconciliation; the city of Bangalore, which had so long withstood every attack, was now forced to capitulate to the truth; preaching-places were erected, and schools established; and while three millions of people were waiting for the bread of life, and every obstacle seemed to be overthrown, and our excellent collectors were entreating us to send them teachers and schoolmasters, that they might do something for the conversion of the people, the only reply we could make to them was "The harvest indeed is great, but the labourers are few; pray ye the lord of the harvest that he would send forth more labourers into his harvest."

Such is a brief and very imperfect outline of the mission to Bangalore. There is not a heathen country in the world that presents so many claims, such providential openings, and such a promising field of labour as this. The province is divided into the four districts of Bangalore, Mysore, Nagara, and Chittledroog. The first has long been in our possession; the second is now occupied, and will when it is strengthened, and well cultivated, become, I doubt not, an important mission; the third and the fourth are prepared of the Lord, and ought to become the seats of Christian settlements, as soon as possible. Many large towns might be enumerated; but where there are three millions of people, it is difficult to say what part of the field is the most necessitous, has the greatest facilities, and is most likely to yield an abundant harvest. In this province more than any other, Providence has gone before us in a pillar of cloud by day, and in a pillar of fire by night; every valley has been exalted, every mountain and high hill has been brought low, crooked paths have been made straight, and rough places plain, that the glory of the Lord may be revealed, and that all the people may see it together.

Let the missionary go from east to west, or from north to south, he is safe under the protection of the law; his temporal comforts are regarded as much by the kindness and urbanity of the natives, as the measures adopted for his convenience by the government; frankness and generosity, he will find, characterize the inhabitants of the province, and standing under the shade of a banyan-tree, or in the porch of a temple, he may preach to hundreds the gospel of God. Many facilities are at hand. The Europeans are kind, obliging,* and ready to give him encouragement and patronage; and if he is endowed with fervent piety and great devotedness, if he is content to labour for souls as one that must give an account, if he is earnest and frequent and importunate in prayer for the blessing and direction of the Spirit, if he is willing to be any thing and to do any thing that Christ may be exalted among the people; then he will no doubt realize his expectations; he will find his Redeemer a faithful master, and though he may have forsaken father and mother, and houses and lands for Christ's sake and the gospel, he will receive a hundred fold in this life, and enjoy the good hope that, in the world to come, he will obtain life everlasting.

* From the superintending surgeons, and other medical gentlemen attached to the regiments stationed at Bangalore, the mission families received, in every hour of need, kind and prompt attendance, and as they would receive no sort of remuneration, they deserve our warmest acknowledgments for their generous conduct.

CHAPTER XXIV.

GOVERNMENT SUPPORT OF IDOLATRY.

BRITISH POWER IN INDIA—DANGEROUS POLICY—THE MALEDICTION OF THE ALMIGHTY—PATRONAGE OF IDOLATRY—LAWS AGAINST CHRISTIANS—INFLUENCE OF THE SYSTEM UPON AUTHORITIES—DECISION OF A MAGISTRATE—ABOLITION OF FLOGGING IN THE NATIVE ARMY—PLOT AT BANGALORE—THE MAHOMMEDANS—INTERPOSITION OF PROVIDENCE.

Of all the dependencies of Great Britain, our Indian empire is unquestionably the most rich, extensive, and distinguished. Nothing has resembled it in ancient, or in modern times. The conquests of Alexander, the triumphs of Rome, the prospects of the new world, and the victories of republican France, dwindle into insignificance, when compared with the extent and the magnitude of our eastern possessions. But in proportion to the greatness of the boon, is the measure of our responsibility. How often have I trembled, lest the blessing should become a curse; lest, lifted up with pride, and infatuated with our power, we should wildly rush against the thick bosses of Jehovah's buckler, forfeit our dominion, and cast this princess of the earth "like a withered weed away." At what have I trembled? Has it been at the internal commotions with which our authority has sometimes been assailed? No. The British power in India is strong in the affections of the people generally,—strong in the order, the peace and the good government which she is endeavouring to secure to all classes of her subjects—strong in the law, the justice, and system of amelioration with which she is attempting to consolidate our empire. At what, then, have I trembled? Has it been at the power, and the number of her external enemies who are said to look at her magnificence with a jealous and an envious eye? No. Let Great Britain only be true to her own interests—true to the welfare and the prosperity of that people—true to the gracious designs for which Providence has committed this trust to her care, and to her rule, and she need not be under any apprehensions from the Great Bear of the North, though all his fury and his craft were sustained by his gigantic power, and though all the independent provinces upon our frontier, were to join him in confederacy against her. At what, then, have I trembled? I have trembled lest the dark and portentous clouds which have sometimes gathered over us above, should burst in storms of vengeance upon our heads; lest the thunders and the lightnings of the Almighty should descend and blast our power and prosperity; lest the curses and anathemas which are sure to cover, with shame and confusion, all the confederates of Satan, should fall upon us; and lest the government being once committed to the support of idolatry and other superstitions, should be slow and tardy in retracing her steps, and thus the kingdom be wrested away from our hands.

In those rash and thoughtless engagements which the government so gratuitously made to lavish her support and her patronage upon these infamous systems, and to take under her protection and her superintendence those grants, endowments, and revenues which other dynasties had left to their natural protectors, little did she think that she was entering into a covenant with death, and making an agreement with hell, and laying a deep and an ample foundation for her own ruin and decline. But nothing could be more evident, than this. Where is the nation that has patronised and encouraged idolatry, which has not suffered, and become a wreck under the frown of the Almighty? Whatever may be the number and the aggravation of our national sins, *this one alone* were sufficient to bring the plague, the famine and the pestilence upon India, to ruin our commercial prosperity, to sap the foundation of our political ascendency, to bring a curse upon our country, and expose all its great interests to the divine malediction.

I allow that our Indian government has given a church establishment to instruct her European subjects, and that she supports bishops and archdeacons and chaplains at a very considerable expense. I allow that she has erected many splendid edifices in which our countrymen may assemble, to worship the Lord God of their fathers, and has established schools in which their children may be educated in the principles of the Bible. But what temple has she ever built for Hindoos, except those in which vile idols are to be served, and a detestable worship was to be performed? What school has she ever established for their children, except those in which heathenism and all its absurdities are to be taught, or those from which the light and truth of Christianity are to be carefully excluded? What system has she ever encouraged among them, except those which will render them weak, cruel, and ungodly now, and which must ruin their bodies and souls for ever? Oh! my heart sickens within me, when I remember that she has delivered over her Hindoo subjects to work all these abominations, that she has sanctioned and patronized their worship to devils, and that this reproach is scarcely yet rolled away. But more than this. Shall I record it or forbear? shall I proclaim the sin and the shame of India, or shall I cover it over with the mantle of love? I wish the system were come to a perpetual end; I wish it could be buried in the depths of oblivion; and I hope ere long to sing its requiem, and to celebrate its death. But tell it not in Gath, publish it not in the streets of Askalon, lest the Philistines should triumph, that in the nineteenth century, and under a professedly Christian government, the divine religion of the Bible, should be rendered subservient to a base and an abominable idolatry; that men nominally Christian should be called upon to fire salutes and to present arms in honour of Baal; and that Christians indeed, should still, according to law, and according to the maxims of the government, be requested to do homage to an idol.

What were the effects which this system was calculated to produce? It led to the formation of laws which if they did not in so many words, exclude native Christians from office, did so in fact, and have ever been regarded as barriers to the advancement of our religion. The following is an extract from the regulations of the Madras government, 1816.

"Par. 6. The Zillah judges shall recommend to the provincial courts, the persons whom they may deem fit for the office of district moonsif; but no person shall be authorized to officiate as a district moonsif, without the previous sanction of the provincial court, *nor unless he be of the Hindoo or Mahommedan persuasion.*" In reference to this regulation, and when he was at Tanjore, Bishop Heber remarks, "Will it be believed that while the rajah kept his dominions, Christians were eligible to all the different offices of state, *while now there is an order of government against their being admitted to any employment?* Surely we are, in matters of religion, the most lukewarm and cowardly people upon the face of the earth."

From this law, it must be evident to the Christian public and to the friends of missions, that the policy of our Indian authorities has invariably been hostile to the progress of the gospel. Nay more. Notwithstanding the moderate tone which was adopted in the late charter, and the clause which professes to lay open all public employments to every denomination, the profession of Christianity would most likely disqualify a native, in the opinion of his superior, for the service of the state; and whatever might be his other gifts, and essential qualifications, it were enough that he was a Christian to drive him from office, and consign him to oblivion. When laws are bad, they are fully and faithfully executed, and when they are unwillingly reformed, they are very easily neutralised by the agents who are appointed to carry them into effect.

When such were the laws, and such the principles upon which the government was conducted, what was likely to be the influence upon the persons who, throughout the provinces, and in all departments of the state, looked up to their superiors for example and for instruction? Just what might be expected. Whether they were civil or military; whether they were high in office, or filled subordinate places; whether they respected the Sunday and went to church, or joined the more fashionable circles to manifest their disregard to both; they were prepared to scowl upon true religion; their consciences perfectly coincided with this iniquitous system; idolatry was, in their esteem, the orthodox faith; every real Christian was an outcast, a heretic, and an impostor; and any attempts made to convert the people, were sure to be regarded as deserving the wrath of official condemnation.

To corroborate these statements, let us appeal to facts. A few years ago, our Baptist brethren at one of the stations in the north, were so successful as to be the instruments of converting two Hindoo females to the faith; and the converts were so bold and so decided in their profession, that they went publicly to the water and were baptized. As soon as their husbands heard of the confession which they had thus made, they entered an action against the missionaries in the magistrates' court. The judge was not unwilling to listen to the complaint; he summoned the missionaries to his bar; and was determined to show his abhorrence of such transactions. At a loss for a law that might be applicable to such a case, his research was long and patient to find one. At length, he lighted upon an obsolete law of Menoo, which declares that the individual who is the means of seducing the affections of a Hindoo female from her hushand, by adultery and other unlawful methods, ought to be adjudged to such and such a penalty. "This," said the judge, "is just the law suited to the case. You, missionaries, have been the means of seducing the affections of these women from their husbands, and of causing divisions in their homes, and I adjudge you to this penalty." It was well for reason, for honour, and for religion that this judgment could be appealed from, and that it was reviewed by a superior court, whose members were more honourable men, and who scouted from them the decision and the sentence of this judge with the contempt and the indignation which they deserved. But the *animus* which actuated this person, has, alas! been too characteristic of the magistrates, the judges, and the rulers of that land.*

One of the last acts which Lord William Bentinck passed, previous to his departure from India, was the abolition of flogging in the native army. Never, I am sure, did it enter his liberal and benevolent

* Two of the native teachers, it appears, were, by the same sentence, put under a bond not to instruct any more married women in Christianity, or to baptize them, without first obtaining the consent of their Hindoo husbands. When the part of the proceedings which referred to the European missionaries, was quashed,—that part which concerned the teachers was allowed to stand, and they are therefore under this singular and intolerant bond. It was thought, at first, there must be some mistake, and there were parties who contended that no British officer would venture to commit an act so unjust and unreasonable. But there is, it appears, from a later statement, *no mistake, and it is most evident that this antichristian sentence was not only pronounced by a British magistrate, but has been connived at by a superior court.* How deplorable! As though the females of India were not sufficiently degraded in their heathenism; Christian magistrates must make laws to prevent their conversion, till their husbands feel the power of the truth, and permit them to renounce their allegiance to Satan and idolatry!

mind that this act should be applied to persons of one religion, while it was withheld from those of another, and least of all, that it should become a persecuting edict against Christianity. But where will the malice and the ingenuity of the enemy not find a ground for hostility to the truth, and for the support of evil principles? The bands of these native battalions are usually composed of Protestants and Roman Catholics, who, in the vocabulary of the army, receive the general name of Christians. During the following year, one of these men deserted, but finding his way hedged up, and that escape was impracticable, he returned to his corps, gave himself up, and entreated for mercy. But no grace was to be shown to such a criminal. He was brought to a court-martial, and was sentenced to receive two hundred lashes. This finding and sentence required to be confirmed by the commanding officer of the district, and this gentleman, understanding the act in the spirit in which it was granted, ventured to call in question the legality of this sentence. But not wishing to trust too much to his own judgment in the matter, he referred his doubts to the judge-advocate. What was the reply of this officer? "There is not room," said he, "for a doubt upon the subject; the act of abolition was only intended for Hindoos and Mahommedans; the boon was never intended for native Christians at all; and the sentence should be carried into execution immediately." What was the conclusion of the affair? This poor native, because he was a Christian, and wore the badge of our holy religion, was taken to the parade, and in the presence of hundreds of Hindoos and Mahommedans, received two hundred lashes, as a testimony to all, that whatever lenity, and consideration might be shown to orthodox pagans, none would be extended to poor, degraded, and outcast Christians. Is it to be wondered at, that men who are perhaps only Christians in name, should abandon a religion which exposes them to such treatment, and should, as it is affirmed, become idolaters and Mussulmen, to avoid such vengeance and such brutality? What do I say? Is it to be wondered at, that our holy religion is trodden in the dust, and that it does not make more eminent progress, when such a system of persecution is carried on against it, and when acts of mercy are abused by those who bear its name, to cover it with shame and contempt in the sight of the heathen? Oh that my head were waters, and that my eyes were fountains of tears, that I might weep and lament day and night over the transgressions of my people.

The year 1832, was a very eventful one in the Madras presidency. In consequence of the oppressions and the rapacity of the Bramins, the Mysore had fallen into the hands of the British government. The Mahommedan population were dissatisfied with the arrangement, and at Bellary, at Cuddapah, at Bangalore, and at other stations throughout the peninsula, they made attempts to regain their ascendency. During the celebration of the Ramzan at Bangalore, they repaired to their Eedgah, which stood on the north side of the cantonment, to worship, and to listen to an address. On their arrival, they found that a pig had been killed there, that its blood had been sprinkled over the place to pollute it, that its head was stuck upon the parapet and the whole was surmounted by a cross. Without any consideration, the large assembly rushed to the Roman Catholic chapel, as it appeared to them all, that none but the party who adopted the cross as a badge, could be guilty of such an outrage. Very soon, the frantic rage of the spoilers, threatened to lay the whole fabric in ruins; but the military speedily appeared, and restored peace and order, and saved the edifice from destruction.

In the mean time, a Naik of the company's service, a Mahommedan, and a disaffected traitor, repaired to the residence of the commandant to give him the intelligence, and he had just cleared his premises, when it was ascertained that he was the perpetrator of the deed. But notwithstanding it was so plain that a Mahommedan was the author of this outrage, and that the views of this part of the community were decidedly hostile to the British power; what was the policy which the Madras government pursued? They sympathized most deeply with the offended Mussulmen; it was seriously debated in the council-chamber whether all the missionaries should not be turned out of Bangalore, to mark the displeasure of the authorities to their exertions; tracts, it was maintained, had been industriously circulated, and had exasperated the minds of the populace; a splendid Eedgah, it was determined, should be erected, instead of the contemptible one that was defiled; and as though they would make it abundantly manifest that they were not only willing to support idolatry and Mahommedan delusion, but, in doing so, to degrade the religion of the Bible, and dishonour those who believe it, they called upon two Christian officers to superintend the erection of this monument of infamy.

"No," was the decided reply of these Christian gentlemen; but they soon fell under the displeasure of the authorities, and experienced the effects of their power. Another officer whose conscience was not so tender, undertook the management of the work; and there it stands on the north side of Bangalore,—a tower of Babel—a gratuitous testimonial to Mahommedan superstition—and a memorial of disgrace to a Christian government. But what was the consequence of this conciliating and temporizing policy? The very reverse from that which was expected. The Mahommedans grew in their own importance, and became more bold in enterprise. Instead of considering this act as one of conciliation, they regarded it as one of cowardice and fear, and drew from it the weight of their influence and the certainty of their success. Scarcely two months had elapsed from the erection of the Eedgah, when a report was circulated among the Mussulmen that the pig's head was buried in the foundation; they resolved to level the building with the ground; and the government were obliged to set a guard over it, by night and by day, to preserve it from the violence of its votaries. Our native teachers could not go out to the villages to preach the gospel, but they were stoned and maltreated; and terrible vengeance was threatened to the missionary in the performance of his duty. Nothing was heard of but insurrections, struggles between the authorities and bands of traitors, proclamations against Christianity and all who professed it, the pollution of tanks to exasperate the Hindoos, and the defilement of mosques to rouse the Mussulmen.

But this was not all. No longer open and public in their attempts, they resorted to secret intrigues and a fearful conspiracy to accomplish their purpose—a *conspiracy*, which, but for the intervention of a gracious Providence, would have rendered Bangalore an aceldama, and a sepulchre. Two native soldiers came to their commanding officer on a Sabbath evening, and gave him the following report. "There exists, sir, a dreadful conspiracy against the government, and against the whole European community. The setting of the moon tomorrow night at elven o'clock, is to be the signal for the horrid massacre. The confederates have tried to trifle with us to-day, to gain us over to their party; but we have resisted, and have determined to give you the information. A Fakeer who has resided here for six months past, under the mask of a button-maker, is the leader in the plot, and has gone out to-night to review his mercenaries for the last time, and give them their orders to act. An individual in your own regiment is to be on centry at the small gate of the fort, and to admit these troops to take possession of it. Great numbers of the infantry, of the cavalry, and of the artillery are seduced from their allegiance, and only await the command of their chief to rise. The native artillery are to bring their guns to bear, and to pour its thunder, on the European barracks, while the dragoon horses are to be cut so as to render them useless in the struggle, and the aid of the Mussulmen servants, is not to be wanting in the hour of trial."

As soon as this gentleman received this statement, he went to the adjutant-general of the forces who was then at Bangalore, and laid it before him. The truth was very soon established; preventive measures were adopted; the Fakeer was caught, returning in his palankeen at ten o'clock next morning; the daring individual who was to be on centry at the small gate of the fort, was not only found to be on guard, but had exchanged with another man to secure his post: the informers pointed out many of the conspirators; and multitudes were apprehended and committed to prison.

Not for our righteousness, O Lord, nor for any good that we have done, didst thou work out for us this great deliverance. No. But for thine own name's sake, that thy name should not be blasphemed among the heathen, and that idolaters should not be able to say, "Where is now their God," thou didst still the enemy and the avenger. The government had been very guilty; it had exerted its power to patronise and to support superstition; it had frowned upon Christians and upon Christianity; and the heavest curses might have descended upon us, in perfect accordance with truth and justice.

But the Lord treated us in mercy. He only wished to expose the folly and inconsistency of such attempts to support a tottering system, and to show that while earthly powers attempted to build superstition up, he would as certainly pull it down to the ground. After this plot was discovered, nothing could prevent the heavy blow which Mahommedanism was to receive. The conciliating policy was at an end. A dreadful example of vengeance was made. Four of the ringleaders were blown away from guns, two were shot by musketry, and great numbers were drummed out of their regiments and banished beyond the seas. The very abettors and advocates of superstition, became the instruments in securing its downfall. From the Eedgah which had been erected, a spectator might almost have witnessed the military execution, might have heard the peal of artillery, might have seen the fragments of bodies flying in the air, and might have heard the "march" with which the many were expelled from the service and from the country. Had the lightnings of heaven descended upon the Eedgah, and shivered it to pieces, it would not have been a more evident token of the divine disapprobation, nor a more overwhelming calamity to Mahommedanism, than the events of that morning. Shame and confusion covered its votaries. The grief, the humiliation, and the wailings which were universal, cannot be described. Hundreds of Mahommedan families hurried away from the Mysore to other parts of the country, unable to endure the odium, and the disgrace under which they fell; and Mahommedanism met with an overthrow from which it will not recover for many a day.

But such has been the policy which the Indian government has hitherto pursued. It has been slow to learn wisdom, and to gather, from the character of events, the designs of Providence. To patronize idolatry, and to support any system of superstition, no measures have been too unchristian, none too unreasonable. What has been the honour of the Christian name! what the extension of the true religion! what the feelings, the principles, the conscience and the morality of their European army!

what the spiritual and eternal interests of the people themselves! what the blessing, or malediction of the Almighty upon their rule! when false principles were to be supported, and a spurious and antiquated system was to be maintained? No. These have been but as the small dust in the balance, when compared with the upholding of systems which are ready to vanish away. To the most superficial observer, nothing can be more evident, than that there has long been a struggle between the authorities of India, on the one hand, to cherish the superstitions of the people, and the events of Providence on the other, to annihilate and destroy them. It cannot be a question, as to the power that will triumph. No. The Lord reigneth; let the earth be glad. He will overturn, overturn, overturn, till He comes whose right it is; and the kingdom, the power, the glory and the dominion will assuredly be given to the Lord.

CHAPTER XXV.

GOVERNMENT SUPPORT OF IDOLATRY.

PILGRIM-TAX—SURPLUS REVENUE—VIEWS OF THE NATIVES—OBJECTIONS OF A BRAMIN—SALEM DISTRICT—STATE OF IDOLATRY IN THE MYSORE—DESPATCH OF 1833—MADRAS MEMORIAL — BISHOP CORRIE — REPEAL OF LIBERAL MEASURES — BRITISH PUBLIC—CHRISTIAN OFFICERS IN INDIA—SIR PEREGRINE MAITLAND.

A PART of the encouragement which the British government granted to idolatry, consisted in the Pilgrim-tax which was collected, at Allahabad, Gyah, and Juggernaut. The cruelties, the degradation, the treachery, and the heart-rending scenes which were associated with these temples, were fearful beyond description. To increase the amount of revenue, every stimulus was given to the cupidity of those who were engaged in the iniquitous traffic. The British collector received a commission upon all the proceeds of the pagoda. Pilgrim-hunters went out to all parts of the country to search for devotees, to applaud the fame and sanctity of the shrines, to speak of the delight which such numbers of votaries yielded to the British government, and to stimulate the ignorant multitude on to the gate of superstition. At the place of concourse, barriers were fixed to prevent intruders from descending to the stream, or from entering into the temple; none could obtain admission without a government-ticket, paid for according to the rank of the applicant, from one rupee, to twenty; the barbers who officiated at an important part of the ceremony, were admitted gratuitously to perform their operation, but were subject to a fine of fifty rupees, were they to shave a votary who could not show his ticket; and every means were adopted to render the festival as profitable as possible to the government. But for the shocking character of the subject, it would be highly amusing to learn that, at one village in the Bombay presidency where votaries paid offerings to Mahadeo, the proceeds were divided between the officers of the village, and the government, and that the latter had lately *farmed* out its share for what? for the large amount of 8*s.* 10*d.*!!

The following are the income and expenditure of the various presidencies upon this point:—

	Annual Income.	Annual Expense.	Annual Surplus.	Annual Deficit.
Bengal, including N.W. Provinces	461,967	233,670	228,297	,,
Madras	4,056,286	3,882,573	173,713	,,
Bombay	40,339	66,850	,,	26,511
Total	4,558,592	4,183,093	402,010	26,511
Deduct deficit.			26,511	
Nett surplus per annum			375,499	

After the expense of collection, patronage, and superintendence throughout the whole of India, the gross surplus of revenue is not more than £30,000 per annum.

The statement is taken from a pamphlet lately published at Calcutta, and lest the surplus should be overrated, the authors reduce it to £25,000 per annum. Is this a sum worth the keeping as the wages of iniquity? Is it a reward for exposing our empire to the curse of the Almighty and to the indignation of a Christian people? Is it to be put in the balance with toleration to our own countrymen, with justice to the oppressed, with emancipation from a thousand evils, with a good conscience and clean hands in a transaction where such responsibility is incurred? No. Whatever respect may be paid to selfish principles, and however loud worldly men may be in their support; it were less wicked to drain such an amount from the veins of the poor, the needy and the fatherless; it were more justifiable to render provinces a desolation and wring out the sum from the spoils of the captives; it were better far to send our vessels to the coast of Africa, to renew the accursed slave-trade, and to render a part of our race, our goods and our commerce, than fill our coffers with taxes on idolatry.

Not to dwell upon the temporal evils which arise from such a system; what is the moral influence which it must produce upon that people? As men, and as Britons, it is impossible that our government in India can be regarded in any other light, than as a Christian one. Whatever may be the character of its members, and whatever may be the principles on which it is conducted, the natives cannot make the nice distinctions which we are in the habit of doing at home, between Christians and the ungodly. What then are the impressions which must be made upon them by the support which the British authorities render to their superstition? I have not been to Juggernaut; I have not seen the horrors which attend the celebration of its festivals; I have not beheld the victims throwing themselves under the wheels of its murderous cars, and the vultures feasting upon the carcases of its slain; I have not heard the multitudes raising their shouts of "Hurree Bol! Hurree Bol!" while the European officer has ascended the idol's chariot, and spread the golden cloth over the abominable thing; I have not witnessed the collectors gathering the tribute from the worshippers, and rendering all necessary power and liberty to bow down to the idol in return. But I have seen the operations of the system in the Madras presidency, and from the effects which it produces upon the natives in the one case, I can judge what it will do in the other. In the estimation of Hindoos, it is tantamount to a renunciation of the religion and the God of our fathers; it is a testimony that Christianity is a worthless and contemptible theory, while idolatry is deserving the respect of the wise and superior classes of society; it is a powerful reason why they should regard missionaries and all who take an interest in the progress of the gospel, as fools or maniacs, and all their labours as the exertions of visionaries; in a word, it stands forth to them a plain and a convincing proof that we love the cruelty, the vileness, and all the diabolical evils of their superstition, since no wise and benevolent government would support and patronize a system which they did not regard and approve.

Taking a mission tour at one time, through the Salem province, we came to a town, named Paulgode. A splendid temple overshadows hundreds of Bramins, maintains them in idleness and sin; and such is the noise with which idolatry is sustained, that you might fancy the shout was ringing night and day in your ears, "Great is Diana of the Ephesians." After the gospel was fully and faithfully declared among the people, and in the neighbourhood of the pagoda, there rose a Bramin to reply, "Who are you," said he, "that come here to find fault with our religion? What may be your names? Is not this temple supported by the British government? The Bramins, the priests, the dancing-women, and all the attendants upon the altar, do they not receive their monthly allowance from the public treasury? The endowments, the internal economy, the times of worship, and the celebration of the festivals, are they not all under the care and superintendence of the collector? Do not European ladies and gentlemen make presents to the god? Why! it was only the other day that a battalion of Seapoys was passing this road; the cholera was among them; their commanding officer gave them fifty rupees to purchase sheep, and to present a sacrifice to Kalee, and when they were offering these sheep to propitiate the goddess, that commanding-officer came himself, and bowed down to the image. Who then are you that come here to scandalize our divinities?" What answer can be made to such statements as these? Nay; how can we justify ourselves and support our declarations, without condemning the government and denouncing its inconsistency?

During this journey through Salem and Coimbatoor districts, there was scarcely a town of any importance where there was not a temple thus supported. Idolatry was seen in a most flourishing condition. The pagodas were kept in excellent repair. At an appointed hour, both morning and evening, the tom-tom was beat to summon the votaries to worship. The full complement of priests, servants, and dancing-girls, was maintained. Nothing was wanting to render the religion of Vishnu and of Seeva, respectable in the eyes of the multitude. But under whose supervision was this grandeur and magnificence displayed? Under that of the British collector, and according to the orders of a professedly Christian government. As we descended upon the Mysore, which, up to that period had been under the rule of an independent and idolatrous prince; what was the state of paganism in that province? Strange as it may appear, the pagodas were neglected and impoverished, and where it might be supposed that Hindooism would be most prosperous, the idols were fast falling into disrepute. But this abandonment did not long continue. No sooner did the British undertake the superintendence of the province, than the neglected system began to revive. In the end of 1835, a festival was celebrated in Bangalore, in honour of the idol Venkuttranmannu. For six or seven years previous, that shrine had been disregarded; but it was now renewed, under the patronage of the government; and the subedar, as the native authority, laid a tax upon every house, and was exacting it with the strong arm of power, to celebrate the feast, while the people were loud in their complaints against this measure, deeming it illegal and oppressive, and declaring that they had never been so taxed under the rajah. This instance proves not only that the government patronage is continued as before in their own provinces; but that in a kingdom which has recently fallen under their authority, where, under its native prince, idolatry was neglected, and where it might have safely been left to the voluntary support of its votaries, the British government has gratuitously given its sanction to its revival and establishment.

After the agitation of the question at home, by the Reverend Mr. Peggs, and great exertions by Mr. Poynder in the Court of Proprietors, the government felt the pressure of the question. Mr. Grant, who was then president of the Board of Control, took a very just and comprehensive view of the subject, and drew up the despatch of 1833. It was sent to the Court of Directors, who, it is said, refused to send it to India, and returned it with their objections to the board. Mr. Grant reminded them that the board had now the power to send out despatches without the consent of the court, and left it for them to say whether it would not be better to comply, than to have their authority superseded. The court sent out the despatch, not only with evident tokens of reluctance, but, if we may be allowed to judge from their subsequent policy, with a determination to neutralise the measure.

The tidings, however, were published in India. After a long night of sorrow, the missionaries, and the friends of humanity, thought that the morning of joy was come. Imagine what was our delight when it was announced in this despatch, and proclaimed throughout the empire, that the pilgrim-tax was to be abolished, that the connexion of the government with idolatry was to cease, that Hindooism was henceforth to be left to its own resources, that a neutrality which ought never to have been departed from, was to be maintained, that the same toleration which was granted to Hindoos and Mussulmen, was now to be given to our own countrymen, and that British officers were no longer to become the ministers of Baal. As cold water to the thirsty soul, so was this good news to us from a far country. We took down our harps from the willows and sang one of the songs of Zion. Then was our mouth filled with laughter and our tongues with singing, and then said we among the heathen, "the Lord has done great things for us whereof we are glad."

But how were these expectations realized? The executive abroad sent these rules and regulations to the collectors of revenue, for their opinions; information was required upon the subject; its bearing upon the dividends,—always a most important question with the court—required to be examined; and thus a measure so full of grace to India, was suspended upon the report which should be made upon this point. For three years, the question was kept in abeyance; nothing, it was evident, was to be done to settle it; and in 1836, and when the advocates of missions were lifting up their voice in England, and rousing the Christian public to action, our countrymen in India, saw their position to be difficult and intolerable. In the Madras presidency, a memorial, signed by one hundred and fifty civil and military servants, and by fifty clergymen and missionaries, was presented to the government of Fort St. George, with a recommendatory letter from Bishop Corrie. What were the grievances of which these excellent Christians complained? Of laws which oppressed their consciences, and obliged them to take an open and an active part in abominable idolatries; of a system which constituted them the masters of heathen ceremonies, and which compelled them to superintend the temples and the festivals of superstition; of regulations which called upon them, at the risk of their worldly prospects, to present arms and to fire salutes, in honour of an abominable thing; and they prayed that their consciences might be relieved from such burdens, by the despatch of 1833 being carried into effect.

When we remember that the measures of relief had been granted by the government at home, and had been published throughout every province of India; when we consider that three years had already been allowed to the executive to signify their approval of the despatch, and to make a commencement of attending to its recommendations; when we reflect upon the advancement of our age in civil and religious liberty, and on the nature of the grievances to be redressed; what request could be more just, more reasonable, more scriptural, and more in accordance with every equitable and beneficent principle of government? Yet what was the reply which was given to the humble and excellent Bishop Corrie, to the friend of Henry Martyn, to the holy man who, for more than thirty years, was an example of piety, devotedness, zeal, and primitive simplicity to India? The secretary of the Madras government, in reply, proceeded to say, "that he was directed to inform the bishop, that the sentiments of the governor were not in accordance with those of the memorialists; and that the governor was sorry the bishop did not attend to his own peculiar duties in moderating the zeal of overheated minds, instead of agitating questions that were calculated to endanger the peace of the country." What man, what Christian, what friend of liberty, of humanity and benevolence does not feel a just indignation at such a reply? I wonder not that the governor, who, in the Ionian Isles, walked with scores of monks in a popish procession, and ordered salutes to be fired at the elevation of the host, could not sympathize with the sentiments and feelings of these honourable men; I wonder not that the secretary and the members of the Madras government, beheld in these measures of relief, the principles of sedition, anarchy, and rebellion throughout our Indian empire, since they have invariably been the advocates of intolerance to our own countrymen, and of support and patronage being granted to the systems of superstition; but I do wonder that, with the despatch of 1833 before them, they did not use more courteous, dignified and respectful language to the amiable and excellent bishop—that, in reply to these memorialists, they could treat, with such haughty indifference, the opinions of men whose nobility of mind, whose principles of action, and whose moral and intellectual worth were so superior to their own,—and that their regard to the principles of liberty and benevolence did not lead them to seize upon this occasion as a delightful opportunity of doing justice to our countrymen, and of removing a scandal from the British name and government.

After the executive in India had thus silenced and brow-beaten these Christian men, and after it was ascertained that the surplus revenue derived from idolatry amounted to thirty thousand pounds, what was the line of policy pursued by the Court of Directors? They ventured to scowl upon Mr. Poynder and the advocates of justice and humanity, and put them to silence in the Court of Proprietors; it was triumphantly announced at the India House that three lacs of rupees were too much to surrender to the orators of Exeter Hall; and a despatch almost tantamount to a repeal of the former, was sent out to India, to render, if possible, unjust laws more binding, idolatrous patronage more decided and unquestionable, and the circumstances of our countrymen more intolerable, than they were before. But no step could be taken, more likely to confound intolerance; the infatuation was complete; the intelligence aroused the advocates of religious liberty at home and abroad; and Providence converted the counsel of Ahitophel into foolishness, to accomplish the rescue of his people. From Birmingham, from Leeds, from Liverpool, from Cork, and other large towns of the United Kingdom, there arose a voice which echoed through the hills and dales of our native land, which awoke a silent and a slumbering parliament, which called forth the zeal and energy and sympathy of the bishops in the House of Lords, and the spirit of liberty and justice among our enlightened members of the House of Commons, till her Majesty's government were compelled to consider the question, and to give an assurance that measures would be adopted which must, in India, satisfy the most scrupulous conscience. Relying on the government that this pledge will be fully redeemed, I cannot but render gratitude to God for this victory, congratulate the Christian public on the progress of truth and principle and religious freedom, and rejoice to think of our own countrymen being able to stand up, like men and like Christians, in the midst of heathens and Mahommedans.

But justice demands still more. I cannot but render a tribute of gratitude to those noble and illustrious men who have carried on the struggle with the government abroad. As soon as this intolerant despatch was received and published in India, what was the spirit and the Christian energy with which it was met? In that hour of trial and of difficulty, when the government at home united with the executive abroad to neutralize the promises of 1833, and when an attempt was made to rivet the chains upon the consciences of our brethren; what was the reply which was given to this despotic announcement? It was the same in spirit, if not in reality, as that which was made by the three children in Babylon of old.—" Ye princes and ye governors, we are not careful to answer you in this matter. If it be so, our God whom we serve is able to deliver us out of your hands. But if not, be it known unto you that we shall not serve your gods, nor worship the golden image which you have set up." I honour the conduct and the character of those men who resolved that they would rather lose their commissions, and resign their offices of trust and emolument, than obey such an order, and bring dishonour upon the worthy name by which they are called. I honour the spirit and principles of Mr. Nelson who, among the judges of India, was a faithful and devoted servant of God and of his country, and who, though he was then residing in England and was not likely to be brought into immediate contact with these orders, no sooner heard that they were forwarded to India, than he resigned his connexion with the Company, stating to them boldly and faithfully that he had nothing more to do with idols,—that he was bound to obey God, rather than man, and sacrificed not only all the prospective honours and emoluments of office, but his retiring pension of a thousand a year, to which a short period of service would have given him a claim. But above all, I honour the name and character and Christian conduct of Sir Peregrine Maitland, who ranks now as high among philanthropists and champions of the truth, as he does among patriots and soldiers, who would have been the first to have led the troops of his queen and his country against the enemy, and would have been the last to have turned his back upon the field of battle, but who was afraid to offend his God, and who, when he received these orders, acted in the spirit of heroism, and declared that he could not carry them into effect, and since there was no alternative but to obey these laws of the Medes and Persians, laid his office of commander-in-chief at the feet of the government, and placed upon the altar of his God, an income of £15,000 a year, as the price of his Christian liberty. Speak we of sacrifices at home, these are the men who have renounced their earthly honours, and their worldly prospects to manifest their attachment to the truth. Speak we of primitive times, these are the men who, with apostles and evangelists, would have rejoiced in being counted worthy to suffer shame for the sake of their Lord. Speak we of martyrdom; these are the men who would have gone with a Cranmer and a Latimer to the stake or to the gibbet. Speak we of our Puritans and worthies; these are the confessors of our own age who take joyfully the spoiling of their goods, knowing that in heaven they have a better and an enduring substance. Thank you, illustrious men! for the noble example you have given to the church and to the world. Happy is India in having such patriots as you to defend her rights and her liberties! Thankful are the friends of religious liberty in possessing such champions to withstand the encroachments of tyranny and sacrifice their own interests to truth! The cause of God and of missions must be triumphant over the earth, when there are such warriors to carry on the contest with the powers of evil, and with the demon of idolatry!

It is, with intense anxiety, that I look to the measures which the religious public are likely to adopt in reference to this important point. Will they stand silently by, and witness such gross injustice and intolerance committed upon these excellent men? Will they have no sympathy, no love, no benevolence, and no energies to expend upon subjects so interesting and so engaging as these? If the executive in India has nothing but oppressive laws and enactments to point to as the support of their authority; if the Court of Directors and the Board of Control will consign the most meritorious officers to obscurity, merely because they will not violate their consciences, rather than that the government should fulfil the solemn engagements which it has made; if the British parliament will connive at proceedings which, in olden times, would have called forth a volley of artillery that would have made tyrants tremble, and would have rolled the peals of indignation over their heads; if her majesty, who has already shown such spirit in her measures, and such determination to uphold law and justice, and the rights of her subjects in every part of her dominions, will not exercise her prerogative and reinstate these noble men in their offices of trust, will there not be justice and truth, and honour and sympathy enough in the people to raise the voice of remonstrance, and make the oppressors understand that Britain is the avenger of the innocent, the protector of the injured, and the friend of the conscientious to the very extremities of the empire? Why should not every congregation in the kingdom, in which the interests of the truth are regarded, present a memorial upon the subject? Why should not the great societies that are formed for the protection of religious liberty, and the boards that represent different denominations of Christians lift up their voice in loud and reiterated protests against these decrees of despotism? Since the days when Captain Dawson and Lieutenant Aitcheson were brought, under the Duke of Wellington's * administration, to a court-

* It is quite distressing to hear his Grace vindicating as he did, in a recent debate, the conduct of the Indian government in this affair. One cannot but admire the military fame which the noble duke has acquired, and the bold and straight-forward course which he pursues in the senate; but it sinks him in the estimation of the wise and the good, when he stands forth as the advocate of such principles. He might still place himself at the head of justice, law, benevolence, and religious freedom, and feeling the vast importance of religion himself, consolidate his fame by becoming the staunch friend of humanity, and of the establishment of Christianity throughout the world. He may contend that pious men have no right in the army, and in places of trust where their consciences would be oppressed; yet Joseph did not cease to be pious when he became the governor of Egypt; nor did Daniel abandon his power and his station because he was a servant of God, and would rather be thrown into the den of lions than bow to an idol; nor did Cornelius leave the service of the Romans and

martial and dismissed the service, because they would not fire a salute at the elevation of the host; nothing has occurred which ought so deeply to interest the religious public, and to call forth its sympathy, and the expressions of its opinion. The Bishop of London has spoken out, with energy and eloquence upon the point in the House of Lords; Mr. Poynder has delivered his sentiments, with his usual zeal and ability in the Court of Proprietors; every friend of India both at home and abroad has raised his voice against an act which has made such honourable men the victims of its cupidity and its faithlessness; it remains for the British public to consummate the triumph, and in defiance of power and threats and influence, to restore the righteous to their honours and their stations, and to sweep from the earth a system which is based in deceit, dishonour and intolerance.

I have more confidence in the promises and in the acts of her majesty's government, than I have in the Court of Directors and the executive in India; and while I hear that in consequence of their

cease to be a centurion, when he embraced the Messiah; nor did the Ethiopian eunuch relinquish, on his profession of Christianity, his office of treasurer to Queen Candace. Woe be to Great Britian when it becomes the law of the land, or the law of the army, that when men become wise and good they must abandon their posts, and when none but the irreligious, and the scorners can remain as the defenders of our queen and our country! It is more than thirty years since the noble duke was in India; and the state of the country is quite changed since that period.

late despatch, the pilgrim-tax is to be abolished, toleration is to be secured to our own countrymen, and a beginning is made of dissolving the connexion between the state and idolatry, I cannot but rejoice. But it is evident that the government of India will not do more, than it is compelled to do. Unable to confer this boon in a noble and generous spirit, it has shown how reluctant it is to part with idolatry as an associate and an ally. It has agreed to dissolve its connexion with Juggernaut and to repeal the pilgrim-tax; but it has determined to confer a donation of £5000 a year upon the murderous shrine! It has granted toleration to our Christian countrymen, and has professed to relieve them from many idolatrous duties; but it cannot dispense with their services* as escorts to Hindoos on their pilgrimage,

* It were well if this system could be entirely abolished. According to the former customs of Hindoos, some have maintained that it is necessary to keep up pomp and parade, and a degree of imposing grandeur, to create respect among the people. Does a heathen dignitary proceed upon a pilgrimage, he must have an escort. Does a bishop go to visit his diocese, the same honour must be conferred upon him. Does a judge go on his circuit to administer justice, a guard must accompany the party. It is all an expensive and nonsensical parade. I can give them a nobler example, and one that made a deeper impression upon the natives who saw it and who heard of it. Lord William Bentinck, on his way to the Neilgherries, had to pass through Bangalore. No sooner did the rich natives and those in power, hear of the approach of his lordship, than they went out many miles to meet him, taking bands of music, presents and great pageantry, to receive him in grand style. His lordship travelled in his palankeen like a private gentleman

and as guards of honour to idols during the processions.

Such leanings to superstition are quite in harmony with other parts of their conduct. Think of a bishop receiving his appointment to India, on the understanding that he would maintain a strict neutrality and perpetual silence on such questions as these; think of a governor* being sent to Bom-

and accompanied only by his private secretary. He stopped not to receive the presents and the adulations of the multitude; he had neither guard of honour, nor escort to attend him; and what was the effect upon the natives? They were all in admiration at the dignity and simplicity of the governor-general!

* On the arrival of Sir James Carnac at Bombay, the community was in a state of the greatest excitement. Two Parsee youths who were educated in the school of Dr. Wilson, had declared for Christ, and were baptized in his name. Instead of granting them toleration, the Parsee inhabitants were highly indignant at the reproach, which was thus brought upon their body; they withdrew their children from the school; and entered an action in the supreme court to recover the youths who had abandoned the system of their ancestors. Dr. Wilson withstood them, and a verdict was given in favour of the missionary and the youths. The greatest ferment prevailed; the missionaries delivered discourses to expose the superstition; and the sympathies of our own countrymen were mingled in the contest. At this juncture, the new governor was announced, and invited to attend a meeting for education two or three days after his arrival; he thought it necessary to take that early opportunity of saying, before the bishop, and clergy and missionaries, "that the religion of the natives must be respected." Had we been ignorant of his views, we might have been disposed to put a liberal construction upon the sentiment; but since he stood forth at home as the advocate of superstition, it reminds me strongly of the announcement made, by the herald,

REPRESENTATIONS OF THE SERPENT-GOD WORSHIPPED IN INDIA.

bay who had not only been in the chair of the Court of Proprietors, when Mr. Poynder's resolution was opposed, but who moved and carried counter resolutions, and who vindicated and approved of the retrograde course which the Court of Directors have pursued since 1836; and where is the confidence that we can place in such a government? How necessary is it that the religious public should watch all its movements, and not suffer liberal measures to be neutralized? How important is it that the public at home should exert a greater influence in the appointment of governors, and in regulating the principles on which the administration ought to be conducted?

On the retirement of the Marquis of Hastings from the head of the Indian government, Mr. Canning received the appointment, and was preparing to embark for Bengal as the governor-general. The pious people in Scotland did not coincide with this nomination. Whatever might be Mr. Canning's religious principles, I know not; but these devoted men believed that they were such as would lead him to oppose the interests of missions

on the plain of Dura, "To you it is commanded, O people, nations and languages, that at what time ye hear the sound of the cornet, flute, harp, sackbut, psaltery, dulcimer and all kinds of music, ye fall down and worship the golden image which Nebuchadnezzar the king hath set up; and whoso falleth not down and worshippeth, shall the same hour be cast into the midst of the burning fiery furnace."

and the progress of the truth, instead of rendering them that assistance and encouragement which his predecessor had done. To counteract the decisions of councils, and the appointment of courts, they gave themselves to prayer; private and public fellowship meetings were held to lay the subject before the Lord, and to plead for his interposition. Fervent interpositions were offered, that God would not suffer the appointment to be carried into effect, that he would provide for India, a man after his own heart—one who would carry on the measures that had been adopted, and give an increased stimulus to missions and to Christianity. The result is a matter of history. In consequence of the death of Lord Londonderry, the appointment was cancelled; Mr. Canning was detained in England as minister for foreign affairs; Lord Amherst was sent to India, and the impetus that was given to the chariot of salvation, has continued yearly to augment till the present time.

In our churches, there is not, I am afraid, enough of special and importunate prayer. Did our ministers in the country, and the devoted members of the congregations, take greater interest in the affairs of India; and on such important occasions as those of the appointment of a governor, or a governor-general, were they to give themselves to united and persevering prayer, that the authorities might be guided in their selection of an individual, and that Providence would interpose to prevent an unsuitable party from obtaining the appointment, they would render most important services to India, would engage Jehovah upon our side, and would secure to the government and to all the interests of the empire, the blessing which maketh rich and addeth no sorrow.

In nothing has the violence of idolatry supporters, been more evident, than in the vituperation, the calumnies, and the misrepresentations which they have heaped upon the advocates of liberty. No matter whether they were missionaries who felt the grievance in all its oppressive bearings, or Christian proprietors who were ashamed of the unholy alliance; no matter whether they were the memorialists of 1836, or the noble worthies of 1839, they have been denounced as anarchists and incendiaries, as wishing to kindle the flame of rebellion through the empire, as aiming a blow at Hindooism only to obtain its funds, its endowments, and its lands to be appropriated to their own purposes, and as enthusiasts who long to turn the power of the government against the religion of the natives for its extermination. Who would believe that these views have, in the most solemn, and explicit manner, been disclaimed? In every petition that has been signed, every memorial that has been presented, every speech that has been delivered, and every publication that has appeared upon the subject; the advocates of toleration have most distinctly avowed that they have only wished the government to remain neutral, to let idolatry alone, and to grant to Christians the same toleration which is granted to heathens. But notwithstanding these disavowals, the abettors have renewed the charge; and since *they* have raised the question and not we, it may not be amiss to examine, with what propriety and justice, they lavish their accusations upon us, and their praises upon idolatry. To the arguments which have been used against us, and to uphold the shrines, festivals, and influence of superstition among the people, a friend of humanity and of good government might perhaps reply, "Well! it is a grave and an important question which you have proposed for discussion. In the history of Great Britain, and in the annals of improvement, have there not been stranger revolutions than these? Look back to the days of the Reformation; were not the endowments and church property which were unquestionably given to the support of Popery, transferred to Protestantism, and are they not held by its incumbents to this day? Nay, to come to our own times, will you tell me by what tenure the honourable Company hold their possessions in the East, and how these immense and invaluable territories have passed from their original proprietors, into the hands of merchants residing in London? I say nothing of your offering crowns and kingdoms for sale; I say not a word about your driving that prince from his throne, and giving his dominion to some friend or ally of your own; I wish not to allude to 'the resumption lands' which, granted by former governments they say, you wish to claim and assess; I speak not of the appropriation which you have made of heathen and Mussulman funds, to instruct the natives in western science and literature—a very different object from that which their donors had in view. No. But as the advocates of vested interests, you have, I conceive, a few questions to ask yourselves, before you scatter your wrath upon others."

"When a vile, a sanguinary, and degrading superstition, is involved, you rush into the breach to save it; all your yearnings and best affections are gathered around it; and vengeance and woes are dealt out to those who would venture to assail it; but why this great love to idolatry? I am afraid you have some *interest* in it yourselves, and that the title by which you hold this part of the spoil, would not be found more valid than that by which you possess the whole."

But without further reference to the party who may be interested in this, or to another who may be profited by that, let us consider the question as one of humanity and of the public weal. Whatever may have been the original views of the donors, is it necessary that through all time, which changes every thing, this property, bequeathed to heathen temples, should remain unchangeable? Is it not possible, on the ground of right and justice, to transfer property granted to a bad object, to one that must be beneficial to the community? Had these testators lived in an age when famines frequently prevailed, and when they saw hundreds and thousands perishing for want, is it not likely that they would have given this property to build granaries, and to collect into them the surplus of abundant harvests, to provide against the recurrence of such calamities? Had they lived in a day when education was popular, and was required and called for, would they not have imitated the example of some of their kinsmen, who, in our own times, have appropriated large sums to this important purpose? Had they lived at a period when sickness, poverty, madness, blindness, and similar evils were common, would they not have erected asylums, and endowed them as receptacles for the poor and the fatherless, the widow, the stranger, and the wretched? Most assuredly. It is not, then, paying a respect to the intention of the original proprietors when we determine, whatever be the change in the circumstances and in the times, to make them the patrons of systems which are now become antiquated, merciless, and diabolical.

To appropriate such funds to any of these objects, would be a blessing, whereas, in their present state, they are a curse to the Hindoos; would it not be worthy of a wise and paternal government to secure the transfer, especially if the people saw the propriety of the change? But if the endowments must be continued to these shrines, why should not the indolent Bramins be called upon to do something for their reward? Why should they not become the teachers in the village schools, and the instructors in the colleges? Why should they not be so educated as to be able to give lectures to their people on mechanics, on science, and philosophy, that improvements might be introduced and happiness be secured? and instead of the British authorities looking after the performance of idolatrous rites, ceremonies, festivals, and superstitions, why might they not superintend a system that would contribute to the wealth and prosperity of the country? You have already abolished infanticide, and delivered helpless infants from the jaws of the devouring sharks; you have already put down the suttee, and rescued the infatuated widow from the funeral pile—vested interests these, far more sacred than any endowments which belong to idolatry; that government will be held in everlasting remembrance, and will receive the blessings of posterity, which will have the courage so to appropriate these ancient funds and bequests, as to contribute to the temporal and everlasting welfare of the people.

Should this connexion between the state and idolatry not be dissolved, it is impossible to say what may be the consequences. Such is the state of our missions, such is the course of policy which the government has lately adopted, and such is the excitement produced among the heathen population, that I cannot but feel the greatest concern upon this point. Persecution, it is well known, has already raged in many quarters, against the native Christians; the young and the old have often been deprived of their property and their privileges, have been impeached, tried, and unrighteously condemned; the apathy and indifference hitherto shown, by the natives of Calcutta and other parts, to missionary exertion, are now bursting forth in scorn, derision, and calumny; and the day, I fear, is not far distant when the Bramins and devotees uniting their power, will commence a persecution as violent and as inveterate as any that has been heard of in ancient or in modern times.

As yet, it is true, the cases which have come before the supreme court, in Calcutta and in Bombay, have been decided in favour of the converts and the missionary; but it would only require a trivial accident, such as the declaration of the new governor at Bombay, to expose the interests of Christianity to danger, and to inspire the Hindoos with fury and rage. What, then, if the government should continue to act upon the principles which have hitherto characterized its policy! what if it should still patronize the idolatry of Juggernaut, and identify its honour, and its prosperity with the support of superstition, instead of seeing that the progress of Christianity would be the consolidation of our power, and the stability of our empire! Will it, in a day of persecution, stand upon neutral ground and hold the balances of justice, without partiality, between the contending parties? Will it in the evil day abandon all its partialities to paganism, and act a different part to the one which it did in the day of prosperity? Will it not rather take the side of the strong against the weak, enact new laws for the suppression of heresy, and should British subjects escape the fury of the storm, will it not arraign the native converts at the bar of judgment, bring dishonour upon our country and the Christian name, and renew, upon the plains of India, the brutal scenes which were once exhibited in the amphitheatre at Rome? I foresee these evils coming; I foresee the result of this patronage being continued to this system; and I wish that the government would begin to act on the principles of toleration and impartiality now, that it may act a liberal and a Christian part in the day of trial. As the churches of Christ love the Redeemer and his cause, and as they wish the prosperity of India and our own country, they will co-operate with us in our prayers and our exertions to remove these barriers to the truth; they will watch the progress of such great questions; they will exercise their rights and privileges for the emancipation of India from this and every other curse; and they will not slumber and not spare till the spirit of religious liberty which beats so soundly and vigorously at the heart, may be extended to the most distant parts of the empire, and be felt in all its power, not only in granting toleration to our religion, but in maintaining its supremacy, and shedding the blessings of peace and order amid the expiring throes of paganism.

CHAPTER XXVI.

EDUCATION OF THE NATIVES.

NATIVE EDUCATION — THE USE OF THE VERNACULARS—PROMISES OF THE CHARTER—MONOPOLY OF INSTRUCTION—TESTIMONY OF THE TWELFTH CENTURY — AMOUNT OF GOVERNMENT PATRONAGE—ENGLISH LANGUAGE—PRINCIPLES OF RULE —SYSTEM OF CONQUERORS—EFFECTS IN ENGLAND AND IRELAND — ENGLISH PARTY AT CALCUTTA—INFLUENCE OF THIS SYSTEM UPON OUR RULE.

IGNORANCE, there can be no question, is a curse to any people. Where the multitudes are illiterate, they are exposed to the wiles of the crafty, to the superstitious fears which their own fancies originate, to all the lies which their priests may propagate, and to all the alarms which the selfish agitator may excite. But when education becomes general, information spreads, and an acquaintance with men and things gains the ascendant; the people judge for themselves; ancient prejudices are removed; society is emancipated from the despotism of priestcraft; facts, truth and evidence gain dominion over the mind; and rational freedom is rendered secure. If the past history of the world has failed fully to substantiate these facts; the history of India will, I hope, very soon render them unquestionable.

As it is at present conducted, no plan of education could be so worthless as that which obtains among the natives. To teach the children to read upon olas,* to write, and to cipher; to load their memories with lessons which they cannot understand; to initiate them into their absurd system of idolatry; to instruct them in the history of their gods, and in the licentious nature of their worship, may be the best method for keeping them in error, but it can never produce those effects which the wise and the good wish to contemplate. The missionaries saw this from the beginning. Convinced that education must become an important instrument in the furtherance of the gospel, and especially in preparing the people for the reception of the truth, they established schools on a better plan. So far as the native system was good, they adopted it. Sets of school-books, containing the elements of history, geography, astronomy, &c., were prepared in the vernacular languages. In the use of catechisms, religious books, and especially the divine oracles, treasures of divine knowledge were enriching the minds of the rising generation, and were preparing them for the abandonment of idolatry, and for the examination of the Bible. Thousands of children were educated in the Serampore mission schools; thousands in the Cal-

* Cajan leaves.

cutta Baptist, and London Mission schools, and thousands more throughout the other presidences; and the brethren affirmed that, if they had funds, schools might be established to any extent. The children were not converted, but their prejudices were shaken; their parents appeared proud of the attainments of their sons; and many were overheard ridiculing the gods of their country. The reports of the School-Book Society can bear testimony to the popularity, and to the extent of education in former days: and had the same system been pursued, we might have had greater victories to record.

In the other parts of the country, and especially in the Madras and Bombay presidencies, the improved system in the native languages, has been carried on, and as far as individual exertions might be expected to avail, the effects have been cheering; prejudice has given way both on the part of the parents and of the children; many have learned to value education as they never did before; a race are springing up to read our scriptures and tracts and books with facility; and a people are prepared to welcome the declaration of the truth. I am not ignorant of the vast work which remains to be accomplished, and of the want of suitable teachers, agents and means to carry it on. No. When I think of the population of Hindosthan, and remember the efforts which voluntary association can make to bring the field into a state of culture; I am ready to sit down in despair, since it must be evident to all that, at the present ratio, we should never be able to perform the task. But when I contemplate the resources and the promises of the government, and think, that, in order to reform its subjects, to fit them for the duties of their stations, to prevent the accumulation of crime, to render prisons and banishment, and gibbets and similar penalties unnecessary, and to advance the moral and intellectual happiness of all, it is one essential principle of political economy to diffuse knowledge and education over the face of society, I am ready to hope for better enactments than have yet appeared. At the passing of the last charter, the following were the sentiments expressed by Lord Glenelg—then at the head of the Board of Control—in reference to that clause which promised that greater things should be done for education. "The great object that we all have in view is the conversion of India to Christ. Some think that this may be better accomplished in one way, and some in another. My own opinion is that it will best be done by the establishment of schools in which the children may be taught the principles of our holy religion, and thus comparing its worth and excellence with their own absurd and monstrous system, they may be led to renounce the one, and embrace the other." In the name of honour and consistency, how, I ask, has this promise been fulfilled? An act of the supreme council has declared "that all the funds appropriated for the purposes of education, would be best employed on English education alone;" but has this edict been sanctioned by the government at home? Is there to be in India a monopoly of public education by the upper classes who are so able to pay for it, while the poor are to be consigned to their ignorance and degradation? Are the benefits of knowledge, instead of extending to the whole population through the medium of native schools, to be confined to a few English colleges where large sums may be expended to educate the wealthy, that they may be prepared to rule and tyrannize over their people? Are we to be told that, on the principles of justice and truth, the maxims of the Norman conquest are to be revived, and the system of the dark ages to be renewed on the plains of India, and that the few who will bow to their masters, are to be regarded with peculiar favour, while the masses are to be delivered up to neglect and to the priests? Then, I cannot but deplore the narrow, impolitic and unreasonable principles on which the government act, and think that the public voice ought to be raised against such unrighteous measures.

The description which is given by the historian Robertson of similar efforts made in the twelfth and thirteenth centuries, will apply with equal force and propriety to the present exertions in India. "Schools, upon the model of those instituted by Charlemagne, were opened in every cathedral, and almost in every monastery of note. Colleges and universities were erected and formed into communities or corporations, governed by their own laws and invested with separate and extensive jurisdiction over their own members. A regular course of studies was planned. Privileges of great value were conferred on masters and scholars. Academical titles and honours of various kinds, were invented as a recompense for both. Nor was it in the schools alone that superiority in science led to reputation and authority; it became an object of respect in life, and advanced such as required it to a rank of no inconsiderable eminence. Allured by all these advantages, an incredible number of students resorted to those new seats of learning, and crowded with eagerness into that new path which was opened to fame and to distinction.

"But how considerable these first efforts may appear, there was one circumstance which prevented the effects of them from being as extensive, as they naturally ought to have been. All the languages in Europe, during the period under review, were barbarous. They were destitute of elegance, of force, and even of perspicuity. No attempt had hitherto been made to improve or to polish them. The Latin tongue was consecrated by the church to religion. Custom, with authority scarcely less sacred, had appropriated it to literature. All the sciences cultivated in the twelfth and thirteenth centuries were taught in Latin. All books with respect to them were written in that language. It would have been deemed a degradation of any important subject, to have treated of it in a modern language. This confined science within a very narrow circle. The learned alone were admitted into the temple of knowledge; the gate was shut against all others, who were suffered to remain involved in their former darkness and ignorance."

More than six years have elapsed since the charter was passed; and what is the amount of exertion that has been made to realize our expectations? Mr. Adam, it is true, was appointed to enquire into the state of education, and he has executed his commission, and has presented his reports full of information, and of plans which, if well received, adopted, and carried into effect, would unquestionably be full of grace and advantage to India. But here, I presume, it has ended. To quote the words of an intelligent speaker on this point, "Works of great national improvement are neglected; and, by similar neglect, the great moral laws of the country are broken down, and sunk in one general abandonment of all that is great, public-spirited, and virtuous in a people. Yet this is not the fault of the natives—they are eager for and highly capable of receiving instruction; nor is it the fault of the executive in India—for one with more paternal feelings towards the country there does not exist; nor is it the fault of the civil servants, the best of whom are over-wrought, and have little time to devote to matters of general improvement. The fault—the *crime* lies with the Court of Directors and the British government in not providing the means for the education of the people. This is the bounden duty of every government. It is by the discharge of this high moral duty, that Prussia has raised her character amongst the nations—but not without a large and necessary expenditure. I find in Berlin, seventeen shillings and sixpence allotted for the education of every child that would not be otherwise educated; and what is the amount annually allotted for the education of India? It is not a farthing for every child that would not be otherwise educated; and it will amount to little more, even although increased by all the sums placed at the disposal of the Committee of Public Instruction. It may be thought that this is foreign to the object of the meeting; but if Englishmen are to suffer so long as the courts of justice are corrupt, it surely behoves us to enquire at what period we may expect an end of our sufferings, as this reform can only be effected by education. And here let me quote the words of Mr. Adam, than whom India has not a truer, a more judicious, or a warmer friend:—'While ignorance is so extensive, can it be matter of wonder that poverty is extreme, that industry languishes, that crime prevails, and that, in the adoption of measures of public policy, however salutary and ameliorating their tendency, government cannot reckon with confidence on the moral support of an intelligent and instructured community? Is it possible that a wise and a just government can allow this state of things longer to continue?

While vernacular education was making progress in Bengal, and the Marquis of Hastings and his lady were rendering it the greatest encouragement, and many were exulting in the effects which the schools were likely to produce; the Hindoo college was established, and was giving to the students an English education. For the first few years, entire failure seemed to threaten it, but the government came to its support. Encouraged by some effects which it ultimately produced, others no sooner adopted a similar method, and held out a high premium to the study of English, in the prospects of office and emolument, than the usual kind of education fell to a discount; there was a rush to those schools where English was to be obtained; the native schools which had hitherto been regarded with esteem, were looked upon with scorn and contempt; the demand for books in Bengalee began to fall, while that for English rose very high; and if my information be correct, the native schools at Calcutta are now almost deserted, and very few think of sending their children to learn their own language.

To some, this effect is a matter of great rejoicing; to me, it is a subject of the deepest regret, and I shall be greatly mistaken if it is not found, in the future, that it has driven back our cause for fifty years.

When the frenzy is over, when the system has done incalculable mischief, and when many a dark and gloomy day has been prepared for Hindosthan, the good will see that they must return to the old system, and begin their march at the point where they forsook the right road. The children in the native schools were receiving western literature and science, through the medium of their own languages; and while they learned all that was good, there was nothing to hinder them from obtaining a respectable education, and from becoming blessings to others. But since that day, English is paramount. In all the government schools and colleges, the children learn to read, to write, and to cipher in English; whatever instructions they receive, are given in the same language; every thing may be learned but Christianity; the teachers may give the students infidel books, and teach them atheism, but they dare not mention the name of Jesus; and such seminaries are to be established over Hindosthan. As this system was unfolding itself, and the government began to show it favour, the missionaries and the benevolent in Calcutta, might have rendered a most important service to the state and to Christianity. Had they pursued their former course with greater assiduity and diligence; had they exerted all their powers to show that a useful, and respectable, and religious education could be given to the natives in their own language; had they remonstrated with the government, and pointed out some of the effects which would certainly arise from the new scheme; then, the system patronized by the Marquis of Hastings might still have triumphed; the languages of the people might have been rendered important, and have become now, as they must hereafter, the vehicle of western science and literature. But I appeal to all who are acquainted with the subject, whether the scheme of the government was not extolled to the skies; whether missionary schools were not established on the very same principles; and whether some did not stand forward as the strenuous advocates of the course which government, and the new committee of public instruction determined to pursue?

This leads me to the discussion of the important question, whether the vernacular language, or the English ought to become the medium of giving education to the natives. I feel the greatest respect for those who have become the advocates of a system which I consider erroneous. I yield to them what I wish to claim for myself,—a regard to the best interests of that people, and a conviction that whatever system will most effectually destroy their idolatrous errors, and establish among them the kingdom of Christ, *that* must be the best, and ought to be adopted. Nay: as I was once an admirer of this theory, but was soon convinced that it was erroneous; and as I have only been a distant spectator of its working in Calcutta, without having at all mingled in the contest, I may, perhaps, be allowed to give an impartial opinion upon the point.

To every one who has investigated the subject, who has perused the documents that have been written, and who has observed the movements of society both in and out of Calcutta, nothing is more evident than that the advocates of English, have stimulated the government to the measures which have been adopted, and that the government, on the other hand, have animated them to adopt the extreme views which are now entertained. Posterity, it is true, will be the best judge in the affair; but in the nineteenth century, after the experience of so many ages, with the history of the world before us, and having the ability to draw from the past, guidance and discretion for the future, it is not wise to enter upon a career of speculation, in the face of well-attested facts; nor to expect success in a race where disappointment has so often attended the best exertions.

I may, perhaps, be told that we have nothing to do with the political bearing of the question. This I cannot admit: it is the business of every benevolent mind to look at measures which are professedly adopted for the moral welfare of any people, and to weigh the reasons, and, as far as possible, the operations and the results, in the balances of truth; and if he finds that such a plan will tend to defeat the great object which he wishes to see accomplished, it is his duty to lift up his voice against it, and to do what he can to prevent it. I regard then this question as having two important bearings—the one upon the present welfare of the people, and upon our Indian rule—the other upon their conversion to Christianity.

If there has been one principle which I have admired in the past government of the honourable Company more than another, it has been the determination they have shown to rule over the people *in their own languages.* Whether the records are to be in Persian or in English, is a matter of trifling importance, when compared with the question, how are the natives to be judged, to be governed, to be instructed, to be elevated in the social scale, and to have their present and eternal welfare promoted. It used to be a rule in the service, that no officer in the military department, is qualified to advancement, except he has studied Hindosthanee, and that no civilian, except he has attended the college, and has made progress in one or more vernacular languages, can obtain a situation of trust and emolument. These rules have been laid down on the principle, that the native dialect should be that of the government,—that it is the best and most direct way to the hearts of the people—that it enlists the sympathies, the passions, the prejudices, and the good feelings of the subjects on the side of their rulers—and that it gives to all in authority, a power which they could not obtain in any other manner.

The experiment has been fully tried, and has succeeded well.

No person who has been employed in offices of state in India, has been more successful in his career, than the late Sir Thomas Munro. When he entered upon his duties in the Ceded districts, they were in a state of the greatest confusion; banditti were prowling among the people, like wolves in the forest; war and anarchy had dissolved the bonds which unite the parts of the social system together; neither peace, nor order, nor security were to be found. But in a few years, this diligent and enterprising officer brought all into subjection, established confidence among the various classes of the community, gave a stimulus to trade and industry, nearly doubled the amount of revenue, and rendered the province tranquil and happy. By what means did he do so? He spoke and used the vernacular language as he would his own. He allowed no interpreters and no expounders of the law to stand between him and the inhabitants. Their complaints, their causes, their grievances were all heard, enquired into, and adjusted in their own tongue. He showed them sympathy and kindness, and in return, met with confidence, gratitude and affection. The birds of prey were scared into their hiding places, and could find no room for rapine and for plunder. The collector became the father and the friend of the people, and when he became governor of Madras, and was accustomed to visit these districts again, they gave him the hearty and the affectionate welcome that is due to a parent, and his name is embalmed in their memories, and will live among them to future generations.

This is only a specimen: go through India—visit with me the north and south, the east and the west. Let us go to the provinces, which have fallen one after another under our rule, and show me the territories where the collectors and all the judges have discarded the Persian and the English, and every foreign tongue alike in the administration of affairs; where they have adopted, in all their courts, and all their official intercourse, the language spoken by the people, and where, like men of honour and of truth, they have laboured to emancipate the poor from oppression and despotism; and I will show you the provinces where peace, and order, and prosperity most prevail; where sympathy and confidence, and the best affections of our nature are called into exercise between the rulers and the subjects; where feuds and rebellions, and deeds of darkness are almost unknown; and where civilization and improvement are making rapid advances in society.

In the days that are past, a very different system from this, has, I am aware, been adopted by conquerors. It must be a shocking usurpation that has not brought some good in its train to posterity. As it is the prerogative of the Almighty to bring good out of evil; so, unquestionably, out of the reign of oppression, insult and tyranny, there has arisen to future generations, some good which neither the advocates of the system, nor the sufferers under it, could have expected or foreseen. It is likely that the Africans who have been stolen from their country, loaded with chains and galled with bondage, may now, in the days of their freedom, bless God that slave-ships touched upon their coast, robbed them of their comforts, and brought them to the West Indies as bondsmen, since they have there heard of deliverance from sin, have obtained the liberty that is in Christ, and may become the instruments of carrying back these tidings to Africa, and of setting their kinsmen free. But no one, I presume, would, on these grounds, regard accursed slavery as a good, or plead for such a system as the precursor of freedom and happiness to men. Now, I might, by trouble and expense, ferret out some good from the systems which former conquerors have adopted. I might expatiate on the conquests of Rome, and show that, in her rule of iron, and her subjugation of the surrounding nations, she imposed her language and her laws upon the people, and has thus "infused her terms into every vernacular language of Europe, and has immortalized her name and her character." I might tell of the conquests of the Caliphs, and show how much the Mahommedan rule was indebted, in the dark ages, to "a celebrated decree that the Arabic should be the universal language of the Mahommedan world, so that, from the Indian Archipelago to Portugal, it actually became the language of religion, of literature, of government, and generally of common life." I might advert to the edict of Akbar, and show how he established the Persian as the language of business and of polite literature through his extensive dominions, and that this has identified the genius of his dynasty with the language of the country.* But a heathen philosopher might reply to me, what then? are these the benefits which you propose to my people in exchange for their mother-tongue? Are these the privileges which you will confer upon posterity, for all the misrule, oppression, and calamities to which the empire must be subject in order to secure their enjoyment? Are we to pass through all the ignominy, the shame, and the degradation which the Romans inflicted upon the Britons, and which Akbar has inflicted for centuries upon India, that after many generations, your names and your nation may be venerated and renowned? Such measures are only worthy of a barbarous age. We live in the days of humanity and benevolence, when better principles should regulate your conduct, and when more respect should be paid to the rights and liberties of men. We shall be glad to receive your laws, your literature, and perhaps your religion; but if we must do so at the expense of our language, our national prejudices, and justice, and

* Dr. Duff, on the New Era of the English Language in India.

law, and right administered to our people as God and nature have given them a claim, then we wish you would wrap them in oblivion, or keep them to yourselves.

Let us see what such an erroneous system has done for past ages. "But the English," says the historian, "had the cruel mortification to find, that their king's authority, however acquired or however extended, was all employed in their oppression; and that the scheme of their subjection, attended with every circumstance of insult and indignity, was deliberately formed by the prince, and wantonly prosecuted by his followers. William had even entertained the difficult project of totally abolishing the English language; and for that purpose, he ordered, that in all schools throughout the kingdom, the youth should be instructed in the French tongue,—a practice which was continued from custom till after the reign of Edward III., and was never, indeed, totally discontinued in England. The pleadings in the supreme courts of judicature were in French; the deeds were often drawn in the same language; the laws were composed in that idiom; no other tongue was used at court; it became the language of all fashionable company; and the English, ashamed of their own country, affected to excel in that foreign dialect."

The very same has unquestionably been the experience of Ireland, Wales, and the Highlands of Scotland. As the authors of this new theory do, I might take the exceptions from the general rule, and might show how agreeable and how useful such schemes were to these countries. But I prefer an appeal to the general sense of the people, to the evils which the workings of an erroneous theory has entailed upon their country, and to the good and the prosperity of which it has deprived them. Though they have been in the very neighbourhood of the conquering kingdom; though they have enjoyed every advantage which power and promise, commerce and friendly intercourse could afford, in order to reconcile them to the English language; though every worldly inducement has been held out to them, extensive establishments have been supported at an enormous expense to wean them from their own tongue, and every measure adopted to initiate them into the foreign one; what, after centuries of grief and vexation, what is the estimation in which the English is held? What is the light in which the people view English judges, magistrates, interpreters, and English jurisprudence? They are all viewed as a badge of conquest and of inferiority; nothing but a want of power obliges the people to submit to the yoke; and whatever privileges the English may have brought in its train, it is still the conviction of the sufferers, that these might have been secured, with the dominion of their own tongue, and with a more just and benignant system of rule.

But I may be told that the natives of India are

anxious that the English language should be used in the courts of law, in the revenue department, in political correspondence, and in all the public offices of state. Such a statement may impose upon those who are ignorant of the condition of India; but it cannot upon those who are acquainted with its affairs. I allow that in Calcutta, there is a rage for English, and that, amongst the young men who are aspirants to office and to power, and who see that the tide is setting in, in favour of English, there are many who think that, if they wish for advancement, they must worship the rising sun; but what has this to do with the vast body of the people? Has it not always been found that a fraction has taken the side of the dominant power, and rendered its obsequiousness, a stepping-stone to office and to aggrandizement? If the government were to make the knowledge of English, *a sine qua non*, to place and to distinction, does not every one see that the path is plain, and that the greatest admirers of the plan, must be the first in the race?

"The sole reason," says Dr. Duff, "why the English is not now more a general and anxious object of acquisition among the natives, is the degree of uncertainty under which they—the natives—still labour as to the ultimate intentions of government, and whether it will ever lead them into paths of usefulness, profit, or honour; only let the intentions of government be officially announced, and there will be a general movement among all the more respectable classes."* Who can doubt it? In such a case, the few will try to gain the monopoly, and rule over their brethren according to law. As soon, therefore, as it was declared that all the sums expended by the government upon education, would be lavished upon English alone; as soon as it was whispered that the language of the conquerors would soon supersede the Persian, and would become the universal medium of transacting the business of the empire, and of course the high-road to office, and emolument; what a rush to the Hoogly college! what an increase to the number of students wherever the essential qualifications were to be obtained! Was this to be wondered at? No. But the great wonder to me, is that a wise and a beneficent government, and that intelligent men, who, no doubt, wish the welfare and prosperity of India, should be misled by such a momentary impulse of native feeling, should mistake this expression of a few at Calcutta, as the wishes of the vast body of Hindoos, and should be carried away, by this burst of popularity, to establish a system which the present generation will ultimately condemn, and which posterity will regard as Utopian. No one who has read upon the subject, can entertain a doubt that what has been termed the English party, wished and hoped and laboured to the last, that English would become the universal medium

* Trevelyan on Education in India.

for the transaction of public business. One of the committee, who from being an orientalist, is said to have become an advocate of this new theory, is represented as stating that if the English was not to be used in every department, the system would completely fail; and in all the records published by the new committee of public instruction, this change is taken for granted, and was to be speedily accomplished. No one can mistake the strain in which all the abettors of the theory have written upon the subject. Whatever might be the regard of the former committee to the learned and to the vulgar languages of India; no one would charge the committee appointed in 1835 with any partiality of this kind. No. English was their watch-word. It became the shibboleth of their party. Persian was to be driven from the courts, but it was that the English might gain the ascendency. The vernaculars were too vile and too contemptible to receive a moment's attention in any discussion upon the matter. If they could all have been amalgamated into one and brought up to receive sentence, like a poor unhappy culprit before the tribunal, this committee would have blotted them out of existence at once, that the English might occupy the place of honour and of station; and that day, the peal of joy would have rung throughout the empire, as loud and as merry as at any jubilee. Will posterity believe it, that, in a committee of public instruction, sitting in Calcutta, and discussing the great and mportant question "what medium should be adopted to give a liberal education to the natives;" the vernacular languages—those spoken by the masses of the people, never once obtained an audience, nor an advocate to allude even to their claims? I say *posterity*, because such an event, I presume, has never occurred in the history of mankind before!

But this strange neglect was attended with some happy consequences. The public was not an inattentive nor a silent spectator of this struggle between parties, and of the treatment which the vernacular languages had received. It awoke to the support of the injured; it raised its voice in their favour; it brought this very committee to make an apology for the contempt which it had shown to them; and when the Persian was abolished, and the question of a successor was to be decided, it sent forth a sound so distinct, and so overpowering on the side of justice and of right, that it exposed the folly of substituting one foreign language for another; it brought in the vernaculars, as the channel of law and equity, victorious over their competitor; it induced this committee to speak a favourable word for the dialects which they had already, in purpose, consigned to oblivion; and it permitted them to take some credit to themselves for coming in to the help of the wronged, when their own favourite had suffered a defeat.

According to the decree of the governor-general in council, the native dialects were to have *a fair trial;* they were, *for the present*, to be employed in the judicial department, as well as in the revenue; and it was to be seen, during a year, whether they were *media* suited to administer law and justice to their people. I understand they are likely to come out of the ordeal triumphant; and after they have been fully tried by better judges, than those who have hitherto so ignorantly denounced them, they will be found, I doubt not, as suitable a medium for giving a liberal education in science, in philosophy and in religion, as they are in securing law, justice and prosperity to Hindoos.

But notwithstanding this defeat, the English party will not rest satisfied; they will soon return to the charge; and every means will be employed to establish the English throughout India, as the language of law and of rule.* It will therefore be

* Lest it should be thought that I am unreasonable upon this point, and that there is not now the least reason for apprehension, since the vernacular languages have gained this triumph, I subjoin in this note, a letter from the secretary of the Bengal government to the committee of public instruction.

"One of the most important questions connected with the present discussion, is that of the nature and degree of encouragement to the study of the English language, which it is necessary and desirable for the government to hold out independently of providing books, teachers, and the ordinary means of tuition. Your committee has observed that unless English be made the language of business, political negociation, and jurisprudence, it will not be universally or extensively studied by our native subjects. Mr. Mackenzie, in the note annexed to your report, dated the 3rd instant, urges strongly the expediency of a declaration by government, that the English will be eventually used as the language of business; otherwise, necessary to glance at the effects which such a system of policy will produce, and to warn the government against it. As soon as this new epoch arrives, dissatisfaction will prevail among the natives in general. English being constituted the chief recommendation to office, hundreds and thousands of meritorious men, scattered through the provinces, will find that it has been their misfortune to have been born a few years too early—that they must sink into utter neglect—that they have not been able to compete with their juniors in acquiring the language of their conquerors,—and that, though they possess every other qualification to render them useful, they have not the one which may throw every other almost into the shade.

with the majority of our scholars, he thinks, that all we 'do to encourage the acquisition must be nugatory;' and recommends, that it be immediately notified that after the expiration of three years, a decided preference will be given to candidates for office, who may add a knowledge of English to other qualifications. The Delhi committee have also advocated, with great force and earnestness, the expediency of rendering the English the language of our public tribunals, and correspondence, and the necessity of making known that such is our eventual purpose, if we wish the study to be successfully and extensively prosecuted.

"Impressed with a deep conviction of the importance of the subject,—and cordially disposed to promote the great object of improving India, by spreading abroad the lights of European knowledge, morals, and civilization,—his lordship in council, has no hesitation in stating to your committee, and in authorizing you to announce to all concerned in the superintendence of your native seminaries, that it is the wish and admitted policy of the British government to render its own

What will be the effect of this feeling so universal throughout the community, pent up it may be from the view of the rulers, but diffusing a sense of injustice and oppression among all classes? It will teach them to hate and despise their governors, as well as the system which has been espoused; the very same complaints which Wales and Ireland have made, will become common; a high and broad wall of separation will be raised between the subjects and the European authorities; and the regulations which have raised the few to office and to wealth, will create heartburnings—discontent and disorder will ensue—and these will lead to anarchy and revolution.

language gradually and eventually the language of public business throughout the country; and that it will omit no opportunity of giving every reasonable and practicable degree of encouragement to the execution of this project. At the same time, his lordship in council, is not prepared to come forward with any distinct and specific pledge as to the period and manner of effecting so great a change in the system of our internal economy; nor is such a pledge considered to be at all indispensable to the gradual and cautious fulfilment of our views. It is conceived, that assuming the existence of that disposition to acquire a knowledge of English, which is declared in the correspondence now before government, and forms the groundwork of our present proceedings, a general assurance to the above effect, combined with the arrangements in train for providing the means of instruction, will ensure our obtaining at no distant period a certain, though limited, number of respectable native scholars; and more effectual and decisive measures may be adopted hereafter, when a body of competent teachers shall have been provided in the Upper Provinces, and the superiority of an English education is more generally recognised and appreciated."

The English party profess to see in the scheme recommended, a bond of union which will unite this Anglo-Indian section to our government, and identify their interests with ours. I may be very defective in vision; but the very reverse is apparent to me. No persons understand their own interests, and what is likely to work for their benefit, better than Hindoos. So long as business is carried on in the vernacular dialects, the Europeans are obliged to learn the languages. Sometimes they apply, with great reluctance, to the labour; but they are under the necessity of doing it; and as interest and advancement depend upon their attainments, they have every inducement to persevere. But what will be the result when all business is transacted in English? Such studies will be thrown aside as useless. As all the natives employed by the government will understand English, and transact affairs of importance among the people, they will become the stewards of the estate; and the Europeans will be enabled to dispense with all trouble and anxiety on the question of language. Superintendence will become the principal business of collectors, of magistrates, and judges; and instead of mingling with the subjects, their time and attention will be devoted to the native assistants. Whatever confidence and sympathy existed before between the governed and their rulers, will now be destroyed. In vain will the former try to make known their complaints and their grievances to the latter. The channel of communication is cut off. The European officer, whose predecessor was accustomed to listen to the wailings of oppression, and to the wrongs inflicted upon the innocent by the native official, is now deaf to every complaint, and understands not the voice of the sufferer. The whole power and management must fall into the hands of those whom this system has formed to rule the country. Rebellions without number will be fomented, and will be carried into effect, without the least knowledge on the part of the government. The state of India at the present period, ruling it on the old system, and with all the knowledge which Europeans have of the languages, has shown the critical position of our power, and the necessity there is for being constantly awake to danger and to intrigue; what will be the state of affairs when we are locked up in security, ignorant of the cabals that may be forming in our own houses, and by our own servants, and exposed, like strangers, in a foreign land? This very party on whom we should depend, would know their time; they could buy and sell their masters at their pleasure; they would know how to improve their position to drive the English from their shores, to emancipate their countrymen from a foreign yoke, and to secure the power and dominion to themselves.

These are neither new, nor extravagant sentiments. "Tippoo Sultan," says Mr. M'Kerrell in his preface to his Carnataca Grammar, "was well acquainted with this—the Hindoo language of his state; and Hyder Ally, his father and immediate predecessor, was quite familiar with it. Both were men of stern and unrelenting dispositions, and little partial to their Hindoo subjects; but they knew mankind too well, not to be aware, that unless those who govern, be acquainted with the language of the governed, a set of middle men will arise, who will ultimately become the scourges of the country."

"In adverting," says Sir John Colbourne, "to the delusion which has prevailed in respect to the character of the rural population of Lower Canada, and to the extraordinary fact, that a people, enjoying, under a mild government, benefits and advantages which were highly appreciated by them, had been prepared and extensively organized for a general revolt, and to blindly enter into the schemes of the factious individuals by whom they have been duped, *without the knowledge of the local government, or doubt being entertained as to their loyalty or intentions*, I consider it incumbent on me to observe that the *executive government, has been, for many years, totally excluded, and cut off from all communication* with the *habitans*, of *every* district; *they being in the hands and under the control* of *avocats*, notaries, and persons of the *medical profession residing among them, have been corrupted by them*, acting under the direction of Mr. Papineau and his faction, and an unrestrained and seditious press. I have no hesitation in conveying this expression of my opinion to her majesty's government, lest too much reliance should be placed on the promises and addresses of a most ignorant peasantry, that have been, for many years, under the control of ambitious and unprincipled individuals to whom I have alluded."

"The facts stated by Sir John Colbourne merit, certainly, the utmost attention. If a fusion of laws and language cannot be obtained, some means should certainly be devised of enabling the government to know what is passing among the governed. To be for years cut off from all communication with the governed, and in ignorance of the state of general feeling, gives a curious idea of government. Epicurus' gods enjoyed themselves in perfect indifference as to the joys and sorrows of mortals; but at all events, they knew something of what mortals were about."

The circumstances of Canada, are a suitable warning to us, in reference to India. I foretel the danger. If the proposed system be persevered in, it will soon be the bane of our empire, and will deprive us of the opportunities of doing its inhabitants good.

But suppose that these predictions will not be realised, and that, in accordance with such a policy, we are able to maintain our power in the East, what heart-burnings! what oppressions! what discontent! what anarchy and confusion! what commotions will not a government, conducted on such principles, create among the people? As I love our fellow-citizens in India, and wish their present and eternal welfare, I venture to warn her rulers of the consequences which must arise from such a course. Experience is not true; the history of the world is a falsehood; mankind have passed through so many revolutions in vain; if such a system will ever succeed, and if it be not attended with the most dreadful calamities to the people. If any case could be more in point, than another, it is Ireland. Look at the dark history of that afflicted country. At the time when its interests became more identified with England, this system was really adopted. The English party gained the ascendency. Every thing that was Irish, was consigned to oblivion. Nothing was heard of but English supremacy, the English language, English law, literature, and science, and English establishments to advance learning and religion. A crusade was especially carried on against the Irish language; it was said to be a barbarous jargon; authority wished to bury it in the tomb; and every thing was printed in English. When any attempt was made to publish a translation of the scriptures in Irish, and works for the instruction of the people, it was opposed with the greatest violence, and the advocates of humanity were thwarted in all their exertions. The complaints of the poorer classes, were disregarded. One rebellion after another, plunged the country in blood and anarchy. Hatred, discontent, feuds, strifes and outrages continued to work in society. No sympathy, nor confidence existed between the rulers and the subjects. The people, regarded as "aliens in blood, in language, and in religion," were delivered over into the hands of their priests. Those who used *their language*, secured the road to their hearts; and while the English might have set them free, might have learned their tongue, and saturated it with science and theology, and might have won them over by kindness and love to the Protestant government and religion, they lost the opportunity; laid up, in consequence of this wretched system, immense stores of misrule and degradation for posterity; and consigned the Irish people and their children to a superstition which now rules them as with a rod of iron. After centuries have passed away, what is still the state of Ireland?

CHAPTER XXVII.

THE EDUCATION OF THE NATIVES.

USE OF TERMS IN THE LANGUAGE—ENGLISH SYSTEM—ARGUMENTS OF THE HEATHEN—IMPRESSIONS UPON THE PEOPLE—EFFECTS OF THE NEW SYSTEM UPON MISSIONARIES—EFFECTS UPON HINDOO STUDENTS—INFIDELITY—LITERATURE OF WALES—HIGHLANDS OF SCOTLAND—IRELAND—THE FORMATION OF A LITERATURE—SUGGESTIONS.

HAVING in the preceding chapter, considered the effects which the English system is likely to produce upon our Indian rule, and upon the temporal condition of the Hindoos; let us proceed to examine the bearing which it will have upon the moral and spiritual state of the community, and upon the interests of science and literature.

In all our plans and operations for the conversion of the heathen, it is well to be guided, as far as possible, by the rules of the New Testament, and by the example of the apostles. Whatever may be the difference in our state and circumstances, the dictates of nature, the voice of reason, and the lessons of the scriptures must be regarded. In their attempts to preach the gospel to the heathen, to communicate instruction to the rising generation, to disseminate divine knowledge by the translation of the scriptures and by the publication of useful works, through the medium of the vernacular languages; modern missionaries thought they were directed by experience, and by the example of primitive times. On the day of Pentecost, they remembered that the Spirit descended upon apostles and evangelists, endowed them with the gift of tongues, and enabled them to address Parthians, and Medes and Elamites, and dwellers in Mesopotamia and in many foreign countries, on the mysteries of redemption. Why, we ask, was not the miracle wrought upon the hearers, rather than upon the preachers? Why, instead of granting the ability to speak so many languages to the few, did not the Almighty agent, grant the ability to the thousands assembled in Jerusalem, and to the vast multitudes in different lands to whom the message was to be proclaimed, to understand his servants who spoke probably the language of Judea? The one miracle would have been as easy to him, as the other; but as it would not have been so much in accordance with nature, and with those general laws to which the Divine Being has attended even in the working of these wonders, he bestowed the gift of tongues. As he did not provide food for millions, when a sufficiency for thousands was all that was required, so he did not grant the gift of understanding the Hebrew or the Greek to the nations, when the other gift to the preachers, was sufficient to accomplish his purposes of love. Though this endowment is not now continued to the church; yet the missionaries deemed it both more scriptural, and more reasonable, that they should toil to obtain the languages of the people, than that the heathen should, either in dozens or in multitudes, learn their foreign dialect; and when God gave them power to accomplish the task, when he commanded his blessing to rest upon their labours, and when idolaters were impressed with the word, they concluded, that they had additional arguments to persevere in their course.

But it has been said that the heathen languages do not, at present, contain terms adequate to convey Christian truth; and it will be better to wait till natives are educated and raised up, to introduce these terms into their own tongues. This is a very old objection. "Among the polished writers of Italy," says Hallam, "we meet on every side the name of Bembo; great in Italian as well as in Latin literature, in prose as in verse. It is now the fourth time it occurs to us; and in no instance has he merited more of his country. Since the fourteenth century, so absorbing had become the love of ancient learning, that the natural language, beautiful and copious as it really was, and polished as it had been under the hands of Boccaccio, seemed to a very false-judging pedantry, scarce worthy the higher kinds of composition. Those, too, who with enthusiastic diligence, had acquired the power of writing Latin well, did not brook so much as the equality of their native language. In an oration delivered at Bologna in 1529, before the emperor and the pope, by Romalo Amaseo, one of the good writers of the sixteenth century, he not only pronounced a panegyric upon the Latin tongue, but contended that the Italian should be reserved for shops, for markets, and the conversation of the vulgar; nor was this doctrine uncommon in that age."

"Can such men assert," says the mandate of Berthold, "that our German language is capable of expressing what great authors have written in Greek and Latin, on the high mysteries of Christian faith and on general science. Certainly it is not; and hence they either invent new words, or use old ones in erroneous senses—a thing especially dangerous in sacred scripture."

But if such an objection, whether made in former times or repeated now, is not the language of ignorance, it must be of prejudice, since the vernacular languages of India are as well qualified to convey divine knowledge, as the languages of Greece and Rome were of old. Did the apostles and evangelists, in their sermons and in their writings, draw their theological terms from the Hebrew, and use them in the languages of the heathen? Instead of employing the term Jehovah or Elohim to express the name of the Divine Being, did they not adopt "Theos" which was used among the Greeks, and

"Deus," which was used among the Latins, and reclaiming the general name from the heathen, apply it to the living and true God? I might pursue this argument with the terms adopted to express sin, conscience, salvation, heaven, hell, adoption, and justification; and did not the apostles take the general terms that were used by the Greeks, and by other nations in an idolatrous sense, and giving them a Christian signification, appropriate them to the doctrines and precepts of Christianity? By this example, modern missionaries have thought that they were justified in taking heathen terms, in giving them a Christian signification, and in making idolaters and Christians understand them either by an explanation, or by the connexion in which they are placed. Nay more; when natives receive an English education, and understand our literature, science and theology; these missionaries cannot see what different plan they will adopt to give their own people the knowledge of the Bible. If instead of pursuing this mode, they attempt to saturate their vernacular tongues with terms from the English as the advocates propose, the barbarity will be extreme; and I will leave those who find such difficulty in pronouncing our eastern words, to judge whether it will be a recommendation, or an act of self-denial to the natives of India to study our religion, when the tracts, the scriptures, and books will be filled with the harsh and disagreeable words which not one in a hundred of them will ever be able to pronounce. In order to consign the Sanscrit to oblivion, Mr. Trevelyan labours to show, that the English language has passed through various gradations to its present stage of perfection; but from whence has it gathered its terms which are now applied to literature and science? Has it not been from Greek and from Latin—heathen languages? And why may not the terms as well be taken from the Sanscrit—a language so copious, and so incorporated already with the vernaculars,—as from western languages whose sounds are so barbarous, and whose etymology is so unknown, to the natives of the East? It is right to speak with modesty of one's country and kindred; but surely it is no arrogant assumption to say that when European missionaries have, in addition to being born in Britain and having obtained an English education, they have studied Latin and Greek and Hebrew in their youth, and have acquired, from many years of labour, a knowledge of an Indian language, that they are as well qualified to introduce terms into these dialects, or appropriate those which will be suitable, as any of the students who may graduate at the Hindoo colleges in Calcutta.

Whatever may be the opinion of others, I cannot but regard this new system, and what has been said to support it, as an injudicious sally against the operations, and the progress of our missions in Southern India. More than a century has elapsed, since the Danish missionaries landed at Tranquebar;

adopted the plan which, as I have shown, was pursued in primitive times, saturated the Tamul language with terms to which they have appropriated Christian significations, and have written works which deserve well of posterity. British missionaries followed in their steps; and in the various translations of the scriptures which have been made into Tamul, Telloogoo and Canarese; in the original works which have been written, and in the translations which have been made of English books, these terms have been used in the same sense; they have long since been rescued from heathenism, and applied to a Christian use; and they are well understood by the large Christian community who are scattered over the peninsula. Since these terms, generally speaking, are of Sanscrit origin; they might be used in Bengalee, or in Oordoo, as well as in the languages of the south, and might become common to our religion throughout our Indian empire; what then? Are the labours, the anxieties and the progress of ages to be thrown away? Is a system to be sanctioned and applauded, which is not only destitute of support from nature, reason, and scripture, but opposed to the genius of the languages, and to the efforts which have so long been successfully made? Are the principles on which Fabricius, Carey, Marshman, Martyn, Hands, Reeve, Gordon, and Rhenius, and many more have proceeded in the translations of the sacred volume to be discarded, and the oracles of truth to be filled with foreign terms which the people can neither pronounce, nor understand? If these are the theories, what must be the practical results?

It has long been an objection raised by the heathen against the missionaries, that Christianity is very well suited to England and to Englishmen; but that their own religion is best suited to Hindoos; what strength does this argument gather from the system espoused? "From the beginning," the Hindoos will say, "we have told you that your religion was not fitted for India. Some among yourselves have now confirmed us in this opinion, since they maintain that it cannot be understood in our languages. If we wish to comprehend your Bible, and your theology we must learn and study English; what cannot be explained in our language, never surely could be intended for us." Indeed, the whole system is calculated to make the impression upon their minds, that it is altogether an English concern. Christianity was intended by its great author, for all languages, nations and kindreds of men. In primitive times, it brought liberty to the Jew and to the Greek, to the Barbarian and the Scythian, to the bond and to the free. But by human systems, how often has the light been obscured, and concealed from their view! During the dark ages, it was shut up in the Latin; and in the nineteenth century and in British India, the English is proclaimed to be the language without which our religion cannot be understood, its evidences cannot be appreciated, its beauties cannot be seen, and its power cannot be felt. When such views are propagated; what are the suspicions they are calculated to excite? That our religion is an engine of the state—that it is a part of our national policy--that it is associated only with our rule—that it has come in to the support of our misgovernment, and all the grievances which may attend our administration—that up to the present time, they have heard very little about religion in English, but now the British think it is proper to consolidate their power, by engrafting their language and religion upon India. "This," they will say, "is just the old system. The Moguls gave us Persian and Mahommedanism; the Portuguese gave us their tongue and Popery; and now we have the English and Christianity." Now, I maintain that this is doing injustice to our religion. It does not require to be mixed up with any language, nor with any government in particular. It is placing it in a false position, and is uniting in the minds of the people, what ought to be kept seperate and distinct. So long as missionaries study and honour their language, and make exertions in Bengalee, in Tamul, and in Canarese; they are recognized as friends to Hindoos; there is a sympathy between them and the people in their sorrows, their trials and oppressions; they are regarded as a wall of defence to shield the helpless from injustice and rapacity, since they will not witness such evils and be silent; and they are everywhere known as the advocates of humanity and benevolence. But the moment that we use our own language, and mix up our religion with it, we appear as Englishmen; the strongest prejudices are raised against us; we are associated with the conquest and with the conquerors of their country. Our religion is only a part of the English rule, and with that government, it must wither and die. If they hate our authority, despise our laws, and complain of our taxation, they will also denounce our divinity. Amongst the few, our language may be popular so long as their ambitious views are promoted; but once let other prospects be rendered more inviting, and they would be the first and the most violent to abuse it, and to aim at its extermination. May that dark and dreadful day be far distant, when the British power will be overthrown in that land! But is it well to adopt plans whose principal importance is derived from the assumption that our rule is to be perpetuated among that people to many generations? Does not the history of the last two years, create within us fears and apprehensions? On the old system, missionaries were in India before the British government was established, and obtained the respect and the confidence of native authorities; but what, in case of revolution, would be the fate of our language, and of our religion as mixed up with it? They would both be swept away in a moment.

The very sound would add inveteracy to the bitterness, and would give energy, to the malice of our foes.

But cultivate the native languages; infuse our science, literature, and religion into every dialect; improve the time and the opportunities which Providence has afforded us, to give the heathen knowledge and Christianity, since we may soon be deprived of them; associate the religious views, principles, and experience of the people with the language in which they were nursed and educated; mix up the zeal, the sympathies, the passions, and the generous impulses of the native converts with the interests of their own country and kindred; and instead of imposing our language upon them, as a badge of their subjection and of our ascendency, let us convince them that it is our supreme wish to do them good, and to convert them to God, in perfect accordance with all their rights and privileges as men and as citizens; then, we establish our religion on a firm and enduring basis; possession is taken of the soil; Christianity is not dependent upon this language, nor upon that government, but it is incorporated with the best interests of the people, and amidst the tempests of revolution, and the fall of dynasties, it will take root, and, like the oak amidst the trees of the forest, it will settle, will continue to grow, and will spread its branches till it fills the land.

The influence which this system is likely to have

upon missionaries and others, will be very prejudicial to the advancement of Christianity. In former days, no sooner did a missionary enter upon his career, than he began to learn the language, and other important subjects engaged his attention. The phraseology that was used; the illustrations with which the natives clothed their thoughts; the figures, the comparisons, and the similitudes which were employed to elucidate the topics; their proverbs, their parables, their questions, their modes of expression, their looks and gestures—all that he could see and hear in the native language, were laid under arrest to imitate, and, as far as possible, to use, that the people might understand, and their attention be gained. His reason, his education, and his hopes of usefulness, demanded of him to lay aside his European fancies and prejudices, and to throw himself, as much as he could, among the people, to cultivate not only their language, but their manner and address. But what is the influence which this English system is likely to produce upon our young missionaries? They find that they can dispense with the toil and the labour of learning a native language. To overthrow Hindooism, and to establish Christianity, the best scheme is to plant English seminaries, and to give the natives an English education. Not one in twenty who advocate this system, will ever obtain a vernacular tongue, so as to use it with any effect. So fully employed are their time and talents with English engagements, that they have none to spend upon the language, the literature, the mythology, the customs, and habits of Hindoos. Teaching in English absorbs every power, and has taken the place of the divine ordinance of proclaiming the gospel. Already nothing is heard of but the establishment of English schools at the mission stations, and many think to accomplish, by this new plan, the greatest wonders, though it be tried under very different circumstances from those of Calcutta, and conducted in a mode very different from that masterly style in which I understand Dr. Duff and his associates have carried it on. Infant schools are planted on the same system, and many of the children, it is announced, are able to *read* the New Testament in English. There is not a word said about their being able to *understand it*, and this, I venture to say, in the face of the church and of the world, they do not. What ridiculous fancies take hold of the minds of men! It were a subject fit to be caricatured, were it not, in another point of view, calculated to excite the deepest mourning and lamentation. When I think of the vast number of children who die in infancy, in childhood, and in youth, and who have only a short time upon earth to learn any thing of heaven and the plan of salvation; I am ready, in the attitude of a suppliant, to beseech every agent in a foreign land to have compassion upon these little ones! Teach them; oh teach them first in their own language! Before you introduce them to a foreign tongue, make them read and understand in their own the scheme of mercy, that should they be called into eternity, they may be able to pray to the Saviour who died for them. With what pleasure do I recollect Canarese children, six and seven years of age, repeating their chapters of the New Testament, and making me feel, with lisping accents, that they understood the tidings of grace.

But if this system produces these prejudicial effects upon European missionaries, diverting them from the native language, leading them to pursue erroneous plans, and unfitting them for usefulness among the heathen; how is it likely to work in preparing the Hindoos for the declaration of the gospel among their countrymen? Mr. Trevelyan contends that Russia—once so barbarous—has been refined and civilized by the study of foreign languages, and the foreign literature which they contain. But is it true that, to accomplish this purpose, the Emperor Nicholas has established *English* schools and colleges in St. Petersburgh, in Moscow, and the great towns of his empire? Whatever foreign stock of learning has been imported, has it not passed through the medium of Russ? and being in its nature and in its growth entirely European, does it not amalgamate almost exactly with the literature of the Tartars? But take Hindoo youths who have never attended school, and many of whom cannot read their own language; place them in a college where they have every thing to learn, and must learn it in English; and what must be the effects of their education upon them? Naturally fond of imitation, they will notice, with intense interest, their European instructors; the looks, the gestures, and the manners which they begin to admire, will be copied; the English tone, accent, and voice must be studied; and Hindoo children are speedily so transformed that they affect the manners and habits of Englishmen. The books which they read, the studies they pursue, the arguments which they hear, the images, the similitudes and the illustrations with which they become familiar, are all European; but is it requisite that they should pass through this process to obtain our stores of learning? Let us look for a moment at our English literature, in whose fields these youths are called to perambulate, and with what does it abound? With allusions to the mythology of Greece and of Rome; to the valleys, the mountains, and the scenery of England; to the frosts, the snow, and the storms of our winter, and to the beauties, the fragrance and sweet melody of our summer; to the strange events that have occurred in our own history, and in those of neighbouring kingdoms; to the great men who have flourished in ancient or in modern times; to the manners, and customs that prevail among our peasantry, and to the splendour, fashions and feats of our court and aristocracy; to thousands of objects which Hindoo students have never seen, and of which it is difficult for them to form an idea. What is there in this literature, to correspond with that required in India? The difference between the east and the west is not greater, than between the former and the latter. Whatever process you adopt, the one will not amalgamate with the style of the other, and in giving these youths such an exclusively English education, you have but ill qualified them for being useful to their countrymen. No. Had this system been reversed; had these pupils learned English in India, as our youth do Latin and Greek in our universities at home; had the professors given their instructions on science and literature in Bengalee, or in Oordoo, and pointed out the books which would be proper for the students to read; had their lectures abounded with eastern allusions and illustrations, while their subjects were so novel and interesting; the same truths would have found their way to the minds of the scholars; the education would have been more Asiatic, but it would have better corresponded with the state and circumstances of the people; English would still have been studied and English essays would have been read, but the latter would have abounded with Eastern figure, allusions, and phraseology; the minds of the students would not be cast in a European mould, yet their thoughts would be Western and dressed in oriental style.

But let us look at the reality. I allude now only to those who, under this system, have become pious, and are devoted to God. How are they qualified for usefulness? Their minds are stored with English illustrations; strange models are held up to their view, and a European standard is the rule of taste and imagination; they live and learn and think in a world of ideality; their speeches are full of illustrations from algebra, geometry,* modern and ancient history, and the various sciences which they have studied; the essays which they compose display considerable talent, abound with European figures and allusions, are cheered by an English

* "As an illustration," remarks Dr. Duff, "of this remark, I may here state, that, about six years ago, I happened to be present at a debating society, composed of forty or fifty young men, who had acquired, or were then acquiring, an English education at the Government Hindoo College. The subject of debate was,—'Whether females ought to be educated?' Another, a youth of about fourteen or fifteen, towards the end of the discussion, rose up, remarking, that he had listened with great delight to the arguments of the other gentlemen, but that one had escaped them, which he would now beg leave to advance. He would prove by *geometry*, 'that females ought to be educated.' All were instantly on the tiptoe of expectation, to hear what this geometrical argument might prove. It turned out to be a somewhat vague and fanciful application of one of the axioms of Euclid, and hence designated a geometrical argument. It was in substance as follows:—

"'Is it conceded that men ought to be educated? Undoubtedly it is. And why is the concession made in their favour? Why not as well educate these cocoa-trees? (pointing to those around the house.) Oh, we are told the reason is, that men have got souls or minds, and these trees have not. And why is it that men's having souls should lead to their being educated? Because these souls are found, from experience, to be susceptible of growth, and consequently of cultivation; and if assembly, and are to be translated* into the vernacular language, and perhaps be published. But are not these young champions less qualified than they might have been for labouring among their brethren? Where are their sympathies now with their own people? Where are those feelings of home and kindred and country which give such a charm to all the realities of life? Instead of having warmed their hearts and their imaginations with the scenes of their childhood, and deepened those impressions which the works of nature and the associations of friendship, had made upon them; you have exchanged them all, for others more distant, indistinct and powerless. You have made them strangers in their own land. They are more

susceptible of cultivation, ought they not to be cultivated? Assuredly they ought, else they must be waste and useless, and not fulfilling the design of their being. It is allowed then, on all hands, that men's souls or minds ought to be cultivated—in other words, that men ought to be educated. Well, and have not females got souls or minds? Many of our Mussulman countrymen think not. But our pundits, (learned men,) in all their folly, have never appealed to the Shasters for any such absurdity as this. So, then, it is quite orthodox for us to believe and assert that females have got souls—and if so, these must, like the souls of men, be capable of growth, capable of being cultivated. And if, because men have got souls capable of cultivation, it is granted that these ought to be cultivated; when it is acknowledged that females have got souls capable of cultivation, ought these not to be cultivated too? Surely they ought; because 'things that are equal to the same thing are equal to one another.' Hence I conclude that females ought to be educated.' "

* Mr. Trevelyan.

prepared to be ministers in England, than teachers to their heathen countrymen. They have lost, in their English education, all that would give life, point and energy to their discourses, delivered to an idolatrous audience. You have made them as much as possible European; but it is not likely that they have become more acceptable and useful to India.

If it be replied that, in reference to the pious and devoted, these fears are groundless, and that they will, no doubt, adopt the style and manner of their country, I appeal to unquestionable facts. Some of the young men who graduated at the Hindoo college, and have become serious, are editors of newspapers, and have the opportunity of sending the streams of knowledge over the land; but what is the style which they have adopted? Have they burst the barriers of habit and education, and in Bengalee, and in language suited to the capacities of their kindred, have they condescended to pour their literature and science through the pages of their journals? Not at all. The English language and style is their standard of perfection; they write more for the European community, than for Bengalees; these newspapers are published in English, and though some of them have columns in the native dialect, they are mere translations from the original, and are the very reverse, of course, of all that is likely to be popular and interesting among Hindoos.

But a champion among the converts, and one who has deservedly been held up as an example to his brethren, has now entered the ministry, and has been admitted, by the Bishop of Calcutta, into deacon's orders; what then? Surely he is an angel of mercy to his benighted countrymen. Whatever direction others may have taken, there can be no doubt that his path is plain, and that, like a zealous and powerful advocate of the faith, he is found, in the towns and in the villages, standing up for the honour of his Lord, calling upon his idolatrous brethren to drink of the waters of life, and to flee from the wrath to come! I hope he would not account this a degradation of his office, though some of his native brethren have written very tauntingly of such missionary exertions! But such, I am sorry to say, is not to be the career of this young man. A new chapel has been erected for him in Calcutta. *He has become an English preacher to his kinsmen, and to all who will go to hear him;* his English education has given a tone to his mind, and a character to his studies and pursuits that have proportionably unfitted him for mixing with his people, and preaching to the poor the gospel of God.

I mention these as specimens of what this English education will do for the converts, even when it is of a Christian kind, as it is conducted in the General Assembly's school; what will be its effects when it is unaccompanied by Christian instruction, as it is exhibited in the colleges established by the government? The results already appear; but these are but the beginning of sorrows. Instead of the glowing picture which Mr. Trevelyan has drawn, and the enlivening prospect which he has described; we have other witnesses at hand, whose authority and testimony are not to be questioned. What say "the friends of religion and humauity" at Calcutta? Have they—the government—not done as much as the missionaries to uproot the ancient laws and institutions of the country, by the establishment of schools and colleges, in which sciences are taught directly at variance with the whole structure of the faith of the people—schools which, as at present conducted, are an unmixed evil?—schools, which deprive the pupils of the miserable comforts of Hindooism, and leave them without even an inanimate God? The government find them the devotees of Kalee, and leave them devotees of brandy-panee and roast-beef.* Let us listen to another witness from Juggernaut. "The Bengalees from Calcutta were *especially ill behaved, and of these, those who were educated, that is who could talk English,* were the cream of the rest, not unfrequently insulting God and Christ in our own language; getting tracts, and immediately tearing them up and throwing them at us, or scattering them in the way."†

* Calcutta Appeal to the Friends of Humanity.

† Rev. W. Lacy's Journal.

But another impartial, and considering the interest which he has taken in this subject, a very important witness remains to be heard. "Once let these leaders of the people, become thorough English scholars, and what will they be? Here opens upon us the glimpse of a dreadful crisis. Give them *knowledge without religion*, according to the present government plan, and they will become *a nation of infidels!* So that, instead of having to contend with the abominations of idolatry, you will have to contend with the wildest forms of European infidelity! If this be the nature of the approaching crisis, who can recall the lesson to be gained from the experience of ages—a dear-bought lesson, deeply imprinted in traces of desolation, and stamped in characters of blood?—Who can look at the convulsions that lately rent asunder the nations of Europe, and beholding, in atrocities that not only outvie savage life, but would, in the comparison, prove the savage to be a sage, eternal monuments of the disastrous power of knowledge unsanctified, and brilliant talents uncontrolled by the power of religious principles;—who, I say, can seriously review all this, and think of the crisis that is impending over India without a thrill of horror?* If these predictions be realized, and I have little doubt they will be, should not some radical change take place in the scheme; what an amount of

* Dr. Duff's Speech before the General Assembly, 1835.

responsibility will devolve upon Mr. Trevelyan, and the members of the Committee of Public Instruction, and upon others who have taken an active part in urging on the government to the adoption of this plan!

Ah! when Christian chiefs visit us from Africa; when Christian refugees, driven from their own land by a persecuting queen, flee from Madagascar, and seek an asylum in England; we are afraid to let them mingle freely with society, lest they should be contaminated; we tremble lest their faith, and piety, and simple devotedness should be injured even by the trifling, and the inconsistencies that are but too visible in the Christian church; we are anxious that the avenues of communication should be shut up, lest they should understand that in this country, so famous for its benevolence and Christianity, there are habits, crimes, and abominations prevailing which would be a disgrace to any people. But what have the friends of English education done to the natives of India? By the adoption of other plans, they might have said to them, "Walk about Zion, and go round about her; tell the towers thereof. Mark ye well her bulwarks, consider her palaces, that ye may tell it to the generation following." But no. They have put the keys of knowledge into their hands; they have laid open Babylon the great to their view; they have taken them into the chamber of imagery to behold the abominations that are there. In order to atone for the manner in which they have condemned, as worthless and vile, the licentious literature, in which the Hindoos would have revelled, whether they gave them liberty or not, the Committee of Public Instruction have taken this people to our theatres, our assemblies, our gaming-houses, our gin-palaces, our fairs, our race-courses, and our "fancy" clubs, to behold the habits, and vices that prevail among a civilized community. As though it were not enough that the missionaries had to contend with their heathen objections, and their depraved propensities, the English party have taken their Hindoo pupils to our schools of infidelity to hear a Hume, a Voltaire, and a Byron; a Paine,* a Carlisle, and an Owen, deliver their lessons of immorality, and to learn the scorn, the ribaldry, and the derision which they can pour forth against Christianity, and its divine Author. Nay: had the government wished to patronise the spread of atheism; to raze the foundations of society; to diffuse an unbounded licentiousness of sentiment and principle; and to cast their Hindoo pupils on the wide sea of scepticism without a helm, a compass and a sail; what more could its agents have done, than to have established, under its high sanction, libraries full of pernicious and infidel publications, to have refused the libraries which the London Tract Society proposed to furnish as an antidote to this poi-

* Calcutta has been deluged from America with the works of Paine.

son, and to have provided an appetite, in their students, for the worst books in the language—books which many persons in Calcutta will not be backward to supply? Who will account for all these evils, and all the calamities, which will unquestionably follow?

A great object which the advocates of the new system have in view, is to provide a vernacular literature for Hindosthan; and the proposal is to educate the natives in English, that they may become the instruments of rendering western literature and science into their own languages. Now, I do not mean to say that this plan may not, after vast trouble, enormous expense, and ages of toil and oppression, be attended with a measure of success. But I must say, that something like the Calcutta plan of steaming round the Cape of Good Hope as a passage to India, in preference to that of going down the Mediterranean, and up the Red Sea, it is neither the most simple, natural, direct, nor promising. As the histories of Ireland, of Wales, and of the Highlands of Scotland, have given us lessons of warning, so they may afford us lessons of instruction upon this point. In these provinces, this scheme has been fairly tried, and the results of the experiment are before us. What is the testimony which may be gathered from the history of Wales? In the principality, this system has been modified by circumstances; the spirit, the energy, and the love of freedom which characterize the people, have tended to counteract the evils which have usually sprung from such measures: schools and colleges, established upon different principles, have secured to the inhabitants some blessings of which this system would unquestionably have deprived them; but what is the amount of literature that is to be found in the Welsh? Alas! after three centuries of English supremacy and favour, how defective is it, according to the evidence of its best friends, when compared with what it might have become under a vernacular administration? So convinced were the inhabitants of Wales, some years ago, of the depressing influence of English upon their national literature, and their interests as a people, that they petitioned the legislature to appoint no bishop to a see in their province, who did not understand their language. But no. It could not be granted. Such is the influence which the adopted system in India, has still in England, that the parliament passed a bill to confirm the grievance which the Welsh complained of; and well might a public journal, in reference to the subject, ridicule the act:—"It is now the law of the land that a bishop need not understand the language of the people over whom he exercises his episcopal functions. The decision is very intelligible. It ought, nevertheless, to be translated into Welsh and pasted inside the covers of the Welsh Bibles. The people should learn, in their own rude dialect, to appreciate the blessings of having aliens in race and language, to superintend their religious instruction. There was a time when a priesthood ignorant of the people's language was held an abomination. The parliaments of Edward the Third, denounced the nuisance. Wicliffe, the patriarch of Protestantism, wrote and preached, with his accustomed fervour, against the gross abuse. The venerable rector of Lutterworth knew nothing of Protestantism triumphant, or of reformed Episcopacy grown old in luxury. The *pastor pastorum* has no connexion with the flock, but the fleece."

The Highlands of Scotland have been rendered another field of experiment. Nothing can show more plainly the prejudices under which Dr. Duff is labouring, than his bringing forward his native language, to support this scheme. If ever there was a dialect that has been despised and neglected, whose literature has suffered oppression and contempt under a foreign yoke, and whose theology remains scanty and cold from the ungenerous plans that strangers have adopted, it is certainly the Gaelic tongue. To a Highlander, what evidence could be more convincing and overwhelming, than that which Dr. Duff has adduced—that her brave and hardy sons should have to travel hundreds of miles, amidst frost and snows, to distant universities—that after centuries during which this system has been at work, they should still be obliged to learn a strange language before they can receive an education—that they should still, far removed from their homes, have to lodge in the midst of strangers, and have to endure all the taunts and the jeers to which they have so often to submit? I allow, with Dr. Duff, that coming from the north and from the west, to English colleges, they have to study a foreign language—that they contend successfully for the prize of scholarship—and that enriching their minds with science, literature and theology,—they return to their native glens to disseminate their knowledge, human and divine; but what system has laid them under such disadvantages? What plans oblige them still to submit to a foreign language, to repair to distant colleges, and to derive their stores from a strange literature? Is it not the scheme for which he is contending? It has, for many an age, been tried in Scotland; and where are the colleges established in the Highlands? where is the literature and theology of which the Gaelic can boast? Ah! Well may the Ossianic Society * send petitions to parliament complaining

* "That there are in the Highlands and Islands of Scotland no fewer than five hundred thousand of her majesty's subjects, entitled, from their patriotic conduct, and by their steady loyalty, to the attention of the British legislature, whose vernacular tongue is the Gaelic, and who are incapable of receiving instruction, religious or secular, to any extent, through the medium of any other language.

"That in the pastoral superintendence of this extensive population, nearly three hundred ministers are at present engaged, to whom an accurate and critical knowledge of the vernacular tongue is imperatively requisite for the effective discharge of their sacred trust, and whose usefulness is almost entirely dependent upon their capacity of diffusing knowledge, and inculcating duty in this the only impressive and intelligible manner. That the momentous object of qualifying such that their language, and literature have been neglected, and praying that professors may be appointed to give the students, from the north, a better knowledge of their own tongue.

If this scheme will confer a literature upon India; it will do for that empire, what it has yet failed to do for the Highlands of Scotland. Another plan would certainly have been more successful. At the time that the Gaelic was assailed,* and measures were proposed to keep those who speak it in ig-

public instructors for officiating effectively, is entirely overlooked in the present constitution of the Scottish Universities, wherein no opportunity is afforded for acquiring that thorough knowledge of the Gaelic language which is so essential and desirable.

"That all Highland students, more especially such as have devoted themselves to theological studies, have long deplored this radical defect in the present educational system in our universities, and various evils and difficulties which it originates; and that they have, for a length of time, endeavoured of themselves to obviate these by convening (under the designation of the Ossianic Society) for the sole purpose of assisting each other to the understanding of the Gaelic language; but they most sadly experience that their utmost efforts are nugatory, and therefore form no adequate remedy; that many others beside lament that they have no proper means of becoming acquainted with the Celtic language, which is not only essential to the divine, but also *per se* of the highest importance to the accomplishment of the philologist, the antiquarain and the historian."

* "Johnson's Court, Fleet Street, 13th Aug., 1766.

"Sir,—I did not expect to hear that it could be, in an assembly convened for the propagation of Christian knowledge, a question whether any nation uninstructed in religion should receive instruction; or whether that instruction should be imparted to norance and deprive them of the word of life; had the government or some generous and wealthy

them by a translation of the holy books into their own language. If obedience to the will of God be necessary to happiness, and knowledge of his will be necessary to obedience, I know not how he that withholds this knowledge, or delays it, can be said to love his neighbour as himself. He that voluntarily continues in ignorance, is guilty of all the crimes which ignorance produces; as to him that should extinguish the tapers of a light-house, might justly be imputed the calamities of shipwreck. Christianity is the highest perfection of humanity; and as no man is good but as he wishes the good of others, no man can be good in the highest degree who wishes not to others the largest measures of the greatest good. To omit for a year, or for a day, the most efficacious method of advancing Christianity, in compliance with any purposes that terminate on this side of the grave, is a crime of which I know not that the world has yet had an example, except in the practice of the planters in America, a race of mortals whom, I, suppose, no other man wishes to resemble."

Boswell's Life of Johnson.

"After such a letter as this," remarks Mr. Anderson, "it may seem strange that schools for the education of our Highlanders, directly and in the first instance, to read their own language, were not established until 1811, more than fifty years afterwards. Such, however, is the fact. After an acquaintance with the state of the Highlands, all along the western coast of Scotland in 1810, the writer could find nothing of the sort. The practice universally was, that of teaching English first; and no small prejudice was then discovered at the idea of teaching at once the vernacular tongue. There was then even no elementary book, save Dr. A. Stewart's large 8vo. Grammar. The letter procured from Mr. Charles, of Wales, was among the steps preparatory. Now the prejudice is gone. His Majesty, on visiting Scotland, through Mr. Peel, with great cordiality became patron of the Society for the support of Gaelic Schools, and since that period the General Assembly have taken up the same idea."

chieftain established a college in the metropolis of the Highlands; had he appointed professors to pour their science, and philosophy, their Latin, Greek and English into the minds of their students, through the medium of the Gaelic; and had he thus raised the language of the North to the rank and station which it deserved; what would have been the effects produced upon the Highlanders themselves?

Instead of their literature being now so barren and impoverished, it would this day have been abundant and interesting; their ministers would be far better prepared to unfold, to their hearers, the mysteries of redemption; the passions and sympathies of the people would respond more fully and more freely to the northern and homely allusions of their pastors, than to their southern phraseology; in lieu of attempts to impose upon their clans, by power and by patronage, a foreign dialect, the pride, the wealth, and the benevolence of the aristocracy would be called forth to uphold their native language, and to replenish it with stores of moral and intellectual wealth; and the sons of Caledonia might now be as renowned for their wisdom and their learning, as they are for their martial courage and impetuous bravery.

But as Ireland is more remote, and has so long been the victim of conquest and oppressive enactments, it bears a greater resemblance perhaps to our Indian empire. What, then, has the scheme done for the literature, the education and the liberties of Ireland? The few who were high, affluent, and noble, have bowed submissively to the yoke, and have assumed the badges of England and its barons; the respectable classes and aspirants to office and to power have pursued learning and philosophy at its university, since that was the path to honour and to renown; but where is the literature which they have given to their language and to their country? Where are the devoted, and laborious ministers whose minds have been filled with English knowledge, and are pouring their treasures of wisdom into the Irish language, and into the minds of its people? Where are the Irish schools that have been established to educate the masses, and to emancipate them from their superstition and their bondage?

"At length," remarks Mr. Anderson, "in the very close of the eighteenth, or rather the opening of the nineteenth century, benevolent feeling haveing come into more lively exercise, a better day seems to have begun to dawn on this long, long neglected people. The time in which their best interest will be pursued, as it relates to the improvement of their minds, is surely now at hand. The time in which their vernacular tongue was thus treated has passed away; and assuredly if the '*English interest,*' in every sense of the term, is to be promoted, such policy and such neglect have passed away for ever.

" In the effectual education of any tribe, there is a course to which nature not only points, but constrains. In every instance, it is demonstrable, that the benevolent visitor or resident must sit down and begin with the people, where God and nature have begun with them. *If we descend not to their level, we shall never raise up any, save a mere fraction of the community, nor will that fraction raise the remaining body. As to the vernacular tongue, whatever that be, if we will not go back and start here, the people, as such, stand still, and are left behind.* But truly, on such a subject as that of a liberal education, naturally and necessarily taking its rise from the first tongue in which a people have spoken, and been accustomed to think, embracing too such an aggregate of human beings under the British crown, and after such a detail as the present, meagre though it be, one is at a great loss what to say. It has been drawn out, and facts placed in this new light before the intelligent reader, in the hope that they will instantly suggest to many the imperious but pleasing duty of pursuing a course more congenial with the love of country and the good of Ireland. If these poor people wish to have education, and let the reader point, if he can, to that class in this kingdom who desire it more, and if the language is dear to them, as dear it is, let them have it to their heart's content, and as the *only basis too of all effectual information and* *happiness* to the Irish mind in its present condition."*

It is a very remarkable event, that after so many ages of oppression and misgovernment, to establish this English system, and to convert the Irish people to the Protestant faith, it should *now* be ascertained that these means are useless; that measures, in the *Irish language*, must be adopted; that *Irish* schools are most suited to give instruction to the children; that *Irish* preachers and readers meet with the most attentive and serious congregations; that scriptures and good books in *Irish* are most acceptable to the people; and that, if we wish to be useful to the Catholic population, we must return to those plans which were rejected and spurned in a former age.

What plan, then, it may perhaps be asked, would you suggest to provide a Christian literature for India? The system, I reply, which has prevailed, from time immemorial among the Hindoos themselves, to provide their own heathen literature, is one whose claims to simplicity and to usefulness cannot be disputed. Whatever may be the difference in the languages, they all belong to the same great family; similar laws regulate the idiom, construction, style, and various kinds of composition, which prevail in the dialects of the north and the

* Anderson on the Native Irish—a book which ought to be read by every friend to mankind.

south; when you describe one part of India, you have, in many respects, described the whole; the manners, the customs, and the habits of the people, with trifling variations, correspond from Cape Comorin to the Himalaya; and their superstition, in all its great lineaments, is exactly the same. Whether, therefore, their present literature was originally written in Sanscrit, or in some other language, the Vedas, the Shasters, the Pooranas, and all their classical writings are to be found in all the principal tongues of India, and are as well understood in the one as in the other. Let this plan be adopted, and acted upon by the friends of Christianity and of India, and every language in Hindosthan will in twenty years have a Christian literature. To supply the growing wants of the people, there is required a General Book Society, whose operations would neither be confined to Bengal, nor to Bombay, nor to Madras; but which would embrace, in its extensive arms, the range of our Indian empire, and which would yield encouragement to Europeans and to natives in the publication of works in every language. So long as the population remains heathen, it is evident that there will be no demand for such books as may be written. The natives must first learn to appreciate the commodity, before they can be expected to purchase it; and such works as are published in the vernacular tongues, must, for a while, either be given for nothing, or sold at a very reduced price, to create the demand. But were such a Book Society established; were European missionaries, and Christian natives, who are qualified to excel in this department of labour, encouraged to unite and to publish useful works, in the respective tongues with which they are acquainted, there is such a similarity in the genius, and in the construction of all the languages of India, that every book which was printed in any dialect from the south to the north, might, with the greatest facility, ease, and advantage, be rendered into every other, and be as much suited to the state, character, and circumstances of the people, as any treatise written in English, might be translated into the language of every Protestant community in Europe.

Let me not be misunderstood; I am no advocate for translations from English or any other European language. Such books as the Pilgrim's Progress, and some others, may, by the greatest labour and by many alterations, be translated, with some advantage, into the vernacular languages of the East. But I appeal to every one who has studied the Oriental dialects, and have become so acquainted with them as to be able to use them like their own, whether there is not an utter incongruity between the English and the languages of India; whether the genius, the character, and construction of the one, are not the most incompatible with those of the other; and whether the modes of expression, the tropes and figures, the allusions and phraseology employed in the East, are not as far removed from those of the West as the space that divides them? Most assuredly they are; and translations made from our literature and our theology, however agreeable to those who make them, will certainly be to those who read them, generally speaking, like the sounding brass or the tinkling cymbal. No; the society to which I refer, would have a very different task to perform, from that of giving encouragement to translations from western literature, science, and theology. Their business and honour would be to patronize, and to assist every book that might be written in the respective languages in the north or in the south, in the east or in the west; and having ascertained that it would be useful, to see that it was translated and published in all the tongues of the empire. Such a society would require great exertions from its directors, and would be attended with considerable expense; but it would do more, in twenty years, to give a Christian literature to India, than any other plan will be able to accomplish for centuries to come.

It has been long laid down as an incontrovertible axiom in India, that the country was acquired by the sword, and that our power there cannot be otherwise maintained. The latter part of this maxim, I venture to question. At present, I allow, the army cannot be dispensed with; but is this state of things to continue for ever? Are the garments of the warrior always to be rolled in blood? Is there to be no cessation to those schemes which require despotism and terror to support them? The past history of India is a frightful comment upon the system of violence and conquest; it is certainly high time that more Christian methods were adopted to give the people peace and prosperity. More of the public revenue must be appropriated to give them education. While sound measures ought to be adopted for the improvement and amelioration of the empire; while the farmers should be shown how productive the ground might be rendered, by better instruments, and new methods of cultivation; while trade and commerce, both internal and external, ought to be encouraged, and every restriction should be removed; while the rich and wealthy should be taught to put out their money to usury, and to form themselves into companies to draw forth the resources of the country, the youth, throughout the land, might be collected into schools, and on the principles which Mr. Adam has suggested, be fitted for useful stations in society, and for giving a greater impetus to science and literature, to wisdom and goodness, in the ages to come. The arts of peace might, at a very trifling expense, supersede the necessity of war. Love, good-will and benevolence, might soon become triumphant over the selfish appetites and passions which heathenism has encouraged, and rendered essential to its own existence. The people might soon be taught, that it is their interest to support a government which aims even at their present comfort and happiness, and to bow to a religion which has secured to them, by its sacred influence, such days of prosperity.

But whether the government will, in this respect, do its duty to the empire, or prefer to run its former career, it behoves the great societies which have the conversion of the heathen at heart, to see that extensive plans are formed, and carried out for the education of the young, and for raising up a more energetic and laborious race of native preachers in India. At the more healthy and principal stations, there ought to be colleges established on broad and liberal principles, where Christian children, promising youths, and candidates for the ministry might receive a suitable education. Instead of the duties of a seminary, the superintendence of schools, and the general business of a mission devolving upon one individual; such stations ought to be well supplied with missionaries who would give themselves to different departments of the great work, and who would become the instruments of raising, to a higher scale, the intellectual qualifications, and the Christian character of our native teachers.

I know of no institution that is better fitted to take the lead in such plans of benevolence, and in bold and extensive measures for the improvement of

India, than the London Missionary Society. Catholic in its principles, liberal in its constitution, simple in its object, already crowned with a signal blessing from on high, and supported by all denominations of Christians, it is well qualified to take up a high and important position in raising a native ministry for Hindosthan. Various plans have already been adopted, but they are not adequate to the exigencies of the case. So long as we depend upon foreign supplies, and are satisfied with maintaining our position, and keeping the enemy in abeyance; so long as we repose our confidence upon those who, converted in their manhood, are apt to bring many prejudices and infirmities into the camp, and are far from being the most devoted and most courageous champions in the field, our army is weak and defective, and we are destitute of the real sinews of war. But let us determine, in the strength of God, to raise up a native army, to instruct them in our spiritual warfare and discipline, to create, as far as possible, between them and their people, a sympathy in their language, their manners and customs, and to render them more efficient by an education superior to any which they have hitherto obtained; then, I feel assured that the money, the labour, and the sacrifice will be well rewarded, and that should these plans require more time to develop their usefulness, they would be more extensive and lasting in their benefits.

In the year 1836, there was a sad want of candidates for missionary work; many of the foreign stations were left destitute, and the wants of others could not be supplied. But appeals were made to the churches to give themselves to prayer, that God would provide for this emergency, that he would raise up evangelists, and qualify them for the service of the heathen, and that he would not suffer the missions to languish and expire for want of devoted agents. These appeals were responded to by importunate intercession, and these intercessions were answered in a host of warriors who have gone forth to the field, and are now contending with the foe. Oh, when will the spirit which gained these triumphs be renewed with increasing fervour and perseverance on behalf of a native ministry for India; when will the churches put on their strength, and wrestle with Jehovah to endow hundreds and thousands of Hindoos, with the gifts and the graces of the Holy Ghost, to proclaim salvation to sinners; and when shall that dark land witness a noble army who, wielding the sword of the spirit, and wearing the shield of faith, and equipped with the helmet of salvation, and the breastplate of righteousness, shall stand forth as the advocates of the truth, and the assailants of the powers of darkness? then, the day of victory will come; persecution will but rage to consummate the triumphs of the truth; grace and strength divine will rest upon the witnesses to enable them to toil, to weep, to pray, to testify and to suffer; and should convulsions drive their European helpers from the soil, there would remain, in the field, a band of faithful, devoted, enlightened and courageous champions, who would lead on their brethren to the struggle, and would, in defiance of bonds, imprisonments and death, continue to propagate Christianity.

THE END.